HEI TAONGA MĀ NGĀ URI WHAKATIPU

TREASURES FOR THE RISING GENERATION

HEI TAONGA MĀ NGĀ URI WHAKATIPU

TREASURES FOR THE RISING GENERATION

The Dominion Museum
Ethnological Expeditions 1919–1923

TE PAPA PRESS

WAYNE NGATA / ARAPATA HAKIWAI / ANNE SALMOND / CONAL McCARTHY / AMIRIA
SALMOND / MONTY SOUTAR / JAMES SCHUSTER / BILLIE LYTHBERG / JOHN NIKO
MAIHI / SANDRA KAHU NEPIA / TE WHETURERE POOPE GRAY / TE AROHA McDONNELL /
NATALIE ROBERTSON / 'THE TERMINOLOGY OF WHAKAPAPA' BY APIRANA NGATA

E tipu, e rea
Mo nga ra o tou ao
Ko to ringa ki nga rakau a te Pakeha
Hei ara mo te tinana
Ko to ngakau ki nga taonga a o tipuna Maori
Hei tikitiki mo to mahunga
Ko to wairua ki to Atua
Nana nei nga mea katoa.

Grow, and thrive
In the days of your world
Your hand to the tools of the Pākehā
For your material wellbeing
Your heart to the treasures of your ancestors
As a topknot for your head
Your spirit to your God
Who created all things.

— A whakataukī written by Apirana Ngata in a young girl's autograph
book in 1949 (trans. with advice from Wayne Ngata)

Tā Apirana Ngata watching a poi dance with his granddaughter,
Wiki White, at the opening of Tamatekapua meeting house
at Ōhinemutu in 1943. Photograph by John Pascoe.

CONTENTS

HEI WĀHI AKE

WAYNE NGATA

Nau mai, haere atu ēnei kupu whakamihi, whakatau hoki i te kaupapa kua horahia atu nei. E mihi ana ki ngā whakaaro, ki ngā rangahau, ki ngā manawanui, ki ngā ringa tuhi i runga i ngā kupu i takutakuhia ai e tahito mā, 'Ka hura, ka hura te manawa uha, ka hura te manawa pore, ko tō manawa, ko tōku manawa, ko te manawa nui o Rangi e tū iho nei…' Mā konei e kotahi ai te manawa hei kawe i te kōrero.

Kāti, he āhuatanga whakaheke tēnei mea te ohu. He mahi ngātahi tōna tikanga. Ka kohia ko te manawa o tēnā, ko te pūkenga o tēnā, ko te whakaaro o tēnā, ko te kaha o tēnā, ko te aroha o tēnā, ko te kupu a tēnā hei whakatutuki i te mahi. Ka whakatūria te kaupapa, ka kauwhatatia kia kitea tōna whānui, tōna katoa, me te koha a tētahi, a tētahi, ka mea hei hākari mā te huihuinga. He wā anō ka whāiti mai te kaupapa ki te ruarua tāngata, ki tōna pūtakenga Māori mai, ka whakamātautauhia, ka whakapakaritia, ka maunu anō. He pēnei nā tēnei o ngā kaupapa i whakaarohia, i whakairohia e Apirana, e Te Peehi, e Te Rangihīroa mā, i whakaahua tonutia e Makitānara, ā, kotahi rau tau i muri mai, ka pērā anō taua ohu hei whakarauora i ā rātau kohikohinga.

Nā reira e mihi ana ki te kaupapa nāna i kohikohi ngā maramara o ngā wānanga o nehe rā, ka tōia mai i tua whakarere ki mua nei whakataki haere ai mā roto i ngā hangarau o te wā, i kīia ai 'hei taonga mā ngā uri whakatipu'. E mihi ana ki te huinga o ngā pūkenga o nāianei; ngā ringa rangahau, ngā ringa tuhi, ngā ringa whakatika i whāriki mai ai te kōrero nei, hei aha, hei whakahoki anō i ō tātau whakaaro ki ngā mahi a ō tātau tīpuna, hei kaupapa ārahi anō i a tātau i ēnei rā, ā, hei taonga anō mā ngā uri whakatipu.

When we reflect on the work carried out by Te Rangihīroa,[1] Elsdon Best, Johannes Andersen, James McDonald and Apirana Ngata nearly a hundred years ago, we find their dreams and aspirations are inevitably balanced with a pragmatic and adaptive approach to achieving those ideals. They were people of their time, responding to matters of that time, using the technologies of that time, with an explicit focus on what they could contribute to their children, grandchildren and beyond. We acknowledge and celebrate what they did and how they did it. We also need to consider what we can learn from that, in this our time—and what is our own contribution to the rising generations after us?

With this in mind, Te Rangihīroa's appeal to his contemporaries gives us pause. 'Kua mutu haere te wa ki a Te Peehi ma, kua riro ma taua ma te Maori taua e korero [The time of Best and that crowd is ending. It is left for us, the Maori, to speak for ourselves].' This line of thought has emerged in various guises and forums since Te Rangihīroa's time, and as recently as 2019 in the build-up to the TUIA 250 commemorations of the first onshore encounters between Māori and Pākehā in Aotearoa New Zealand between 1769 and 1770.

Some occupy the cultural high ground in advocating strongly for owning the storytelling, and rightfully so. Others would carry on, regardless of cultural connection to a subject. The space in the middle where researchers and writers of various cultural hues work together to make sense of what was, and posit what could be, is therefore challenging, but nonetheless needs the mix of cultural translators, negotiators and facilitators to get things done, and to help shift the dial towards the 'tino rangatiratanga' of storytelling.

This work is a product of negotiation and collaboration, as it was one hundred years ago. The product itself is important, as is the way in which it has been built. The depth of shared expertise and experience, the passion and commitment to research about and for our own people, the facility to utilise current technologies and forums and the contribution to the body of mātauranga and to the way of wānanga help to ensure that we continue to provide treasures for the rising generations.

Inā te kaupapa, inā te kōrero hei taonga mā ngā uri whakatipu.

MIHI

ARAPATA HAKIWAI, KAIHAUTŪ
MUSEUM OF NEW ZEALAND
TE PAPA TONGAREWA

Tēnā koutou kei ngā mana, kei ngā reo, kei ngā mātā waka tangata. He kupu whakamihi tēnei ki a koutou e kai ō mata ki tēnei pukapuka, ki ēnei taonga whakahirahira i kohia i tērā rau tau. Ko ngā taonga me ōna kōrero kua whārikihia he hononga o mua me ngā tūmanako o ngā reanga o nāianei tonu. Nō reira, he tautoko ake ahau i te taitara *Hei Taonga mā ngā Uri Whakatipu*.

He hōnore nōku kia tuhia he whakaaro e pā ana ki ngā kaupapa taonga i whakahaerehia i te wā o Apirana Ngata me Te Rangihīroa mā.

Ko te kupu kōrero o te whakaaturanga taonga Māori a Te Māori e rere pēnei ana 'He Toi Whakairo, He Mana Tangata'. He tika tērā kupu kōrero mo ēnei taonga maramara whakapūmau nō te mea he whakapapa tonu ki ngā uri whakaheke, ki ngā whānau, ki ngā hapū me ngā iwi nā rātou kē ēnei taonga. Nā, kua tae te wā kia riro mā te Māori anō e kōrero ā rātou ake taonga, ō rātou ake hītori. Nō reira, me tuku te reo taketake kia rere, kia hono anō ēnei taonga ki ōna rahi me ōna uri hei oranga tangata, oranga taonga, oranga reo, oranga ahurea. Tēnā tātou katoa.

The title of this publication, *Hei Taonga mā ngā Uri Whakatipu: Treasures for the Rising Generation,* is very appropriate. The Dominion Museum Ethnological Expeditions were globally unique, being led by visionary leaders like Apirana Ngata and Te Rangihīroa, in association with like-minded 'museum' people including James McDonald and and Elsdon Best. As Dr Wayne Ngata notes, there were many reasons and motivations for undertaking these ethnological expeditions, but what's important now is that the voices and space for Māori to speak about them and to them has arrived.

At that time there was a real fear that valuable dimensions of Māori culture would be lost and something needed to be done to ensure their survival. As old boys of Te Aute College, leaders like Apirana Ngata, Te Rangihīroa and Māui Pōmare were ever present at the kura as a source of inspiration and leadership. The active involvement of the Dominion Museum in this work and the collecting of waiata, karakia, taonga and traditions should be acknowledged. Today, however, museums and cultural institutions are coming under much scrutiny, challenging their colonial and Western histories, policies and practices. Decolonising museums and their practice and working towards reconciliation and healing is a growing international initiative as museums confront their colonial past. In Aotearoa New Zealand, Māori are calling for museums to recognise Te Tiriti o Waitangi, our nation's founding document, and to reconnect them with their taonga and ancestors held in their care. Rather than perpetuating colonial Western museum practices, museums know that they must change and transform themselves. Cultural ownership and tino rangatiratanga are important dimensions that Māori are demanding of museums. How true are the words of Apirana Mahuika, chairman of Te Rūnanga o Ngāti Porou, at a Tairāwhiti cultural heritage wānanga at Waihīrere marae, Gisborne, in June 2002, when he said, 'The process of colonisation will never end unless the process of rangatiratanga is acknowledged and respected.'

Ngata's foresight and vision are unquestionable, as is his plea that 'Maori should be treated as equals and not as objects in museums'.[2] It is appropriate that iwi descendants are involved in this publication, for the time has come for Māori to reclaim the space and speak for and about their taonga, histories and worldviews. This publication is a strong reminder that taonga remain embedded and forever alive in the Māori psyche. The taonga collected during these expeditions connect with tribal descendants today, providing tangible links to their ancestors and the Māori world. Recognition and mihi should be given to Ngata, Te Rangihīroa, McDonald and Best as the legacy of this work remains in cultural institutions awaiting full reconnection to their descendant kin communities. These enduring taonga must not be left on shelves and in cupboards as collections and passive artefacts for museums, libraries and cultural institutions. Their trajectories have a greater cause, helping to uplift the foundations of language, culture and identity.

Museums have a greater purpose and mission now than perhaps at any other time in our history. The challenge and opportunity is for these taonga to be released and set free, to be reunited with their descendants to enable language, identity and culture to flourish and grow. Let's honour the legacy and reconnect the taonga for this and future generations. Me whakatinana te wawata o ngā rangatira o ērā wā ki ngā reanga o ēnei wā, āpōpō ake.

INTRODUCTION

ANNE SALMOND
CONAL McCARTHY
AMIRIA SALMOND

'Ka waiho i konei hei taonga mā ngā uri whakatipu' (We're leaving these [songs] here as treasures for the rising generation)

TUTA NGĀRIMU, dedicating his recording, with his wife Mākere, of taumaunu sung at the arrival of Te Rangihīroa, Elsdon Best and their friends at Whareponga, Tairāwhiti, 19 March 1923[1]

The 1919–1923 Dominion Museum Ethnological Expeditions were world-leading. Inspired by the determination of visionary Māori leaders to save their people and ancestral ways of life from extinction, the expeditions featured active collaboration with iwi (tribal) communities and central government; close relationships with Pākehā colleagues at the Dominion Museum (now the Museum of New Zealand Te Papa Tongarewa); a vigorous and critical engagement with international anthropology; and the use of cutting-edge technologies in photography, film and sound recording to capture ancestral tikanga feared to be fast disappearing.

The driving force behind these expeditions was Apirana Ngata, MP for Eastern Maori, a charismatic, tireless champion of his people. On 1 December 1918, while working on the revision of the Williams' *Dictionary of the Maori Language,*[2] Ngata wrote to Hon. GW Russell, Minister of Internal Affairs, urging him to support phonographic recordings of the various dialects of Māori, along with their songs and speeches, and filming of life in Māori settlements:

A group of women, including the Kaua Sisters, Heneriata Te Paea Collier and Erana Heihi, making kete at Waiomatatini during the fourth expedition in 1923. Photograph by James McDonald.

Referring to our conversation on the above matters this afternoon, I have much pleasure in placing on paper the suggestions I then made. Your Department has shown during the last few years that it is taking an interest in the preservation of records relating to the language, customs and ethnology of the Maori Race.

The completion of the enlarged edition of Williams' Dictionary of the Maori Language sets at rest any anxiety that students may have had as the preservation of a complete record, so far as writing can record any language, of the vocabulary of the language of the aboriginal race.

The ethnology is, in its different aspects, the subject of close study and constant investigation by many capable men here and in the islands. The words of the old songs and incantations, comprising the poetry of the race, have been saved to us by Grey and others.

But a language, which lacks a literature like Maori, and which depends for its preservation in the finest form on the inflection and modulation and for its correct use on principles of euphony, must be recorded in the 'speech' form — must be heard spoken by the fast passing generation of elders.

I, therefore, make the suggestion that phonographic records be made by the Government throughout the islands. There are numerous dialects, and records of songs and speeches in each of the principal dialects should be taken. Of course great care would have to be taken to secure really good characteristic records.

The still life, characteristic of this Country in its lakes, forests and snow-clad mountains, has been, I believe, 'filmed' by the Tourist Department. But no whole-hearted attempt has yet been made to record characteristic scenes from Native life. My second suggestion is, therefore, that the Government should undertake the 'filming' of the hakas and pois, and of Maori village life, showing 'tangis', meetings, life on the cultivations and so on.

One of the largest Native Meetings in my electorate will be held the first week of March, 1919, to augment the Maori Soldiers' Fund and to unveil the monument to the late Wi Pere. That would be an excellent opportunity for taking good records, for there will be no more representative gathering of Maoris in any part of this Dominion.

I am assured of your interest in the above matters and trust that you will move your Department and the Government to undertake this further service to the Maori race.

For these expeditions, timing was everything. Just two weeks earlier, on 11 November, the First World War had ended when the Armistice was signed in Europe. More than 18,000 New Zealanders had died in the fighting. At the same time, an influenza pandemic was raging, brought to New Zealand by soldiers returning from the battlefield. Between October and December 1918, 9000 New Zealanders died in the pandemic—half as many as had died during the whole of the war. It was a terrible time, seared into the memories of survivors. As one reported later: 'In that 'flu, when they died, the bodies turned black … In one house, I looked into a bedroom and there was the wife, still fast asleep, and her husband dead and black beside her.'[3]

James McDonald (left) and Johannes Andersen filming during the
Hui Aroha in Gisborne in 1919.

In this pandemic, between one-third and one-half of New Zealand's population was infected. It hit the Māori community particularly hard. Over that two-month period, more than 2500 Māori died,[4] including many experts in ancestral arts and knowledge—the Māori death rate of fifty people per one thousand was eight times higher than the death rate for Europeans.[5] It is no wonder Ngata was desperate to ensure that the Māori language and tikanga were put on record as soon as possible.

Later that month James McDonald, formerly government 'kinematographist' (one of the first official filmmakers in the world),[6] and now Acting Director at the Dominion Museum, took up the challenge in a letter to the Undersecretary of the Department of Internal Affairs:

> The opportunity to secure phonographic records of Native songs and incantations and also moving picture films of Poi dances, haka, etc., at the Maori gathering in March next is one of which every advantage should be taken. As the Hon. Mr Ngata truly says the elders are fast passing away, and the chances of securing such records are steadily diminishing.
>
> At the first meeting of the Board of Science and Art in 1916 the desirability of having a phonographic recording machine was suggested by Dr. Thomson. Since then a machine — the Dictaphone — has been procured. It has been tested both for office work and for recording native speech and works satisfactorily. So far only the Hon. Te Heuheu Tukino, M.L.C., and Mr. H. Stowell (Hare Hongi) of the Native Department have recited short pieces in the native tongue and these reproduce very clearly.
>
> The Native meeting to which the Hon. Mr. Ngata refers would appear to present a most favourable opportunity of securing records, and with Mr Ngata's assistance much valuable material might be preserved for future use.

> So far but a few films only of Poi dances, and haka by the Arawa natives have been secured. These were taken during my period of service in the Tourist Department, and are now stored at the Museum. They are, however, far from complete and much remains to be done before the collection can be called a representative one.
>
> If the Hon. Minister approves of Phonographic and Kinematographic Records being at the forthcoming meeting it would be helpful if the Hon. Mr. Ngata could visit the Museum some time beforehand so that a list could be prepared and an estimate made of the wax records, films and plates likely to be required.

In February 1919, the Museum Director, Dr James Allan Thomson,[7] wrote to the Minister of Internal Affairs, noting that the Minister had authorised museum staff to attend the Hui Aroha, the meeting referred to by Ngata, to film and record Māori speeches and songs, and suggesting that the Museum should be represented by Elsdon Best and James McDonald. He added that Johannes Andersen, the Turnbull Librarian and a keen student of Māori music, was eager to go with them, and that he approved of this request. In this way the team for the first Dominion Museum Ethnological Expedition came together.[8]

Elsdon Best, an eminent ethnologist and fluent speaker of Māori who had long studied ancestral beliefs and practices, was very clear about the illustrations that he wanted for the Museum's occasional publication, the *Museum Bulletin*. He drew up a long list of the games and tikanga that he hoped would be performed at the Hui Aroha, so that McDonald could photograph and film them, including 'Karetao—Jumping Jack, Reti—toboggan, Aka—swings, Potaka ta—tops, Whai— string games, Pirori—hoops, Pou toti—stilts, Piu— skipping and Koruru—knuckle stones,'[9] along with haka and songs, and performances on Māori musical instruments. To illustrate his forthcoming monographs and museum exhibits, Best also wanted photographs of groups of Māori, eating, singing, making speeches,

generating fire and fighting with taiaha and tewhatewha (hand weapons), cutting greenstone, making stone tools and using the old cord drills.

When Thomson forwarded this list to Ngata, he suggested it would be helpful to get the old people and children to practise some of these ancestral arts so that they were familiar with them before filming began. He added that the Museum could supply stone tools from its stores, and that it would be 'desirable as far as possible to eliminate any Pakeha costume in the groups to be photographed'.[10] In the event, most of these suggestions were cheerfully ignored.

From left: James McDonald, Hēnare Te Raumoa Balneavis, Elsdon Best and an unnamed man making a recording during the Hui Aroha in Gisborne, 1919.

Once it was agreed that the expedition team would attend the Hui Aroha in Gisborne, Ngata delegated the practical arrangements to his close friend and colleague Hēnare Te Raumoa Balneavis, Secretary to the Minister of Native Affairs, who himself was deeply interested in Māori proverbs and ancestral knowledge.[11] Like Ngata, Balneavis had attended Te Aute College, an Anglican boarding school for Māori boys in Hawke's Bay.[12] Another Te Aute old boy, Te Rangihīroa (or Peter Buck, as he was then known), doctor, politician, military hero and up-and-coming ethnologist from Taranaki, had worked closely with Ngata and Balneavis in the Te Aute Old Boys' Association. Although Te Rangihīroa played

a leading role in the third and fourth Dominion Museum Ethnological Expeditions, and helped to organise the second, he did not accompany the team on this occasion.

After the First World War broke out, Te Rangihīroa had volunteered as the Medical Officer for the Maori Contingent (Te Hokowhitu a Tū, later the Maori (Pioneer) Battalion). He was decorated and mentioned in despatches and became the Pioneer Battalion's second-in-command. Instead of attending the Hui Aroha in Gisborne on returning to New Zealand, however, he accompanied other Māori troops to the South Island, where he and his wife visited her family.

Richard Aldworth Oliver's depiction of a large feasting stage: *Feast at the Bay of Islands, September 1849*, c. 1849. Watercolour, 375 × 530 mm. Museum of New Zealand Te Papa Tongarewa.

Weaving the relationships

In his unpublished paper 'The Terminology of Whakapapa' (see Appendix), Apirana Ngata explored many different ways in which whakapapa experts were able to memorise and master a vast array of genealogical knowledge.[13] This included the creation of the cosmos itself with its array of ancestral forces; the emergence of islands from the ocean, along with their mountains, rivers and harbours, plants, animals and people; and intricate networks of relationships among groups and individuals, with stories of their births, marriages, battles, alliances and migrations down through the generations.[14]

According to Ngata, in one of these strategies, known as takiaho, the expert imagined an aho or kaha (string) on which ancestors were strung one by one (taki). When the string was lifted up (hāpai), the ancestors were displayed. Ngata explains it as follows:

> Aho, kaha. Literally a line, string or cord. In relation to a pedigree or genealogy this is a figure that would naturally occur to a weaving, cord-making, net-making, fishing people. The reciter conceived a connected string on which the persons concerned in the matter of his recitation were strung along in sequence and by lifting the string displayed them prominently. The string was the aho or kaha. The act of tracing it along in memory was 'taki', and of lifting it 'hapai'.
>
> Aho is most commonly used in the expression 'aho ariki'. Takiaho is a cord on which fish or shellfish are strung, and also a line of descent.[15]

In another mnemonic device, kauwhata, the reciter conjured up a stage on which an array of ancestors could be displayed. Ngata notes:

> 'Kauwhata' is to display as on a stage or frame in tied bundles, as of fish or articles of food, the elevation giving prominence.

A kauwhata was a stage or frame built on which to suspend fish or bundles of food, which were tied together in such a way that the bundles straddled the cross-beams of the stage. There was a horizontal and a vertical method in the arrangement and display.[16]

In yet another way of reciting whakapapa, tāhuhu, the expert thinks of a cloak woven from its original weft (tāhuhu); or a decorated whare with its ridgepole (tāhuhu), rafters (heke) and carved ancestors (poupou). As Ngata recalls:

> In the cult of genealogies, 'tahu or tahuhu' has a technical meaning. It is the act of setting out or arranging the main ancestors (connected with a common ancestor) from whom you may derive the tribe or tribes occupying a more or less extensive area.
>
> It has the idea of a horizontal arrangement with connected suspended lines that fits with both the conception of a weft and of a ridge-pole.
>
> The expert reciter was he who could most vividly impress on his hearers the array of related ancestors so that he might at will follow down any strand or rafter or poupou with the connected details of kaho, covering thatch or decorative tupuni.[17]

In researching this book, the takiaho strategy became a conceptual tool for tracing and recalling lines of connection, while exploring the social context of each of the four Dominion Museum expeditions initiated by Ngata—the Hui Aroha in Gisborne in 1919, the 1920 welcome to the Prince of Wales in Rotorua, the 1921 expedition up the Whanganui River, and the expedition to Tairāwhiti in 1923.

The film segments that James McDonald shot during these four expeditions, when strung together, are the most visible surviving trace of these explorations. Each sequence in the films, and the people who appear in it, can be understood as being strung on a relational cord of connection — similar to the way in which photographic prints are pegged along a string in the darkroom to dry, which has become a display method for viewing. The master catalogue that our research team has compiled of McDonald's photographs taken during the expeditions seeks to string the images as accurately as possible in their original sequence, providing information about the people and places that appear in them, and the archives in which they are held. In the same way, in this narrative, key figures in the expedition are introduced one by one, and their relationships are explored.

The kauwhata strategy is another invaluable way of organising ancestral materials. In the chapters that follow on each expedition and its afterlife, different scholars have crafted their understandings of each expedition, along with the particular individuals who feature in them and the records that were produced, displaying them on a kauwhata or stage composed of text and images.

The tāhuhu, the original weft of the Dominion Museum expeditions, was woven by Apirana Ngata and his lifelong friend Te Rangihīroa, as Ngata's vision of recording te reo on wax cylinders, and tikanga in film and photographs, entwined with Te Rangihīroa's fascination with the ancestral arts of fishing, weaving and netting. From this powerful tāhuhu, the idea of the expeditions emerged. Letters to the relevant authorities were written, the expedition teams were assembled and funded, arrangements were made with local people in each of the communities they visited, and complex networks of relationships were woven.

The interior of the whare whakairo Porourangi, at Waiomatatini, photographed in 1923 by James McDonald.

THE EXPEDITION MEMBERS

Apirana Turupa Ngata
(1874–1950)

Sir Apirana Turupa Ngata photographed around 1934, when he was
Minister of Native Affairs in the Liberal Government. He was first
elected to Parliament, for the Eastern Maori seat, in 1907.

This is my gift to you for the immediate future. Here is my story...your protégé. I was born a descendant of Maui, a spirit of the ancestors, in the period when man, food and good health flourished. It was indeed you all who cast me into the distance onto the marae of another people to be fed with Pakeha weed. What for? As a slave perhaps for the Pakeha; I who am the descendant of Maui and the blood of the chiefs of these islands, a slave?...

I thought...that perhaps I was selected by the people and the chiefs of these islands to seek redress within the fortifications of the Pakeha, who brought the ills and sorrow amongst us. I thought that I was to seek knowledge and that I was to extract from the Pakeha the solutions for the injuries he has done.

Oh my elders, this might only be the daydreams of a youth that he should desire to undertake the responsibility of the elders. Nevertheless take heed of the following; ignore them if they are childish; if they are sensible then perhaps it is right they should be discussed. However this is what my heart reveals for examination by the elders and learned men of the Maori people.

APIRANA NGATA 1897, Introduction to the first conference of the
Te Aute Students' Association (Māori version), trans. Koro Dewes[18]

The relationships that inspired the Dominion Museum Ethnological Expeditions were of long standing, and in many ways pivotal to the history of twentieth-century Aotearoa. Perhaps the story begins in the remote, hilly landscapes of Tairāwhiti, with Ngata's Ngāti Porou forebears. During the New Zealand Wars of the 1860s, some Ngāti Porou allied themselves with the Māori King and hoisted the Kīngitanga flag at Niu Tireni (the Great House of the Māori King of New Zealand) at Waiomatatini;[19] while others, including Ngata's tipuna whāngai (adoptive grandfather) Rāpata Wahawaha,[20] forged an alliance with the Crown.[21] Both factions were intent on protecting their ancestral lands, and in this they were largely successful. This strategy of drawing from both Te Ao Māori and Te Ao Pākehā — the Māori and Western worlds — to preserve land and tangata whenua (literally 'land people') was instilled in Ngata from a young age.

Gottfried Lindaeur's portrait of Apirana Ngata's tipuna, *Major Ropata* [Rāpata] *Wahawaha NZC*, 1890. Oil on canvas, 1558 × 1090 mm. Auckland Art Gallery Toi o Tāmaki, gift of Mr HE Partridge, 1915.

James McDonald photographed three old friends at
Waiomatatini in 1923. From left: Iehu Nukunuku, Elsdon
Best and Apirana Ngata's father, Paratene Ngata, on the
verandah of Ngata's home, the Bungalow.

In 1865, Rāpata Wahawaha and others of Ngāti
Porou fought against supporters of the Pai Mārire
religion known as Hauhau (followers of the
Taranaki prophet Te Ua Haumēne) who had
entered Ngāti Porou territory. He appealed to
the provincial superintendent, Donald McLean,[22]
for reinforcements. When the fighting ended,
an amnesty was signed and many of the Hauhau
prisoners were sent to Napier; the remainder
were forced to take an oath of allegiance to
Queen Victoria and the Church of England.[23]

Later that year, McLean implored Rāpata, his
nephew Paratene and 300 Ngāti Porou warriors
to join government forces in an attack on Hauhau
supporters at Waerenga a Hika pā in Gisborne —
a battle that would not have been forgotten when
Apirana Ngata organised the Hui Aroha in Gisborne
more than fifty years later.[24] At Waerenga a Hika,
Paratene met the prophet leader Te Kooti Arikirangi,
who with his followers was catching horses from
abandoned Pākehā farms in the district.[25]

When Rāpata and Paratene returned home to Waiapu after this battle, food was scarce. They were called back to Gisborne, where Paratene gathered blankets, clothes and food for a feast for his relatives at Hautanoa, north of Tokomaru. Impressed by his generosity, a young woman named Katerina (whose father, Abel Enoch, was part-English, part-Jewish)[26] fell in love with him and, in a dream, composed a waiata aroha for Paratene. With the approval of their elders, the couple were married at Tupāroa in late 1867, and Rāpata put his nephew and protégé in charge of the sheep run at Waiomatatini. Paratene also set up a store at Te Araroa and became a trader.[27]

After seven years of marriage, Paratene and Katerina were still childless. During this time, Paratene had a child, Hone Te Ihi,[28] with Hāriata Fox, daughter of Rāpata's sister Ritihia Te Riunui and Mathew Fox. At first, Hone was raised by Paratene and Katerina. Although Katerina was fond of the boy, she yearned for a child of her own. During bouts of depression, she would starve herself and say to Paratene, 'I am finished with your child.' Concerned for her, Paratene eventually sent Hone to his half-sister Pane and her husband Apirana Tatua, who raised him at Whareponga.[29]

At this time of crisis, a kuia named Mere Tūrei came to the young couple and advised them to go to Hākopa, a tohunga from Te Tāperenui a Whātonga whare wānanga. Paratene, a staunch Anglican,[30] was reluctant but finally agreed. Hākopa conducted a ritual that included an invocation to 'te tipua, te tahito, te taniwha' (all ancestral beings). As smoke plumed up from a pāua shell and a rainbow stood in the sky, Hākopa exclaimed,

> Katerina, I have done my best with you. You shall have two children, both boys, but take great care of your children. If you should ride a horse, ride slowly. Ill omen lies with me. When your son is born I shall die. He will bring me bad luck. Why did you come to me? Why did you not go to somebody else?[31]

On 3 July 1874, Apirana Turupa Ngata was born; and during the speech-making at his christening, it was announced that Hākopa had just died. From his birth, Apirana was marked out as someone remarkable—a taniwha like his whale-rider ancestor Paikea, a man with ancestral powers.[32]

Not long after he was born, Paratene and Katerina went to live at Reporoa with Rāpata and his wife Harata Te Ihi, both of whom schooled the boy in ancestral knowledge. In 1871, with the support of Donald McLean, Rāpata established the first native school on the East Coast at Waiomatatini, which Apirana attended.[33] He later described the night classes in which the teacher, Mr Green, put the children through their times tables, greeted by loud applause from the watching elders.[34] Seven years later, when Queen Victoria awarded Rāpata Wahawaha a sword of honour for his war service, he decided to build a carved meeting house, Porourangi, at Waiomatatini, hoping to reconcile Ngāti Porou and bring them back together. Porourangi (named after their eponymous ancestor), which was finally opened in 1888, was the setting for much of the work carried out by the fourth Dominion Museum Ethnological Expedition in 1923. It was located next to Apirana's home, Te Wharehou (also known as the Bungalow), almost on the site where Niu Tireni had stood, and below his ancestral pā, Puputa.[35]

Ngāti Porou were early adopters of sheep farming, and by 1873 there were 14,000 sheep on land to the south of the Waiapu River. Three years later, when the Native Land Court began holding hearings in Waiapu, Rāpata urged his people to ratify their claims to their land through the Land Court, and to make lands they were not using available for Pākehā settlement. He and his wife Harata, a feisty battler in the Land Court, shared their knowledge with Paratene, who became a Native Land Court assessor.

While these new battles over land were being fought, Ngata, at nine years old, was sent to Te Aute College in Hawke's Bay to get a Pākehā education.[36] Te Aute had been founded in 1854 by Samuel Williams, a Church Missionary Society (CMS) minister, as a college for Māori boys, with support from Donald McLean and a leading Hawke's Bay rangatira, Te Hāpuku, whose people gave land for the school. In 1878 when John Thornton, a dedicated teacher from England who had served as a missionary in India, was appointed as headmaster, Te Aute was transformed: it offered mathematics, science and New Zealand law as well as Anglo-Saxon, Latin, French and English, and prepared students for the professions.[37]

In 1884, James Pope, Inspector of Māori schools, wrote a pamphlet entitled 'Te Ora mo te Iwi Maori' (Health for the Māori people), arguing that scientific ideas about health and sanitation should be applied in Māori schools and communities to rescue the Māori people from oblivion. John Thornton took notice. The Māori population had fallen from about 200,000 at the time of European arrival to a low point of about 40,000, and many were lamenting, 'Ka ngaro a moa te iwi nei – like the moa, our people are heading for extinction'.[38] Thornton decided that Te Aute old boys, inspired by Christian morality and equipped with modern science and legal skills, should rescue their people from this fate.

While Apirana was still at Te Aute, his elders betrothed him to Te Rina Tāmati, a Ngāti Porou student at Hukarere College; and subsequently, when she died prematurely, to her younger sister Arihia, hoping to ensure he would stay close to his people. Apirana did well in his studies, and when he passed matriculation with high marks in 1890, Thornton encouraged him to go to university.

In his will, McLean had established a Makarini Trust to give scholarships to Māori boys, and the trustees offered Apirana a grant to study at Canterbury College. When he wrote to his father, asking for his approval, saying 'Maku pea e ora ai te iwi Maori' (Perhaps I can help to bring the Māori people back to life), although some of the elders were reluctant, fearing that he would become a stranger, Rāpata gave him his blessing: 'Tukua kia haere' 'Let him go'.[39]

Te Aute College headmaster John Thornton with staff and students, c. 1910.

Apirana Ngata graduated from Canterbury University College (now the University of Canterbury), with a BA in politics in 1893. His subsequent law degree was from Auckland University College (now the University of Auckland).

In the summer of 1891, before Apirana headed off to university, he and nineteen other Te Aute students, supported by Thornton, established the Association for the Amelioration of the Condition of the Maori Race. The Association aimed to suppress traffic in alcohol, disseminate sanitary knowledge, and abolish 'injurious customs and useless meetings'.[40] A year later, three Te Aute students — Rēweti Kōhere, Māui Pōmare and Timutimu Tawhai — toured the Hawke's Bay, preaching this message to their elders, but the kaumātua were preoccupied with Te Kōtahitanga, a movement to set up a Māori Parliament, and did not take them seriously.[41]

At Canterbury, Apirana studied arts and law, gaining second-class honours in jurisprudence and constitutional history. Well liked by his fellow students, he worked hard and attended Anglican service each Sunday. He composed a waiata in praise of the college rugby team, and in 1892, 'A Scene from the Past', an ode celebrating the arts of poi and haka that won first prize in the Canterbury College Dialectic Society's poetry competition.[42] In 1893, Ngata was awarded a scholarship and, at the age of nineteen, published his first article, 'The Past and Future of the Maori', a personal lament for the losses his people had suffered since colonial times:

Where are the mana and prestige of the ancient chiefs, the tapu, the chants and incantations of the priests? Surrendered to the white man, disdained by him and laughed to scorn, nay, abused by those of his own race.

Where are those lands over which his ancestors held such absolute sway? Gone, sold, stolen, robbed, the chief source of perplexity to his day, the bane of his race. And the hosts of warriors that traversed forest and plain, on the war path?

They, too, are gone, they, too, have disappeared before the advancing tide of immigration. Then he recoils startled and trembling, for the gain of civilisation fails far short of the loss he has suffered.

But now he ceases from retrospection. He has to face greater problems than have been worked out in his past. He has to consider the land question and the best means of government, he has to discuss the education of his children, but, above all, he must set about to find means for staying the alarming decrease of his race.[43]

In 1895, when Apirana was twenty-one and Arihia was sixteen, they began to live together, and the first of their fifteen children was born a year later. That same year, Ngata completed a Masters of Arts in political science, and joined the Polynesian Society, showing a keen interest in its research into Māori ancestral ways of living, and in anthropology as a discipline. The following year, he completed his LLB, the first New Zealander to gain the double degree BA, LLB.[44]

When his fellow student Ernest Rutherford, later a world-leading physicist, urged him to follow him to Cambridge University, Ngata replied, 'I bid you well that you go, while I remain here to help the people.'[45] This dedication and commitment to his people, instilled in him by his elders and by Thornton, stayed with him for the rest of his life.

The following year, when Ngāti Porou gathered to protest to Wī Pere, the MP for Eastern Maori,[46] about land purchases by government agents, Ngata was appointed clerk for the proceedings. The iwi also asked for a bridge to be built across the Waiapu River, and they expressed their concern about the decline of native birds because too much native bush was being logged, saying that the Crown should prohibit further felling of the remaining forests and declare them as reserves.[47]

In 1897, Apirana and Arihia moved to Auckland, where he was articled to the law firm Devore and Cooper to complete his legal training.

Te Rangihīroa /
Peter Henry Buck
(1877–1951)

Te Rangihīroa, Sir Peter Henry Buck, photographed in Wellington
during a visit home to New Zealand in 1935, after several years in
the United States. The following year he was appointed Director
of the Bernice Pauahi Bishop Museum in Honolulu.

Her name was Kapuakore, which means Cloudless, an apt name for one who never brought a cloud of sorrow to any living being. She was an old lady as I first recollect her. I do not remember when first we met, for she was my Maori grandmother, and she must have been about when I made my entry into the world. She often visited us, and I remember my mother saying to me, 'Press noses with your grandmother.'

Sometimes we crossed the river in her canoe to gather a commercial fungus that grew on dead trees and logs. After she sold the fungus to the village storekeepers, she would come to our house and gravely hand me a 2/- piece as my share in the partnership. While gathering drift firewood on the ocean beach, she pointed out the tapu spots to be avoided lest monsters of the deep carried one away.

On a deserted village site she pointed out a hollow that had formed the sunken floor of the house of my great-great-grandfather. When I helped her weed her potato patch on the Motunui plain, she showed me the trace of an old path that crossed her plot. She said, 'That was the swept-path of Kapuakore, and this plot was assigned to me because I bear her name.'

TE RANGIHĪROA, quoted in Condliffe, JB.[48]

Te Rangihīroa (second boy from right, middle row) with
his classmates at Urenui School, c.1885.

Peter Buck's upbringing was very different from Ngata's.[49] He was born in 1877, in Taranaki, to Rina, a close kinswoman of Ngārongokitua, his high-born, childless 'mother', and William Buck, an Irishman who had fought in the New Zealand Constabulary during the New Zealand Wars. Peter Buck (or Te Rangihīroa, as he later became known) spent his childhood in a whare near the Urenui River.

His Māori relatives, Ngāti Mutunga, had suffered greatly during the Musket Wars, when they were driven off their lands by tribes from the North. When they returned to try to stop their ancestral territories being acquired by European settlers, Ngāti Mutunga were attacked by the Crown and most of their land was confiscated.

Buck was raised by his Irish father, William, and Ngārongokitua (also known as Ngārongo), whose mother Kapuakore had gone with her people in the great heke (migration) south. He attended the local school, where he did very well, having a quick mind and a good memory. As a 'half-caste' in a European school, he later recalled, he was determined to be top of the class. According to one of his teachers, 'Peter was a perfect pupil, and practically taught himself. Though he appeared serious-minded, he had a great sense of humour.'[50]

Buck was very fond of his kuia Kapuakore, and often stayed with her. She told him ancestral stories and took him to the local marae, and sometimes to Parihaka, where the Taranaki prophets Te Whiti and Tohu had led a campaign of non-violent resistance against European land acquisition. His first language was English, however, and he did not speak Māori fluently. When Ngārongo died in 1894, Buck and his father packed up their possessions and left Urenui at night, going to Wellington first, and then to work on a sheep station in the Wairarapa owned by Reverend JC Andrews, Vice-Chancellor of the University of New Zealand.[51] Andrews was impressed by Buck, and encouraged him to apply to Te Aute, where he was accepted, beginning his studies there in 1896.[52]

At Te Aute, Buck was interviewed by Thornton, whom he described as 'an English gentleman with all the best traditions of his class, tall and dignified, with a well kept gray moustache that enhanced the character of his face'.[53] Gifted at sports, Buck trained assiduously, won the athletics championship and was made captain of the Te Aute rugby team. He was also a fine scholar, studying English, mathematics, physiology, Latin and Anglo-Saxon.

At the end of Buck's first year at Te Aute, Thornton decided to invite past and present students, along with various rangatira and other leaders, to a conference at the school in February 1897. After delivering an address, 'Labourers together with God', Thornton helped to draft a constitution for the Te Aute College Students' Association (TACSA), which, like the association Ngata had tried to establish five years earlier, aimed to improve buildings and sanitation, foster higher education and the Māori ministry,

suppress 'the drink traffic' and 'discourage and abolish objectionable and pernicious customs in connection with Maori meetings of all kinds'.[54]

Ngata played a leading role at this conference, issuing a clarion call for young Māori leaders to forge a new future for their people. He read papers on politics, employment, social reform and sexual morality; advocated university education as 'the royal road' to the professions; argued that Māori should create wealth by developing their own land, thus ensuring that it was not alienated; and offered a brief summary of the laws relating to Māori land, drafted during his legal apprenticeship in Auckland.

Peter Buck and fellow Te Aute student Hēnare Te Raumoa Balneavis (Ngāi Tāmanuhiri and Te Whakatōhea) were deeply impressed by Ngata and decided to follow in his footsteps, Buck attending university, and Balneavis becoming a law clerk in Gisborne. Meanwhile Thornton decided to raise funds for a travelling secretary for TACSA. He wrote to potential donors: 'The Maori, although he may not know it, is going to his doom; and his death is to a great extent chargeable to the English. Your plain duty then is to save him before it is too late. Every penny given to us is used for that object.'[55]

Later that year, according to Buck, Ngata visited Te Aute, brandishing a copy of the *Journal of the Polynesian Society* that included an article by Archdeacon Herbert William Williams on how ancestral Māori houses were constructed, and he discussed this with Thornton. At the second TACSA conference, in Gisborne in December 1897, Buck presented a paper describing Te Whiti's settlement at Parihaka, praising the wooden houses, public dining rooms and metal roads, but highlighting problems with gambling, alcohol and 'immorality'.[56]

With the encouragement of one of his teachers, Buck added Greek to his list of languages at Te Aute so that he could qualify for a government scholarship to study medicine at Otago. He sat the exam in Gisborne at Te Rau Kahikatea (the Māori theological college), where he first met Archdeacon Williams, the Māori language scholar whom he and Ngata respected and admired. From Gisborne he went with a school friend to Tairāwhiti, Ngata's home territory, where he attended the third TACSA conference in 1898. At the conference, Ngata presented a paper in which he traced the demographic decline of Māori to a low point of 39,854, recorded in the 1896 census.[57]

Amiria Stirling (Ngāti Porou) photographed by Jeremy Salmond at Rauru Nui a Toi whare tīpuna meeting house at Taumata-o-Mihi, near Ruatōrea (Ruatoria). In 1897, Te Rangihīroa lived here for a time with the Anglican minister Eruera Kāwhia.

After the conference, Buck stayed on to earn money scrubcutting and to learn more about the Māori language and ways of life. He was a guest of the Anglican priest Eruera Kāwhia, living in the wharenui at Taumata-o-Mihi, a small village south of Ruatōrea (Ruatoria).[58] Here, Buck first heard the saying, 'Ka pū te rūhā, ka hao te rangatahi' 'Set the old net aside, let the new net go fishing'. Ngata wrote to Buck at Taumata o Mihi, sharing his dreams for their cohort of Te Aute graduates:

> Hector, Kohere and Bennett, [as] parsons; Hei and myself lawyers, you and Tutere [Wī Repa] doctors—these are the men on whom a tremendous responsibility has devolved by virtue of their position and education. We the parsons & lawyers will do the talking and some practical work, we will 'clear the land, drive the road & bridge the ford' for you that come after—it is ours to remove prejudice, to argue out of existence fallacious doctrines, to lay the foundations of a healthier, more compact, more powerful social opinion among our people, that your future work may be easy.

> I only wish you had your M.B. or M.D. now and you could come with me...to begin the field-work of the Association [TACSA], to devote ourselves body and soul to it. I can't sleep for dreaming & thinking of it. I hope you are acquiring knowledge of Maori life amongst my people—don't pick holes in them, we have done that time & again, but seek rather for the good qualities such as may be perpetuated for the good of the race.[59]

During this visit, Buck fell in love with Materoa Ngārimu, a high-born, beautiful young woman. The elders ridiculed his pretensions, and composed a haka, 'Who is this man from Taranaki?' After this galling experience, he decided to take Apirana's advice and learn te reo Māori, and about Māori life.

> My Maori words unconsciously flowed along an English channel of grammar, and I was horribly conscious that I was talking to my own people like a foreigner...I early realised that to gain the interest and support of chiefs and leaders older than myself, I must overcome the handicap of youth by an exhibition of Māori scholarship that would not only earn their respect but indicate clearly where my sympathies lay.

> I commenced an intensive study of Maori mythology, legends, tradition, and the details of customs, manners and etiquette. I learned the pattern of ceremonial speech, and the forms of metaphor and simile that went with it...

> With others of the younger leaders, I became a home-made anthropologist—not to obtain a university degree, but to gain an inner understanding of our own people in order that we might better help them through the problems and trials created by civilisation.[60]

It was probably at this time that Buck adopted his ancestral name, Te Rangihīroa.

When he learned that he had passed his medical preliminary examination, Te Rangihīroa joined his fellow Te Aute student Tūtere Wī Repa, who had also passed the exam, and in February 1899 they headed south to the Otago Medical School in Dunedin as the school's first Māori medical students. Te Rangihīroa studied hard at Otago, and gained a reputation as 'a student of excellent abilities, hardworking and conscientious, [who] never failed to take a good place in his class and earned the good opinion of all of his teachers'.[61] He was popular and amusing, and became captain of the university rugby and athletics clubs, subeditor of the Otago University *Review*, and in his final year, was elected president of the Otago University Students' Association.

**Te Rangihīroa graduated with a Bachelor of Medicine and Bachelor
of Surgery from the University of Otago in 1904.**

Te Rangihīroa and his university colleagues Wī Repa and Nuku, in the
Dunedin Botanical Gardens in 1899, staging a stunt in which they
stalk a stuffed moa.

Te Rangihīroa was fond of practical 'stunts', as he called them. When Dr Thomas Hocken, founder of the Hocken Library, asked him to perform an ancient Māori christening ceremony at a local bazaar, and gave him an English text of a karakia to recite, Te Rangihīroa and Wī Repa decided to use a chant that was well known to Māori children instead. Dressed in a cloak provided by Hocken, Te Rangihīroa took a karamū twig and dipped it in water, then sprinkled the stage 'baby' and chanted 'E rere te kotare' 'Fly, kingfisher', to tremendous applause. After repeating the ditty, he improvised in Māori, 'Who are these people in the audience. They are Pakeha. They are the people who have stolen your land.' Dr Hocken mercifully did not understand, but an officer in the Native Affairs Department who was in the audience called out, 'No, not at all!'[62]

After graduating from Otago, Te Rangihīroa was appointed as a junior house surgeon at Dunedin Hospital, and then worked briefly at Sunnyside Mental Hospital in Christchurch. He met and married Margaret Wilson, an Irishwoman who had arrived in New Zealand as a young girl. This was an unusual marriage at the time, when prejudice against Pākehā women marrying Māori men was strong. Margaret was a determined woman, however, and intensely loyal and ambitious for her new husband. At the end of 1905, Te Rangihīroa took up an appointment as a native health officer, working under Māui Pōmare, another Te Aute old boy who was also from Taranaki and a trained doctor, at the Department of Health.[63]

At this time, while Te Rangihīroa was studying medicine at Otago, Ngata was fighting for his people.

In 1899 he became the travelling secretary for TACSA, campaigning on health issues, including ventilation in meeting houses, strengthening tribal committees, arguing for papatipu rūnanga to deal with ancestral lands instead of the Native Land Court, and fostering Māori arts including haka, poi and whakairo. During his travels around the country, Ngata built close relationships with leading rangatira, and in 1901 he was elected chairman of the Horouta Maori Council. The following year, he was appointed the organising inspector of Māori councils, campaigning for the preservation of Māori lands.[64]

In 1905, at the age of thirty-one, Apirana Ngata was elected to Parliament, defeating Wī Pere to win the Eastern Maori seat.[65] He remained closely associated with TACSA, and at its tenth conference at Ōhinemutu in December that year, moved a motion to ask the Minister of Native Affairs to have waiata and whaikōrero collected 'in the recording machines of the Pakeha'.[66]

In June 1906, a Royal Commission into Te Aute College issued its report. Despite (and perhaps because of) Te Aute's academic success and TACSA's best efforts, Thornton was pressured to abandon his academic programme for Māori boys, and to shift to a technical curriculum based on agricultural studies. When he refused, the provision of scholarships to Te Aute was curtailed. According to the Inspector of Native Schools, 'the purpose of Maori education was 'to prepare Maori for life among Maori, not to encourage them to mingle with Europeans in trade and commerce'.[67]

James Ingram McDonald
(1865–1935)

In the late summer of 1815, an elderly man sat in front of his farmhouse on the Hebridean island of Mull in Scotland, singing ancient songs and reciting poetry handed down to him by his grandfather, and recounting legendary feats of their ancestors and tales of extraordinary beings that used to roam their island home.[68] Iain MacMhuirich, the local schoolmaster and a native-speaking Gaelic scholar and collector of poetry and lore, sat beside him, recording the old man's words on paper.

MacMhuirich (known to his English-speaking associates as John Currie) was engaged in a project to capture Gaelic songs and poetry from the Scottish Highlands that were in danger of disappearing, threatened by the encroachment of the English language and radical changes in the lives and lifestyles of the people of the region.

A century later, after MacMhuirich's descendants had been forced to leave their island home and many were scattered around the world, his great-grandson James McDonald was at work on a similar kind of project, this time with Māori elders in the North Island of New Zealand.

This self-portrait of James McDonald was taken at the Dominion Museum around 1925.

James McDonald, the son of Gaelic-speaking Scottish immigrants to New Zealand, was born in 1865 in the Tokomairiro district in South Otago. His father, Donald, a ploughman from the island of Ulva, had left Scotland with his wife two years earlier. Donald, his parents and siblings had been removed from their ancestral land during the Clearances, a series of events that forced thousands of rural Scottish people from the lands they had farmed for generations. After working for the owner of a large Otago sheep run, Donald saved enough to buy a small farm at Lovells Flat in the Tokomairiro district,[69] near the lake now known as Tuakitoto (but properly Rotonui a Whatu) that was said to have been dug by the South Island ancestor Rākaihautū, on land that was formerly contested between Ngāti Māmoe and Ngāi Tahu, and had since been purchased by the New Zealand Company as part of the Otago block in 1844.[70] The family then shifted to Waihola, where James and his brothers and sisters were educated at the local school. Eventually, Donald purchased a larger farm at Milburn.[71]

In the McDonald household, education was greatly valued, a legacy handed down from Iain MacMhuirich. For centuries, the MacMhuirich lineage had acted as keepers of genealogies and composers of poems celebrating the deeds and conquests of the MacDonalds, Lords of the Isles[72] — and latterly of Clanranald — in a rich oral tradition, not unlike the tohunga who passed on ancestral knowledge across the generations in Aotearoa.[73] James McDonald's later interest in Māori culture and traditional life may well have been sparked by this ancestral precedent.

As a young man, McDonald moved to Dunedin to study at Otago Boys' High School, where he first became interested in art. He enrolled in drawing and painting classes, probably at the Dunedin School of Art (founded in 1870 by another Scot, David Con Hutton). He also studied bookkeeping, and around 1889 went to work as an accountant in Melbourne, Australia. There he became an active member of the local arts scene, studying painting with Frederick McCubbin at the National Gallery of Victoria Art School and becoming a founding member of the Yarra Sculptors' Society.[74] In 1891 he married Mary (May) Brabin, and the couple had three children while living in Melbourne.[75]

McDonald moved back to New Zealand with his young family in 1901, and worked in Wellington as a freelance newspaper cartoonist while developing his skills in photography and cinematography. The Lumière brothers had devised a portable Cinématographe which had made its Australasian debut in 1896, and McDonald was among the earliest pioneers of the medium. He was appointed as a photographer and cinematographer in the newly established Department of Tourist and Health Resorts in Wellington,[76] headed by TE Donne, in 1902[77] and became a member of the Silverstream group of painters, led by the Scottish artist James Nairn. McDonald worked closely with his friend James Cowan, a Māori-speaking journalist who also worked at the Department.[78] As Cowan later recalled:

> 'Mac' was not only a good artist but a good sport, a capital travelling mate, always cheerful, resourceful in camp. I write with knowledge and affection for 'Mac', for we travelled some thousands of miles together and camped in all sorts of queer corners in those days. There was the faithful trio of us, with T.E.D. to boss the party in his genial capacity as official head.
>
> I see them now, 'Mac' jogging along on his horse with a brace of cameras slung over his shoulders; far down the bush tracks of Westland — we had a wild week of it there once, a hundred and fifty miles from the Franz Josef Glacier over the Haast Pass and out to civilisation again at Lake Wanaka.
>
> He was almost constantly in the field for the Government Department of Tourist and Health Resorts, in the pioneer days of that office under its very energetic head, Mr. T.E. Donne, now living in London. ['Mac'] was an all-round able man in the artistic side of our national advertisement work, before that much-used term publicity had been coined.[79]

FROM THE PAINTING BY J. McDONALD.]

"HE TAUA! HE TAUA!"

In ancient Maori times, when every tribe's hand was against its neighbour's, and when the Maori warrior ever had in mind the adage of his fighting race, "Me mate te tangata me mate mo te whenua." ("The death of the warrior is to die for the land")—the Maori equivalent of the ancient Roman's "Dulce et decorum est pro patria mori,"—such a scene as that depicted by the artist was quite a frequent one.

The cry, "He Taua! He Taua!" ("A war party!" "A war party!") has been raised in the sentinels in the watch-towers, or fighting-platforms, which project from the upper walls of the carved stockading encircling the hill fort. It is early morning, and the watchers have just descried a fleet of war canoes sweeping into the bay. The man in the immediate fore-ground is sounding an alarm on a Triton conch-shell (pu-tatara) such as were commonly used in the olden days and were quite recently to be heard in the villages of the Urewera country. These pu-tatara emit a most doleful sound, which can be heard for a great distance. Another excited warrior is putting his soul into the blowing of a long pukara, or war trumpet, made of wood bound round with aka vines, and fitted with a blunderbuss-like mouth; these were used in olden times to call the tribe to arms. On the citadel within the topmost holding the pole, or wooden war drum, is being beaten, while the inmates hurry to the cliffy sides of the pa to grapple for battle. Just such a scene as this is inimitably described... the pending in that Maoriland classic, "Old New Zealand."

THE ARMORIAL BEARINGS
OF
THE DOMINION OF NEW ZEALAND.

*Authorized by Royal Warrant, dated
26th August, 1911.*

In 1905, perhaps attracted by the opportunity to use his artistic talents, McDonald took a job at the Colonial Museum in Wellington as a draughtsman and museum assistant, helping with displays, and making a detailed model of a Māori pā. The following year, he began work on a monumental group of Māori figures, also intended for display in the museum's Maori Hall.[80] Later that year, McDonald was transferred from the museum back to the Department of Tourist and Health Resorts to work as an 'art assistant' for the New Zealand

International Exhibition in Christchurch, where he completed his sculpture, described by Cowan in the exhibition's official report:

> The two principal figures were a Maori man and woman, standing, the *wahine* finely draped in a long *korowai* mat and carrying a baby *pikau*-fashion on her shoulders. Seated were a youth, playing a *putorino* or flute, a carver at work, a beautiful girl (modelled from a young Canterbury half-caste girl) making a *poi*-ball, and on the western side an old warrior *mere* in hand, gazing with introspective eyes to the past.

**James McDonald's design for the New Zealand
Coat of Arms. Salmond Family Archive.**

James McDonald took this photograph of his sculpture
for the International Exhibition in Christchurch in 1906,
at the exhibition building.

On each face of the pedestal was a panel, two of which represented the ancient art of cutting green-stone, the other two the olden-practice of *hika-ahi* or producing fire from wood by friction. A heroic emblematic Māori group of this kind, based on Mr. McDonald's ideas, would be a remarkably appropriate sculpture set, at any future New Zealand exhibition.[81]

At the exhibition, McDonald photographed many of the events held in the model pā, including waka paddling on the lake, haka, poi dances, demonstrations of tattooing and fighting, ceremonial welcomes to visitors, Fijian kava ceremonies and firewalking. He worked closely with the Museum Director, Augustus Hamilton, and with Neke Kapua and his two sons Eramiha and Tene Neke, Ngāti Tarāwhai carvers from Rotorua who had been recruited to work on the carvings for the pā, which included a large gateway that is now in Te Papa, and a pātaka that was first exhibited in the Dominion Museum and is now at the Canterbury Museum.

The Ngāti Tarāwhai carvers played a prominent role in the ceremonial welcomes to visitors, along with other iwi and groups from the Pacific Islands.[82] It is probable that McDonald first began learning the art of whakairo from the Kapua men at that time, a practice to which he became devoted in his retirement. He also produced artworks for a series of postcards illustrating key themes at the model pā.

During his time as government kinematographist, McDonald had been with ethnologist, historian and collector Thomas Hocken when they discovered a copy of the Treaty of Waitangi (now on display at the National Library in Wellington) in the basement of Parliament Buildings, chewed by rats. In 1910, McDonald won a competition with his design for the New Zealand coat of arms, which received its royal commission in 1911. Many of his photographs had been published by the Tourist Department as postcards, and he filmed a number of historic occasions, including the Dominion Day celebrations and Shackleton's departure on the *Nimrod* to Antarctica. As Donne noted:

The Department's photographer is also an expert cinematographer operator, who secures bioscope records of geysers in action, Maoris in their dances and the many picturesque incidents of life in these islands that lend themselves particularly to reproduction by kinematograph. Lately a set of films of this character, illustrating life in geyserland, travel and scenery on the Wanganui River, among other things was despatched to London, for use at the Franco-British Exhibition.[83]

In 1912, the Liberal government fell from power, succeeded by William Massey's Reform government, and Ngata found himself in opposition. A year later, after five years as government kinematographist, James McDonald found himself high and dry when one of his official patrons, Thomas Mackenzie, Liberal MP and Minister in charge of tourism (and briefly Prime Minister), was appointed as New Zealand's High Commissioner in the United Kingdom. His other patron, TE Donne, an enthusiastic collector of Māori traditions who had been head of the Department of Tourist and Health Resorts, had already shifted to London as New Zealand's Trade and Immigration Commissioner.

With the departure of McDonald's patrons, funding became scarce, and he decided to return to the Dominion Museum. Hamilton, perhaps looking for a good-tempered foil to Elsdon Best as well as a gifted all-rounder, appointed McDonald as photographer and art assistant, with responsibilities including illustrating the *Dominion Museum Bulletins*, helping set up exhibits, and looking after the paintings and drawings in the museum's collection.[84]

When Hamilton died of a heart attack in 1913, McDonald applied for the post of Director. Instead, the trustees appointed James Allan Thomson, a geologist and New Zealand's first Rhodes Scholar, who had a deep interest in museums and ethnology. Thomson was hard-working and well respected, but he suffered from tuberculosis, and frequently had to take sick leave.[85] This meant that, over the next thirteen years, McDonald would often serve as the Museum's Acting Director—a post he did not enjoy.

Elsdon Best
(1856–1931)

Elsdon Best, in 1931, not long before his death.

By the time Elsdon Best joined the staff of the Dominion Museum in 1910, he had already secured an international reputation as an ethnologist. His parents had grown up in England, married there and immigrated to New Zealand. They settled on a farm at Tawa Flat, south of Wellington, where Best was born in 1856. When he was ten years old, the family moved to Wellington, where his father Will became chief clerk and cashier in the Colonial Treasury. Best missed the farm, where he had worked in the bush with his father and brothers — memories his father captured in a poem:

> When we started from home last Tuesday morn,
> Three happy boys were we;
> As we wended our way to the back of the ground
> We and our axes three,
> To hack and slash at the underbrush
> And cut down the greenwood tree.
> Walter came first with his long, long legs,
> Striding over the lea,
> Fred came next with his impudent face,
> Full of his fun and his glee;
> Whilst Elsdon he followed up behind,
> The sturdiest of the three.[86]

After only five and a half years of formal schooling, Best passed the Junior Civil Service examination, and his father decided that he should join the staff of the Registrar-General. Best endured a year of office work, then resigned in 1874 and went to join his sister Isabel in Poverty Bay, where she had married a cattle farmer. In the wake of the battle of Waerenga a Hika in 1865, many Pākehā families had fled the district, and when Best arrived in the Bay, Te Kooti Arikirangi was still at large in the Urewera. Although Best sympathised with local Māori, he saw the conflict and the confiscations that followed as inevitable:

> Sooner or later the two peoples had to struggle for mastery. It would have been too much to expect of the Maori that he should fall in line with the methods, customs and ambitions of a race differing so widely from him on these lines and in general culture. Such a thing could not be.
>
> On the other hand, no civilised folk could have adopted the methods and ideals of a barbarous people. The only way in which the struggle could have been prevented would have been for the white man to have kept away from these isles, to have left the Maori in sole possession…
>
> The concrete fact is that neither of these peoples understood the other, their language, habits, methods or aspirations and herein lay the principal cause of the quarrels that arose between them.[87]

In Poverty Bay, Best became fascinated with ancestral tikanga, and spent much of his time with local Māori. As he recalled, 'I was always interested in these people, and between work and bedtime I was ever on the lookout for fresh material. Hour after hour I would listen to their tales, their traditions and their songs—and there were hundreds of the latter.'[88]

Nevertheless, when work dried up in Poverty Bay in 1877, he joined the Armed Constabulary as a volunteer to fight against Māori in Taranaki. William Buck, Te Rangihīroa's father, had left the Armed Constabulary in 1871, but was still living in the district.

In Taranaki, Best met Percy Smith, a surveyor who had served in the local militia and was deeply interested in Māori history, and Edward Tregear, captain of the Patea Rifle Volunteers and also a surveyor, who later wrote a comparative Māori dictionary. Like Best, they were fascinated by Māori life, providing Best with books on the subject and encouraging him in his researches. Best's commander Captain WE Gudgeon, also a keen Māori scholar who had married another of Best's sisters, supported his application to join the Native Contingent, which was dominated by Te Arawa warriors, because he thought it would be helpful to have a young European who spoke Māori attached to the forces. In 1881, Best participated in the attack on Parihaka (and Te Rangihīroa's Māori relatives) that resulted in the devastation of the settlement and the arrest of Te Whiti and Tohu, along with hundreds of their followers.

After a brief stint in Kāwhia, guarding the boundaries to the King Country, Best decided to return to Poverty Bay, although his sister Isabel and her husband had by now left the district. In 1883 he set sail for San Francisco, and for the next three years worked in logging camps and sawmills and on railways across the United States. When he returned to New Zealand in 1886, Best helped his brother Walter to set up a timber mill in Horowhenua, hoping to make enough money to spend his time studying and recording tikanga Māori.

At this time the Māori population had reached its nadir, and it seemed that the Māori people were heading for extinction. Best, like many others, was convinced that Māori were a dying race, and was eager to record their customs and beliefs before it was too late. In 1891, when the timber mill failed, Percy Smith invited Best to come to Wellington to discuss the establishment of a society devoted to Polynesian history and culture. Best responded with alacrity: he moved to Wellington and found himself lodgings close to the Colonial Museum.

In January 1892 the Polynesian Society was established, with Her Majesty Liliuokalani, Queen of the Hawaiian Islands, as patron; Judge H Seth-Smith, chief judge of the Native Land Court, as president; Sir George Grey as an honorary member; and Smith, Tregear and Best as council members.[89] They began publishing the *Journal of the Polynesian Society*, which from the outset printed articles by

Māori experts in Māori. By 1893, the honorary members were joined by professors Max Muller from Oxford and Horatio Hale, who had headed the United States Exploring Expedition of 1838–42; and among the corresponding members were Major Rāpata Wahawaha from Waiomatatini (Ngata's tipuna); Hoani Nahe from Thames; and Major Te Keepa Te Rangihiwinui from Whanganui. After

forging friendships with local elders in Porirua, Best travelled around the Wellington region—often wearing a Scottish plaid, the uniform of the Armed Constabulary in Taranaki[90]—recording pā sites and ancestral stories. He began to write articles for newspapers and for the *Journal of the Polynesian Society*, although he still felt that he had seen 'only the outer palisades of the hidden pa of knowledge'.[91]

Elsdon Best (left) and his friend Tom Wyatt in 1883, not long before Best left for San Francisco. Photograph by Edgar Richard Williams. Alexander Turnbull Library.

The Tūhoe elder Paitini Wī Tāpeka, photographed with Elsdon Best
by James McDonald in Rotorua around 1920, during the second
Dominion Museum Ethnological Expedition. Paitini is wearing the
kaitaka later presented to James McDonald which is now held
in the Otago Museum collection.

The government was intent on opening up the Urewera, and when they sent in a survey party to mark out a road, Tūhoe resisted. Percy Smith suggested that Best should join the survey team as a storeman, paymaster and mediator. He joined in 1895, and over the next few years formed close relationships with Tūhoe elders, including Tūtakangahau and Paitini Wī Tāpeka of Maungapōhatu, both of whom had fought with Te Kooti against the Crown in the New Zealand Wars.[92]

In 1920, Paitini and Best met again when they attended the welcome to the Prince of Wales in Rotorua — Best in his capacity as a member of the second Dominion Museum Ethnological Expedition. In Rotorua, James McDonald photographed Paitini and his wife Makurata demonstrating various tikanga, including string games. At that time, a kaitaka worn by Paitini (and no doubt woven by Makurata) was given to McDonald; it is now in the Otago Museum.

Best's time in the Urewera was transformative. Many knowledgeable elders were still living, and Māori was spoken everywhere. Best's appointment as Secretary of the Urewera Commission, investigating land boundaries and lists of owners, gave him access to a wealth of ancestral stories and whakapapa; and Tūtakangahau, Paitini and a number of other Tūhoe elders became his teachers. He recorded a treasure trove of material in Māori on a wide range of subjects, often using an idiosyncratic shorthand to keep pace with the speakers,[93] to the despair of later generations of scholars. After a heavy fall from a horse, he was nursed by a friend's daughter, Adelaide Wylie, a Native School teacher whom he married in 1903. In 1904 he was appointed as a Native Health Inspector, and he and Adelaide spent the next six years at Rūātoki, where he wrote his 1200-page magnum opus *Tuhoe: The Children of the Mist*, although this was not published until 1925. During his time in the Urewera, Best published more than 100 articles, mostly about tikanga Māori.

Before Tūtakangahau died at Maungapōhatu in 1907, however, he and Best had become alienated. When Tūtakangahau became a follower of the prophet Rua Kēnana, whom Best abominated, they parted ways.[94] In 1906–07, Paratene Ngata also spent a good deal of time in the Urewera as the sole Māori member of the Urewera Commission — a controversial appointment, since Paratene's tipuna Rāpata Wahawaha had pursued Te Kooti into the heart of the Urewera during the New Zealand Wars.[95] The decisions of the commission provoked inter-hapū conflict, and were often followed by government land purchases.

At the same time, Best's work as a Native Health Inspector was frustrated by apathy and resistance, and he complained bitterly to Māui Pōmare about his inadequate travel allowance. A standoff with the local Maori Council led to his dismissal in 1909.[96] In his *Tuhoe* manuscript, he wrote: 'The last two years have wiped my old teachers off the slate of life…And I alone am left.'[97] In 1910 Best and Adelaide moved back to Wellington, and Augustus Hamilton, with support from Te Rangihīroa, Percy Smith, Walter Gudgeon and Edward Tregear, appointed him on a small salary as a clerk at the Dominion Museum.

In 1908, Hamilton had published the first *Dominion Museum Bulletin*, on Māori fishing. He was eager for Best to produce a series of similar bulletins about Māori life for the Museum, and recruited him for this purpose. When the first of Best's monographs, Bulletin 4, *The Stone Implements of the Maori*, was published in 1912, however, it led to a bitter dispute. Hamilton, who had contributed a few illustrations, inserted his name as a co-author, enraging Best, who threatened to 'publish the facts to every scientific body in the world'. Although Hamilton was very ill with heart disease, Best was bitter and kept up his attacks, even after Hamilton died the following year.[98]

Johannes Carl Andersen
(1873–1962)

Johannes Andersen, photographed in Wellington in 1928.

Johannes Andersen, the last member to join the Dominion Museum Ethnological Expeditions, was born in Denmark in 1873. A year later, his family immigrated to Christchurch. After attending Papanui High School, where he was dux two years running, he trained as a surveyor, and worked as a clerk in the Department of Lands and Survey.

Andersen was a fine sportsman, gifted in gymnastics and tennis. In 1890 he married Kate McHaffie, a teacher — although, judging from his diary from the 1923 East Coast Ethnological Expedition, he had a roving eye. He wrote and published poetry, and after trying his hand at translating Danish literature into English, turned his attention to Māori mythology.

In 1906, Andersen composed an ode that was performed to music at the opening of the International Exhibition in Christchurch, where he heard Māori music for the first time.[99] It is likely that he met Ngata, Te Rangihīroa, Best and McDonald during his visits to the exhibition. The following year he published a popular book, *Maori Life in Aotea-roa*, which earned him a reputation as an 'expert' on Māori traditions, although McDonald wrote to him afterwards, perhaps on Best's authority, correcting his use of the term tekoteko in *Maori Life*; he said that 'the word should be pou-teko'.[100] Andersen also studied the songs of birds and tried to reproduce these in musical notation; and Māori and European New Zealand place names, linking these with his work in Lands and Survey. In 1916, he published a mammoth history of Banks Peninsula.[101]

When Andersen was offered a post as assistant in the General Assembly Library in 1915, he and Kate moved to Wellington, where he joined the Wellington Philosophical Society. There he met James Thomson, Director of the Dominion Museum, who was interested in using sound recordings to capture Māori music[102] and who encouraged Andersen to use his skills to record waiata in musical notation. It seems to have been Thomson, rather than Ngata, Te Rangihīroa, McDonald or Best, who encouraged Andersen to contribute to the museum's work in this area despite his having little lived experience with Māori, then or later.

Towards the end of July 1918, when Thomson called a meeting to discuss the formation of a Historical Section in the Philosophical Society, Best was elected chairman, and Andersen, who had recently been appointed Librarian at the Turnbull Library, was made honorary secretary. Andersen also had an interest in string games, and when Thomson wrote to the Minister of Internal Affairs in February 1919 about the expedition to the Hui Aroha in Gisborne to 'obtain records of Maori speeches and songs, and films of Maori life and action', he enclosed a letter from Andersen asking if he might attend the gathering in an official capacity to study Māori songs, music and games. He added, 'Mr. Andersen has lately been making a special study of music from the Maori flute, using specimens in the Museum, and has been able to get notes from the mouth-flute, but none so far from flutes played by the nose. I heartily support the proposal that Mr. Andersen should accompany the party, which I suggest should consist of Mr. McDonald and Mr. Elsdon Best.'[103]

THE EXPEDITION TEAM COMES TOGETHER

Apirana Ngata (far left) and Te Rangihīroa (second from
left in front row) during a haka at the International Exhibition
in Christchurch, 1906.

FOLLOWING PAGE: Philip Robert Presants' illustration *A Bird's-
eye View of the International Exhibition in Christchurch 1907*, 1906–07.
Chromolithograph, 260 × 660 mm. Alexander Turnbull Library.

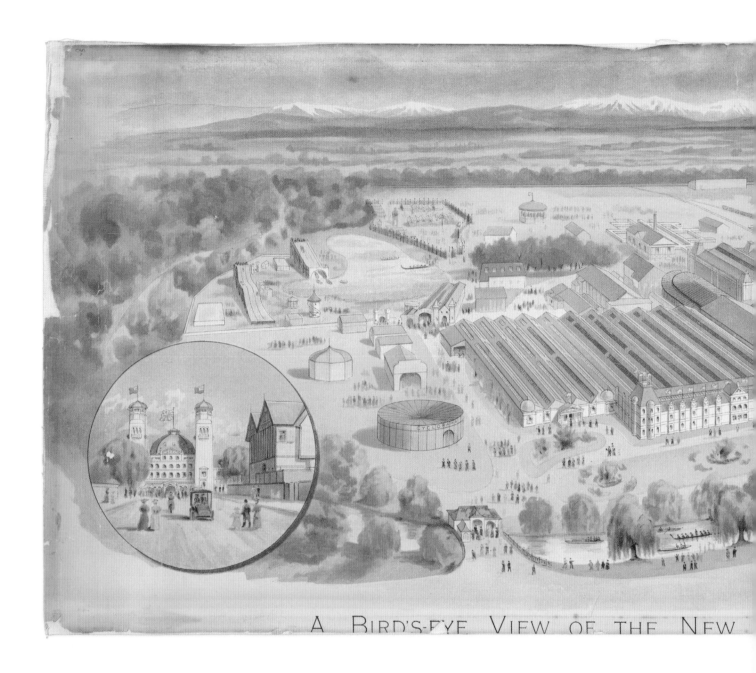

A BIRD'S-EYE VIEW OF THE NEW

The New Zealand International Exhibition in Christchurch in late 1906, with its efforts to celebrate and revive tikanga Māori, was an important precursor to the four Dominion Museum Expeditions that followed thirteen years later. Apirana Ngata, James McDonald, Te Rangihīroa and Johannes Andersen all spent time at the Exhibition, built in Hagley Park and featuring an impressive central building, a dragon train, water chute, toboggan course, helter-skelter

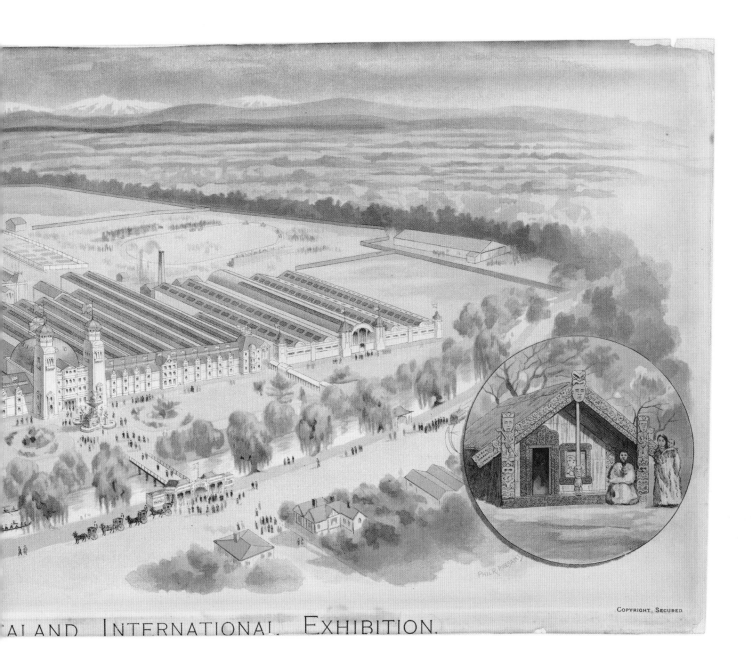

ALAND INTERNATIONAL EXHIBITION.

COPYRIGHT. SECURED.

and gondola, and a model Māori village located beside a man-made lake, with river waka from Whanganui and Waikato. In the pā, the meeting house was decorated with carvings borrowed from various New Zealand museums, or commissioned from Te Arawa and Whanganui carvers, who had worked on them at the Colonial Museum. A storehouse, destined for a model pā in Rotorua, stood nearby.

Augustus Hamilton,[104] who had met Te Rangihīroa during his studies, was ostensibly in charge of laying out the model pā, although Māori experts such as Hori Pukehika from Whanganui and Tuta Nihoniho of Ngāti Porou also played leading roles.[105] When it was opened, the pā was occupied by a contingent of fifty-seven Arawa and Whanganui people and twenty-five men, women and children from the Cook Islands, who lived in whare built of raupō, wore traditional costumes, and demonstrated 'ancient social customs, handicrafts and amusements' for visitors. The group included a number of elderly men who had fought both for and against the Crown during the New Zealand Wars.[106]

Perhaps through Hamilton's influence, or that of Sir James Carroll (Timi Kara), the leading Māori politician, who was a strong supporter of the Exhibition, Te Rangihīroa was appointed as the medical officer in charge of the village. As journalist James Cowan wrote in the official report of the exhibition:

> Not only did the different tribes benefit by witnessing each other's competitions and ceremonies and by the exchanging of ideas and information, but they were also given an excellent lesson in hygiene. They learned the necessity for ventilation in houses and for cleanliness in all respects. For this the credit is due to Dr. T. Rangihiroa, the young Maori tohunga of the pa.[107]

Apirana Ngata and Te Rangihīroa were photographed at various events at the pā by James McDonald.[108]

Women photographed by James McDonald performing at the International Exhibition in Christchurch in 1906.

Tene Waitere, another Ngāti Tarāwhai carver, who later carved a flagpole that was presented to the Prince of Wales at the 1920 welcome for the Prince in Rotorua (see page 147), also visited the exhibition. In December 1906, Samuel Heath Head photographed some of the Te Arawa party, including the well-known rangatira Mita Taupopoki, Mākereti Papakura (who later trained as an anthropologist at Oxford)[109] and Gilbert Mair, former commander of the Te Arawa Flying Column and an avid collector of taonga Māori.[110] Mair would later be interviewed by members of the second Dominion Museum Expedition at Ōhinemutu in 1920.

Te Arawa representatives photographed at the International Exhibition in Christchurch in 1906. From left: Te Rangikatukua, Mita Taupopoki, Iharaira Hikairo, Makareti (Maggie) Papakura, Hekemaru Kaiawha and Tutanekai Haerehuka. Gilbert Mair is in front. Mita Taupopoki, Hekemaru Kaiawha and Gilbert Mair hold patu. Te Rangikatukua and Tutanekai Haerehuka hold taiaha. Iharaira Hikairo holds a tewhatewha.

Sir James Carroll, photographed by James McDonald c. 1914, when Carroll was in his fifties.

Hēni Materoa Te Huinga Carroll (Rongowhakaata, Te Aitanga a Māhaki), wife of James Carroll, photographed in Wellington in 1909.

At this time, Ngata was serving his political apprenticeship as a Liberal MP, having recently joined Carroll in Parliament. Carroll (Ngāti Kahungunu), a revered Māori statesman and eloquent orator, would have a profound influence on Ngata's career.[111] The son of Tapuke, a Ngāti Kahungunu woman of mana, and Joseph Carroll, an Irish trader, he was a native speaker of Māori who had attended a European school. He joined the Native Department as a cadet, and McLean transferred him from there to Wellington. He was also a gifted sportsman. Carroll worked on sheep stations for a time before returning to Wellington as a parliamentary interpreter. In 1887 he married Hēni Materoa (Te Aitanga a Māhaki), a high-born young woman from Gisborne and a tribal leader in her own right.

Carroll defeated Wī Pere to win the Eastern Maori seat. In Parliament, he fought against the Crown's 'right of pre-emption' (first right of purchase) for Māori land, and worked closely with Rāpata Wahawaha and Paratene Ngata to develop management committees for blocks of Māori land with multiple owners. As land sales accelerated, he tried every tactic to delay them; this earned him the nickname 'Timi Taihoa' (Jimmy take-your-time). He was elected as the MP for Waiapu, a general electorate, in 1893. A gregarious, affable man, Carroll served as Minister of Native Affairs and Acting Prime Minister for a time, and he remained an MP until 1919.

Once Ngata entered Parliament, James Carroll became his mentor. He made sure that the young lawyer was appointed alongside Sir Robert Stout to run the Stout–Ngata Royal Commission, inquiring into Māori land in 1906.[112] By now Ngata was running a number of communally owned farms in Ngāti Porou, with financial support from Samuel Williams on modern sheep-farming methods, and advice from local members of the Williams clan. Seventeen years later, he proudly demonstrated the results at his home farm at Waiomatatini to the fourth Dominion Museum Expedition.

In 1907–08, Stout and Ngata issued a remarkable report that documented Māori land losses, sought to limit the further alienation of Māori land, and proposed that shares in multiple-owned estates be consolidated into workable blocks and farmed as incorporations, a collective approach to farm management that they also recommended for European land.[113] Afterwards, Ngata worked with Carroll, and law lecturer and later Solicitor-General John Salmond[114] on the 1909 Native Lands Act, consolidating the laws relating to Māori land.[115] At the same time, Ngata was engaged in a programme of restoring Porourangi, the ancestral whare whakairo at Waiomatatini, an exercise designed to revitalise Ngāti Porou's mana and pride.[116]

In July 1908, TACSA held a high-profile conference in Wellington, attended by the Chief Justice, Sir Robert Stout; the Governor, Lord Plunket; and Prime Minister Sir Joseph Ward. Te Heuheu Tūkino V, ariki of Tūwharetoa, one of the highest-ranking figures in the Māori world, represented iwi leaders, and Apirana Ngata represented the rising generation. In his speech to the conference, Ngata urged Pākehā to stop regarding Māori as objects in museums, or as only good for performing the haka; rather, they should be treated as equals.[117]

With his growing interest in physical anthropology, Te Rangihīroa (who was now working as a medical officer in the central North Island and writing his MD thesis 'Medicine among the Maoris in Ancient and Modern Times') presented a paper to this conference called 'The Evolution of the Maori', which later

developed into a Cawthron lecture and his classic book, *The Coming of the Maori*.[118] This session was chaired by Augustus Hamilton, and at its close a motion was passed, setting up a heavyweight committee to confer with the Senate of the University of New Zealand about establishing a chair in Polynesian Studies.[119]

In August 1908, Admiral Sperry, commander of the US 'Great White Fleet', visited Rotorua with a party of his officers. They were welcomed by a group that included the Arawa rangatira Mita Taupopoki. James McDonald, recently appointed as government kinematographist,[120] filmed the pōwhiri or ceremonial welcome;[121] and Te Rangihīroa, formally dressed in frock coat and top hat, acted as interpreter. Tom Seddon, a fellow MP and a close friend of Te Rangihīroa, later recalled that when Mita Taupopoki stood to speak:

> Taiaha in hand, the orator worked himself into a frenzy. Sentence by sentence Te Rangi Hiroa interpreted him: 'Greetings, greetings to you, our kith and kin, who like our ancestors of old have crossed the Great Ocean of Kiwa.'
>
> Bennet [sic] began to chuckle as words poured from the speaker and Dr. Buck maintained the even tenor of his interpretation. 'You have come to this land in your canoe—just as did your ancestors from the English motherland in the *Mayflower* to found a new nation. So did our ancestors sail the tempestuous seas to another land.'
>
> Asked why he was laughing, the future Bishop explained, 'Peter is making it all up as he goes along! The old man is working himself up into a passion because of the neglect of the drains at Whakarewarewa!'[122]

In February 1909, when Ngata's close friend and colleague Hōne Heke, the MP for Northern Maori, died, Te Rangihīroa accompanied the cortège to Heke's home marae at Kaikohe. Carroll was also present, and when Heke's wife asked him to nominate Heke's successor, he sent a telegram to Ngata to seek his advice. Ngata telegraphed

back simply: 'Te Rangi Hiroa'. Te Heuheu Tūkino's name had also been mentioned in this connection, and when Carroll spoke on the marae, he praised the ariki: 'How can the lord of Tongariro descend from his mountain to the plains below? No, he cannot be a husband for the widow.' He turned to Te Rangihīroa, who was sitting at his feet, and declared, 'Here I have a husband who has the learning of both races — Te Rangi Hiroa! He is a fitting husband for the widow.'[123] As Te Rangihīroa later told Eric Ramsden, when he heard this, he nearly fell over backwards in shock.

Te Rangihīroa easily won the by-election for Northern Maori, and joined Ngata in Parliament. Like Carroll, he was popular with his fellow MPs, who respected Ngata but found him a little austere. Te Rangihīroa enjoyed the Parliament bar, Bellamy's, was good-natured and amusing, and was an accomplished golfer, a game that Ngata described as 'a form of marbles'. He belonged to a Masonic lodge and the Savage Club, a 'gentlemen's club' that featured Māori motifs.[124] When he spoke in the House, which was not often, it was generally about health, education, or Māori land.

Te Arawa during the reception for the officers and crew of the United States Navy battleships, known as the Great White Fleet, in Rotorua in 1908, photographed by James McDonald.

By now the Liberals were in power, Carroll was the Minister of Native Affairs, and Ngata was a junior minister, taking close friend and former schoolmate Hēnare Te Raumoa Balneavis as his private secretary. Te Rangihīroa joined them on the Native Affairs Committee, which dealt with most Māori questions, and as one of the 'Scarlet Pimpernels' — an informal society of Carroll, Ngata and Te Rangihīroa — would send an image of a scarlet pimpernel to an MP, indicating that they intended to filibuster his bill in the House unless an offer of hospitality at Bellamy's was forthcoming.[125]

Carroll was a wise mentor, calling Ngata and Te Rangihīroa his 'two colts', and winning their respect and admiration. When Carroll died in 1926, Ngata paid tribute to his 'statemanship;

From left: Te Rangihīroa, Apirana Ngata and Māui Pōmare at the Avondale Military Camp in Auckland in October 1914, during a visit to the Maori Contingent (later more correctly known as the Maori (Pioneer) Battalion).

his unrivalled oratory; [and] the fact that he represented in his person the ideal of the future New Zealander; the interpreter of the minds of two races, the link between the two'. He added:

> No one saw more clearly than Carroll the significance of the Young Maori Party Movement or welcomed it more warmly. For he was hoping for something like it to emerge, and had been watching us youngsters out of the corners of his very wise and cunning eyes.

> He saw it fill every sphere of affairs, and so warned of one which might be belittled in our eagerness — 'Kia mau ki to koutou Maoritanga' [hold fast to your Maoritanga] — thus handing us his ultimate treasure, the key to his life.[126]

Te Rangihīroa also recorded his thoughts about their mentor:

> Carroll was a lovable soul as well as a great leader. In some respects I was closer to him than the others, for I shared certain social tendencies with him.

> We sat at his feet, and we learned and supported his policy which Api has aptly termed 'masterly delay'. We wanted, with him, to delay the sales of Maori lands to the Pakeha until the Maoris could farm their own lands. Carroll was a philosopher and a theorist, and he required a younger, an active man to put his theories into practical effect.

> The man who took over from Carroll was Ngata. Api carried out his ideas with his own people, and it was only through his influence in commanding tribal cooperation that the ideas came to fruition. Api and Ngati Porou —

> a unique combination. Nobody else could have done it even if he had tried, for our people did not have the lands to work with. I could not have done it, because my medical training had diverted me to another field.

> Ngata was born and created for what became his life work. Carroll may have been the master, but his pupil grew in stature beyond the master though, with the humility of the truly great, he assumes the lower role.[127]

When TACSA held its conference in 1909, along with innovative initiatives in health, education and land reform, the 'Young Maori Party' (as it was now called) stated in its manifesto that it aimed to 'preserve the language, poetry, traditions and such of the customs and arts of the Maori as may be desirable and by promoting research in the Anthropology and Ethnology of the Polynesian race to contribute to science and provide a fund of material which should enrich Literature and Art of the future'.[128] On this matter, the influence of Samuel Williams and John Thornton had waned, and Carroll's was in the ascendant.[129]

At the New Zealand International Exhibition in Christchurch, Te Rangihīroa had become friendly with Augustus Hamilton, an avid collector of taonga Māori and a passionate proponent of establishing a national Māori Museum.[130] In 1909, when Hamilton asked Te Rangihīroa to help him arrange a job at the Dominion Museum for the distinguished ethnologist Elsdon Best so that he could write up his lifetime researches on ancestral Māori beliefs and customs, Te Rangihīroa was supportive. Shortly after the conference, however, he wrote to Ngata to suggest that they should organise a comprehensive programme of research into Māori life, and carry this out themselves.

According to Te Rangihīroa, this programme would include an anthropometrical survey of 'the race' (noting that he had already taken some measures of Māori school children); the collection of songs and incantations, as part of Ngata's proposed revision of Sir George Grey's *Nga Moteatea*; phonograph records of Māori music (here he added that the well-known Australian-born composer Percy Grainger had offered to set the songs to music); and a survey of Māori social organisation, with information to be recorded on forms adapted from those outlined in the Royal Anthropological Institute handbook, *Notes and Queries on Anthropology*.[131]

In 1910, during the parliamentary recess, Te Rangihīroa set off for the Cook Islands, where he served as a temporary medical officer and carried out fieldwork on material culture in Mangaia.[132] The following year, when fellow Young Maori Party member Māui Pōmare won the Western Maori seat, joining Ngata and Te Rangihīroa in Parliament, the three men divided up the research programme between them:[133] Ngata would tackle Māori songs and poetry; Te Rangihīroa would focus on physical anthropology and material culture; and Pōmare would record myths and legends[134] — fields to which they devoted themselves for the rest of their lives.[135]

Later that year Te Rangihīroa published his first substantive work on Māori material culture, an article in the third *Dominion Museum Bulletin* called 'On the Maori Art of Weaving Cloaks, Capes and Kilts', along with several other articles on Mangaian material culture.[136]

LEFT: The Director of the Dominion Museum, Augustus Hamilton, photographed by James McDonald in 1904.

RIGHT: Dr James Allan Thomson, Director of the Dominion Museum, 1914–1928, photographed by James McDonald c. 1919.

Dr Māui Pōmare signed this photograph taken
by James McDonald around 1910: 'Me te aroha'.

By this time, Te Rangihīroa's resolution that Māori should record their own ancestral tikanga, and his fascination with the Pacific and with weaving — usually a women's art — was becoming an obsession. As he wrote later to Ngata, he realised that:

> Maori ethnology could be made a monument of real research work that would be second to none in the world as regards a native race. All these other native cultures are being worked out by pakehas with all the drawbacks that they have as regards language and viewpoint.

> Kua mutu haere te wa kia Te Peehi ma, kua riro ma taua ma te Maori taua e korero [The time of Best and that crowd is ending. It is left for us, the Maori, to speak for ourselves.] It is left to us to straighten up what has been written by our pakeha pioneers and to carry on the work in intensive detail.[137]

Ngata agreed, emphasing the importance of te reo Māori in offering deeper understandings of ancestral tikanga:

> It seems to me that the language must be maintained. Indeed the English language fails in appeal to those subtle things that influence the mind & heart of the Maori, no matter how well educated he may be. And no pakeha, no matter how accomplished a Maori linguist he may be, can use the instrument of the Maori language to move the Maori mind and heart. With language goes the poetry, the whakatauki, the history and traditions, the whakapapa & so forth that enrich it.

> So also we must hang on to Maori art & the crafts. Happily these are finding a ready place in the native-born New Zealanders' scheme of life. I hope that the possession of a superior carved house with accompanying tukutuku

panels & painted rafters &c will do something to influence the Waikato people. It is bound to influence the pakehas round about.

> So when you ask, 'are we trying to hang on to too much or are we jettisoning valuable freight that the canoe may reach the haven?' I answer that the Maori is reacting on himself & his native culture, equipped with the 'taonga' the pakeha has laboriously gathered for himself. He is no longer puzzled by the innovations of the pakeha. In the higher reaches he can take the scientific view that many so-called inventions are merely additional & probably overrated methods of doing the same old things.

> Our best people will hold their own anywhere. Our faith now is to go our own way to build on what has, without design in most cases, persisted of the old tikanga with eye and brain made keener, with hand surer by the education of the pakeha & the experience of his methods.[138]

At the same time, both Ngata and Te Rangihīroa acknowledged the contribution of the older Pākehā scholars associated with the Polynesian Society, especially Herbert Williams, whom they both admired for his deep knowledge of te reo Māori, and Elsdon Best (or Peehi, as they called him); as Te Rangihīroa wrote later, 'We can never appreciate too much the work that Peehi has done.'[139] In another letter, he added:

> Percy Smith, Elsdon Best and others were voices crying in the wilderness to members of their own culture for support. Sir James Carroll was ridiculed by the higher culture because he recognized that cultural adaptation takes time. I have come to the conclusion that all the old Maori chiefs who tried to smooth things over and the succession of people with Maori blood from Jimmy to ourselves were all empirical anthropologists.[140]

In August 1914, the First World War broke out in Europe. At that time a delegation led by King Mahuta Tāwhiao was visiting London, where they presented a petition to King George V, asking for the return of confiscated Māori lands.[141] All of the Māori MPs—Ngata, Carroll, Pōmare and Charles (Taare) Parata (Ngāi Tahu, Ngāti Māmoe and Waitaha, the member for Southern Maori)—saw the war as an opportunity to lift their people to a position of equality with Europeans. According to Te Rangihīroa, although the British government had ruled that 'no native race should be used in hostilities between European races',[142] they argued that soldiers should be sent to Egypt as fighting troops, not on garrison duties.[143] The Māori troops were recruited along tribal lines, and in December, Te Rangihīroa, after unsuccessfully contesting a general seat in Parliament, joined the first Maori Contingent (Te Hokowhitu a Tū, the war party of Tū, the war god, as they were known in Māori) as their Medical Officer.[144]

In April 1915 when they arrived in Egypt, the Maori Contingent was inspected by General Sir John Maxwell, commander of the British forces.[145] At the pōwhiri, Te Rangihīroa spoke on behalf of the troops, asking that they be allowed to serve on active duty:

> Our ancestors were a war-like people, constantly sending out war parties on their intertribal campaigns. The members of this war party would be ashamed to face their people on the conclusion of the war if they were to be confined entirely to garrison duty and not given an opportunity of proving their mettle at the front.
>
> I speak now not so much as a soldier, but as a representative of the old Maori chiefs who would have spoken to you had they the opportunity. I voice their views and the thoughts that are in them. If we transgress the rules and forms that govern soldiers, then forgive us, for we speak as Maoris. We would sooner die from the bullets of the enemy than

from sickness and disease—for what says the Maori proverb? Man should die fighting hard like the struggling ururoa [shark] and not tamely submitting like the lazy tarakihi, which submits without a struggle.

> Though we are only a handful, the remnant of a remnant of a people, yet we consider that we are the old New Zealanders. No division can be truly called a New Zealand Division unless it numbers Maoris in its ranks. We, therefore, ask you, as the old chiefs of our people would ask you, to give us an opportunity for active service with our white kinsmen from New Zealand. Give us a chance![146]

His argument—and that of the Māori MPs at home—succeeded, and the Maori Contingent, after a stint garrisoning the island of Malta, was sent to fight at Gallipoli. Before they went into battle, their chaplain Henare Wainohu, who had attended Te Aute with Te Rangihīroa, spoke to the troops with tears in his eyes:

> The name and honor of the Maori people lies in your hands today. When you charge the enemy, never turn back, but go on, and on, and on to victory. I know that some…now here will never again stand together with us. But it would be better for us all to lie dead in these hollows and on the tops of these mountains than for a whisper of dishonour to go back to the old people at home.[147]

Later, Te Rangihīroa vividly described the fighting on the peninsula:

> As we went along, we heard the sudden burst of machine-gun and rifle fire on a ridge. We knew that an attacking party had neared a Turkish trench and had been discovered. Then suddenly the fire ceased, to be followed by a burst of three British cheers. I knew that a Turkish trench had been captured in the darkness at the point of a bayonet.

But more wonderful to me was that the night air was broken vigorously by the Maori war cry of 'Ka mate, ka mate! Ka ora, ka ora! We may die, we may die! We may live, we may live!' I knew that a platoon of Maoris had shared in the capture of the trenches. Hardly had the sound died down than another burst of rapid fire occurred on another ridge with the same impressive sequence; silence, then British cheers accompanied by the Maori war cry.

And so it seemed perhaps to my excited imagination that the various slopes beyond kept repeating the same sequence of success and my heart thrilled at the sound of my mother tongue resounding up the slopes of Sari Bair. The Maoris had passed through the baptism of fire with courage and dash surpassed by none and had proved themselves worthy of their ancestry.[148]

During this campaign Te Rangihīroa was twice mentioned in despatches, and was awarded the DSO. In 1916 he was promoted to the rank of Major, became second-in-command of the NZ Pioneer Battalion (as it was now called)[149] and was sent to Europe. After their arrival in France, when Sir James Carroll visited the battalion, he was greeted with a spine-chilling haka; and Te Rangihīroa spoke, naming his comrades who had died and recounting their feats at Gallipoli.[150]

In August 1916 at the Somme—a campaign he recorded in his war diaries—Te Rangihīroa cared for many casualties, including Lieutenant Hēnare Kōhere, another Te Aute graduate from a Ngāti Porou rangatira family, who had been mortally wounded. On his deathbed, Kōhere asked Te Rangihīroa to ensure that his close relative Pekama Kaa would take command of his platoon.[151] During the fourth Dominion Museum Ethnological Expedition to the East Coast in 1923, Te Rangihīroa was warmly greeted by the Kaa and Kōhere families, who were still mourning the loss of their sons.

The Maori Contingent, later the Maori (Pioneer) Battalion, is farewelled from Wellington as HMNZT *Warrimoo* prepares to set sail in February 1915.

In February 1917, when the commander of D Company was wounded, at his own request Te Rangihīroa relinquished his position as Battalion second-in-command[152] and took over D Company's command.[153] He fought in the battle of Ypres (in which James McDonald's son also fought and was wounded), before transferring to the New Zealand Medical Corps in January 1918. In May 1918 he was sent back to England, where his wife Margaret joined him (she later received the MBE for her war service as a VAD in Egypt and England). In England he met the British social Darwinists Arthur Keith and Karl Pearson, who lent him instruments that he used to measure the men of the Pioneer Battalion on their way home, publishing the results in the *Journal of the Polynesian Society* in 1922–23. Many of McDonald's portraits of Māori men and women show them face on and in profile – images intended to assist Te Rangihīroa with his physical anthropology inquiries. On 5 April 1919, Te Rangihīroa and Margaret finally returned to New Zealand with the remnants of what was now known as the NZ Maori (Pioneer) Battalion on HMT *Westmoreland*.

The New Zealand Maori (Pioneer) Battalion performs the
haka for Prime Minister William Massey and Sir Joseph
Ward at Bois-de-Warnimont, France, 29 June 1918.

Te Rangihīroa with New Zealand's High Commissioner
to the United Kingdom, Sir Thomas Mackenzie, during
a visit to troops in France, 9 September 1917.

On the home front, throughout the war, austerity reigned. Best and McDonald were too old to fight, and Thomson was too ill. Early in 1915 there was a flurry of excitement when William Halse Rivers Rivers, ethnologist and lecturer in experimental psychology at Cambridge University, visited New Zealand after attending a meeting of the British Association for the Advancement of Science in Sydney.[154] In Wellington, Rivers delivered a public lecture, 'The Peopling of Polynesia',[155] and encouraged Best to join the Royal Anthropological Institute. He must also have told Best about the 1898 Cambridge University expedition to the Torres Straits, led by Alfred Cort Haddon, accompanied by Rivers and three other Cambridge graduates, including a photographer and filmmaker, and a musician who knew how to make wax cylinder recordings. This pioneering use of cutting-edge technology in anthropological fieldwork helped to inspire the Dominion Museum Ethnological Expeditions; and—as Best noted in the Museum's annual report—during his visit Rivers recommended that 'a series of monographs…be compiled on other ethnographical subjects, such as Maori sociology, mythology, anthropogeny, and religion'. Rivers may also have delivered copies of the Torres Straits Expedition reports to the Dominion Museum, or suggested that they order some from England.[156]

This contact with Rivers, along with Best's prior field experience, helped to ensure that Dominion Museum ethnological staff would carry out and publish research and, with their Māori associates, often spend time in Māori communities—although due to the war effort, there were no organised expeditions until those initiated by Ngata between 1919 and 1923. Hare Hongi, parliamentary interpreter and iwi scholar, carried out collecting and research with Hamilton; and Best visited Whanganui, Northland, Taranaki, Hawke's Bay and Wairarapa, and kept up an extensive correspondence with Māori scholars around the country.[157]

For the rest of the war years, Best and McDonald worked together at the Museum under challenging conditions, McDonald cataloguing the collections of artefacts, films and photographs, arranging displays and cleaning, oiling and painting rotting carvings,[158] while Best translated Māori manuscripts into English, because publication of the bulletins was no longer possible due to wartime paper shortages.[159] In 1915 McDonald reported:

> Nearly one thousand plates of Maori life, art and industry made by myself during my term of office in the Department of Tourist and Health Resorts have been transferred to the Dominion Museum. Also cinematographic films of Maori hakas, poi dances, and incidents of Native life which I had opportunities of taking have been added to the photographic records.
>
> The historical moving picture records in the possession of the Museum are: The visit of their Royal Highnesses the Duke and Duchess of York; visit of the American Fleet; visit of Field Marshall Lord Kitchener; visit of the battleship H.M.S. New Zealand; celebrations on the first anniversary of Dominion Day; several films of Mining Jubilee celebrations.[160]

The following year, Best wrote in the Museum's annual report:

> No. 5, 'Maori Storehouses and Kindred Structures' is still in the printers' hands, the long delay in its issue being due to the difficulty of obtaining a suitable and permanent paper. No. 6, on Maori Fortifications, awaits illustrations before being sent forward to printers. During the year No. 7, a monograph on Maori canoes and their manipulation, has been compiled, and awaits illustration…It is proposed to make Bulletin No. 8 a monograph on Maori games and exercises, for which a considerable amount of matter has been collected.[161]

Conversations with Cambridge University ethnologist William Halse
Rivers Rivers, and his use of cutting-edge technology on expeditions
to the Torres Straits, helped inform and inspire the Dominion
Museum expeditions. Rivers was photographed in London in 1917.

The medicine depot in Cathedral Square, Christchurch, from
where the government's standard influenza medicine was dispensed,
in 1918. Rural Māori communities did not have access to the same
supplies, and therefore the spread of the epidemic was more severe
and mortality rates higher than in urban centres.

In 1917, while McDonald was again Acting Director, Best was offered access to a number of old whakapapa books if he travelled to Whanganui to meet Hoani Te Whatahoro Jury, a scholar and prolific recorder of customs and traditions, who later provided access to Te Mātorohanga's famous whare wānanga manuscripts.[162] During this visit Best met a number of Whanganui elders with whom he would renew his acquaintance in 1921, during the third Dominion Museum Ethnological Expedition to Whanganui.[163]

Throughout this period, McDonald pursued his artistic work and from 1915 to 1918 served as Secretary and Treasurer of the Academy of Fine Arts. In this capacity, he had a strong influence on the establishment and early selection of the country's national art collection, and later played an important role in the establishment of the Rotorua School of Maori Arts and Crafts in 1926, and the Tūwharetoa School of Maori Arts and Crafts in 1932.[164]

The war was drawing to an end, and the Armistice was signed on 11 November 1918. At the same time, a virulent influenza pandemic broke out in New Zealand, brought by soldiers returning home from Europe. More than 8000 people died, and the death rate of Māori was eight times greater than that of Europeans. In the midst of this cataclysm, in December 1918, Apirana Ngata wrote his letter to the Minister of Internal Affairs, urging him to fund the use of phonographs to record different dialects of Māori, and the filming of tangi, meetings, village life, haka and poi dances.

There was a widespread sense of alarm that many experts in ancestral arts were dying and cultural practices were being abandoned, and Ngata was desperate to ensure that their skills and knowledge were not lost to future generations. As he told the Minister, GW Russell, early in 1919, there would be an unrivalled opportunity to try out these new technologies when the Pioneer Battalion was welcomed home in Gisborne. On the last day of the year, McDonald wrote to the Undersecretary of Internal Affairs, supporting this proposal, and adding, 'As the Hon. Mr Ngata truly says the elders are fast passing away, and the chances of securing such records are steadily diminishing.'[165]

In February 1919 Thomson, now back at work, wrote to the Minister: he noted that he had approved a Dominion Museum party to record speeches and songs at the Hui Aroha in Gisborne, and suggested that James McDonald and Elsdon Best should represent the Museum, and that Johannes Andersen should join them.

Now that the team for the first Dominion Museum Ethnological Expedition had been assembled,[166] the practical arrangements got under way. With the approval of the undersecretary, three saloon berths to Gisborne were booked and, as the *Poverty Bay Herald* reported on 3 April 1919, 'Mr. J. C. Andersen, Turnbull librarian, Mr. Elsdon Best, ethnologist of the Dominion Museum, and Mr. J. W. McDonald left Wellington yesterday morning for Gisborne to attend the Maori hui and collect phonographic and photographic records of song, speech, haka, and poi, dances.'

'KIA ORA TE HUI AROHA'

The First Dominion Museum
Ethnological Expedition
2–16 April 1919
Gisborne

MONTY SOUTAR

1

During the 2019 re-enactment in Gisborne of the return of
the Maori (Pioneer) Battalion in 1919, Pat Makiri follows the troops
with a camera on gimbal, while onlookers take photographs with
their phones. Photograph by Natalie Robertson.

Tatau tatau i roto i nga ra o te mamae, o te tauwhainga. Tatau tatau i roto i nga ra o te rangimarie, o te maungarongo.

We were together in the days of anguish and contention. So, let us come together in these days of peace and harmony.

Te Kopara, February 1919[1]

'The Pioneer (Māori) Battalion band' marches through Gisborne during the Hui Aroha commemorations in 2019. Photograph by Natalie Robertson.

FOLLOWING PAGE: Two horsemen in Mounted Rifles garb — Tawhai Aupouri (left) of Waiorongomai and Reihana Tipoki of Rangitukia — and troops marching across the Gladstone Road bridge in Gisborne. Photograph by Natalie Robertson.

'Parade! Parade shun! Parade! By the left quick march!' The officer's command echoes across the asphalt in front of Te Poho o Rāwiri marae and immediately 100 pairs of heel-plates click together. They are mostly young men, kitted out in First World War period uniforms, led by two horsemen dressed in Mounted Rifles garb and followed by two young women in nurses' attire. At the command they set out for the Gisborne CBD, where a crowd of over a thousand are gathering to commemorate the centenary of the Hui Aroha.

The articles they wear or carry — New Zealand Maori (Pioneer) Battalion replica hat and shoulder badges, webbing, waistbelt, slouch felt 'lemon-squeezer' hat with its red puggaree, and the SMLE Mk III, the standard rifle for the New Zealanders on the Western Front — recall military life of a century ago. Between the two platoons, each forty-five strong, the colour party escort positions itself to troop the Battalion's silk 'Union' flag, while a solitary base drummer marks the cadence, and the young men strike up the song 'Tipperary' in Māori and English.

Cameras are everywhere, from high-end media gear capturing soundbites of the parade, songs and haka for national television or for live-streaming to social media platforms, to individual smartphones recording the moment for posterity. The use of the latest technology to record the occasion, the dense throng of onlookers clapping and cheering, and the tramp, tramp, tramp of 100 pairs of brand-new army-issue boots echo across a century to 8 April 1919 and the largest Māori gathering of its time.

In early 1919, *Te Kopara*, the Māori-language newspaper printed in Gisborne, explained why the Hui Aroha was being held, reproduced below.

1. He hura i te kohatu whakamaharatanga ki to tatau kaumatua, ki a Wi Pere. Na te Kawanatanga i awhina tenei kohatu, a ma tetahi o nga Minita o te Kawanatanga e hura.

2. He whakanui mo te Maunga-rongo nana nei i whakamutu te pakanga.

3. He mihi ki o tatau aitua i hinga ki te pakanga.

4. He tangi ki o tatau aitua i hinga i te mate-uruta i mua tata ake nei, a he kimi i tetahi tikanga e taea ai te whakangawari te pa a nga mate pera a muri ake nei.

5. He powhiri ki a tatau tamariki i hoki mai i te pakanga. Kua whakaaetia e te Kawanatanga kia whakauria ratau ki Turanga i roto i nga ra o Aperira.

...Me powhiri ratau e te iwi Maori ki te marae kotahi, a koia tenei te marae kei Turanga. Ko nga ohaoha o te Hui kei runga kei nga iwi o te Tai-Rawhiti, o Te Arawa, o Matatua, o Horouta, o Takitimu, o Kahungunu, o Tamatea, o Rongokako. E hiahiatia ana kia eke ki te £25,000 te moni hei tapiri i te £25,000 kua kohia e nga iwi o te Tai-rawhiti i roto i nga tau e rua kua pahemo ake nei hei tahua oranga mo nga Hoia Maori. Heoi. Haere mai! Haere mai! Haere mai!

1. An unveiling of the memorial monument to our elder Wī Pere. The government contributed to this monument, and a minister of the Crown will unveil it.

2. A peace celebration to mark the end of the war.

3. An acknowledgement to our war dead.

4. A mourning for our loved ones who were recently struck down by influenza, and to look at ways of ameliorating the impact of such diseases in the future.

5. A traditional welcome to our young men who have returned from the war. The government has consented to them being disembarked in Gisborne in April.

...They should be formally welcomed by the Māori people on one marae, and this is to be at Gisborne. The tribes of the Tairāwhiti, Te Arawa, Mātaatua, Horouta, Takitimu, Kahungunu and Rongokako districts will underwrite the cost of the Hui. The aim is to raise another £25,000[2] and thereby double the funds collected by the tribes of the Tairāwhiti over the past two years for the maintenance of Māori soldiers. And so. Everyone is welcome! Come join in![3]

The group of soldiers relaxes during the Hui Aroha
commemorations in 2019.

The haka 'Ka mate' is performed by volunteers, including
Carlos Paenga (foreground) and Te Rakato Symes (far right),
in front of the Wī Pere Memorial in Gisborne, 2019.
Photographs by Natalie Robertson.

At the end of the notice was the phrase quoted at the start of this chapter: 'We were together in the days of anguish and contention. So, let us come together in these days of peace and harmony.'

The name Hui Aroha reflected the main purpose of the hui — an opportunity to show gratitude for all the sacrifices that the people had made over the course of the war. As Tūtere Wī Repa, a member of the Maori Soldiers' Fund (MSF) executive, explained:

Hui aroha ki nga morehu o te iwi Maori i te kainga nei. I te wa i karangatia ai tenei hui i te Aperira 6, 1919, kaore i maharatia tera e mutu te pakanga i roto i te 12 marama i muri iho o taua ra i karangatia ai te hui; a, kaore rawa hoki tetahi tohu kotahi nei i kitea e nga matakite Maori, Pakeha ranei, kua tata te mutu o te pakanga. Ka mutu ano nga tohu o era ra, ko te heke a te toto i te pae o te riri, ko te aue a te iwi i nga marae o muri nei. No reira ka kiia me tu he hui hei karanga i nga morehu o te iwi, kia huihui, kia kitekite, kia tangi, kia mihimihi kia ratou. Ka tapaia taua hui, he 'hui aroha', a, kei tu kohakore taua hui ka whakaurutia mai ki roto nga take e whai ake nei...[4]

A gathering of compassion for the remnant of the people here at home. When the gathering was announced for 6 April 1919 it was not realised that the war would be over within a year of the day the hui was called; for there was not one omen noticed by either the Māori or European seers that the war was near its conclusion. The symbols of those days have also ceased — the spilling of blood on the battlefield and the subsequent grieving of the people on the marae. So, it was said that a hui be held where the remnant of the people are invited to gather, to take stock, to mourn, and to acknowledge themselves [i.e. their efforts, sacrifices, losses]. The hui was dubbed a 'gathering of compassion', and so that it was not held without the opportunity for financial support the following purposes were included...[5]

Planning for the hui had begun a year earlier, before anyone knew when the war would end.[6] At first the organising committee intended to unveil a memorial to the late Wī Pere, the last in a series of fundraising events in aid of the Maori Soldiers' Fund.[7] This fund for the Eastern Maori electorate (Rotorua to Greytown) had been established in February 1917 at Waiomatatini, Apirana Ngata's home. A target of £25,000 (equivalent to $3.35 million in 2020)[8] was set and fundraising hui were held in Horouta (Te Araroa), Te Arawa (Rotorua), Mātaatua (Rūātoki), Kahungunu (Nūhaka and Frasertown), Tamatea (Hastings) and Rongokako (Wairarapa) districts of the electorate.[9]

Although the Gisborne tribes and those as far north as Tokomaru Bay, the Takitimu district, had contributed generously at these hui, there had been no special gathering in their area. On 16 March 1918, at the Frasertown (Te Kapu) hui, Lady Hēni Materoa (Te Huinga) Carroll, on behalf of the tribes of the Takitimu district, announced that a final rally would be held in Gisborne in March 1919. The committee was expecting to cater for about 2000 people.[10] The sudden end of the war

on 11 November 1918, when Germany surrendered and signed an armistice with the Allies. This and the influenza pandemic, which also reached its peak in November, cut across these patriotic arrangements.[11] Nevertheless, in December 1918, Ngata wrote to the Minister of Internal Affairs to suggest that films, photographs and wax cylinder recordings should be taken at the rally in Gisborne to assist 'in the preservation of records relating to the language, customs and ethnology of the Maori Race'.[12]

In the new year, the executive committee of the MSF heard that the Maori (Pioneer) Battalion, unlike other New Zealand battalions, would be returning as a complete unit.[13] The committee made representations through Ngata and James Carroll (MP for Gisborne) to the Minister of Defence (and Acting Prime Minister), James Allen, that a hui aroha should be held, in keeping with ancestral custom, to welcome home the Māori troops. They also requested that the Battalion be landed at Gisborne.[14] Shortly afterwards, the first Dominion Museum Ethnological Expedition team was assembled to carry out recordings at the hui.

With a population of over 8000, Gisborne was the fifth largest borough in the North Island after Auckland, Wellington, Palmerston North and Napier.[15] The Māori people of the electorate bombarded the minister with telegrams and letters in support of the committee's request.[16] In late January 1919, the government announced that Gisborne would serve both as the port of disembarkation for the Maori (Pioneer) Battalion, and the venue for the Battalion's official public welcome.

28 February 1919

On the night of 28 February 1919, 1033 members of the New Zealand Maori (Pioneer) Battalion left Liverpool aboard HMT *Westmoreland*.[17] The journey was expected to take six weeks, with Colón in Panama the only stop. Meanwhile, in New Zealand, the government's approval for the Battalion to disembark at Gisborne drew criticism from an unexpected quarter.[18] It came after Captain William Tutepuaki Pitt, a returned serviceman and secretary of both the executive committee of the MSF and the Hui Aroha organising committee, announced that one of the reasons the government had agreed the Battalion should disembark at Gisborne was that more than half the Māori soldiers who had gone overseas were from the Eastern Maori electorate; and that, since the Hui Aroha had already been arranged at Gisborne, the government regarded it as a timely opportunity to welcome them home.[19]

Pitt's statement drew adverse reaction from Māori returned servicemen from North Auckland, and a deputation of three veterans asked Auckland's mayor to lobby for the Battalion to land there instead. They argued that Auckland was centrally located, the troops could come ashore there in any weather, and its greater population would ensure a larger welcome from both Māori and Pākehā.[20] They argued that most of the returning men were in fact from North Auckland, and that Ngāpuhi had sent more men to the war than any other tribe.[21]

In fact the number of volunteers from the Northern Maori electorate was proportionate to its Māori population, which in 1914 had been 22 percent of the national Māori total of 49,595, whereas 41 percent of the Pioneers returning aboard the HMT *Westmoreland* were from the Eastern Maori electorate. Whanganui Māori joined the debate: they suggested the ship should land their boys at the Heads Wharf and they would escort them to Pūtiki pā aboard a number of large waka.[22]

The northerners' challenge succeeded. A fortnight before the *Westmoreland* was expected, Defence Minister Allen decided that the transport would dock at Auckland. Captain Henry Te Reiwhati Vercoe, another veteran on the Defence staff, had travelled as far afield as the King Country and the East Coast to get an indication of which iwi would attend a function in Auckland. Māori across the country, including Waikato, wanted the Pioneer Battalion to have a fitting welcome home, and were keen to help the citizens of Auckland and the authorities to plan an appropriate programme, but Māori on the eastern seaboard would not attend, as they were already committed to the Hui Aroha in Gisborne.[23]

Allen also approved a coastal steamer, the SS *Mapourika*, which belonged to the Union Steam Ship Company, to take the 428 soldiers from the Eastern Maori electorate to Gisborne after the Auckland event.[24] The Defence Department publicised the new arrangements, along with the names of the returning men.[25] When some of the soldiers on the *Westmoreland* learnt that they would be taking a detour past their tribal districts, however, 157 men from Rotorua (Te Arawa), Whakatāne (Ngāti Awa), Ōpōtiki (Whakatōhea) and East Taupō (Ngāti Tūwharetoa) decided not to travel to Gisborne, although their tribes had already agreed to attend the Hui Aroha.[26] They were keen to go directly to their home marae to be reunited with their loved ones.

The editor of *Te Kopara*, writing about the imminent return of the Maori (Pioneer) Battalion, took the opportunity to have a dig at Waikato and other iwi who had fought conscription:

Kei te hoki rangatira mai a tatou tamariki
i te marae o te pakanga. Kaore rawa he mea
kotahi o ratou e hoki mai nei i waiho ma te
Ture Puruma e akiaki. Ko nga Ture Puruma
i konei tonu e whawhai ana. He aha ra nga
tohu honore i riro mai i a ratou?

Our boys are returning from the battlefields
with their heads held high. Not one of those
returning was compelled by the conscription
law to enlist. The shirkers are still here resisting.
What emblems of honour have they gained?[27]

After thirty-six days at sea, the *Westmoreland*
dropped anchor in Waitematā harbour at 7pm
on Saturday 5 April.[28] The following day the Maori
(Pioneer) Battalion attended a grand public welcome
at the Auckland Domain. Afterwards, the soldiers
broke away into their tribal groups and boarded
transports to their home regions.

The 271 men from the East Coast and Hawke's
Bay, who were travelling to Gisborne on the
Mapourika, were the first to leave. They had been
disappointed not to see their iwi at the Auckland
Domain, but Carroll, who had travelled from the
East Coast to escort them home, told them of the
formal welcome that awaited them in Gisborne.[29]
The soldiers assembled at Queens Wharf at
6.30pm and were on their way within half an hour.
'Many had to be assisted aboard,' wrote Company
Sergeant Major Tawhai Tamepo, 'wobbly under
the influence of drinking over the mark.'[30]

They were joined by Allen, Major Boswell
representing Defence headquarters, the Battalion
commanding officer Lieutenant-Colonel WO Ennis,
and Majors Henry Peacock and Alex Main—two
Pākehā officers who had been responsible for
training the first Maori Contingent in 1914, and all
Māori and Pacific Island reinforcements since 1915.
The names of the soldiers aboard the *Mapourika*
were sent to the Gisborne Defence office, which published
them in the local paper the following day.[31]

Soon after their departure, 196 men from the
Western Maori and Southern Maori electorates
marched to the railway station, where they left
for Whanganui on a special train. Māui Pōmare
(MP for Western Maori) and Hopere (Billy) Uru
(MP for Southern Maori) accompanied this
group, which included Te Rangihīroa and his wife
Margaret. Tau Hēnare (MP for Northern Maori)
accompanied the northern contingent.[32]

Days before the *Westmoreland* docked in Auckland,
planning for the Hui Aroha was reaching a fever
pitch. The Gisborne Borough Council had met and
had voted to extend a civic welcome to the troops.
Mayor WG Sherratt dissented: he preferred to wait
for the arrival of the last of the overseas troops
and then hold one public welcome for all the
returned men, Māori and Pākehā. Other councillors,
however, insisted that the return of hundreds of
Māori troops was an occasion not to be missed.
A council subcommittee, headed by the deputy
mayor, HE Hill, was set up to make the necessary
arrangements, including the train to convey the
troops from the Gisborne wharf to the local park
racecourse at Te Hāpara.[33]

Ngata had persuaded the Poverty Bay Racing
Club to make the racecourse available as a venue
for the huge crowds who were expected to attend
the Hui Aroha. The ablutions were long overdue for
replacement and as a way of thanking the Racing
Club, the MSF's executive committee agreed to
build a new ablution block and to meet half the
cost of upgrading it with a septic tank system and
running water.[34]

On 2 April, the council subcommittee and the hui
organising committee agreed to a series of resolutions,
including closing the town from 10am until noon
to allow shopkeepers and their employees to join in
the festivities; that the mayor and other dignitaries
would deliver short speeches of welcome at the wharf;
and that the Civic and Salvation Army bands would
accompany the soldiers on a march up Gladstone
Road to the railway station.[35]

James McDonald took a series of photographs at Hui Aroha, Gisborne, 1919, showing the preparation of food (left, above), digging the hāngi pit (left, below), and lifting the hāngi (above).

A team of tradesmen and labourers, under the leadership of Ngata, Pitt, Carroll, Lady Carroll and the organising committee, had been busy for weeks preparing the hui grounds. They had transformed the racecourse into a contemporary pā, with a large 'marae' area in front of the main grandstand. The grandstand was to serve as the wharepuni (guesthouse) where the returned soldiers would sleep. A stage was constructed at the head of the marae where visitors would be welcomed and performing groups could entertain. They also built cooking facilities, temporary dining rooms, and extensive accommodation for the large number of tribal visitors expected from many parts of the eastern North Island. Under the careful watch of the Health Department and local authorities, special attention was paid to sanitation and hygiene matters.[36]

It was organisation on a massive scale, greatly helped by the fine weather. Pitt controlled the running of the camp. Volunteer workers from other iwi arrived from all over the Eastern Maori electorate, bringing their experience and skills honed at the other MSF fundraisers. Two local sheep stations each loaned an engine and a dynamo to light the tents and the camp. There was hot and cold running water for the kitchen, toilets—and the laundry, which was run by Pitt's wife, Kitty, and her team.

Local Māori communities contributed firewood and potatoes. Taranaki Te Ua was in charge of the catering. Te Ua was an experienced chef, and had been in charge of the Maori Contingent that had travelled to London for the coronation of Edward VII in 1902. Local stations donated cattle and sheep that were butchered at the Taruheru Freezing Works. Liquor was prohibited at the venue and policing of the event was placed in the hands of Thomas Halbert— a younger brother of the late Wī Pere, who had three sons in the Battalion. The issue of liquor was a significant one, as 10 April had been set down for a national liquor referendum on prohibition or continuance (preserving the status quo). Many Māori leaders involved in the hui hoped that prohibition would carry the day.[37]

The total outlay for the hui was estimated at £3600: this would cover crockery, cutlery, bedding, rugs, enamelware, linen, tinned food (apart from the koha of meat and vegetables), hire of marquees, cartage, freight, possible breakage and depreciation. This cost was to be met by a combination of money already raised by iwi specifically for the hui; the sale of surplus stock; the admission charge to the grounds; and proceeds from entertainments, canteens, stalls, permits and licences. 'No part of the money raised for the Maori Soldiers' Fund,' Ngata said in an interview, 'is to be touched for camp expenses.'[38]

Ngata personally supervised the large dining room, which was staffed by young men and women from all the tribes involved in the hui. The food was cooked in steam casks; crockery and cutlery were washed in wooden troughs; and steam was blown through the drains to keep them free of grease. Large hāngi were laid down to feed the hordes of visitors. The dining hall was 124 feet (37.8 metres) long, with a canvas roof and walls made of raupō and corrugated iron. A special canteen, run by Pare Keiha (Hēni Materoa's brother), was set up, from which Pākehā visitors could purchase cups of tea and light refreshments. There was even a merry-go-round for the children.[39]

The MSF advertised the hui in the *Poverty Bay Herald* as 'The Largest Meeting of Maoris ever Attempted', and informed the public that it could inspect the layout of the extensive grounds from Thursday 3 April, with entry at one shilling a head; the admission fee was set to double once the Hui Aroha officially got under way.[40] Local residents, who were used to seeing the grounds on race days or A&P show days, were pleasantly surprised to see how the facilities had been adapted for the hui. By this stage, local Māori were gathering at the park racecourse and visitors were beginning to pour into Gisborne.[41]

On 4 April, after collecting a contingent of Ngāti Kahungunu from Napier, the *Tangaroa* doubled back to pick up about 150 from Wairoa and Nūhaka. The next morning the *Mako* steamer brought about 100 people from Waiapu and Te Araroa; the *Arahura* picked up a group from Tokomaru Bay; and the Tūhoe people came overland through Motu.[42]

Te Hui Aroha camp carpenters with Apirana Ngata in 1919. Most of
this group were Ngāti Rangi from Reporua marae. From left at back:
Topi Pōkai, Tipiwhenua Houia, Hōri Kōnia, Kāwhia Milner, Haare Mūmu,
a not-yet-identified man and Herewini Te Hei. From left at front: Hūrae
Mākarini, Apirana Ngata, Paretītoki Rangi, Hāmiora Aramākutu,
Kereama Aupouri and Apirana Aupouri.

HUI AROHA

PARK RACECOURSE, TE HAPARA

Maori Reception

TO THE

Maori Battalion.

The Largest Meeting of Maoris ever attempted.

Camp Now Nearing Completion.

Open to the General Public as from

THURSDAY NEXT.

ADMISSION TO GROUND, 1/-. EXCEPTING ON DAYS TO BE NOTIFIED.

WM. T. PITT,
Secretary.

The Hui Aroha advertisement placed in the *Poverty Bay Herald* by the Maori Soldiers' Fund, April 1919.

Crowds gather at Te Hui Aroha, 1919. Tairāwhiti Museum.

2 April 1919

Amid this frenzied activity, the Dominion Museum team of Best, Andersen and McDonald arrived in Gisborne on board the *Arahura* on 2 April.[43] Ngata had arranged for Raumoa Balneavis, now private secretary to William Herries, the Minister of Native Affairs, to come to the hui from Wellington to take care of the team and organise their recording sessions. Balneavis's Ngāi Tāmanuhiri people of Muriwai were fully involved in the hui preparations: they had already supplied raupō for the accommodation buildings and to fill 1200 mattresses. The *Gisborne*

Times announced the arrival of the Dominion Museum team whose purpose, it said, was 'to attend the Maori hui and collect phonographic and photographic records of song, speech, haka and poi dances'. The knowledge that the government had gone to such lengths to document the event only added to the growing excitement among the public in Gisborne. When the *Times* reporter interviewed Best, the ethnologist explained the traditional significance of the hui and added that he expected it to be bigger than any Māori gathering since the visit of the Duke and Duchess of York in 1901.[44]

THE HUI: ITS HISTORIC SIGNIFICANCE. REVIVAL OF ANCIENT MAORI CUSTOMS.

Mr. Elsdon Best, in the course of a chat with a representative of the *Times*, said that the object of the visit is to obtain materials and data to serve as illustrations in several forthcoming works which would deal with Maori ethnology and serve as records of ancient rites and customs. He expected that the coming ceremony would probably be the largest of its kind that has been held since the visit of our present King, then the Duke of York. In connection with the coming function, the newly imported dictograph would be used to obtain records, not only of songs, but also of the ceremonial speeches — which will be such a marked feature of the great gathering. It is anticipated that some of the oldest Maoris will consent to intone some of their ancient chants, and thus preserve a permanent reminder of these fast disappearing features of Maori life.

A Hui, continued Mr. Best, is an assembly; it was derived from a verb meaning to assemble and a noun signifying an assembly. The Maori prized meetings of this kind because of their social nature — it brought the natives together in pleasurable social reunion which their barbaric mode of life did not generally provide. The Maori was much given to ceremonial speech-making, but dearly loved it. This penchant stood in place of several activities in our civilised life. It was a substitute for almost anything that would be proclaimed by the European in printed page or by writing.

The spoken word was with our aboriginals practically the only method of verbal expression and of public discussion. Even matters which we regard as private and of individual and personal interest only were made by the Maori the subject of discussion at the Hui. Even wills, family quarrels, individual disputes, as well as tribal differences and politics were made the subject matter of these public utterances and deliberations. Consequently, the anticipated event affords an unusual and most interesting insight into certain aspects of disappearing native customs.

It would therefore be seen, continued Mr. Best, that the Hui was to the Maori as a magistrate's court, a municipal council, and even as a Parliament. The Maori was a born orator and the idioms of his language lent themselves to poetic expression. The mytho-poetic faculty of this race was very strongly developed, as was usual with neolithic people. Therefore the speeches at these gatherings contained a world of imaginative imagery unknown in our tongue.

Eloquence became a fine art, to which no European could aspire. The public utterances of Sir James Carroll afford an excellent illustration of the astonishing command of soul-stirring eloquence. The native concept of the abstract was amazing, hence he delighted in the use of personification. With all deference to the views of other authorities, he believed that this grasp by the Maori of the sense of abstraction has enabled this people to evolve sublime ideas of God and the human soul. This may astonish those unacquainted with Maori modes of thought, but of it the student could find much evidence. It was eminently fitting and highly noteworthy that the return of warriors of this fine race to their native land should be marked by such functions as prevailed in pre-European times and which eloquently reminded them of the traditions and life of their ancestors.

The *Gisborne Times* printed its record of an extensive interview with Elsdon Best on 4 April 1919. It has been re-typeset here for ease of reading.

On 7 April, the programme for the civic reception was published in the *Poverty Bay Herald*, just a day before the *Mapourika* was expected in Gisborne. Children were given a half-day off school so they could join in the civic reception and line the parade route to throw flowers at the soldiers. The local Returned Soldiers' Association (RSA) requested that returned soldiers meet at their clubrooms so they could parade for the welcome, and the local cadets were invited to do likewise.[45]

On the morning of 7 April, the Tūranga tribes staged a combined pōwhiri for all the visiting iwi groups.[46] The canteen and stalls did brisk business all day; and Joe Gardiner, a well-known jiu-jitsu expert, packed out his performances. The *Gisborne Times* reported 'the grounds were well lighted, and everything pointed to good organisation and management'.[47]

The Dominion Museum team set up their dictaphone amid the festivities that day, but only managed to make a few recordings—three songs, three pātere (songs of derision in response to slander) and a karakia, performed by Tupaea Rapaera of Tūhoe and Koopu Erueti of Te Whānau a Apanui, from Maraenui.[48] Most of those attending the hui were swept up in the excitement of the occasion, and were too busy to spend time with the team.

In the evening, the Fisk Jubilee Singers gave a free open-air concert to an enthusiastic crowd of about 1500 Māori and 500 townspeople. The African-American a capella ensemble, which had been touring the country performing 'negro melodies, plantation songs, ragtime ditties and excerpts from the grand opera'[49] and was about to return to Fisk University in Nashville, Tennessee, donated a sum of £10 to the hui coffers.

Despite the last-minute arrangements, the council's civic reception on 8 April was a huge success. The *Gisborne Times* went into rhapsodies:

> Bright, clear and cloudless, the long hoped for day came. The sun shone out in majesty and glory and with the smile of rosy morning waked life and nature to the activity, beauty and joy of a great day. Hill and dale laughed in the sparkling light, and the birds sang their chorus of welcome. The world around, in consonance with man, seemed to say, welcome, welcome, welcome! Welcome ye brave warriors to the home of your ancestors and your own native-land.[50]

After a calm, pleasant voyage, the *Mapourika* anchored in the harbour in the early hours of the morning, and at 7am the harbour board launch took the reception committee, led by Deputy Mayor Hill, out to the ship (Sherratt had been called away on urgent private business). When he saw the rows of men drawn up on the decks of the vessel, Hill led three hearty cheers; and a karanga of 'Haere mai, haere mai, haere mai' rang out over the bay. Allen, Carroll and the non-battalion officers accompanied the reception committee to the wharf, where people were already lining streets bedecked with flags, streamers and emblems. The *Times* described Reads Quay as 'a mass of pulsating human beings tingling with expectation, and the excitement of a great occasion'.[51]

It was low tide: the soldiers had to wait until 9.30am before they could disembark. The *Tuatea* ferried them from the steamer, and as it came alongside the wharf, the City and Salvation Army bands struck up 'See the Conquering Hero Come' to loud cheers from the spectators. Thousands of local people and visitors had gathered, keen to show the soldiers their gratitude for the acclaim that the Maori (Pioneer)

Battalion had won overseas, and the part they had played in bringing the war to an end. Returned servicemen, with senior and junior high-school cadets on each wing, formed a guard of honour as the soldiers assembled in front of the official platform, which was festooned with bunting in red, white and blue. Various local politicians and dignitaries made short welcome speeches from

The East Coast and Hawke's Bay troops of the New Zealand Maori (Pioneer) Battalion are greeted by a huge crowd as they arrive in Gisborne on the *Tuatea* on 8 April 1919.

the platform, including Hill, JW Bright for Citizens Defence, representatives of the Cook County Council and the harbour board, Reverend Packe on behalf of the borough's Christian ministers, Colonel Fletcher from the local branch of the RSA, as well as Allen and Carroll. During Bright's address, Carroll obliged his request by leading the soldiers in a haka. Bright concluded with a patronising exhortation: 'He hoped the men who had been so strong to save the Empire would be equally zealous in preserving it and building it up, and that they would all be good citizens. "Remember," he said, "the dignity of labor, and show the world that though your skins are dark, your hearts are white."'[52]

The soldiers then marched in formation into Gladstone Road and through the town, led by their officers, Lieutenant-Colonel Ennis (Dunedin), captains Edward 'Tip' Broughton (Ōmāhu) and Paumea 'Jim' Ferris (Wainui, Gisborne), chaplain-captains Wepiha Wainohu (Mōhaka) and Pēni Hakiwai (Ōmāhu), lieutenants Hāwea Mason (Carterton), Joseph Paku (Waipukurau) and Tūpara Rotoatara (Wairoa) and second-lieutenants Apiata Apanui (Kahukura), Percy Fromm (Gisborne), Charlie Goldsmith (Rangitukia), Jack Ormond (Ōpoutama), Waiheke Pūha (Te Araroa), Kahutia Te Hau (Muriwai) and Rota Waipara (Te Kuri a Tuatai, Gisborne). The soldiers marched behind the bands and returned servicemen, with the cadets bringing up the rear. At the station, they boarded the train along with their Pākehā comrades, the bands and the cadets for the short journey to Te Hāpara Park Racecourse. The train stopped short of the park so that the soldiers still had a short distance to march. From Chalmers Road to the entrance there were outbursts of cheering from the public, and school children pelted the troops with confetti and flowers.[53] After a wero and karanga at the park entrance, they marched towards the makeshift marae. People were 'massed across the marae', and as the soldiers approached 'the thin screen of women and men, waving handkerchiefs and greenery', at the front of the welcoming groups, they heard plaintive cries ring out above the haka pōwhiri: 'Haere mai! Haere mai! Haere mai!'

James McDonald had set up his camera and filmed the ceremonial reception, although much of this footage has evidently been lost.[54] The iwi who were present included Ngāi Tai, Te Whānau a Apanui, Ngāti Porou, Te Whānau a Ruataupare, Te Aitanga a Hauiti, Ngāti Konohi, Ngāti Kahungunu, Whakatōhea, Tūhoe and Ngāti Tūwharetoa (from the Mōkai district), all wearing their tribal colours[55]—the purple and black of the Horouta group, the black and red of Takitimu, the red, white and blue of Tamatea, and the khaki and pink of Ngāti Kahungunu.[56]

Since Ngāti Tūwharetoa and Tūhoe had travelled the greatest distance, they were given the honour of performing the first poi of welcome to the Battalion. Their poi swung from much longer strings than are usual in modern poi. The women wore red dresses and blue and white sashes, and 'with their striking piupiu hats, made very picturesque figures'. They were followed by a group from Moteo, Te Hauke and Pakipaki, and a combined East Coast, Wairoa and Hawke's Bay party who performed the popular military poi, 'The Noble Sacrifice', which Ngata had composed in 1917. As the strains died away the group was reorganised to perform 'Karangatia Ra!', another song composed by Ngata especially for the Hui Aroha:

Karangatia Ra!

Karangatia ra! Karangatia ra!
Powhiritia ra! Nga iwi nei;
Ngā mate tini, haere mai!
Te Hui Aroha
Mou e Wi Pere.
Ngau nei te aroha me te mamae.
Nga mate tini! Nga mate tini,
Kei Paranihi! Haria mai ra.
Kia tangihia ki te marae!
Te Hui Aroha
Mou e te Wiwi
Ngau nei te aroha me te mamae.
Nga toto heke! Ngā toto heke!
Maringi kino, e toha mai ra
I te whenua pamamao
E karanga ana i
Te Hui Aroha,
Kia pumau te aroha me te mamae!

Summon them! Summon them!
Bid the tribes foregather;
Our tributes to the dead, bring hither;
To this Assembly of Love
Let us mourn in memory of thee, Wi Pere
In loving respect and pain
The dead, they call from afar,
From France! Bring hither
From France! Bring hither
And commingle our sorrow
At the Assembly of Love
At the Assembly of Love
Let us weep in memory of the brave
For whom our hearts are torn.
The red blood they gave,
That spread befouled
On fertile soil,
It calls to this
Assembly of Love
To preserve its sacred memory![57]

The Battalion's soldiers march down Gladstone Road through the borough centre to a tumultuous public welcome, 8 April 1919.

Three impressive haka followed: a peruperu performed with weapons by the Tūranga tribes; an ancient posture dance, 'Rūaumoko', performed by Ngāti Porou; and the well-known tūtū ngārahu in preparation for battle, 'Kia Kūtia!' given by the combined tribes.[58]

The haka were followed by a heart-wrenching tangi. The East Coast tribes had lost eighty-seven young men during the war, a sacrifice that was expressed in the long-drawn-out laments for sons and husbands who had died. The *Gisborne Times* reported, 'No one with a sympathetic heart could fail to be touched with the lamentations of the elders for those brave boys who will never return.'[59] The mourners sat on the grass on one side of the marae, facing the soldiers, who hid their eyes and were visibly affected. At this point the chaplain, Wepiha Wainohu, a man much loved by the troops, 'rose with taiaha in hand and inched towards the grief-stricken women'.

Chanting in Maori, he stated that their sons had been given into his hands, and he knew not how to greet them. They were very kind to let him stand before them. In the olden days they would have killed him. The answer was merely the outstretched hands of the stricken relatives, as with eager, tear-stained eyes, they look[ed] into the face of the padre...then slowly, very slowly the soldiers moved towards the mourners...the men lay wailing with their relatives on the ground, with no words spoken and an occasional caress from the mothers to their sons.

But the mothers whose boys would not return sat in a group by themselves, with Chaplain-Captain Wainohu standing in their midst, the faces of the women still eagerly searching the countenance of the padre...Little groups of relatives occasionally withdrew silently and after about an hour and a half the tangi was concluded.[60]

After this intense outpouring of grief, the soldiers, their families and guests were summoned to a meal in the large dining hall, until a bugle call summoned them to muster again. Wī Repa, reporting on the hui for *Te Kopara*, listed some of the well-known kaumātua he saw there: 'Ta Timi Kara [Sir James Carroll], Mohi Te Atahikoia, Meiha Tunuiarangi (Wairarapa), Paratene Ngata, Te Kairakau (Waiapu), Ihaia Hutana (Heretaunga), Te Otene Pitau (Turanga), Wi Ngara Houkamau, Te Hati Pakaroa, Te Moana Tautau, Arapeta Rangiuia, Koroneho Kopuka Rangimatemoana, Paora Haenga.' Those he considered among the next generation of elders were: 'Te Kani Pere, Tipiwai Houkamau Remuera Te Urupu, Patu Te Rito, Paetai Kaimoana, Tame Arapata, Te Moana Tatae, Takurua Tamarau, Hatara Te Awarau.' Among the well-known women who were present he listed: 'Te Rina Whaanga, Mako Kara Tamaheni Toheriri, Peti Ata.' He included as the rising stars of the race: 'Apirana Ngata, Peneti, Taranaki Te Ua, Paraire Tomoana, Tipiwai Houkamau, Hamiora Hei; Te Kani Pere, Reweti Kohere, Kopu Erueti, Henare Te Wainohu, Waikura Tautuhi-o-rongo, Hori Tupaea, Hemi Huata, Wiremu Potae, Paetai Kaimoana, Timi Heihi, Kapene Piti [Captain Pitt],' and among the women: 'Heni Materoa [Lady Carroll], Hikihiki Turoa, Niniwa-i-te-Rangi, Tangiora Mohi, and the younger women: Arihia Ngata, Materoa Ngarimu, Rutu Tawhiorangi, Rotu Kereru, Heni Houkamau and Matehaere Arapata.'[61]

Groups at Te Hāpara Park Racecourse welcome the Pioneers from a makeshift marae with a stage behind it. The racecourse grandstand, seen in the background, served as a wharepuni or principal guest house for the Battalion soldiers.

The afternoon programme began with the Defence Minister presenting the French Croix de Guerre to Private Toi Karini of Mangatuna, who received a standing ovation. Then the City Band played 'God Save the King' to open the thanksgiving service, which was conducted mainly in Māori and presided over by the bishop of Waiapu, Bishop Sedgwick, supported by reverends Fred Bennett (Hastings) and Rēweti Kōhere (Rangiata, East Cape), and Reverend WT Fraser (Te Raukahikatea College, formerly chaplain at Narrow Neck Māori military camp).

The bishop received loud applause for his opening remarks in which he made reference to a widely reported incident in France: 'Whether we believe in the angel of Mons or not, we believe that had God not been on our side we would have been swallowed up at once. You may remember how a young officer in the evacuation of Gallipoli summed it up: "Not unto us, oh Lord, but unto Thy name give the praise."'[62] Bennett's address, which the Dominion Museum team recorded a few days later, captured the storm of emotion engendered by the return of the soldiers.

> Mai anō i te taenga o te rongo, kua hiki te pakanga, he anga tonu atu te mahi a te whatu ki te mōana, te ara i haere atu ai koutou. 'He pō te tatari; he rangi, he wawata!' Nō tēnei rā koutou ka puta mai, anō rā te ūranga o te rā.

> Ever since word was received that the war was over, our eyes have been turned upon the ocean, the path by which you went. 'Nights were spent waiting, days were spent longing!' Today you have appeared, and it is as if the sun has risen again.[63]

Apirana Ngata, the late Wī Pere's son Te Kani Pere and Lady Carroll welcomed the official visitors on behalf of the local iwi. They thanked the Acting Prime Minister for arranging to ship the soldiers home, and encouraged him to stay longer. Originally the *Mapourika* was to spend twenty-four hours in Gisborne, but Allen had wired a memo from Auckland to say that duties now 'required his

attendance in Wellington'. Speaking in praise of Major Peacock, Ngata declared that 'there was no better man … for training the men'; the major 'had felt his way to the heart of the Maori people'.[64]

When Sir James Allen led the speeches in reply, he apologised for not being able to bring the whole of the Maori (Pioneer) Battalion to Gisborne:

> He had done the next best thing — he had gone to Auckland to meet the Pioneer Battalion, and he had brought this lot of his 'children' to Gisborne with him. He wished that he could stay for the morrow … and he was sorry he was unable to accept their invitation. He had other 'children, Pakeha children' who needed his care, and he must go and look after them. (Laughter.) He wished he could have stayed for the unveiling of the memorial, but as it had been fixed for the morrow it was not possible for him to do so.

> Every dark cloud had its silver lining … One of those silver linings was in the early part of 1915 when 515 men of the Maori race decided to stand alongside their Pakeha brothers. (Applause.) You have gone and fought, you warriors. You have been victorious and have come back to your people with peace and honor. You chiefs of the East Coast, and all these men of the Pioneer Battalion, you should be proud of the fact that of all the 2227 Maoris who went to fight, every single man of them was a volunteer. (Applause).[65]

A family photograph of Private Toi Karini, who was awarded the French Croix de Guerre during the Hui Aroha. On 12 July 1917, he was hit in the leg by a shrapnel fragment from a high-explosive shell. About forty Maori Pioneers were taking ammunition to the front line at the time. The *Gisborne Times* reported that the Maori Pioneers 'were under heavy fire the whole time, and from the moment they left on their perilous errand they commenced to drop down. Toi succeeded over three parts of the way, and was then badly wounded in the knee and, in his own words, "knew nothing more" until he found himself at base hospital. Then he was removed to a hospital in England and invalided home.' As a result, he missed the presentation from the general commanding the French First Army. When Toi was interviewed at the hui, he disclaimed credit for the award, stating that 'his comrades' on the occasion were as much worthy of the honour as he was.[66]

Lieutenant-Colonel Ennis thanked their hosts for the warm reception, and said he was proud to have the honour of bringing back the men he had taken away. 'On the word of the Corps Commander and the Divisional Commander,' he said, 'these men were the best Pioneers in the British Army.' This comment drew tremendous applause.[67] That evening a huge open-air church service was held at which Chaplain Wainohu gave a 'stirring and powerful address'. The service was followed by a performance of poi dances and haka.[68]

McDonald filmed most of the pōwhiri that day, although only a short clip showing the long-poi dance by Ngāti Tūwharetoa and Tūhoe women

survives. McDonald also filmed the catering team peeling great piles of potatoes and kūmara and putting down a huge hāngi; and he photographed the returned soldiers dressed in suits, white shirts and ties surrounded by people in the large dining hall. Most of the participants in the hui were too caught up in the emotional proceedings to work with the Dominion Museum team that day. Just three waiata tangi sung by Kaha Kerekere of Ngāti Kahungunu were recorded on the dictaphone, including a lament for Rangiuia, the famed tohunga from Te Rāwheoro, the school of learning at Ūawa Tolaga Bay.[69]

Photographers Luther Mence and Joseph 'Zak' Zachariah arrived from Wellington on the *Arahura* earlier that morning. A local entrepreneur had hired them to film the Hui Aroha, and they had also shot film aboard the *Mapourika*, in Gisborne itself, and at the unveiling of the Wī Pere memorial on 9 April.[71] When their moving pictures were screened four months later at His Majesty's Theatre in Gisborne, the advertisement in the local newspaper read: 'Come and see yourself in this picture. Views of the Great Gathering on the Show Grounds, Poi Dances, Haka and Tangi, Street Scenes in Gisborne, a trip up the Waimata.'[72]

9 April 1919

On 9 April, the official public welcome to the Māori soldiers opened with more speeches. Ngata and many East Coast people were staunch Anglicans, and once again the bishop of Waiapu was invited to open the proceedings. He thanked the parents for encouraging their sons to go to war, but reminded them that these boys, after years of being together 'in a fight for righteousness against a common enemy', were about to disperse. He hoped that the mothers and fathers would not allow their sons to exchange the fellowship of the Battalion 'for that of the billiard saloon and the public-house bar', but would 'encourage them to a daily fight against the devil'. Sedgwick also asked the people to support the reconstruction of the main building at Te Aute College, which had been destroyed by fire a month earlier, as a memorial to the soldiers.[73]

In a brief response to the bishop's address, Ngata noted that his people had almost exhausted themselves raising £50,000 for the Soldiers' Fund, and that although the school's old boys would surely support the bishop's proposal, others might have different ideas. In fact, 124 boys from Te Aute had gone overseas to fight, and they had already made a huge contribution to the war effort.[74]

Maori (Pioneer) Battalion soldiers photographed by James McDonald at the Hui Aroha hākari in Gisborne. Catering for the hui was an enormous task: an estimated 1.7 tons of meat was required daily, along with 2000 loaves of bread, 120 pounds of tea, 900 pounds of sugar, 100 pounds of fat and 2.3 tons of vegetables. Five hundred people could be seated under cover at each sitting, and a tea room was erected for Pākehā visitors, of whom there were 2000 over the two days of the hui.[70]

Ngata was followed by Lady Carroll, who regretted that other tribes had not allowed their sons to be welcomed in Gisborne. When Sir James Carroll stood to speak, he explained that at the Auckland welcome for the Battalion, the chiefs and relatives of the men of the other tribes had asked to take their sons with them to their homes, and 'he had fallen in with their desires'. The Tūranga people responded by singing a song of welcome, and when Carroll praised the soldiers for the honour and distinction they had won, and urged them to carry on the heritage of their fathers, they performed a haka.[75]

Other speakers on this occasion included Pene Heihi (Ben Hayes) from Ngāti Porou, who gave a poignant speech in which he remarked, 'We gave up our children for death. Some passed away. We grieve not for them. We honor their memory.'[76] Major Brown (Tūnuiarangi Paraone), a rangatira from Wairarapa who had commanded a Māori contingent at Queen Victoria's diamond jubilee celebration in 1897, spoke; as did Reverend Hēmi Huata of Mōhaka. The Hawke's Bay Maori Entertainers, dressed in khaki, closed the official welcome to the soldiers with a performance of popular military poi and other action songs.[77]

At about 3pm, the Gisborne and Hawke's Bay soldiers boarded the train for town to attend the unveiling of a handsome memorial obelisk that had been erected in memory of Wī Pere in the heart of the town, beside the Taruheru River. The memorial,

HONOUR FOR AN EAST COAST MAORI CHIEF: THE UNVEILING OF A MONUMENT AT GISBORNE TO THE LATE WĪ PERE LAST WEEK, WHEN MEMBERS OF THE RETURNED MAORI BATTALION WERE PRESENT.

C. Troughton Clark, Photo.

This photograph of the Wī Pere Memorial in Gisborne appeared in the *Auckland Weekly News* in April 1919. The imposing structure stands over 7 metres high. An inscription on one side reads: 'I whakaarahia i te wa o te hui aroha mo te tahua ma nga hoia Maori, Aperira, 1919, Unveiled at the time of the Māori hui to raise money for the soldiers.' On the opposite side: 'I hurahia i te wa i u mai ai te ope hoia Maori te Hokowhitu a Tu, Aperira, 1919. To commemorate the landing of the Māori troops at Gisborne, April 1919.' The Ministry for Culture and Heritage refurbished the monument in 2017.

funded by the government and local Māori, was significant because Pere, a former MP for Eastern Maori, had helped to raise the Tairāwhiti recruits for the first Maori Contingent, and had named the contingent Te Hokowhitu a Tū when it was formed in October 1914. He died on 9 December 1915, while the contingent was fighting at Gallipoli. In uncovering the memorial, Carroll said that it was fitting that it was unveiled on the day of the return of the men whom Pere had sent to the front.[78]

Addressing the largely Māori gathering, Ngata explained that although James Carroll and he had both run against Wī Pere in elections for the Eastern Māori seat, they knew that he had always had the interests of local Māori at heart.

There [are] standing in front of [us] this afternoon men of that first Maori contingent, the contingent which had been constantly reinforced by the men of Wi Pere's tribe. Wi Pere never drew back an inch. He had said to his son, Te Kani, and to Lady Carroll that they must put all their resources from Gisborne, Wairoa, East Coast, and Hawke's Bay into the war. (Applause.) The Maori people never departed…from that word.

All this land belonged to the Mahaki and Gisborne tribes which he represented… and the very soil this monument now rests on, that was once his…What greater honour could there be to him than the erection of the memorial on soil which he once owned?[79]

Wī Pere Halbert's portrait and taonga flanked by his sons Moananui and Te Kani, photographed by James McDonald in Gisborne, 1919.

Speaking for the soldiers, Wainohu said that few of the original men of the Maori Contingent were present; those who had returned home 'regretted that Wi Pere did not live to welcome them back, as he sent them forth'. Lady Carroll presented the mats that decorated the base of the monument and £250 to Wainohu and his soldiers to mark their return to Gisborne. Of this sum, £50 had been donated by the widow and relatives of the recently deceased Hori Mahue of Te Araroa, and the balance by Wī Pere's family. After the ceremony, McDonald photographed Wī Pere's sons Moananui and Te Kani standing beside a portrait of their father, flanked by two kahu kiwi, with a kaitaka with a tāniko border draped in front of the portrait, plus two mere and a kotiate.

In the evening, there was more entertainment back at the park, including a dance that was very popular with the young people.[80]

During the day the Dominion Museum team recorded eleven different items on six wax cylinders,[81] including a pao of welcome and a tangi sung by Karaitiana Ruru of Te Aitanga a Māhaki; an ancient lament with the names of noted young rangatira who fell at Gallipoli and in France added in, performed by Eruera Ngātoto from Ngāti Porou; four waiata tangi performed by Rangi Te Rito of Ngāti Kahungunu; a summons for Ngāti Porou to resist the Ngāpuhi attack on Tōtara pā, chanted by Paora Haenga of Ngāti Porou; and a waiata aroha or love song, also sung by Haenga. Haenga was a well-known Waiapu chief. His father Arapeta Haenga had been involved in the war against the Pai Mārire adherents in 1865, and Paora himself had joined the Pai Mārire movement.

Aporo Paerata of Ngāti Kahungunu sang a love song and a lament composed by his grandfather, Enoka Te Pakaru, a tohunga who had been widowed. Johannes Andersen later described Paerata as 'a man of parts, proficient in string-games, a bird-tamer, a teacher of speech to the tui, a weather-prophet, something of an impromptu poet and singer, and a dog trainer' whose dog could do 'super-canine tricks'.[82] McDonald filmed and photographed Paerata demonstrating a series of fifteen whai (string games)

for Andersen, who remarked that 'Comparatively few of the Maoris were able to give any information about the games, and very few were able to make the figures. Only one was learnt from the children; the others were learnt from grown men.'[83] McDonald also recorded Paerata's attempts to play a nose flute that Andersen had brought with him from Wellington. When Paerata failed to get any sounds out of it, he turned the flute over and, finding worm holes near the aperture, remarked to Andersen, 'It's no good, worm eaten; it wants some putty.'[84]

The soldiers, led by Chaplain Wainohu, replied to the welcome they had received, and more songs and poi dances were performed. The soldiers sat on the stage, where cloaks and other gifts presented to them by their people were displayed, along with an enormous four-decker cake cut by Wainohu, using an officer's sword.[85]

It is likely at this point that McDonald filmed several sequences of three groups of women and girls demonstrating the short poi, standing on a grassy lawn away from the marae, with willow trees and a stream in the background. The first performance features a group of women wearing dark dresses and piupiu; the second, a group dressed in white sailor shirts and piupiu over long dark skirts, accompanied by a man carrying a large Union Jack; and the third performance involved a team of young girls with white bows in their hair, white blouses, short pleated skirts, long socks and black sandals, led by an older girl who stepped forward and demonstrated each move.

The group was escorted by a man and a woman carrying a large flag with a Union Jack, emblazoned with the words 'Te Hokowhitu-a-Tu' and a striking image of two warriors with hair dressed in topknots, one of whom is wearing traditional costume and wielding a taiaha. Perhaps because the dictaphone was not able to record group performances, these teams are not singing, and no wax cylinder recordings were made on the day.

In filming these performances, McDonald was assisted by Te Raumoa Balneavis. As Best recognised in his report on the Hui Aroha, Balneavis's diplomacy was crucial to the success of the expedition:

Aporo Paerata (Ngāti Kahungunu), left, attempting to play the nose flute as Elsdon Best, right, and an unnamed man look on. This photograph was taken by James McDonald in 1919, during the Hui Aroha in Gisborne.

Long experience has taught me that social meetings of the Natives do not, as a rule, afford a collector good opportunities for collecting ethnographical data. The attractions and distractions are so numerous that it is usually difficult to obtain matter the procuring of which demands the close attention of Natives. Moreover, Europeans going among Natives to whom they are quite unknown are heavily handicapped in any attempts to collect such data.

It is therefore with much pleasure that I acknowledge our indebtedness to M. Balneavis, private secretary to the Minister of Native Affairs, who, at the request of Hon. Mr. Ngata, placed himself at our disposal, and was indefatigable in his efforts to induce Natives to fall in with our wishes...His own interest in the work resulted in that enthusiasm that ensured success. The interesting collection of Native songs, games &c. may truly be said to be almost entirely due to his efforts. I found that my best course was to stand aside, and hence my share of the work is best represented by profound silence.[86]

With Balneavis's help, McDonald was also able to take photographic portraits of several Māori who attended the Hui Aroha, some of them dressed in fine cloaks; and a group portrait of Balneavis and his family.

Andersen records that on one of these occasions he noticed a group of young girls setting up a string game: this turned out to be the whai known as moti, which features two loops—one representing a man and the other a woman. As the fingers of the left hand wriggled the strings, getting the 'man' to chase the 'woman', the audience chanted:

Moti, moti, moi haere, moi haere
Moti, moti, moi haere, moi haere
Ana kapeape au noa, ha raparapa noa
Aue! Arara!
Haere ki te tihoihoi...E![87]

According to Andersen, the conclusion of this graphic whai—when the man 'caught' the woman—was an unfailing source of amusement. During the hui, Paerata taught Andersen a number of other whai, including one called 'Tutae takahuri',[88] and Hēnare Ruru taught him three others. Best recorded the names of each whai as McDonald filmed them. On several occasions the daughter of Herbert Williams helped Andersen to work out the sequence of figures.[89]

McDonald reported that during the Hui Aroha he collected 200 photographic plates of 'Maori types, string games (whai) and cooking in the old-time way', along with moving pictures of the haka of welcome and poi dances, cooking with steam and setting up whai.[90] However, most of these images—including those of the haka—do not seem to have survived. Only sixty plates that can be confidently attributed to the Hui Aroha now remain in the photographic collection of Te Papa.

The following day, 11 April, as the hui wound down, the Dominion Museum team collected a rich haul of chants, songs and incantations. From the Ngāti Kahungunu contingent, Mohi Te Ātahīkoia of Waimārama sang a moemoeā matakite or prophetic song about war, an oriori (lullaby) and a pao aroha, and chanted Tamatea's karakia, sung while that ancestor was undergoing circumcision; Pora Hakere of Whakakī sang a waiata aroha, and Īhāia Hūtana of Waipawa gave a whaikōrero, sang a waiata aroha and performed a peruperu.[91] From Gisborne, Tiera Tapunga of Rongowhakaata sang four waiata aroha and a waiata tangi; Waatara Mirangi of Te Aitanga a Hauiti gave a whaikōrero interspersed with two waiata tangi and a tauparapara; Wī Repa from Te Araroa sang a waiata aroha and a pao whaiāipo; and Pihitahi Tamaikoha of Tūhoe sang a waiata tangi.[92]

Te Raumoa Balneavis (Ngāi Tāmanuhiri and Te Whakatōhea), private secretary to the Minister of Native Affairs, and his family, photographed by James McDonald at Te Hui Aroha in 1919. From left: Mihikore Te Kani, Te Raumoa Balneavis, Kura Te Kani (later Hayes), an unnamed baby and Irma Balneavis.

Tiera Tapunga (Rongowhakaata and Ngāi Tāmanuhiri) was a leader and a war veteran. Tapunga fought in the New Zealand Wars in the 1860s and was awarded the New Zealand Medal in 1914. He was born in the 1840s to Herewini Hotuariki and Ruihi Koihe. He later married Heniriata Mangere, and was the father of Mōtoi Tapunga. Tapunga, who died in 1932, was among the last Tūranga rangatira of the ancient Māori world who retained the ancient customs, whakapapa, kōrero tuku iho (oral traditions) and waiata. He was recorded by the expedition team as he recited a number of old waiata at the Hui Aroha on 11 April 1919. Photographer unknown. Photograph originally held by Hēni Sunderland.

Aporo Paerata photographed by James McDonald demonstrating 'Tutae takahuri' whai at Te Hui Aroha in Gisborne in 1919.

That same day, the tribes met to discuss repatriation, the application and investment of the Maori Soldiers' Fund and other matters relating to the welfare of the returned soldiers. The goal of raising £25,000 at the hui was reached when recent fundraising efforts were included.[93] This brought the amount raised in the Eastern Maori electorate since 1917 to £55,000, the basis for what became known officially as the Maori Soldiers' Trust Fund. None of the costs for the hui came out of that fund.[94]

Some of the officers addressed the large audience, and told them about the Battalion's work at the Front. Captain 'Tip' Broughton's address was particularly compelling, as he recounted notable feats by some of the local men who, he felt, had performed exceptionally well overseas.[95] After the evening church service, the Savage Club Orchestra provided the entertainment, assisted by Chaplain Wainohu as master of ceremonies and Lance-Corporal Noho Toki of Greytown. Toki, a tenor, had been one of the singing sensations of the Battalion overseas, and had appeared before royalty.[96]

Te tāhua mā ngā hōia Māori

Contributors	Pounds	Shillings	Pence
Takitimu	£7612	14	8
Arawa	£381	13	0
Mataatua	£173	1	8
Horouta	£8049	0	0
Kahungunu (Wairoa)	£1628	0	0
Kahungunu (Tangoio ki Tahoraiti)	£3000	0	0
Rongokako	£1000	0	0
Rotorua Hui, 31 August 1917	£1300	0	0
Ruatoki Hui, 26 July 1917	£1000	0	0
Whenua o Tuhoe, te wariu*	£3150	0	0
Nga riihi a Te Arawa†	£2000	0	0
Total	**£29,294**	**9**	**4**

* 'Value of Tuhoe lands'. Tūhoe donated about 3000 acres of land with a capital value of roughly £3000 to the Maori Soldiers' Fund. This land was to be leased to the executive of the fund for forty-two years, rent-free for the first twenty-one years.

† 'Te Arawa leases'. Te Arawa donated rents from their lands for five years. The committee had already received £1700, leaving a balance of about £2000.[97]

(Source: *Te Kopara*, 30 April 1919, no. 64, p. 10.)

12 April 1919

Most of the visitors and soldiers left Gisborne on Saturday 12 April. The East Coast people boarded the *Mako*, along with their soldiers: there would be other welcomes on marae in their district. This left the camp free for the carpenters to pull down the temporary buildings. The organisers held a sale at the grounds of firewood, produce, rugs and other items, and raised a good amount.[98] The Ngāti Kahungunu soldiers were the last of the Battalion to leave the camp, on Monday 14 April. They left in two contingents: the Hawke's Bay and Wairarapa parties went by the *Arahura*, and the Wairoa soldiers, accompanied by Carroll, travelled on the *Mako*. They received huge welcomes in their home towns and again on their marae.[99] By 15 April everyone had left the park racecourse.[100]

Over the final weekend of the Hui Aroha, on 12 and 13 April, the Dominion Museum team made many more recordings, including Reverend Fred Bennett's speech to the soldiers, and a series of love songs: two performed by Wī Repa from Te Araroa, another by his wife Merewhati Wī Repa from Gisborne, and two others that they sang together; and two more by Pora Hakere from Whakakī.

Waimārama Hawaikirangi Pūhara from Heretaunga performed the sacred karakia for the *Tākitimu* waka. Mohi Te Ātahīkoia and Rapihana Koopu Hawaikirangi, also from Ngāti Kahungunu, performed the famous oriori 'Pinepine te Kura', and Hawaikirangi also sang two waiata tangi, and recited the oration he had given to the returned soldiers. Tūtāwake Rāmeka from Ngāti Kahungunu sang two whakaaraara (watch songs) and a lament. The Hawke's Bay Maori Entertainers, who had performed often throughout the Hui Aroha, recorded several songs that Ngata had published in his pamphlet 'A Noble Sacrifice', including Ngata's recruiting song by the same name, the canoe poi song 'Hoea mai te waka nei' in English, 'Hoki hoki tonu mai', and a lament for a departed lover, 'Haere mai e hine mā'.[101]

Mohi Te Ātahīkoia also recorded his welcome address to the soldiers. Te Ātahīkoia had become the recognised senior chief and leader of Ngāti Kahungunu after the death of the rangatira Henare Tomoana. In 1919 he was in his late seventies. He was an eloquent speaker who made people laugh, despite the solemnity of the occasion. He warmly acknowledged Wī Pere, and recalled his words when they farewelled the East Coast section of the Maori Contingent in Napier in 1915: 'Haere koutou ki te whawhai, a, kia motu rawa mai te ūpoko o te Kaiha, me mau mai ki a au.' 'Go to the war and sever the head of the Kaiser, then bring it back to me.'[102]

The Dominion Museum team collected a few more dictaphone recordings on 14 April, including a whakapapa and two whakaaraara from Paora Te Kohu of Ngāi Tāmanuhiri; a well-known waiata tangi by Rangiuia, the great tohunga from Ūawa; an oriori performed by Taake Kerekere; and another for Rangiuia, recorded by Kaha Kerekere of Te Aitanga a Māhaki in Gisborne.[103]

That evening, Best (touted as 'one of the highest authorities on the subject of Maori lore'[104]) gave a public lecture in the Holy Trinity Church schoolroom, sponsored by the Poverty Bay Institute. The *Poverty Bay Herald* reported on the film and sound recordings that the Dominion Museum team had collected, and remarked that Best had lived in Gisborne in the early 1870s, when he purchased the Pukepapa block near Te Karaka where, at that time, the only European dwellings in the vicinity were a few slab houses. Best had built the original homestead at Lorne, which was later demolished.

The following day, Best went inland to inspect some old pā sites, while McDonald and Andersen returned to Wellington.[105] Before they left Gisborne, Ngata asked McDonald to convey his thanks to the Minister of Internal Affairs for authorising their visit to the Hui Aroha. The following week, McDonald wrote to the undersecretary to pass on this message.[106]

Post-hui

The first Dominion Museum Ethnological Expedition was hailed as a great success.[107] In the Museum's 1919 annual report, Best and McDonald described in detail the material they had collected, and thanked Ngata and Balneavis for their invaluable support. Best wrote:

> The photographs and moving pictures of various old Native games that were procured are not only of much interest as permanent records, but will also provide illustrations for Museum Bulletin No. 8 on Maori games. Those of certain domestic occupations and scenes are also much wanted, and inquiries on this subject have lately been received from English sources.
>
> A long-cherished desire for phonographic records of Maori songs has at last been fulfilled. The collection of dictaphone records is exceedingly good, and comprised Native songs of many kinds, from old-time laments, watch songs and ritual chants of past centuries to the simple songs composed as a welcome to the returning Native troops.
>
> From my own point of view the most interesting feature of the collection of these dictaphone records is the fact that it provides material for a proper study of Native songs and singing by an expert. This is a highly interesting subject, but unfortunately I am not capable of dealing with it. I have long hoped that someone would take up this line of study, and am exceedingly pleased to hear that Mr. J.C. Andersen has resolved to do so.

For the first and last time, Johannes Andersen contributed his own section to the Dominion Museum report. He wrote that Elsdon Best had recognised many of the songs they had recorded as 'true Maori, and typical of the old Maori style'. He acknowledged that many of the tunes would be very difficult to record in musical notation, since tangi featured intricate arrays of quarter-tones; and he added:

> There is much fine recitative, and even a style approaching operatic music of the florid Italian school. [Some of] the rhythms show to perfection the old Greek and Latin quantitative rhythm. Copying out the songs and analysing the various styles will be a revelation. There is music of a kind I have never heard before.[108]

Wī Repa's impressions of the hui were published in Māori in *Te Kopara* at the end of April. He described the camp setting as a canvas forest of tents, some green and some white, the largest of which was the wharekai catering for 500 at each sitting. There were no serious accidents at the park, although he did mention that Wī Kaipuke had been knocked down by a car in town on the day the soldiers arrived. He acknowledged the fine weather throughout the whole of the hui. Pākehā visitors had made many complimentary remarks, he noted, about the way the hui was run and he put this down to the military way it had been organised. The entertainment, he felt, was well varied so that speeches were interspersed with poi, Māori songs sung to European tunes, and new haka. Wī Repa praised the lighting of the camp, especially as it was overseen entirely by Māori supervisors. Lastly — and interestingly — he remarked on the changed tikanga that he had witnessed at the hui and he used the examples to strike a progressive note.[109]

> Kaore he powhiri, karanga ranei i nga ope. Na nga ope noa i haere mai ki te marae. Kaore he 'haere mai! haere mai!' Kaore he tangi. Na nga mea tino kaha tonu ki te rapa tangi haere ma ratou ka whiwhi. Te whiwhinga ka wehe i te rekareka. He mea ano ka haere ngaro etahi ki roto i nga teneti o etahi tangi ai. Otira, i te korenga o enei tikanga o te ao tawhito e whakatutukitia, kaore he aitua, kaore he aha. Nga tikanga tawhito nga tikanga hou, o ia ao o ia ao, na te tangata i hanga, ma te tangata ano e wetewete. Kia ora te hui aroha. Kia ora te hunga aroha.[110]

There was no formal welcome, or traditional call to the groups as they arrived. The groups just proceeded onto the marae. There was no 'haere mai! haere mai!' Nor was there any tangi ceremony. Those who were determined to go through the mourning ceremony, they did so. That took away from the festiveness of the occasion. Others did so out of sight, they mourned under the cover of the tents. But the thing is this, despite these protocols of the old world not being properly carried out, there were no mishaps, indeed nothing bad happened. Ancient and new protocols, belonging to each successive generation, are established by people and the people can also unravel them. Greetings to the gathering in compassion. Greetings to the people of compassion.[111]

In the aftermath of the hui, the Carrolls, Ngata and his wife Arihia and other members of the Maori Soldiers' Fund travelled to Hawke's Bay and Wairarapa to complete the tangi ki ngā mate (mourning for those lost during the war) across the Eastern Maori electorate. They were accompanied by local Māori soldiers who gathered again for this occasion. The group arrived by train in Masterton on the morning of 28 April from Hawke's Bay, accompanied by Wainohu and Hakiwai, Broughton, Paku and Mason, Te Hau and Waipara, and twenty-six others. They were met at the station by local Māori and Pākehā and taken by vehicles to Te Oreore pā, where the group was welcomed and a tangi took place for those who had been killed or who died in the war. That afternoon, their last stop was at Pāpāwai pā near Greytown.

The Maori Soldiers' Fund representatives and officers of the Battalion joined the Wairarapa men to complete the kawe mate ritual for the men who had died overseas, carrying their wairua to marae across the Eastern districts. This reflected the enormous responsibility borne by these leaders, and Wainohu in particular; the Battalion's long-serving padre had buried so many of those who died in foreign lands, and was committed to visiting as many marae as he could. After completing the Hawke's Bay and Wairarapa visits, at the beginning of July Wainohu went with some of the Battalion officers to East Coast marae to mourn Ngāti Porou's dead.[112]

Commemorations in 2019

Fast-forward 100 years, to 8 July 2019, and 100 volunteers, one for each year since the First World War, mustered for the centenary of the Hui Aroha in Gisborne. Most of the young men were from the same tribes that had been present at the original Hui Aroha. Some were direct descendants of the soldiers who had marched up Gladstone Road in 1919 as returning members of the Battalion.

A hundred years later, the parade gave a general salute at Heipipi Park, where the soldiers had disembarked from the *Tuatea* and again at the Wī Pere Memorial, where one of Wī Pere's descendants marched out from the ranks and laid a wreath. The Mayor of Gisborne, Meng Foon, and the Minister of Defence, Ron Mark, addressed the gathering, just as their predecessors had done in 1919. The songs performed at the Hui Aroha came to life again through the voices of the 100-man troop and the crowds who assembled to mark the occasion. What's more, the weather was as glorious as it had been a century earlier.

In documenting the Hui Aroha the Dominion Museum team was grabbing at fragments of Māori culture as they were scattered by the winds of change. We should be thankful to them and to Tā Apirana Ngata, who had the foresight to persuade the government of the day to seize the moment. They left us glimpses of Māori culture in 1919, just as future generations will look back at Māori culture in 2019, when the centenary of the Hui Aroha was captured on film and in photographs. It will be interesting to see what they make of the changes. They might agree with Wī Repa's statement, made at a time when such sentiments were not well received: that people can adapt tikanga to suit changing circumstances without the fear of exposing themselves to supernatural retribution.

Kia ora te hui aroha. Kia ora te hunga aroha.

'E TAMA! E TE ARIKI! HAERE MAI!'

The Second Dominion Museum
Ethnological Expedition
12 April–8 May 1920
Rotorua

ANNE SALMOND
JAMES SCHUSTER
BILLIE LYTHBERG

Tene Waitere's carved pouhaki, with iwi flags flying, photographed
by James McDonald in Rotorua in 1920.

On 27 April 1920, a bright sunny day with southerly
breezes, thousands of people at Rotorua welcomed
the Prince of Wales. Six days earlier, Prince Edward,
heir to the British throne, had arrived in Auckland
to thank New Zealand and its troops for their role
in the First World War, a visit promised by his father
King George V at the 1917 Imperial War Conference
in London 'when peace comes'.[1] The Prince arrived
on HMS *Renown*, the mightiest of the battleships built
in Britain during the war.[2] At the Auckland domain
he was greeted by Prime Minister William Massey
and 20,000 citizens at a military review attended
by disabled veterans, nurses, officers and soldiers,
including three winners of the Victoria Cross.

In his reply to the Prime Minister's speech of welcome,
the Prince expressed a sense of fellowship with those
who had fought alongside the British:

> I have served with my New Zealand brother
> officers and men in the great war, which
> made all nations of the British Empire
> doubly and trebly kin. I have seen the
> Ministers of New Zealand taking their place
> as representatives of a nation in the framing
> and signing of peace. I have shared to the full
> your pride in that achievement, the sign that
> this young nation has nobly won its spurs,
> and I have felt as deeply as you for those
> brave men and women who sacrificed their
> life, their health, or their happiness for the
> victory of our cause. You will understand,
> therefore, gentlemen, that my thanks to your
> most cordial welcome is no mere form.[3]

After receiving gifts, Prince Edward pinned medals on
the coats of those who had fought with distinction,
and was driven back to Government House along
streets lined with cheering crowds.

From Auckland, the Prince travelled by train
to Rotorua for the official Māori welcome. His
parents, King George V and Queen Mary, had
been welcomed there almost twenty years earlier,
and had been showered with an impressive array
of ancestral taonga that were then taken back
to Britain, inspiring a move to ban the export of Māori
'artefacts', led by Sir James Carroll, Percy Smith
of the Polynesian Society and Augustus Hamilton,
later the Director of the Colonial Museum.[4]

The official Māori welcome for the Prince, which
some predicted would be the last great gathering
of its kind,[5] created great excitement, and iwi across
the country organised representatives to travel to
Rotorua to meet him.[6] The only stand-outs were the

Tainui tribes, who requested that Prince Edward should visit Ngāruawāhia to meet King Te Rata before heading to Rotorua, although this insistence on recognising the status of the Māori King was treated with scant respect.[7]

In 1920, Carroll and Apirana Ngata were still in opposition in Parliament; the Reform Party led by William Massey was in power, with Māui Pōmare as their leading Māori MP. The influenza pandemic had subsided, but local outbreaks (in Christchurch and Hawke's Bay, for example) raised serious concerns about staging such a large intertribal gathering.[8] Te Rangihīroa, now Director of the Maori Hygiene section of the Department of Health, was put in charge of health matters at the iwi encampment

in Arawa Park, the racecourse at Rotorua.[9] He worked closely with Lieutenant Kepa Ehau, another Te Aute graduate who had served in the Pioneer Battalion, a rising leader among local iwi and an accomplished linguist, regarded as perhaps the best interpreter in the country.[10]

The government estimated that at least 5000 Māori would attend the hui, and offered to pay their travel costs.[11] As the time of Prince Edward's visit approached, hundreds of bell tents, double- and treble-poled marquees, raupō houses and other temporary buildings were erected at Arawa Park, laid out in streets and blocks like a town, with each of the blocks named after a particular iwi.

His Royal Highness the Prince of Wales leaves Queens Wharf in Auckland with the incoming Governor-General, Lord Jellicoe, in 1920.

Members of each hapū (kin group) slept in bell tents, using the marquees for their meetings and raupō structures roofed with tarpaulins as dining halls, with steam cookers powered by traction engines. Electric lighting and water pipes linked the different blocks, there was a tramway for shifting food and luggage, and a marquee was erected with a wooden floor and a stage for dancing and picture shows. It was like a cluster of kāinga, in which each iwi had its own dwellings, wharenui and wharekai.[12] When Sir William Herries, Minister for Native Affairs, and Māui Pōmare inspected the encampment,[13] the estimated cost of staging the hui was £30,000, inviting a caustic response from some Pākehā commentators.[14]

Like the Hui Aroha in Gisborne, this gathering offered an excellent opportunity to record ancestral tikanga. It was thought that at least twenty-three tribes would be represented, including 'Te Arawa, Te Rarawa, Ngapuhi, Ngatiwhatua, Ngatimaru, Ngatipaoa, Waikato, Ngatimaniapoto, Ngatiraukawa, Whanganui, Taranaki, Ngatikahungunu, Ngatitoa, Te Aitanga-a-Mahaki, Porourangi, Whanau-a-Apanui, Ngaitai, Te Whakatohea, Matatua, Ngaiterangi, Te Patuwae, Ngaitahu and Tuwharetoa.'[15] According to the *Evening Post* in late 1919:

> Preservation of records of Maori songs and incantations was commenced at Gisborne. The Hon. A.T. Ngata (Eastern Maori) urged that more should be done in this direction. They had the manuscript of Maori songs in the Grey collection, but they should have a record of the lines and inflexions. There was little time to spare, for the old Maoris were passing away quickly.[16]

At Ngata's request, Dr Thomson wrote to the Minister of Internal Affairs, who gave his permission for Johannes Andersen, Elsdon Best and James McDonald to travel to Rotorua a fortnight ahead of the official event.[17] By that time, all the accommodation in town had been booked, so the Public Works Department loaned them three tents for their stay in Rotorua,[18] while the Dominion Museum provided Best and his

companions five crates filled with long spears to distribute to the warriors who were participating in the ceremonial welcome.[19]

Around the country, iwi groups chose their gifts and rehearsed their presentations. In Gisborne, Lady Carroll organised a poi party, Ripi Wihongi set up a brass band in Kaikohe, various iwi commissioned illuminated addresses in carved frames, and ancestral taonga and other gifts for the Prince were chosen.[20] According to the 'Women's Page' in the *New Zealand Times*, Mrs Andersen and Mrs McDonald, eager to see the Prince of Wales, planned to accompany their husbands on this expedition.[21] On 20 April 1920, when the team arrived at Rotorua, the *Sun* reported:

> Some months ago, on the occasion of a great Native gathering in Gisborne, a party of ethnologists of the staff of the Dominion Museum went to the gathering to collect information about Maori history and lore, and to get kinema records of ceremonies, and to get also dictaphone records of old Maori chants and songs.
>
> The same party has gone to Rotorua to the big Maori camp there, for the purpose of gathering more of the same information. The Gisborne expedition was a huge success, from the point of view of the information collected, and much is hoped from the present further study of the subject.[22]

Ngata, meanwhile, arranged for Ngāti Porou to attend in large numbers. As John Hyland, a resident of Port Awanui, recalled:

> In 1920 when the Prince of Wales visited New Zealand, Sir Apirana Ngata arranged for the Maoris to go to Rotorua for the welcome. Well, they left from Port Awanui. They went out in the big surfboats and were stacked in tight like short pieces of wood. There were hundreds of them going. A southerly got up and I remember seeing them go up and down, up and down. It was the only form of transport from here then, so they went to Auckland by boat and to Rotorua by train.[23]

The Dominion Museum Ethnological Expedition camp,
photographed by James McDonald in the iwi encampment
at Arawa Park, Rotorua, 1920.

Makurata Paitini weaving a korowai. This photograph, taken in the
1900s, was copied by James McDonald; the original photographer
is not known.

Paitini Wī Tāpeka (Tūhoe) and Makurata Paitini (right),
both photographed in Rotorua in 1920, by James McDonald.

As soon as they pitched their tents in the tribal encampment, the members of the second Dominion Museum Ethnological Expedition set to work. The Tūhoe contingent who travelled to the hui included a number of Best's old friends, who began recording karakia and waiata with him the day after the expedition team arrived. Paitini Wī Tapeka and his wife Makurata Hineore, who had looked after Best while he lived in the Urewera between 1895 and 1910—first near Te Whaiti and later at Ruatāhuna—were among the Tūhoe manuhiri.

Paitini had fought against the British at Ōrākau in 1864, where he was wounded and many of his comrades were slain. At their last stand at Ōrākau, King Tāwhiao's supporters fought furiously until their bullets ran out; they fired peach and plum stones at the British while their leader Rewi Maniapoto cried out in defiance, 'Ka whawhai tonu mātou, ake ake! We will fight on forever!' Later, Paitini became a follower of the Māori prophet–warrior Te Kooti, joining the 1869 attack on Mōhaka in which several Pākehā families were killed.

During their work together in the Urewera, Paitini had dictated more than 300 Tūhoe waiata to Elsdon Best.[24] After Best moved to Wellington and worked at the Dominion Museum, he wrote to Paitini about ethnological matters. His wife Makurata was an expert weaver, and provided items of weaving for the museum collection.

4455 1643

At the iwi encampment, over the days that followed, members of the Tūhoe contingent worked closely with Best and the rest of the expedition team. Despite the large number of iwi who had gathered in the encampment, Best did not seek out experts from other tribes. From 21–24 April, Te Amo from Ruatāhuna, and Hinewaho, Wharemutu and Te Rangiua from Tūhoe, sang into the phonograph — although unfortunately the machine that the team had brought to Rotorua didn't work very well, and many of the recordings are almost unintelligible. By 25 April, however, the team had managed to get

the machine working better, and over the next two days Te Amokokouri recorded a waiata aroha, a whakaaraara pā (sentry song) and a waiata tangi; and Toki Wharetapu recorded a whakaaraara pā, a pātere (chant), a waiata aroha, a kaioraora (curse), a chant for the *Mātaatua* canoe and a short chant sung to a humming top, and led a haka taparahi with other Tūhoe performers,[25] including Makurata.

McDonald filmed and photographed Paitini listening to Best, smiling as Best wagged his finger; and Makurata performing string games and hand games. Makurata, who had a keen sense of the ridiculous, ended her demonstration of whai with a dramatic pūkana, rolling her eyes down as she held up a string figure.

Elsdon Best (far left), Makurata Paitini, an unnamed woman and Johannes Andersen (far right) photographed by James McDonald performing whai or string games in Rotorua in 1920.

Whai demonstrated by Te Rangiua (centre), his wife, Te Urikore (left), and Johannes Andersen (right), to expedition members and photographed by James McDonald in Rotorua in 1920.

Trucks piled with army tents arrive at the iwi encampment in Rotorua in 1920. Photograph by James McDonald.

A younger Tūhoe couple, Te Rangiua and his wife Wharemutu, performed action songs and string games for Best, and recorded a love song, a waiata tangi and a haka. Rangiua also demonstrated the use of a cord drill and made a fire using a hika ahi (fire plough), while McDonald filmed him at work. According to Andersen, American ethnographers had not been able to discover how Native Americans used their cord drills, and he was eager to send McDonald's film showing the Māori technique to the United States.[26]

As streams of trucks arrived at the encampment with boxes and sacks of food, bales of hay and large bundles of raupō, McDonald filmed the proceedings. He photographed raupō being spread on the ground inside the tents to serve as bedding, and a group of men serving food from steaming buckets, waving their pannikins and hats and laughing and clowning at McDonald and his camera.[27] Excitement was mounting; according to the *Otago Daily Times*:

> Nearly all the tribal representatives have now arrived here, and never before have there been so many Maoris in Rotorua. They seem to have taken possession of the town, and the camp from hour to hour presents an ever-changing scene.
>
> This morning the South Island Maoris from Canterbury and Otago came in, and were welcomed with the usual quaint and fascinating ceremonial. In the afternoon the Taranaki people arrived, and were similarly welcomed. In all these ceremonials Sir James Carroll — or Timi Carroll, as he is more often affectionately called by his intimates — takes a prominent part.
>
> So far, the Maoris have been too busy settling down to spend much time in practising their dances of war and of welcome, and there has been no grand rehearsal of all the tribes. Indeed, this is almost an impossibility, for each tribe has its own ideas, and it is impracticable to combine them. Today also some of the Taupo Natives, headed by the famous Heuheu, came in, but they took up their residence at Whakarewarewa. A few of the tribes in camp practise their hakas, and the town Maori maidens' singing is delightful.[28]

The Te Arawa people treated Arawa Park as a marae, and as each visiting iwi arrived, a warrior was sent out to challenge them, brandishing his taiaha. Andersen wrote:

> The challenge would be accepted by one of the visitors, who, similarly armed, would leave the ranks of his party; these two after a mock encounter, returned to their respective parties, the visitors slowly advancing amid welcoming cries. They passed where a space of about 30 feet separated the two bodies of people, when the keening took place. Suddenly the keening stopped and the visitors began their chant. The local people immediately followed with a rhythmical monotone. The usual speeches by both parties followed the chant, and the local people then sang a third song.[29]

McDonald filmed one of these pōwhiri, which began as a large group led by men dressed in hats and suits and holding greenery walked slowly across the marae. A grey-headed challenger greets them, brandishing his taiaha, then a line of local women, also holding greenery, perform a chant as another challenger dances before them. The visitors reply, the men lifting and lowering their greenery in unison as they perform a haka. This is followed by an exchange of speeches: the noted Te Arawa chief Mita Taupopoki, dressed in a kahu kiwi and feather headdress, speaks first, followed by other local orators, before the visitors reply. Finally the visitors walk along a long line of local people, and hongi with them. As they pass McDonald's camera, some of these people stare; others laugh and smile. That night in the encampment, the expedition team could hear the different iwi practising their chants and poi dances, hoping to keep them secret from the other tribes.[30]

Then, just before the Prince arrived, there was an outbreak of influenza among the Ngāpuhi contingent, and a number of people were taken to hospital in Rotorua.[31]

The Prince arrives

On 27 April 1920, Prince Edward's train steamed into Rotorua, just an hour after the train carrying the Governor-General Lord Liverpool[32] and his entourage had arrived. King George V had commanded that during the visit, the Governor-

General — as his representative — should take precedence over Prince Edward.[33] Herries, Māui Pōmare and the Hon. Tureiti Te Heuheu Tūkino were on the platform to greet him, along with a party of wounded soldiers accompanied by their nurses, and a guard of honour made up of 100 members of the Pioneer Battalion in mufti, many wearing ancestral cloaks. They were led by Captain Henry Vercoe, a noted rugby player who had been decorated in the Boer War and in the First World War.[34]

The Prince inspected the guard of honour, and was driven to the Grand Hotel, where he was greeted by cheering crowds and karanga from Māori women standing in front of a decorated arch emblazoned with the motto 'Greetings to our future King'.[35] After the reception he went for a stroll with three of his retinue to the grounds of the Government Sanatorium and Baths, where they watched the artificial geysers and he had a ride on a merry-go-round run by a returned soldier — until the engine stalled. That night an impromptu dance was held at the hotel, and Prince Edward danced with Māui Pōmare's wife Mīria and with the daughter of William Massey. Afterwards he unburdened himself in a letter to his mistress, Freda Dudley Ward, bemoaning the lot of a travelling prince:

> Fredie my precious darling beloved
>
> Just back from a desperate little party here where we arrived about 5pm after leaving Auckland... Its not till today that I've had my first proper glimpse of NZ not that I'm in the least bit thrilled darling one & contrary to all popular notions I think it looks far more like Canada than the Old Country!
>
> There were practically no stunts here this evening altho the Liverpools came here too and are staying in this hotel tho thank God they came in another train 1 hr. earlier!! Still I got a good walk before dinner... then came a pompous dinner party merely because of the presence of Their Exc.s & we went to the bloody party at 9.30 tho I loathed it.
>
> The women could not dance except one & I didn't have more than a couple of dances with her (and then I cant dance any more as you know only too well beloved) & the band was impossible.

And then there's a big hospital for returned men here (both wounded and TB cure) & I've got to visit that tomorrow too so that's going to be as heavy a day as any angel tho not worse than the last 4 days that's impossible!![36]

Visits to Ōhinemutu and Whakarewarewa

The next day dawned damp and bleak, although the rain lifted as the Prince arrived at Ōhinemutu, escorted by Herries, Māui Pōmare and Admiral Lionel Halsey, commander of the *Renown*. The distinguished rangatira Te Kiwi Amohau, and Rangi Te Aorere, a 'youth of magnificent build, dressed in the traditional costume of his people', with Captain Kepa Ehau interpreting, delivered their whaikōrero in front of Tamatekapua meeting house, recalling the 1901 visit by Edward's parents to Rotorua, and reminding him of the loyalty to the British Crown that Te Arawa had shown over many years.

These speeches were followed by a haka performed by about fifty warriors 'in a manner so realistic as to cause bystanders to marvel and wonder if the time had not arrived for an incontinent departure', and a canoe song with poi performed by 100 women sitting in three lines, wearing cloaks over white blouses, blue scarves and red skirts:

> A clear alto voice rose, leading the poi song, while the women kept time with poi balls. At intervals the warriors behind joined in the refrain, the effect being delightful, captivating all in the stand. The colour and movement of the dancers were almost obscured at times by steam rising from the bubbling vent holes in the ground and mingling with the thick drizzling rain.[37]

After the canoe poi, another rangatira, Wheoro Te Poni, stood up and spoke before presenting the Prince with a kahu kiwi, a taiaha, two carved pipes inlaid with pāua shell and a huia feather, which Edward stuck in the band of his military hat.

Prince Edward spoke briefly in reply, acknowledging the speeches and thanking Te Arawa for their gifts. After donning the cloak, he took the taiaha in his hand and stepped down to shake hands with the

line of poi dancers. When one pretty young woman curtseyed, called out 'Hail the King' in Māori and kissed the Prince's hand, this evoked 'a round of applause, and much merriment on the part of the girls, every one of whom now kissed his hand amid a continued ripple of merry laughter'.[38] According to the *Auckland Weekly News*, 'the Prince blushed becomingly, [and] one ambitious maiden put up her face, either with the intention of rubbing noses or kissing the Prince's cheek, but he gave a startled backward movement, and so missed this token of regard. But he laughed gaily and carried on.'[39]

Prince Edward's party then visited the old church at Ōhinemutu, and stood in silence in front of the statue of Queen Victoria before boarding their vehicles, girls waving Union Jacks and singing 'God Save the King' as they drove away.

From Ōhinemutu Edward went to King George Hospital to inspect the wounded soldiers, then carried on to Whakarewarewa, where he was met by young boys carrying flags that had been presented to Te Arawa by Queen Victoria in 1870 and by King George V in 1901. Well-known tourist guides, Bella Papakura and Miria, escorted him to a nearby carved meeting house where he was greeted with a haka and poi dance, and where Mita Taupopoki delivered a speech of welcome, interpreted by Captain Vercoe. The Prince was presented with a feather cloak, an illuminated address of welcome in a carved frame, a prized ancestral tiki, a tewhatewha and a miniature greenstone mere.

Afterwards, he strolled through the pā, looking at the carvings on the houses and the boiling springs. By now it was pouring with rain, and the Prince was getting soaked. Although his guides 'soaped' Pohutu, the geyser refused to blow, and he grumbled that they must have used the wrong brand of soap. To cheer him up, a group of local women chanted 'Rotorua, where the water boils all day. If only we had the Kaiser sitting on Pohutu geyser, we'd all shout hip hooray!'[40] After an hour of waiting in the rain, it was decided to postpone the intertribal welcome at Arawa Park until the following day.

As the Prince of Wales rode back to the Grand Hotel, crowds lined the streets. According to the *Colonist*, 'The Maoris are greatly excited, and could not restrain their enthusiasm in having among them one in whom they had visible reminder of the great King for whom so many of their sons and brothers had gone to the war, some to rest in foreign lands.'[41] This enthusiasm was not reciprocated. That night Edward wrote to Freda:

Today's stunts altho terribly boring and irritating would anyway have been a little interesting if it hadn't poured in sheets till 3.00PM. I had to go thro long & tedious Maori ceremonies at both the native villages & had to submit to being made to look the most hopeless B.F. dolled up in mats and other things, while more Maories danced or made weird noises at me!!

Some of the Maori women sang & danced quite nicely tho they spoilt their stunt by revolting me by kissing my hand when I shook hands with them all. That was too much sweetheart & was the last straw & then my boredom turned into bloody mindedness when they made me stand for a whole hour by a hot geyser to watch it blow off and it never did!

What a hopeless state the world is in just now & each day I long more & more to chuck this job & be out of it all and free for YOU sweetie; the more I think of it all the more certain I am that really the day for Kings & Princes is past & monarchies are out of date tho I know its a rotten thing for me to say and sounds Bolshevik!

However I'll turn in and try and sleep it off Fredie mine & so good night & bless you bless you forever![42]

With their patronising dismissal of New Zealand and Māori in particular, the Prince's private letters to his mistress make uneasy reading. They foreshadow the passionate self-absorption and hatred of royal duties that led to his eventual abdication ten months after ascending to the throne as Edward VIII in 1936.

Sir Joseph Ward (left, holding a hat), the Prince of Wales (centre) and Dr Māui Pōmare (right) at Ōhinemutu, Rotorua, in 1920.

Guides Bella and Miria escort the Prince of Wales in the pouring rain at Whakarewarewa, Rotorua, in 1920.

Women perform at the welcome ceremony for the Prince of Wales at Arawa Park in 1920. Photograph by James McDonald.

Arawa Park

On 29 April the 'day of days' for the official Māori welcome at the racecourse arrived. The morning was windy and cold, but bright and clear. According to the Rotorua correspondent for the *Otago Daily Times*:

The stands were packed with people, and a great concourse surrounded the marae, eagerly awaiting the arrival of the tribes. On a flagpole carved by the Maoris fluttered the huge tribal flags — Union Jacks bearing the names of the different tribes. This flagpole had been specially carved for presentation to the Prince.

On a high, slender pole, cut from the forest, fluttered a great New Zealand flag, with a crescent moon in the middle of the Southern Cross. Beyond was the tent field, and for a background a grand panorama of fern and forest clad hill and dale. On the left Ngongotaha, the scene of tribal fights, raised its rounded back, crowned with forest of sombre green, while to the right Mokoia — the island of legend and story — stood clear cut against the sky, and the shimmering silver of the lake.[43]

After the hui, the great pouhaki carved by Ngāti Tarāwhai carver Tene Waitere, which carried the tribal flags given to Te Arawa tribes by Queen

Crowds gather at Arawa Park's covered grandstand
for the reception of the Prince of Wales. Photograph
by James McDonald.

Victoria and King George V, was presented to Prince Edward. It later made the journey on the *Renown* back to England, where the Prince gave it to the Portsmouth naval base HMS *Excellent*.[44] The pouhaki now stands in the Museum of Archaeology and Anthropology in Cambridge. Its story, and that of Tene Waitere, is told later in this chapter by his great-grandson, the carver and wānanga expert James Schuster.

About 6000 Māori had gathered at Arawa Park— 1000 more than were expected. When Prince Edward arrived, accompanied by Admiral Halsey and officers from the *Renown*, he was wearing the cloak presented to him the previous day. As he entered the racecourse, one of the stands collapsed, although fortunately no one was badly hurt.

There was a tangi of welcome for the Prince, and after Te Arawa warriors performed the challenge, Edward took his seat, and students from Hukarere, Te Aute and Waerenga a Hika Māori boarding schools sang the national anthem in English and Māori. Sixty male and female rangatira accompanied Herries to the dais and stood to attention as he read in English the address that had been written for the Prince in Māori:

James McDonald photographed kaumātua chanting as the Prince of Wales approaches.

Son! Lord! Welcome! Majesty! Return once more following the way your Father trod. Least among the peoples that acclaim his 'mana', we give place to none in service and loyalty, and thus we greet Thee.

Bring with you memories of our beloved dead. They live again, who strove with you on the fields of Tu [Tūmatauenga, the god of war] in many lands beyond the Seas. Your presence there endeared you to the hearts of our warriors. Your brief sojourn here will soften the sorrows of those whose dear ones have followed the setting Sun.

Royal Son of our Illustrious Line, King that is to be, we are proud that you should carry on the traditions of your Race and House. For it is meet that those who sit on high should turn an equal face to humble as to mighty. Walk therefore among your peoples, sure of their hearts, fostering the love they bore Queen Victoria and those who came after.

Welcome and Farewell! Return in peace, without misgiving, bearing to His Majesty the King, and to Her Majesty the Queen, the renewal of the Oath we swore to them on this Ground a generation ago, an oath rooted in the Treaty of Waitangi, hallowed by time and manifold trials. The Maori people will be true till death, and so, Farewell!

The text in Māori read:

E Tama! E te Ariki! Haere mai! E te Whatukura! Hoki mai ano, whaia mai nga tapuwae o to Matua. Haere mai kia matou ki te iti rawa o nga iwi e tau nei i raro i tona mana. He iti, otiia e nui ana i to matou piripono. Koia ka karanga atu nei.

Haere mai e Tama! Kawea mai te ahuatanga o a matou tamariki e tangihia nei. Kua ora mai ra ratou, i ngana tahi na me koe i nga marae tini o Tu i tawahi, ko wai e hua kei hea. Nou i tae tahi ki reira ka awhitia koe e o ratou ngakau. Ka tae mai nei koe, ka mahea te pouri o te hunga kua wehe atu ra a ratou i kaingakau ai.

E te Uri Rangatira o te Kawai Tapu, a muri ake nei Kingi ai, e koa ana matou ki a koe e whakatutuki nei i nga tikanga o tou tatai. E tika ana hoki kia pera koutou e noho mai na i nga wahi teitei, kia rite te huri o te kanohi ki te iti, ki te rahi. Na reira, haere mai ki waenganui i o iwi. Kaua e hopohopo, e whakahohonutia nei e koe ki roto ki o ratou ngakau to ratou aroha ki a Kuini Wikitoria me ona uri.

Haere mai ra, a haere ake! Hoki atu i runga i te rangimarie ki o matua, ki to matou Kingi, ki to matou Kuini. E kore e taka ke te kupu i hoatu ki a raua i te marae nei ano. He ohaki, i takea mai i te Tiriti o Waitangi, he kupu tapu no nga whakatupuranga, i honea i nga whainga maha. Ka mau to te iwi Maori, a mate noa. Na reira, Haere![45]

The tangi of welcome to the Prince of Wales in Rotorua.
Photograph by James McDonald.

When Prince Edward stood to speak, a magnificent kahu kiwi was placed around his shoulders, to thunderous applause. He declared:

> A mighty war has shaken the world since my father came to this place, but the Maori people have held true to the oath which they swore to him upon the day when he stood here.
>
> Your warriors went forth to fight and conquer his enemies in many distant lands. I saw and spoke with them often on the hard fields of Tu. They fought and endured most gallantly as Maori warriors ever do, and many gave up life or health for the sake of those of us who remain.
>
> Chiefs and people, it is Queen Victoria's great grandson who speaks to you today. Under her just government, to which your fathers swore fealty at Waitangi eighty years ago, the Māori people, secure in their lands, found true contentment and peace under her wise guidance. Maori and Pakeha grow ever closer together in understanding and good will. The welfare and happiness to which Queen Victoria first led you have been assured to you in like measure by King Edward and King George. I rejoice to hear that your children make good progress in the Schools which the King's Government provides for you; for thus only can the youth of Aotearoa, Maori and Pakeha alike, grow up worthy of this free land and of the mighty Empire to which they belong. For my part, I will ever keep before me the pattern of Victoria, the Great Queen, whose heart was with the Maori people from the day they swore allegiance to her rule.
>
> Chiefs and People, I greet you from my heart, and so Farewell.[46]

In the Māori newspaper *Te Kopara*, this was translated as follows:

> No muri mai i te ra o taku Matua ka ngarue te ao i tetahi pakanga nui whakaharahara, otiia i tino mau te Iwi Maori ki ta ratou kupu i whakaoati ai ki a ia i tona ra i tu ai i te marae nei. I haere a koutou tamariki toa ki te pakanga, ki te raupatu i nga hoa riri o te Kingi i nga topito o te ao. I kite au ia ratou, a i korero tahi matou i nga marae papamaro o Tu. I kakari ratou, i tohe ratou i ta te toa i tana tohe, pera i o ratou tupuna onamata iho; a he tokomaha o ratou i mate kai-a-kiri, i mate rawa atu mo tatou, mo nga morehu. I kite te Kingi i to ratou toa, nana au i whakahau mai kia mihi ki te Iwi Maori mo to ratou toa, ahakoa tutuki noa ki te mate.
>
> E nga rangatira, e te Iwi, ko ahau ko te mokopuna tuarua a Kuini Wikitoria tenei e korero atu nei. Na nga ture i tukuna mai e ia, i na runga mai i te kupu oati a o koutou tupuna i hoatu ai i Waitangi, ka waru-tekau tau te pahuretanga atu, i tau ai te rangimarie ki te Iwi Maori, i mau ai kia ratou o ratou take whenua, i tatu ai o ratou ngakau. Nana i atawhai i tupu tahi ai te Maori raua ko te Pakeha, i whakatata ai tetahi ki tetahi i runga i te whakaaro pai, i te whakaaro kotahi.
>
> Ko tera pai, ko tera ora i matua horahia mai ra e Kuini Wikitoria i whakapumautia ki nga uri e tana tama e Kingi Eruera, e tana mokopuna e Kingi Hori. E koa ana au i toku rongonga kei te piki te matauranga o a koutou tamariki e whakaakona nei ki nga kura i hangaia e te Kawanatanga a te Kingi mo ratou. Ma tena anake hoki nga taitamariki o Aotearoa, Maori, Pakeha hoki e tupu ai hei tangata tika, e tau ai hei rangatira mo nga Moutere nei, mo to tatou Emepaea hoki. Na moku, ka mau au ki te tauira a Wikitoria, te Kuini Nui, i awhi tonu nei tona aroha i te Iwi Maori mai ano o te ra i whakaae ai ratou ki tona mana.
>
> E nga Rangatira, e te Iwi, tena koutou, a Hei konei![47]

In his speech, the Prince invoked the spirit of his great-grandmother Queen Victoria, in whose name the Treaty of Waitangi had been signed in 1840. His claim that the treaty had been followed by 'true contentment and peace', however, ignored years of bitter fighting during the Northern Wars of the 1840s and the New Zealand Wars of the 1860s, and subsequent land confiscations and land losses through the Native Land Court.

While warriors from Te Arawa and various Mātaatua tribes had fought alongside British troops during the New Zealand Wars, other tribes had refused to sign the Treaty and had fought against the British, including the Waikato people under King Tāwhiao, who came together to protect their lands against the incoming settlers. According to the *London Star*, the Waikato tribes had decided not to attend the welcome in Rotorua:

James McDonald photographed a section of the attentive crowd at the welcome ceremony at Arawa Park.

The Waikato tribe of Maoris, formerly our enemies in the Maori War, refused to be represented at Rotorua in the welcome to the Prince of Wales, as they would have had to associate with other tribes. They threatened that if the Prince did not stop at their village to receive them they would hold up his train and lie in front of it in order to prevent his going to Rotorua. They finally promised not to create a disturbance if they were permitted to welcome the Prince.[48]

Nevertheless, some Waikato rangatira defied the boycott, and one, Tupu Taingākawa Te Waharoa, presented a pounamu mere to the Prince; this later led to a court case, because his kinsmen had not authorised the gift.[49]

Sir James Carroll acted as master of ceremonies in the entertainment that followed the speeches. Te Arawa opened with a haka and poi, and then Bay of Plenty iwi also performed a haka, led by a rangatira brandishing a claymore that had been presented as a sword of honour to his grandfather, Major Hemana, who had fought alongside the British troops in the wars of the 1860s. Next came Ngāpuhi and other northern iwi, each carrying a taiaha (probably those supplied by the Dominion Museum) with a bunch of dried flax tied on its point. The *Otago Daily Times* Rotorua correspondent wrote:

They were challenged as they advanced by a grimacing, gesticulating warrior, who pranced before their ranks. A warrior dashed out, pursued the challenger, overturned him, and placed his foot on the recumbent form in triumph. The tribe followed with a roar and a stamp, and swung into the wildest war song yet heard, followed by a combined haka and poi.

Both a haka and a poi dance were performed for the Prince of Wales in Rotorua. Photographs by James McDonald.

Next came the Raukawa, who gave a
poi emblematic of the Prince's journey
overseas [accompanied by a fiddle and an
accordion]. Following them came the men
and women from the East Coast, including
the Ngatiporou. At their head was the Hon.
A.T. Ngata, in full warrior costume. Stripped
to the waist and barefooted, greenstone mere
in hand, he led the dances — all Maori for the
day, with Parliament, Law Courts, and
University forgotten.[50]

Ngata, who had instigated this second Ethnological
Expedition, attended the hui in his capacity as
a tribal leader.

After Ngāti Porou left the ground, the Wairarapa iwi
gave a haka, followed by Whanganui and Taranaki,
who performed poi and haka. During one of these
performances, one of the women brandished a

white-backed hand mirror instead of a mere, and
blew kisses towards the royal stand. Then, at the
end of the entertainment:

Following a wailing chant that came from
the left, men and women, rank behind rank,
went through a final dance with long stringed
single pois, and the back ranks with the
smaller double pois were very graceful.
As they finished their dance a pretty maiden
was seen advancing. In one hand she carried
a mere and in the other a camera.

Very graceful she was as she repeated the
movements of the poi. Thus she came to
the foot of the stand where the Prince was
seated, and having taken his picture she
curtseyed and retreated as gracefully and
as enchantingly as she came. She was a
born actress — a comedienne one moment,
a tragedienne the next.[51]

Prince Edward now left the stand and inspected the Māori police before mingling with the crowd, who surged around him; then he and his retinue drove away from the park, pursued by hearty cheers. They dined at the hotel, and later that afternoon, the Prince attended a parade at which he presented medals to Corporal M Otene, Sergeant Pomana and privates Tapu and H Mau. That night he wrote another querulous, self-pitying note to his mistress:

'Christ! I've had such a terrible day of Maories and their comic stunts. All I was thankful for was that YOU didn't see me looking such a fool beloved tho they gave me some fine presents when all the 'hakas' and 'poi dances' were over.'[52]

That evening he went to bathe in the Duchess Pool opened by his mother in 1901, then boarded the train and stayed inside until it left Rotorua late that night.

The Māori police, photographed by James McDonald as they line up for inspection at the Māori police reception for the Prince of Wales in Rotorua, 1920.

Matangireia, the Maori Affairs Committee Room of the House of Representatives at Parliament, Wellington, around 1922.

Aftermath

During the formal ceremonies of welcome to the Prince of Wales, the Dominion Museum team was able to do very little work, although McDonald managed some filming. On 30 April, however, they resumed their recordings, and Paitini and Makurata sang a waiata and two oriori, including the famous lullaby 'Pōpō', and Hiahianui, a Te Arawa woman, recorded a pātere.

That same day, Te Kiwi Amohau, the high-born Te Arawa elder, Anglican lay reader, carver and authority on ancestral knowledge,[53] recorded a greeting to the team 'who had come to see the Prince', a pātere, a whakaaraara pā and a tapatapa kūmara (chant for planting kūmara), although the sound quality was poor.[54] He also tried to play a kōauau that Andersen had brought with him, but was not able to draw sound from the instrument. After explaining some design features of this small mouth-blown flute—for instance that the holes were called wenewene, and that each had a different purpose in strengthening, softening or 'correcting' the sounds—he told Andersen that no one now living at Ōhinemutu had heard the pūtorino, and that the kōauau was no longer played.[55]

Ngata and McDonald already knew this eminent elder. The previous year, a small committee consisting of Herries, Ngata and McDonald had been set up to oversee the decoration of the Maori Affairs Committee Room in the new Parliament House. McDonald modelled kōwhaiwhai rafter patterns in plaster relief that were placed on the cornice and ceilings,[56] and Ngata asked that the woven tukutuku panels and carving be carried out by Ngāti Tarāwhai experts.[57] At about the time of the welcome to the Prince, the timber was sent to Rotorua, and Te Kiwi Amohau and Te Ngaru Ranapia set to work with a team of carvers and weavers, later travelling to Wellington in 1922 to finish the decorative work on the room, with McDonald as supervisor.[58] Amohau also helped Johannes Andersen with his work, giving him information about ancestral games.[59]

Over the following week in Rotorua, the Expedition team visited Whakarewarewa, where James McDonald photographed the model pā, and Ōhinemutu, where he shot images of various whare whakairo and lines of palisades running out into the lake. McDonald also took portraits of Neke Kapua's whānau, including his son Eramiha's wife, Wairata Neke, and his grandson, Paora. On 7 May the team met Gilbert Mair, the former commander of the Arawa Flying Column that had pursued Te Kooti (and perhaps Paitini as well) during the New Zealand Wars.[60] Mair, whom most of the team had previously met at the New Zealand International Exhibition in Christchurch, and who had been closely involved in organising the welcome to the Prince of Wales, recorded the speech he had made to welcome the manuhiri to Ōhinemutu on 27 April, a waiata and several kōrero tuku iho (ancestral stories). He also told them a story about

Wehipeihana, a warrior given to nervously firing his musket when silence was necessary, until Mair expelled him from the Flying Column. In mortification Wehipeihana jumped into a boiling thermal pool at Ōhinemutu. After Mair pulled him out, he jumped in again and later died of his burns. Mair indicated that the boiling steam pool where Wehipeihana had died was just behind them, in a hut. He also told them the story of Hinemoa and Tūtanekai, saying that in former times, the soft sounds of the kōauau could be heard every evening at Ōhinemutu at about dusk.[61]

Just before the official party left Rotorua on 8 May, Hēnare Balneavis told McDonald that the taiaha used in the welcome were being taken away by departing groups. When McDonald, Best and Andersen searched the camp, they found five crates of taiaha, two still closed and three that had been opened. They collected the remaining spears and organised for them to be sent back to the Dominion Museum in Wellington.[62] The use of artefacts in cultural performance, rather than their preservation

The whare whakairo at Ōhinemutu, Rotorua, in 1920. Photograph by James McDonald.

Carver Neke Kapua's grandson Paora, photographed by James McDonald in Rotorua around 1920.

in museums, made more sense to tangata whenua, however, and the missing spears eventually turned up and were used by Te Arawa performers associated with the School of Maori Arts and Crafts set up in Rotorua a few years later under Augustus Hamilton's son Harold Hamilton.[63]

A month later, Dr Thomson told the Government Printer that a case containing 5000 feet of moving film entitled 'Visit of HRH the Prince of Wales to New Zealand' had been sent to the museum.

Andersen wrote a paper on Māori string games, reporting that he had collected eighteen new whai at Rotorua, but adding that 'a gathering of this kind, whilst it brought many Maoris together, was not the best for obtaining ethnological information'.[64]

He noted that at Ōhinemutu, Guide Bella had showed him a figure she called Te Moana nui a Kiwa, which she told him represented the seven lakes in the area and Mount Tarawera.[65] Some of these figures are included in Andersen's book *Maori String Figures*, published in 1927 by the Board of Maori Ethnological Research.

Eramiha Neke's wife Wairata, photographed by James McDonald in Rotorua around 1920.

Palisades at Ōhinemutu, Rotorua. Photograph by James McDonald.

In the 1920 annual report of the Dominion Museum, McDonald (now Assistant Director) reported on his work for the new Maori Affairs Committee Room in Parliament; and Best reported in some detail on the Rotorua expedition:

As our sojourn at Rotorua occurred at the time of the visit of HRH the Prince of Wales, we encountered a very large number of Natives, and witnessed some remarkable illustrations of pre-European usages. Many of these scenes were enacted not as a spectacle for the Royal visitor but in connection with the reception of successive parties of Native visitors arriving from other districts.

Messrs McDonald and Andersen were enabled to produce a large number of photographs and moving pictures of old Native games and occupations, among which that of the generation of fire by means of the primitive 'fire-plough' of Polynesia is the most interesting. Mr. Andersen collected a considerable number of string games, and a fair number of songs were recorded on the dictaphone.

As the Rotorua district is remarkable for the number of carved Native houses it contains, the opportunity was taken to obtain a considerable number of photographs of such illustrations of Maori art. The so-called model pa at Te Whakarewarewa, although of modern design [a gun-fighter's pa] supplied some very good details for photographing. The party was indebted to Te Kiwi Amohau and Captain Gilbert Mair, NZC, both of Ohinemutu, for much kindly assistance, and to Major P. Buck and Captain Vercoe, of the reception camp for help in many ways.[66]

A POUHAKI FOR THE PRINCE

JAMES SCHUSTER AS TOLD TO BILLIE LYTHBERG

James Schuster in 2016 with the tā moko panel carved
by his great-great-grandfather, Tene Waitere.

James (Jim) Schuster, great-great-grandson of the renowned great Ngāti Tarawhai carver Tene Waitere, explains the story of the huge pouhaki that Tene Waitere carved for the Prince's visit to Rotorua, and its journey to Portsmouth, England.

In 1906, when the New Zealand International Exhibition was happening, the Whakarewarewa people were in Christchurch, but my great-great-grandfather Tene Waitere was back in Rotorua,[67] because at that time he was doing the carvings for the model pā Rotowhio at Whakarewarewa.[68] He went down to Christchurch on a visit with Gilbert Mair, who took him to see all his relations. There's a photograph of them all at the exhibition, standing in front of the whare. Tene is in the picture with Gilbert Mair, who is sitting in the middle (see page 58).

As well as carving the model pā, he was also doing the carving for the Government Gardens in Rotorua. It was a lot of work but this was how he kept my kuia and the rest of the whānau alive. He had to provide for them because their father, Te Mangō Rātema, had left their mother and had headed back down to Rotoiti to live down the road at Te Waiiti. Their mother, Tuhipō, had married again, to Hori Kereopa, and had another family. They lived with Tene at Whakarewarewa, and the carving kept them going.

Tene was also a builder and a carpenter. He built things. He also did a lot of hunting and gathering. In her book, Guide Rangi described how she would go out hunting with him—mainly for pigeons and things. They would leave early and walk across the hills via Tarawera to come down to Okataina round the old places, the old pā sites around Lake Okataina where Ngāti Tarāwhai lived. She remembered wild cherries growing up at Okataina. By the time they got to Ruatō, on the southern shores of Lake Rotoiti, they'd have bags full of berries they'd picked on the way. They had hunting dogs, so if he could, he'd get pigs as they went. In a way, he was doing his shopping as he went home through the bush. Tene was a good provider.

It was 1920 when the Prince of Wales came to Rotorua, and Tene carved the pouhaki specially for that visit, to be put up for the big gathering at the Racecourse. Now it's called Arawa Park, but back then it was called ANZAC Park.

Tene had to recruit somebody to give him a hand to carve the pouhaki quickly. By then the carver Te Ngaru Ranapia was coming into prominence. Te Ngaru worked for Apirana Ngata on the Māori Affairs Committee Room in Parliament, which is now called Matangireia. When I went in there for the first time in 2020, when they wanted us to go down and do some restoration work, I said, 'Oh, this looks like Ngāti Tarāwhai carvers have done this!' They told us that Te Ngaru Ranapia and Kiwi Te Amohau of Ngāti Whakaue were the carvers, and the tukutuku panels were done by Te Arawa weavers.

Tene called on Te Ngaru to give him a hand to finish the pouhaki in time for the Prince's welcome but you can tell they didn't quite get it done because it's carved on all four faces except the back. On the front face they left a space where a copper or brass plaque was put on, which named the carvers. There are figures shaped out on the back, but they haven't got any surface decoration. There's no pākati or haehae or spirals covering it. They ran out of time so they left those unfinished; formed them and shaped them out but didn't decorate them. So that was a result of their hurry to get the pouhaki up, with all the flags hung off it, for the Prince of Wales.

I don't know quite why they carved a pouhaki for the Prince, but they probably tried to outdo somebody else who was giving him a taiaha. The Prince had enough patu and mere and things like that, so perhaps they were just thinking of something different. I think Tene liked to think out of the box. On some of his whakairo he left little tohu or signs. Perhaps he thought 'Oh we'll outdo those East Coast fullas and carve something big and tall, and see if the Prince will take it back and put it up at Buckingham Palace.'

What I do know is before that, Tene had carved a miniature waka about two metres long for the Duke and Duchess of Cornwall when they visited in 1901. They had sent it to the British Museum to be looked after. I saw it there when Professor Nicholas Thomas, the Director of the Museum of Archaeology and Anthropology at the University of Cambridge (MAA), took my wife Catherine and me to look at it in London. It was in offsite storage in Soho. Later, when I told Greg McManus, who was at the Rotorua Museum at the time, about it he said, 'Oh, we can apply to have that returned. It will still belong to the royal family, but we'll be looking after it.' So it's now here and on display in Rotorua.

I was recently reading something written by Don Stafford, who used to give a local history component on our tourism course at Waiariki Polytech. Don wasn't a fan of the royal family and he described how the Prince of Wales would only shake hands with his left hand, so he could keep his right hand on his gun. Don said of the Prince's visit to Rotorua, 'Good job he got rained on most of the time.' But that whole welcome was for the Prince. There were Māoris for miles here in Rotorua — mostly from Mātaatua and

Tūhoe. I think Tainui people didn't want to come down and meet Victoria's grandson. They were still hurting after all the land confiscations and the wars there, so the Waikato didn't come as part of it.

My kuia wrote an action song, 'Nau Mai', to welcome all the tribes that came for that welcome to the Prince of Wales at ANZAC Park, and the Tūhourangi people still sing it today; it's one of their number one favourite songs when they have to welcome people to Te Arawa or Whakarewarewa. It's been popular ever since.

The pouhaki was gifted to the Prince of Wales, and it was put onto the train to Auckland and went up with him when he returned. Then it was put onto the *Renown*, the ship he came on, and as soon as the *Renown* berthed in Portsmouth, the Prince got off and went back to London, leaving everything that had been given to him on the ship. The navy commandeered the pouhaki, I suppose; they put it up in the Rose Garden at Portsmouth, and it stood there from the 1920s until I first got to see it a few years ago with Dean Sully, who is the associate professor of conservation at the Institute of Archaeology at University College London.

I was staying with Dean in Norwich at the time. He'd asked me to come and help write a couple of chapters in his book *Decolonizing Conservation*.[69] When I told him I'd heard about a flagpole that my koroua carved that was down in Portsmouth and said that I'd never seen it, had never even seen a picture of it, he said, 'We'll go down and have a look. We've got to find it.'

One Sunday we drove from Norwich all the way down to Portsmouth, where we met retired Lieutenant Commander Brian Witts. He was a nice man, a real card, and it was through him that we met Nicholas Thomas from Cambridge.

The pouhaki was stuck in a huge concrete slab in the middle of the rose garden and braces were stabilising it. They'd made sure the pou wasn't going to get blown down in a storm. It had stood there all through the Second World War. German bombers used to offload the bombs that they hadn't dropped on their targets all over the English countryside on their way back to their bases in Germany, and quite often the bombs would land around Portsmouth. But they missed the pouhaki.

It had been standing out in the rain and the weather for close to eighty years. 'The way I see it,' I said to Brian, 'Either it's got to be restored and covered with protective paints, or you've got to take it down and bring it inside. Because water does more damage to tōtara than anything else—all those cracks!' Woodpeckers had eaten holes in it too. However, Brian said that there was no building in Portsmouth where it could be erected.

Some time later, when Nicholas Thomas heard about my discussion with Brian, he suggested that the navy give the pouhaki to the MAA, where

it could be installed. And so they did a deal with the British Navy. Later, my wife Catherine and I went back for the dismantling at Portsmouth.

Nicholas came too, and he brought with him from the museum a tokotoko that was believed to have been carved by Tene Waitere. I held it while I did the karakia to settle the mauri of the pou before it was moved. Some naval ratings were practising the hymn 'Oh God, our help in ages past', and were singing loudly about 100 metres away while I was trying to do my karakia. I just stopped and waited till they'd finished and then I carried on.

Tene Waitere at work in 1905, shaping the outlines for a whakawae.

The conservators who came down from Cambridge had built a frame for the pouhaki, and it was all boxed in. A crane came to lift it up. They had to run a chainsaw through the base of the pou as they wouldn't have got it out any other way. We had no idea how much was in the ground—there could have been another two or three metres of the pou down there. It was a bit sad to hear the chainsaw cutting through the pou but they cut below the surface and the base was not carved. I don't know if they were going to dig out the rest of it but I said, 'That piece in the ground could be still in good nick. It might be just a few centimetres on the outside that is a bit soft. But it's good heart tōtara.'

The pōwhiri and dedication ceremony for the pouhaki, following its restoration and installation at the Museum of Anthropology and Archaeology at the University of Cambridge. James and Cathy Schuster, Anne, Jeremy and Amiria Salmond, Esther Jessop and (then High Commissioner) Derek Leask were present.

It was put onto the back of a big truck and sent off to Cambridge. Catherine and I followed it up there, and then we worked with Dean Sully's conservation students to do what restoration we could. It wasn't so much about restoration, it was more about stabilisation so that the pou didn't deteriorate anymore.

We cleaned off the moss that had grown on it in places and replaced all the pāua eyes. We put in little inserts of tōtara where the woodpeckers had made holes. Before it went into the museum they put it in a freezer for a couple of days to kill any bugs that might have been living in the cracks. We worked on it for just over a week, and Nicholas put us up during that time in the halls of residence at the university. The pou is now standing upright in the museum, braced to the balcony.

Catherine is an expert weaver, and she gave a lecture in Cambridge about making muka and preparing harakeke for weaving. She showed them how to use a mussel shell to extract muka from flax. We were invited down to Kew Gardens to have a look at some of the old cloaks in the botanic collection there. I think they had wondered what this mussel shell was doing in amongst some of the muka in their collection, and all installed in a little box! Some of the muka we saw had been dyed with paru, an iron-rich mud that can cause fibre deterioration, and it was so fragile we couldn't touch it. It was so fine that at first I thought it was human hair. I believe that cloak was from the collection of Joseph Banks, made during James Cook's first voyage, 1768–71. They took us again to Kew later to have a look at a tikumu cloak made from the mountain daisy from the South Island. It's beautiful. It felt like a chamois cloth. It was made just of the leaves, which were softened.

Eventually we went back to Cambridge for the unveiling of the pouhaki. I brought a couple of flags from my marae, the Ngāti Hinekura marae at Te Waiiti, Rotoiti, with the same names that were on the flags that hung on the pou during the welcome for the Prince of Wales in 1920. One of them bore the name of Hinekura, the other Puwhakaoho — Hinekura was the father of Puwhakaoho. We put the flags on the pouhaki for the opening, and afterwards I brought them back home again. The pouhaki is in shelter now. It's out of the rough English weather — those winds that come off the English Channel. It will last forever inside a museum now; it won't deteriorate any more.

My grandmother, my kuia Ngātai, was Tene Waitere's granddaughter. He died twenty years before I was born. It was his granddaughters, Guide Rangi and Ngātai, who he stayed with. They looked after him, so they had lots of stories to tell me when I asked about him.

When I told my kuia that I was interested in learning how to carve, they said, 'Oh, your koroua was a carver, and he did this and he did that, and his chisels are still in a box in the shed.' They brought them out for me to have a look through, and to play around with bits of tōtara. I've never been taught how to carve, I sort of learnt it from all of the whakairo around me. But, hey, I think I just had to hold his chisels and they did all the work.

Although Tene was a well-known carver in Te Arawa, he didn't hold a prominent position in the tribal politic, because he was born part Ngāpuhi. His mother, Ani Pape, was taken as a slave by Hongi Hika when he came down to Rotorua. She was only about nine years old, we figured out, when she was taken away. I think they took all the young ones because they had to walk all the way back to Tai Tokerau, and they didn't want to take old slaves with them. She lived up in the North, up in Mangamuka, for a long time, and Tene's father was Ngāpuhi. She wasn't freed till after the arrival of the missionaries, when Samuel Marsden told Ngāpuhi it wasn't a Christian thing to do to keep people in slavery. They had to let them go.

Tene's uncle was Anaha Te Rāhui, another well-known Ngāti Tarāwhai carver. Anaha went up to the North to get his half-sister Ani and Tene, and Tene's younger sister Mereana, and he brought them back to Rotorua. Tene was only about six years old when he came back to live at Ruatō.

That's where I'm living now, at Ruatō, on land that's been in the family for a long time. Tene is buried just down at the end of the bay, in an unmarked grave. Mum took me up there one day and she said, 'We'll go up and have a look and see if we can find him'. But there were no markings or anything. She knew he was up on the hill; she said he wanted to be buried overlooking his beloved Ruatō Bay. So that's where he lies, upon one of the points at the end of the bay. This was where he learned to carve, too. He was only nine, my kuia reckoned, when he picked up his first chisel.

There was a Ngāti Tarāwhai school of carving here in Ruatō. It had been based at Okataina to begin with but had moved to Ruatō. The tohunga whakairo was Wero Tāroi. Tene used to sneak over when the carvers put their chisels down and went off to have a smoke or a cup of tea. He watched them, and he watched for a long time. He just watched them carve for about three years and the carver, old Wero, didn't say anything.

But one day Tene decided to pick up the chisels and have a go. He'd been watching for so long that he just picked up the chisel and started finishing the old tohunga's work. When Wero came back, Tene dropped the chisel and his patu whao, his mallet, and stepped back but the old man said to him, 'No, you carry on, you finish it now.' And so he took him under his wing, and in his later years, Tene was his apprentice.

I think Wero was eighty when he carved Hinemihi o Te Ao Tawhito—the carved meeting house that's in Surrey, England. Wero and Tene were working on that whare together for Aporo Te Wharekaniwha, the chief at Te Wairoa at the time.[70] While they were carving that whare, they were also carving Te Tiki a Tamamutu in Taupō for the Spa Hotel: Tene was travelling there, working between those two jobs. But Tamamutu didn't pay them in the end so they left that job, and that's why a lot of the carvings in that whare Tiki a Tamamutu are only half finished.

After Tene came back to Rotorua, Wero died, and Tene had to finish off the carvings for Hinemihi. This was in the 1880s. Hinemihi was opened in 1885, and then the Tarawera eruption happened in 1886 and the whare was buried. Tene was in his twenties by this time, so he was only a young man. He was a bit ostracised by some of the people down here because he'd been born up North. So he just stuck to himself, stuck to his carving, hunting, providing for his family. He didn't get any positions of responsibility like Neke Kapua, his brother-in-law. Tene, Neke Kapua and Tene's uncle Anaha were quite often photographed together, working on all of the early whare around here, and especially ones up at Whakarewarewa and the whare Rauru that is now in the Museum für Völkerkunde in Hamburg. It was at Whakarewarewa, beside the Geyser Hotel.

Anaha was a translator for the court, he was a land surveyor. Neke was in the Maori Armed Constabulary, and he got to be a sergeant for a while in Gilbert Mair's Te Arawa Flying Column. Because he didn't have any official positions, and just stuck to his carving, Tene was more prolific as a carver than the other two, because they had so many other things to do.

After the Tarawera eruption, Hinemihi was sold to Lord Onslow, then the Governor-General, who took the whare to his family home, Clandon Park, in Surrey. After the recent fire at Clandon Park, a group of us from Te Arawa went to England, taking a koha of $10,000 to help if they should decide to let Hinemihi come home. They had put a security fence around the burnt-out Clandon house, and left Hinemihi outside the fence. I said to them, 'Look, if you're going to do that, you might as well take these carvings off, because they'll become a target for fossickers or artefact dealers.' I told them, 'You've got more than a million dollars' worth of whakairo sitting out there outside the security fence. You need to take them off and put them into storage.'

So they did; they flew me across to take the carvings off. Again Dean Sully and his students came down from University College and gave us a hand. We found a few secret things on the carvings as we took them down … just names, telling us which figure actually was Hinemihi. We had to stop work one day when we found a bat stuck against the back of one of the carvings. Apparently it's a protected animal in the UK, so we had to stop work until someone came to take it away.

When the carvings were all cleaned down and packed up and put in a big container on the back of a truck, I said another karakia for the carvings and told them, 'This is the start of your long journey home.' And it has turned out that way. Well, hopefully, the pandemic isn't going to cause the people in Surrey to change their minds.

We owe our lives to this house, Hinemihi, because our great-grandparents sheltered there and she protected them and that's how they survived the Tarawera eruption. That's why she's special to us.

Even though the Onslow family owns the physical house, the wairua still belongs to us. And when we explained this to the current Lord Onslow, he was quite happy to let her go back home. The National Trust were the ones who weren't going to let her return, but now they've changed their minds.

When she comes back, we'll welcome her back with open arms and decide as a people what to do with her. Hinemihi needs to be kept warm. That's how you look after these taonga. They need to stay in touch with the people.

The rūnanga house Hinemihi, photographed by the Burton Brothers at Te Wairoa in 1885, before the eruption of Tarawera a year later.

'TŌIA MAI! TE TAONGA!'

The Third Dominion Museum
Ethnological Expedition
17 March–18 April 1921
Whanganui River

ANNE SALMOND
JOHN NIKO MAIHI
SANDRA KAHU NEPIA
TE WHETURERE POOPE GRAY
TE AROHA McDONNELL
BILLIE LYTHBERG

Pā tuna on the Whanganui River at Hiruhārama,
photographed by James McDonald during the third
Dominion Museum Expedition in 1921.

At the turn of the twentieth century, the Whanganui River was a major tourist attraction, dubbed 'the Rhine of Maoriland',[1] with steamboats plying between Whanganui township and Pipiriki near the top of the river road. During his time as the first government kinematographist, James McDonald had filmed the scenery along the river for the Tourist Department.[2] Elsdon Best had also visited various Whanganui River communities, carrying out two weeks of fieldwork there for the Dominion Museum in 1915, and recording material in Māori from local elders about the origins of the cosmos and other esoteric matters.[3] In mid-February 1921, the team of McDonald, Best and Johannes Andersen were given official leave to travel up the Whanganui River on the third Dominion Museum Ethnological Expedition to collect 'phono-graphic and photographic records of Maori life'.[4]

On 1 March 1921, McDonald, as Acting Director of the Museum, wrote to the Undersecretary of Internal Affairs to request permission to purchase gifts for the local people.[5] Best, for his part, wrote to Thomas Downes, Supervisor of River Works for the Wanganui River Trust and an amateur ethnologist who knew the river communities well, seeking his assistance. Shortly afterwards, Downes replied:

I have had a reply from headquarters saying that I may spend part of April with your party and also that I may take the motor canoe. Now as April is getting late I would advise you to get it partly done (at least) by Hatrick's boats.[6] Ratana is meeting the natives of the river at Pipiriki towards the end of the month, and there is no saying when the gathering will be over.

The fruit and Tuna heke [eel migration] is also on this month, first fresh and may interest you, there are pa tuna [eel weirs] at Te Autemutu above Pipiriki, one now being built at Paparoa Pipiriki and one at Hiruharama. Trusting you will have a good time and that I may participate a little. I can let you have tents and camping gear.[7]

This was sound advice. Once the autumn rains arrived it would be much safer to travel up the river by steamer, and with a visit by the prophet leader Tahupōtiki Wiremu Rātana looming, the sooner they reached Pipiriki the better. Te Rangihīroa, whose interest in Māori material culture — especially weaving, fishing and netting — had become a passion, found the prospect of studying local weaving and observing the eel weirs in action along the Whanganui River irresistible. By 10 March he had decided to join the expedition.

A few days later McDonald received permission to buy a dictaphone that could be used without electrical power, since this had not yet reached the upriver communities.[8] Tickets were purchased for the team to travel by steamer to Koroniti (Corinth),[9] Hiruhārama (Jerusalem) and Pipiriki.

Koroniti

On 17 March 1921, when the expedition team arrived in Koroniti, McDonald filmed the passengers disembarking, and local boys skipping stones across the river. In the village they were greeted by the local rangatira, dressed in a 'tatterdemalion' grey shirt and trousers—although, as Andersen remarked, this reflected 'neither poverty nor ignominy'. He added that while their houses were built in European style, the river people were still very Māori in their ways of living, and that 'very little of value can be obtained unless the collector knows and speaks their language, or in default has with him a mutual friend who may interpret for him; but complete ignorance of the language is an almost insuperable obstacle'.[10]

Best had worked with various of the Whanganui elders before, but seeing him and Andersen with their notebooks, some of the local people thought they might be tax collectors and regarded them with suspicion. At the same time, McDonald's camera was 'a thing to be avoided as not being familiar'.[11] Fortunately, Te Rangihīroa was well known in the Whanganui communities in his former role as second-in-command of the Pioneer Battalion, and as Director of Maori Hygiene at the Department of Health. When he arrived at Koroniti from Auckland the next morning, he was received with a hongi and tangi. During the formal welcome at the local marae, after listening to speeches from the local rangatira and another elder, he delivered a lively address that allayed their fears and won their support.

The wharepuni at Koroniti, photographed by James McDonald during the third expedition in 1921.

After that, as Andersen noted, the expedition team were 'given the keys of the city ... That is no empty phrase; for without their goodwill we could not have written or photographed anything worth while, but with it we had to send for more pencils and more films.' Although the team had brought tents with them, a small house was set aside for their use; and as they soon learned, in these communities, 'Your house is everybody's house, in return for which everybody's house is your house.'[12] The Koroniti people gave them 'royal hospitality', with meals that included boiled and roasted meat, potatoes and parsnips, and rice with stewed quince.[13]

According to Andersen, the Whanganui iwi had their own ideas about time: 'Why hurry to get anywhere?— there will be somewhere else to go to. Why hurry with your work?—there will be something else to do.' All the same, he and the members of the team often worked long hours during the expedition, beginning at eight in the morning and ending at about midnight. 'If some of our friends grew tired, others would come on, and whilst information was flowing we must be there with our pitchers.'[14]

Heremia Rāwiri, a veteran of the New Zealand Wars, photographed at Koroniti in 1921.

Johannes Andersen watching a local woman demonstrating whai at Hiruhārama, Whanganui River, in 1921. Photograph by James McDonald.

The new dictaphone was immediately put to use: on their first day at Koroniti they recorded twenty-seven songs and chants by different performers, including seventeen by Heremia Rāwiri of Oneriri, a blind old man[15] from Ngāti Pāmoana and Ngāti Tamataira[16] who had fought with the Whanganui troops in 1866 when they were sent to Ōpōtiki to avenge the killing of the German missionary Carl Völkner.[17] As the steamer carrying the troops approached Ōpōtiki, the tohunga Patiwha (also known as Titau) had climbed out onto the bowsprit and chanted a prophetic song, which Heremia recited into the dictaphone.[18] Heremia also performed songs about fights with the Pai Mārire supporters and at Operiki pā, four whakaaraara pā or sentry songs, haka, laments, a karakia, several waiata aroha, pao (short songs), an oriori or lullaby, and songs that were accompanied by a flute, or performed by messengers from one village sent to invite the people of another to a feast, traditionally sung to the accompaniment of the pūtātara.[19]

The old soldier Heremia lived at Oneriri, and over the next few days he recorded another thirteen songs, chants and stories, including tales about patupaiarehe and taniwha, and a chant that accompanied a string figure or whai, 'Te Ara Pikipiki a Tāwhaki.' Presumably this was for Andersen, who was fascinated by this art form. As Andersen described it, it took some time to record this chant: 'The game was familiar to me, but the song was new. It was a lengthy one, and it took a couple of hours before the whole could be recollected, some ten or a dozen men, old and young, discussing and reciting until the song was secured, and taken down.'[20]

Rihipeti Aperaniko photographed by James McDonald as she weaves a basket at Koroniti in 1921.

Another of the singers, Rihipeti (or Irihāpeti) Aperaniko, a chiefly woman from Ngāti Pāmoana and a skilled weaver,[21] sang a ngeri (canoe launching chant) composed by her grandmother, a tangi and another lamenting her solitary life (although she had five children).[22] Other performers included Toka Peni, who sang two waiata tangi, a waiata aroha, a tau marae, sung to welcome visitors onto a marae, and chanted two ngeri; and the high-born elder Ropata Rangitahua, who sang a love song[23] and a lament for a plundered kūmara pit.

In addition to these recordings, a number of the singers presented the team with taonga, some of which were closely linked with the ancestral knowledge they were sharing with the expedition team. Rihipeti, for instance—a raranga expert who demonstrated harvesting, splitting, stripping, dyeing and weaving techniques for Te Rangihīroa—presented the team with a kete made of kiekie vine (*Freycinetia banksii*), another made of tī (Cordyline), a kawe rapa (carrying cord) and a makawe (narrow flax belt), which were later accessioned into the Dominion Museum collection.[24]

With great good humour, Rihipeti and her friends also demonstrated their art on film and in photographs—stripping and splitting flax leaves, beating hīnau bark and steeping it in water from a calabash to act as a mordant; soaking strips of harakeke in paru to dye them, then washing them in a stream; and stripping muka and beating it with a pounder, 'making a glossy soft fibre, and the weaving was most artistic'.[25] Te Rangihīroa recorded all these processes, and two years later published a superbly detailed article in two parts, 'Maori Plaited Basketry and Plaitwork', in *Transactions of the New Zealand Institute*.[26] McDonald enjoyed working with Te Rangihīroa to document these arts, noting, 'I got interested in kit weaving & mat making.'[27]

Together, McDonald's record of these processes and Te Rangihīroa's sketches and writings give an exceptional portrait of an early-twentieth-century weaver at work, images that have recently been used by weavers, conservators and researchers in reviving these art forms and the practices associated with them. Some of the photographs were taken at a local pā harakeke; Andersen noted that there were several of these 'small enclosures where from twenty to thirty flax plants grew to supply the constant need for blades in the manufacture of food-baskets, kete of all kinds, kawe or carriers etc'.[28]

Another of the singers, Ngārongo Pokiha, performed a song that accompanied the ritual presentation of prized foods, describing the ceremony and presenting the team with two poti taro that were used on such occasions. As Best recorded in his field notebook:

> These poti were used to put food in at a hakari. At these hakari a number of stakes stuck upright in rows perhaps 1 foot apart and each man of [the] community filled a space between two stakes with his contribution of food. Baskets of kumara [...] at the bottom then other foods, & then birds, huahua [preserved flesh in calabashes] on top. Certain special kai carried in poti by persons singing. Sometimes a number of ruru obtained and made into huahua and then song of person carrying poti was as follows: ... Get from Nga rongo.[29]

After he had recorded his songs, Ropata Rangitahua gave the team a patu muka (muka beater) made of maire taiko, a stone adze, a mutu kākā (kākā snare) named 'Rerehau' and a mōria kākā (stone or bone leg-ring for a captive kākā) named 'Ngā wai takahia', which was made out of kiwi bone.[30] Rangitahua's gifts of a snare and a leg-ring were associated with a series of photographs taken by McDonald to illustrate the art of bird snaring and the use of decoys, although Best identifies the man who features in these images as Apirana Tukairangi.

Rihipeti Aperaniko and her friends demonstrate the processes
of preparing and dyeing flax for weaving at Koroniti in 1921.
Photographs by James McDonald.

McDonald also photographed snares for kiore—which, according to Best, have black, brown or reddish fur and could swim across rivers, each kiore holding the tail of the one ahead in its teeth; if one kiore let go, the ones behind it would drown. Māori baked these rats with their skins on, so that the skin and fur were easily stripped off.[31]

Although he did not record any chants or songs, Wēneti Nopera of Koroniti presented the visitors with a fine wooden bailer carved by his father Nopera for the river canoe *Tahuhuroa*.[32] Nopera's gift, which Best recorded in his notebook, was followed by descriptions of seven canoes that were hauled up on the riverbank at Koroniti, which he measured at 45 feet, 44 feet, 34 feet 6 inches,

Wēneti Nopera makes a trap for kiore at Koroniti. Photograph by James McDonald.

Rihipeti Aperaniko photographed by James McDonald standing in *Te Wehi o te Rangi* at Koroniti in 1921. This waka is now on display in the Whanganui Regional Museum.

47 feet 6 inches, 52 feet 3 inches, 61 feet 6 inches and 31 feet 6 inches long respectively — and which McDonald also photographed. Best noted that the largest of the river waka, a very old canoe named *Te Wehi o te Rangi*, was 61 feet 6 inches (19.75 metres) long and could be paddled rather than poled over the rapids.[33] The second largest, at 52 feet 3 inches (nearly 16 metres) long, was named after John Ballance, founder of the *Wanganui Herald* and later Minister of Native Affairs, who had died almost twenty years earlier. In his field notebook, Best's records of the gifts they were given were often accompanied by a note reminding him to write to the donors and present them with gifts in return.[34]

Best and Te Rangihīroa were both fascinated by the Whanganui art of eeling, but few artefacts associated with this work were presented to the team—no doubt because the eeling season was in full swing. They had to be content with McDonald's photographs of two large hīnaki and his images of a catch of tuna being distributed during their visit to Koroniti. Best collected stories about battles at Operiki pā—a large fortified site upriver that McDonald photographed—and he later published a pamphlet about this site.[35] Best also recorded the names of other pā close to Koroniti.

Distributing a catch of tuna at Koroniti in 1921.
Photograph by James McDonald.

Stacked firewood for fuel at Koroniti.
Photograph by James McDonald.

Stringing tuna, ready for cooking at Koroniti.
Photograph by James McDonald.

As Andersen could not speak Māori, Best transcribed the words of several songs for him and the names of the singers who featured in the wax cylinder recordings, often using his distinctive Māori shorthand. He collected terms associated with eeling and catching piharau (lamprey), weaving and bird snaring, games including walking on stilts and hand games, how to use the body to measure distances, and a tale about the local kaitiaki—a ngārara or monster named Tipaeara that lived at the paepae tuatara (village latrine, a sacred place where karakia were performed), and which showed itself in times of danger.[36]

Best collected terms for body measurements at Koroniti, and it is likely that a series of film and photographic sequences featuring Apirana (or Aperahama) Tukairangi demonstrating this and other arts[37] were recorded in this village. These include a set of photographs demonstrating how to make twelve different measurements using the body as a yardstick, as well as film sequences showing him drilling stone with a cord drill, sharpening an adze against a stone set in a stream, snaring birds in a hide made from mamaku fronds and, finally, performing a niu (divination) ritual.

Boys photographed by James McDonald playing upoko-titi, a hand game, at Koroniti, 1921.

A niu divination rite photographed by James McDonald at Koroniti in 1921.

This involved setting up a line of vertical sticks in the ground and casting fern stalks towards them; and, in another ritual, chanting and wagging a forefinger as sticks jerked along the ground towards twigs of karamū; each twig standing upright on a small mound and representing a hapū. For each man doomed to die in the approaching battle, a karamū leaf would fall, and if the whole twig was knocked over by one of the moving sticks, that whole hapū would be defeated.

The team found that evenings in the local wharenui were the best time for gathering ancestral information. Old tales were told, specialist terminologies collected and puzzling words discussed. Sometimes this process was confusing, for example when Te Rangihīroa asked an old man about two terms for particular

kinds of fences that Best had collected, and how these fences differed.[38] At first the elder insisted that these were simply two names for the same kind of fence, but later he changed his mind:

> Towards evening he came strolling along with the negligent indifference of definite purpose. 'About those two kinds of fence,' said he, 'The difference is so and so,' entering into minute details. 'But you said they were the same thing,' said our half-caste friend.[39] 'What I said five minutes ago we will wipe out of the memory,' said he, passing his hand through the air before us as if actually wiping it out: 'I have just proved to you that they are two different things', and proven it remained.[40]

Four days after arriving at Koroniti, Te Rangihīroa learned that his wife was seriously ill, and on 22 March he left for Auckland.[41] By then he had already gathered many anthropometric measurements (for cranial and other bodily indices), and recorded each stage of the weaving process for kono, kete and whāriki.

The rest of the team stayed on in Koroniti for another week, and during this time, McDonald photographed more fine mats, cloaks and baskets. Thomas Downes was not present; instead the team were assisted by Teko N (Rangi) Chadwick from

Koroniti, who appears in a number of McDonald's images, adzing wood and entertaining the visitors at his home, while his wife demonstrates how to make a kono. Chadwick was later paid £10 for 'assisting with camera and Dictaphone, hire of canoe, interpreting and work, arranging with natives at Maori villages for preparation of specimens for photographic work'.[42] Teko Chadwick and his wife Rākera may also have helped to organise the exuberant display of communal skipping in Koroniti village that McDonald recorded on film, with men (some wearing white shirts, waistcoats and hats), women and children skipping in groups or pairs, the dust rising as they demonstrate their skill, running in and out and turning as they jump to a long single or a double rope.

Mrs Pokai displays a whāriki she wove at Koroniti in 1921. Photograph by James McDonald.

Teko Chadwick, photographed by James McDonald, adzing timber at Koroniti in 1921.

On 29 March McDonald wrote to James Thomson, the Museum's Director, who had recovered from his most recent illness and returned to work. Enclosing a strip of film for testing, McDonald remarked:

> Basket and mat weaving with flax, ti and kiekie have been done for us, and all the processes of preparation and working from start to finish have been noted and photographed...
>
> A fair number of dictaphone records have been made. The Wanganui natives are not a singing people like the East Coast folk, and there are not many of the old people left, the younger ones did not seem to care to learn the old time songs. I quite expected we should have been able to get a number of canoe songs but they are pretty well forgotten. I understand that there are more of the older men at Hiruharama and we may be fortunate there...
>
> So much has been done for us here in the way of basket & mat making, and in other things for photographs that we feel we cannot leave with out giving the Maoris something in return. Mr. Best thinks this can only be appropriately done by way of a gift of flour & other food... I certainly think that we ought to present these people with goods to the value of 10 or 12 pounds for what they have done. A very fine canoe baler has been presented to us for the Museum, a stone adze, food baskets of various kinds, belts & several other things.
>
> I shall be glad if you will bring this under the notice of the Under-Secretary and advise me by telegram as early as possible if a gift as proposed is approved.

There has been a good deal of rain and the river has risen. At Hiruharama there are large eel weirs erected and the eels are beginning to move down the river. In a hinaki turned out here a few mornings ago there were 220 caught in one night. Best, Andersen and myself are well and join in kind regards.

In a postscript, he added:

> My fountain pen has run dry and we are without ink.[43]

As they were about to leave Koroniti, a telegraph arrived from Wellington, authorising McDonald to buy goods 'not exceeding £10 or £12 in value'.[44]

On 4 April, after a friendly exchange of speeches, the team presented their hosts with gifts of flour, sugar, tea, rice, tinned meat, honey and treacle, which were gladly received.[45] As McDonald noted in a letter to Thomson, 'A number of speeches were made all round, and we parted with regret.'[46]

The following day the Ethnological Expedition team boarded the steamer, and they arrived at Hiruhārama four hours later. The river was exceptionally low and progress was slow, especially up the rapids.[47] During the journey, Best recorded the names of pā along the banks, utu piharau (lamprey weirs) and pā auroa (eel weirs), rapids and cliffs and notable rocks in the river.[48]

James McDonald's photograph of expedition members visiting the Chadwick house at Koroniti in 1921.

A still from the Whanganui River expedition film of people skipping at Koroniti in 1921.

Hiruhārama

When they landed at Hiruhārama, the Catholic missionary settlement upriver from Koroniti, most of the local people were away from the village, digging potatoes. Nearby they found an old man named Te Kehu who was building an utu piharau on the riverbank,[49] assisted by a younger man, Tau Tamakehu, who also features in several of McDonald's photographs.[50] During this encounter Best recorded terms for different parts of the weir in his notebook.[51]

Although McDonald filmed a hīnaki tuna made from aka and kiekie hanging from a tree, and these men allowed him to photograph the construction of the pā, they refused to let him film the process of setting and lifting the hīnaki, saying that this 'would be an aitua [ill omen] for the owners of the pa'.[52] The following day they discovered several more eel weirs about half a mile downriver, but it was pouring with rain and too wet and misty to film. When the people returned from the potato gardens that afternoon, the team were formally welcomed in the wharepuni and, according to McDonald, 'Best made a great oration in Maori which was enthusiastically received.'[53]

A James McDonald photograph of Hiruhārama village as seen from above in 1921.

Elsdon Best (far right) talking with Father Venning at Hiruhārama in 1921. Photograph by James McDonald.

People gathered on Hiruhārama marae in 1921. Photograph by James McDonald.

As they had expected, there were more elders at Hiruhārama than at Koroniti, since this settlement was further upriver; and on 6 April the team set about recording chants, laments, haka, love songs, songs of welcome and poi songs from these experts, who included Tamatea a Urunui, Aterea Te Whetū, Mirita Reihana, Metiria Tamahea, Kopeke and Ngāpare. Over the following week they collected laments for Māori soldiers killed in the First World War,[54] two haka pōwhiri[55] and a tau (song of welcome) that had been performed for the Prince of Wales at Rotorua when the Whanganui iwi attended that hui, led by a woman named Te Hāpai Rangitauira. The tau referred to the Treaty of Waitangi, the Prince's whakapapa, and the Māori soldiers who had died in the war.[56] They also recorded a tinatina or comic ditty in English: 'One, two, three! Mata caught a flea; Flea die, Mata cry, Mata pour tea.'[57]

As at Koroniti, some of the local people were fascinated by the process of making sound recordings. Although Best remarked that 'people here don't like to speak [chants] in the Dictaphone lest other tribes get them',[58] an elder named Taaia Toheriri recorded a tau, four waiata tangi, a pātere, a pao and a highly tapu karakia—an invocation for the paddle of Turi, captain of the Aotea canoe;[59] while Ihaka Toitupu performed six items—three tau, two haka and a waiata poi. Among the women, Matapārae Moari Whareoka sang two poi songs, a waiata, several pao, a tapatapa kai and a waiata kaioraora or cursing song, while Mātarena Enoka sang three pao and two waiata tangi.

At Hiruhārama, Best concentrated on collecting specialised terms associated with eel and lamprey weirs, and various waiata and karakia, which he transcribed in his Māori shorthand in his notebook. He noted that when a pā tuna was being built, a piece of the vine used in its construction and a stone were taken away as an iho and hidden as a mauri, a talisman to protected the structure.[60] He added that the 'river natives have lost most of old time knowledge, as details of processes &c and as to names of things, much confusion follows enquiry & such names given by one are often derided by another'.[61]

At Best's direction, McDonald photographed and filmed pā tuna, utu piharau, the hīnaki or traps that were attached to the weir—both completed and in the process of being woven—along with river canoes and scenes of the river. He hoped to film people gathering eels from the local pā tuna, but after another downpour the river rose rapidly, and several of the eel weirs were washed away.[62] McDonald also filmed men and women demonstrating ancestral gardening techniques with kō and hand picks, and photographed children playing or standing in the tobacco gardens; tobacco being dried; tombstones in the cemetery; the wharenui and dwellings; and Andersen trying out string games with the local people. One intriguing portrait features a young Pākehā woman, later identified as Violet O'Connor, who had been adopted by a local Māori family, with two friends, wearing traditional costume.

In one evocative film sequence, Elsdon Best speaks into the trumpet of the dictaphone to introduce a female singer, while Johannes Andersen brushes wax off the cylinder, and women in the background demonstrate whai. In another, Andersen is setting up a whai in the middle of a group, each of whom is demonstrating their skill in the art. Andersen later reported that he had recorded a number of new whai at Hiruhārama that he intended to publish in the Journal of Science and Technology, along with two songs to accompany the making of particular figures.[63] The only record of artefacts being presented to the team at Hiruhārama were three calabashes in a basket, given to them by a person named Matarena.[64]

An utu piharau being built by Tau Tamakehu (right) and an unnamed man, photographed by James McDonald at Hiruhārama in 1921.

FOLLOWING PAGE:

Pā tuna at Hiruhārama, 1921. Photograph by James McDonald.

Working on a hīnaki, Hiruhārama, 1921. Photograph by James McDonald.

A child photographed by James McDonald working in a tobacco garden at Hiruhārama in 1921.

Violet O'Connor (left) with friends at Hiruhārama in 1921. Photograph by James McDonald.

Pipiriki

After distributing gifts among their Hiruhārama hosts, on 12 April the team boarded the steamer and headed further upriver to Pipiriki, where they stayed at the fine new hotel, Pipiriki House, which McDonald also photographed. After being greeted by the rangatira, a man they called Rua (but identified by his descendants as Neri Erueti), they set up the dictaphone at the marae and a number of people recorded greetings to the team, including a karakia or mihi ki te taonga performed by a man named Te Ākihana Rangitāroia that began 'Ira! Ira mai tau taonga, ki te whai ao, ki te ao mārama!' 'Look, gaze at your taonga, in the daylight, the world of light!', followed by a waiata aroha.[65]

At Pipiriki, it seems, the team was treated with particular ceremony, and their devices to record ancestral knowledge were greeted as taonga, powerful treasures. One woman recorded a karanga for the 'taonga' (the dictaphone itself, or the cameras), hauling them like a canoe onto the marae: 'Tōia mai! Te taonga! Ki te urunga! Te taonga!' 'Haul! The taonga! To its resting place! The taonga!' Another woman, Hakaepa Marie of Ngāti Rangitautahi, performed a pao to welcome 'the men from the Government who have come to Pipiriki, who do all the work and who work for the Maori'; while Kume Tarake of Ngāti Rangitautahi chanted a pao 'about the actions of the Government in the past', two pao lamenting the loss of family members and another lamenting her advancing age. Other performers included Tarake Mai, Wiiwii of Pipiriki, Nika Erueti Toerangi and Te Ākihana Rangitāroia of Ngāti Kura, Ngāwai Whakarake of Ngāti Ruakā, Ruku Anihana, Rukuhina Te Ākihana, Wirihine Rerekura and Te Rangikauruera. Ruihi Gray of Ngāti Kura sang a number of 'Hawaiian' songs into the dictaphone. There were also waiata tangi, pao or short songs; and Matewai Tuatini of Ngāti Kura recorded a tapatapa huahua (chant) that the bird snarers intoned as they returned from the forest carrying bark vessels filled with birds, which are preserved in fat.[66]

To McDonald's relief, at Pipiriki he was able to take 'all the photographs of eel-catching arrangements that were wanted'.[67] He filmed hīnaki being set up by men dressed in white shirts and dark ties, no doubt in honour of the camera, as they poled canoes against a fast-running current to the end of eel weirs; and the eels being grilled and distributed by the local rangatira. He also made many portraits of Pipiriki people, including children.

While they were in Pipiriki, however, McDonald caught the flu, and the filming was curtailed.[68] They also heard that Thomson had suffered a relapse. When McDonald recovered, he wrote a short note of sympathy to the Director, saying, 'I was greatly distressed when I heard of your illness.'[69] Before they left Pipiriki on 18 April, a woman named Anihana presented the team with a 'fine korotete

or basket for holding eels after capture',[70] and Erueti gave them a plaited band for a pig's leg. In return they distributed a number of gifts.

As Andersen noted in his account of the Whanganui expedition:

> Much has been said of the lovely Wanganui, but the true beauty of this river can never be known to those who merely sail up or down its waters. One must live on its banks for a time, and see it from above early and late, in shadow and in shine. We spent some weeks in this way, living with the Maori people at one or other of the villages on its banks, and those weeks have given us a great love, not only of the beautiful river, but of the Maoris who live there.[71]

James McDonald's photograph of the view of the Whanganui River from Pipiriki House, Pipiriki, 1921.

Rangatira Neri Erueti 'Rua', photographed by James McDonald at Pipiriki in 1921.

2186

PREVIOUS PAGE: Pā tuna at Pipiriki, 1921.
Photograph by James McDonald.

Setting a hīnaki in the river at Pipiriki in 1921.
Photograph by James McDonald.

Two unnamed children photographed
by James McDonald at Pipiriki, 1921.

In the Dominion Museum's 1921 annual report, both McDonald and Best spoke warmly of their experiences on the Whanganui expedition. McDonald recorded that he had shot over 300 still photographs, and more than '5000 feet' of cinematographic film. Best remarked that the expedition had been very successful, due to 'the extreme kindness' of the Whanganui people, and added:

> They not only treated us with great hospitality, but also placed themselves at our disposal in regard to the obtaining of illustrations pertaining to old time industries &c; also, they presented the Museum with a number of Native artifacts of an interesting nature. So helpful, indeed, were these folk that to insert a list of the names of those who afforded us generous aid would add seriously to the length of this report.

> Dr. P. Buck joined us at Koriniti and conducted further anthropometrical work, also investigating thoroughly the manufacture of baskets, mats, &c., in view of preparing monographs on these subjects. A very large number of photographs were taken of old Native games, industries, implements &c, also moving pictures of a number of manufacturing processes and other activities of pre-European life.

> Dictaphone records of Native songs were taken to the extent of over fifty cylinders, and some interesting data were obtained as pertaining to old tribal and racial lore. Since our return letters have been sent to many of the Natives thanking them for donations and much kindly assistance.[72]

Later that year, when Andersen sent Ngata a copy of a paper on string figures he had collected at Rotorua in 1920, Ngata replied:

> I am glad to see that the good work commenced at Gisborne is being continued. I suggested to Mr. McDonald the other day a visit to my district with the dictaphone to secure records of Maori songs. There is a tremendous lot to be done yet in that direction — the tunes must be recorded now if they are to be caught at all.[73]

A group of three children, who are unnamed,
photographed by James McDonald at Pipiriki in 1921.

LIKE HE'S SITTING HERE AND TALKING

JOHN NIKO MAIHI
AS TOLD TO BILLIE LYTHBERG
AND SANDRA KAHU NEPIA

We've seen the Expedition films quite often and they stir amazing memories for our people. Now we get to see the photos, read the written histories and hear their voices on the recordings. The connections with our tūpuna are very close; they're direct and they help me recall what our old people used to tell us. Sometimes I'll look at the photos and documents that Sandy Nepia shares with me, and go away and have a dream, and it all comes back.

Rihipeti Aperaniko is my great-grandmother, my grandfather's mother. She was called Irihāpeti sometimes but we know her as Rihipeti. Rihipeti is in many of the expedition photos and she was probably directing things a fair bit. In those days you didn't just jump in to be photographed—you would have been told who was going to be in the films and photos, and what they would be doing. You would be chosen.

Rihipeti was a rangatira woman. In some of the expedition photos you can see her moko kauae clearly, her sharktooth earrings threaded through her ears on satin ribbon, and the tāniko on her sash and the waistband of her piupiu. She was dressed for the occasion.

You know, you hear the voices of the men in the expedition recordings, but Rihipeti was very significant. She forged a relationship with the expedition and did some weaving for them later, after they'd returned to the Dominion Museum.

When I look at the photo of Rihipeti and my grandfather Niko Maihi and grandmother Mere Te Hau Potaka-Osborne, and maybe even my father

Paeroke Aperaniko, under that tree, with samples of their weaving—wow, it gives me shivers. Because I can see all my nieces and nephews in her face, as a young woman. Man, do they look like us! Or rather, we look like them. This is my family, my blood.

Rihipeti had standing at Pūtiki, Kahawai, Parikino, and of course up at Koroniti, Matahiwi. She could probably go anywhere she wanted without too many problems. She stayed most of her life at Paetawa, which is across the river from Parikino marae.

Another of the photos shows Rihipeti standing in the war canoe *Te Wehi o te Rangi*, the largest of the Whanganui River waka. I was in my twenties or thirties when it last came out on the water, and I was arguing that I should be allowed on it but they said, 'You haven't had any training—get on the side!' *Te Wehi o te Rangi* was in so many battles it's a story on its own, and it now rests in the Whanganui Museum. There are still waka by the marae when you travel down the river. At Putiki, *Mangaone* belongs to the marae.

The photo of women weaving on the porch of Te Waiherehere at Koroniti shows Rihipeti next to Naima Peni.

Heremia Rāwiri, the old soldier who lived at Oneriri and recorded so many songs and chants on the dictaphone for the Expedition, was Rihipeti's uncle. Seeing him brings back lots of memories about Operiki. That was the main village until it became overcrowded and our whānau moved out of there and down to Koroniti. And listening to him … it's like he's sitting here and talking.

Five women making kono inside Te Waiherehere at Koroniti, 1921.
From left: Rangi Pokiha's mother Ngāreta, Naima Peni, Rihipeti Aperaniko, Puti Ngātaierua and an unnamed woman.

The person who was making the kiore traps, Wēneti Nopera, was my grandmother's father. It's another line of my whakapapa. My grandmother was from Pāmoana, she was a Tangaroa; Nopera Tangaroa was her father.

As for Aperahama (Apirana Tukairangi), he was very clever. He demonstrated the old ways of measuring using the body and the niu divination rites for the Expedition. He was using his computer! Our old people were clever and had skills in all areas.

Reading the expedition narratives in this book is awesome. I can hear the kōrero coming out of the wānanga we had in the 1980s. We don't do those anymore because the people have gone, but now I'm thinking that I need to do something about that. I'll get onto it. I've got to get as old as them first!

From left: Puti Ngātaierua (sitting), an unnamed man (standing), Naima Peni, Ngāreta Pokiha, Niko Maihi (standing), Te Hau Potaka (daughter of Naima Peni) with Paeroke on her lap and an unnamed woman, photographed by James McDonald next to Teko Chadwick's homestead at Koroniti in 1921.

MY TŪPUNA ARE REVEALING THEMSELVES

SANDRA KAHU NEPIA AS TOLD TO BILLIE LYTHBERG AND JOHN NIKO MAIHI

I've been looking at my whakapapa and now my tūpuna in the photos are revealing themselves more clearly—our veteran koro Heremia Rawiri, who is the brother to my great-great-grandmother, Riria Rawiri, who married Wi Ngātoa; and my nan Rākera Chadwick (née Ngātoa), who is the sister to my koro, Iharaira Ngātoa.

There are photos where the eels are all stacked up and the wood is ready to burn, to smoke them. One of our Ngātoa homesteads is situated around the back of the area shown in these. The marae cooking facilities were centred around the walnut tree, and the tree is still there, it's huge! I remember playing with the fire there.

My mum talked about a certain time of year when the river would flood and the waters rose, and they would go the water's edge and be able to flick the eels out onto the bank.

Nan Rakēra married Teko Chadwick, and when I look at photos of her, I see her facial characteristics in my family (the mokopuna of Iharaira and Hapai ki te Rangi). This is all fascinating to me.

In the photos that show her weaving and wearing a korowai, it looks like she had a costume change, because when she was at the house she was dressed differently—in 'civvy' clothes. She was very glamorous. I don't know where those korowai are now, but I can recognise them being used in other photos.

The weaving skill that Rākera demonstrates in the images gives me a sense of pride in knowing that this has been handed down from her, too; one of my aunties is the go-to when you want things woven, including korowai. When I shared these photos with my aunties they talked about all the flax bushes that were up on the hill. Koroniti was known as the weaving place. Beyond korowai and other time-intensive weaving there were also gifts they could create quickly, like table centrepieces for celebrations.

I see the strength in Rākera. Whanganui is known for its strong women. Even though they might seem to be in the background sometimes, they are arranging and sorting things out. The women make it happen and the men jump! And I see that in her. The expedition records say that the river people had their own ideas about time; that time could carry on and things would be done in their own good time when the people were ready. But in my family, when a job's got to be done, we get on with it.

Rākera's husband, Teko Chadwick, was the kaiwhakahaere for the expedition, setting things up and organising things; he and Rihipeti together. Teko was educated, possibly at Te Aute or Wanganui Collegiate. He ran businesses, and he had a shop up at Operiki.

Teko and Rākera had a beautiful house at a time when most of the neighbouring homes were small huts. It wasn't easy to get building materials up the river. In town, in Whanganui, Major Kemp had a home like Teko's in Koroniti. It makes you realise why wharenui were so important, when lots of people were living in such small places. Wharenui allowed you to come together.

When Rākera died, Teko moved back home to Putiki. He had been in Koroniti and Operiki because that was Rākera's place and we think he moved because he had a broken heart.

I've listened to the soundtracks and I've read the kupu. And a lot of what is written in this book starts to come alive. There's a lot that goes on in your mind when you listen. You think about the old people and you also reminisce about yourself. The accent is still the same but it's like the river flowed faster in their time, and we've slowed the river down.

A photograph of Rākera Chadwick taken by James McDonald at Koroniti in 1921.

WHERE THERE WAS AN ASTRONOMER THERE'S A PŌHUTUKAWA

TE WHETURERE POOPE GRAY AS TOLD TO SANDRA KAHU NEPIA AND JASMINE RATANA

You can see Upokonui, the clearing by the hill, to the left in this photograph. That's where we used to catch piharau and ngaore, little fishes like smelt, and īnanga. Karewarewa is the mountain to the right, Upokonui is the one in the middle. Karewarewa is named after Mercury, the planet closest to the sun.

In our history, Wi Pauro was a tohunga ki te ao, a stargazer. They used to tell all the people when it was time to go catch fish, or when it was time to grow spuds. If you've been to Koroniti, they've got a pōhutukawa tree down there that they got from my koro. There's another one at Ōtoko on the Whanganui road, a third one at Pipiriki, and the last one is at Kauangaroa. Pōhutukawa don't grow up the Whanganui River, but wherever there were astronomers, they've got a pōhutukawa tree at that place: Koroniti, Ōtoko, Pipiriki, Kauangaroa.

Fishing at Pipiriki, Whanganui River, 1921.
Photograph by James McDonald.

THE KNOWLEDGE INSIDE THE WORDS

TE AROHA McDONNELL AS TOLD TO SANDRA KAHU NEPIA AND JASMINE RATANA

From left: Koro Taaia Toheriri, his wife Te Ara Toheriri and their daughter, Te Hukinga, photographed by James McDonald at Koroniti in 1921.

I've seen this image before. I think one of my aunties has this particular photo but we don't have a copy of it ourselves at home. I instantly knew that the man on the left is Koro Taaia Toheriri, and in the middle is his wife Te Ara, Te Aratu Parewhakairo. On the right is their daughter Te Hukinga with a piupiu around her. Nanny Te Hukinga always wore dresses.

I like the clean-shaven look of Koro Taaia in this picture, and the style of his haircut.

I am fascinated that he's wearing a white polo neck. The material looks like it's ribbed and possibly made of wool. There's also great detail on the kahu kiwi that Koro Taaia is wearing and the tāniko pattern that's on there. I like to think that we could work out the pattern and perhaps recreate that tāniko pattern one day.

This photo was taken out the front of our house at Hiruhārama. You can see the fence in the background and where it joins at the corner. That fence join is still there, and the tree that's immediately behind Nanny Te Ara is still there today too. It's instantly recognisable for me because we had a rope-and-tyre swing on one of its branches. I remember as a young girl spending hours and hours spinning round and round on that swing, and back the other way, and twisting the rope. So, I'm really familiar with that corner of our place and the activities that we got up to there.

Koro Taaia Toheriri was also known as Taaia Kingi or Taaia Toheriri Kingi. He lived at Hiruhārama and married Te Aratu Parewhakairo from Ngāti Maru ki Taranaki. They had one daughter, Te Hukinga Huia Parewhakairo or Te Hukinga Huia Kingi. Te Hukinga married Mahia or Masha Mahia Potaka from Rata/Utiku over in Ngāti Hauiti. They all lived together at the house that our whānau now looks after at Hiruhārama. That house was already built by the time that James McDonald and Elsdon Best visited Hiruhārama in 1921.

Masha (Mahia) Potaka, the husband of Te Hukinga, had a brother called Tiopira Potaka. Tiopira Potaka married Miera Reone and had a child called Niurangi. Niurangi was whāngai by Koro Taaia and Nanny Te Ara and raised as their child, at the house at Jerusalem, together with Te Hukinga.

Over time, Te Hukinga and Mahia weren't able to have any children of their own and they knew that Koro Taaia and Nanny Te Ara were aging, so they decided to adopt. They adopted the first two children of Niurangi, Pene or Fanny Kingi, as well as Genevieve (Genny) Potaka and Wikitoria (Tukapua), who then became Wikitoria Potaka. These three children were formally adopted, confirmed by the Māori Land Court, and their records are held there in the archives.

Koro Taaia and Nanny Te Ara passed away and then a little while later Te Hukinga and Masha also passed on. All of them left their Māori land interests to their three adopted granddaughters, including the house where they were all raised.

They're all buried in our whānau urupā near the house. Koro Taaia Toheriri Kingi, Te Ara Kingi and Te Hukinga Potaka are buried side by side, and each of the three daughters is right beside them together with their husbands; except for my grandmother's, Fanny Bell. Her husband is buried at Pipiriki, where he came from. He wanted to go back there so she happily obliged, although she was quite clear that she wanted to be buried by her sisters and her parents and grandparents. So that's where our kōrero is and where we all are.

Amongst the collections made during the expedition are recordings of Koro Taaia reciting a number of waiata and pao and karakia—about eight or nine of them, I think. The first time I got to hear Koro Taaia's voice was by listening to one of these, a waiata tangi. I listened, and just allowed the waiata to play, and experienced how it resonated with me. I chose that waiata to listen to first because it is continuous. There's just one interruption in it, and in that moment of silence I reflected on how overwhelming it is to hear his voice after 100 years. That was a moment that sank in and connected with me internally. I was thinking about Nanny Te Ara sitting there listening in, and then wondering what Te Hukinga also got to hear, the delivery of the kupu and the language. I was remembering my grandmother and thinking, this is her Koro and the waiata and the ori that she would have listened to and been taught.

I remember my grandmother always saying to me that Koro Taaia was an orator. He was always on the marae doing all the whaikōrero and he must have had to sing his own song too. He carried a lot of knowledge.

My grandmother went to school at the convent so Koro Taaia and Nanny Te Ara were heavily involved with the Catholic Church. I believe that's the reason why Koro Taaia was involved with this visit of Elsdon Best and James McDonald: because of his ability to converse in English as well as te reo. He would have accompanied Best and McDonald when they went on to the marae and engaged with the whānau down at Patiarero. There's a photo outside Whiritaunoka with Father Venning greeting Best. Koro Taaia is standing in the background holding a suitcase or a satchel.

One of the karakia recited by Koro Taaia in the recordings is about the *Aotea* waka and some of the names, the kōrero, the essence, the richness of it all, makes me want to be able to repeat it and learn it and share it so that it's given life again. Because it does have a place. It had a place back in 1921, and for whatever reason my grandmother didn't retain it or impart that knowledge on to her children and then to her own grandchildren. I've shared these waiata and the kupu with my aunties and uncles and my cousins and we're all just in awe of this treasure of listening to Koro Taaia sing, and the knowledge inside the words.

Koro Taaia Toheriri Kingi (centre at back, carrying a small box), and Te Ara Toheriri (seated in the foreground, front row at left), at Koroniti in 1921. Photograph by James McDonald.

'OH MACHINE, SPEAK ON, SPEAK ON'

The Fourth Dominion Museum
Ethnological Expedition
18 March–12 April 1923
Tairāwhiti

ANNE SALMOND
BILLIE LYTHBERG

Unnamed man with a tāruke kōura ready to be set in the Waiapu
River. Photograph by James McDonald at Waiomatatini in 1923.

On 10 April 1923 at Waiomatatini, in Tairāwhiti, James McDonald filmed Riwai Te Miringa o Rangi making a crayfish pot from mānuka and vines. As he heard the camera whirring, the old man addressed it, saying 'Oh machine, speak on, speak on. I shall go with the pictures to London, to Japan, to so and so.'

JOHANNES C ANDERSEN, diary: Waiomatatini, 1923, p. 11

In September 1922, impressed by what the team had achieved during the Whanganui expedition the previous year, Apirana Ngata invited them to visit his home region to record the ancestral practices of his own people. Supported by two other Māori MPs, Māui Pōmare and Tau Henare, he wrote to Native Affairs Minister William Herries to request a grant to fund this fourth Dominion Museum Ethnological Expedition, to Tairāwhiti.[1] The following month, McDonald, who was once again Acting Director of the Museum, followed up with a letter to the Undersecretary of Internal Affairs, reporting that during their visit to Koroniti, he, Elsdon Best and Te Rangihīroa had decided that a series of further expeditions should be undertaken to the East Coast, the Bay of Plenty and Taupō, and perhaps later to Rotorua and the Urewera, 'to make a complete survey of the North Island cultural areas'. He added, 'The Hon. Mr. Ngata is very desirous that Messrs. Best, Andersen and myself should visit the East Coast district at an early date to obtain records from his people—the Ngati Porou.'[2]

Te Rangihīroa's interest in international anthropology had been fuelled by a visit to New Zealand in 1922 by John Stokes of the Bishop Museum in Hawai'i, who met him to discuss his work on Māori weaving.[3] Te Rangihīroa had also begun planning a British and American tour that would be illustrated with films and photographic slides from the expeditions;[4] and McDonald had alerted him to the forthcoming Pan-Pacific Science Congress in Australia, and printed a copy of the Whanganui expedition film that could be shown at the congress.[5]

In his letter to the Undersecretary, McDonald noted that 'February is the most suitable time for our particular work. Shearing is over; crops are ripening, and the men are not so busy as at other times of the year, while in that month the women folk are preparing baskets etc. for storing the food crops and flax fibre for use during the winter months.'[6]

Typhoid and influenza had hit the East Coast, and in early February, Te Rangihīroa decided to visit the district in his official capacity as Director of Maori Hygiene, and wrote to McDonald:

Dear Mac

I am leaving today for Gisborne to work the district and be ready to link up with the expedition when you come along after the Session at present. It has occurred to me that if not entailing the bringing of too much gear, how would it be if you brought the films along and we gave the Gisborne people a demonstration.

They would also interest the Maoris at Ngata's place and perhaps make them vie with one another to produce good stuff to put on record. Keep the British and American tour steadily in mind and work towards it in the getting of material. I am thinking out things as regards the lecture but I am sure we would do all right if we get the chance.

Drop me a note to the Gisborne PO as to what the movements are.

Cheer oh

Yours, Te Rangi Hiroa.

James McDonald's photograph of Kaiti Beach,
Gisborne, in 1923.

On 28 February, McDonald wrote again to the Undersecretary of Internal Affairs to report:

> The Hon. A.T. Ngata has very kindly offered us hospitality among his people at Waiomatatini and is prepared to assist us in every way possible to further the object of the Department.
>
> He has proposed that I take up the film secured on the Wanganui River in 1921, and that lectures be given at the towns where electric light is available, viz, Waipiro, Tolaga Bay, Waiomatatini, Tokomaru and Te Araroa. This is recommended for your approval.
>
> Dr. Buck, Health Officer is now at Gisborne and proposes to journey through with us to the Northern towns where he has some inspection to carry out. While with us he proposes to do some anthropometrical work, ie. measurements mainly cranial of varying types — in conjunction with our photographic work.[7]

Once again, Raumoa Balneavis made the arrangements. McDonald, Best and Andersen travelled to Gisborne on the *Arahura*, a coastal steamer; by motor car to Waipiro Bay; and then by buggy with Ngata to the coastal settlement of Whareponga, where they arrived on 18 March 1923. By now they knew each other well: Te Rangihīroa addressed Andersen in his letters as 'Tarawhai', McDonald as 'Mac' and Best as 'Peehi', remarking to Andersen, 'You see how I have to come to the Wellington triple alliance for comfort.'[8]

Whareponga

On their arrival at Whareponga, the expedition team were given a formal welcome on the marae and a lavish meal of roast meat, crayfish and onion fritters, jelly and plum pudding. After dinner the team got to work, sitting with local experts including Hēni Tūrei, Kataraina Ngawati, Rīpeka Te Irikaraka, Turuhira Whāki, Mere Arihi Huinga, and recording ancestral songs on wax cylinders until late that night.[9] These waiata included the well-known lament 'I hoki mai au i Kererūhuahua', composed by Rāpata Wahawaha's grandmother Hinekaukia for her son, who had been burnt to death at Kererūhuahua near Waipaoa in the Gisborne district, and performed by Henare Teowai and his wife Te Kurumate. This waiata came from Ngata's own family, and this and other songs included many references to local ancestors and landmarks.[10] The session ended with the haka taparahi 'Kura Tīwaka Taua', performed by Apirana Ngata himself.[11]

Over the next three days the team recorded a range of other songs and chants with Te Hati Pakaroa, Rīpeka Te Irikaraka and Kataraina Wi Kahukahu, including a sexually explicit song traditionally accompanied by a flute.[12] As a finale, Tuta Ngārimu and his wife Mākere performed several taumaunu, ending with a chant to commemorate the arrival of Te Rangihīroa, Te Peehi and their friends at Whareponga, 'hei taonga mā ngā uri whakatipu (as a treasure for the rising generation)'.[13]

During this visit to Whareponga, McDonald filmed string figures for Andersen; men fishing for kehe (granite trout) and women diving for kōura (crayfish) on the beach for Te Rangihīroa; men and women preparing food in an umu or earth oven; and competitive hand games on the porch of the meeting house, including one that ended with a woman diving on top of the man (probably her husband) who had just defeated her. In these filmed episodes, the mood is exuberant and relaxed. Before they left Whareponga, they also recorded a poroporoaki (speech of farewell) addressed to the team by Te Hati Pakaroa: 'Hei kōnei rā koutou e te rōpu hopuhopu o ngā takenga a te iwi Māori (Farewell until we see you again, the group who capture the ways of the Māori people).'[14]

Waiomatatini, Tikapa, Tikitiki, Te Araroa and Rangitukia

The team travelled next to Ngata's home at Waiomatatini, near the mouth of the Waiapu River. When they arrived there on 22 March, a bright, hot day, an old man, Riwai Miringa o Rangi,[15] began making a tāruke kōura (crayfish pot) for Te Rangihīroa, who was working on a study of fishing and netting techniques that he later published in the *Transactions of the New Zealand Institute*.[16] Over the next few days McDonald shot a series of still photographs of the process, and filmed Te Rangihīroa smiling broadly as he walked a small black kitten into the tāruke kōura instead of a crayfish, while Johannes Andersen recorded a number of string figures in a field notebook (now lost), many of which appeared later in his book on this topic.[17]

On 24 March, Ngata was summoned to meet his parliamentary colleague, Native Minister Gordon Coates, at Rotorua, so he left his friends in the care of his wife Arihia and Tūtere Wī Repa, another Te Aute old boy. The team stopped at Tīkapa, where they recorded Te Irimana Te Kawa Tikapa performing the karakia 'Te Whakakau a Paikea'.[18] Afterwards, at Tikitiki, an inland settlement, they stayed in a boarding house and showed a film of their 1921 Whanganui River expedition to a packed hall, aiming to inspire a competitive spirit in the East Coast people, as Te Rangihīroa had suggested.[19] Although the film was silent and the lights kept going out, people called out to those who appeared on the screen, giving them advice and talking to them as though they were in the room.

A young man remarked that he had often heard of people fighting over eel weirs, but he couldn't understand why until he saw the pictures of the impressive pā tuna along the Whanganui River.

After the screening, Ngata's son-in-law Te Kani played Chopin on the boarding-house piano, while Best, who had caught a bad cold, went to bed. According to Andersen, both the boarding house and the store at Tikitiki were owned by the tribal cooperative—one of Ngata's initiatives and a source of great pride for the local people.[20] As Ngata had suggested, the proceeds from the screening were donated to the village committee.[21]

Over the next couple of days Buck and Andersen scoured the streams for kōkopu, the native freshwater fish, but found only one specimen. During these excursions, Andersen noted kūmara and maize plantations fenced with mānuka, and dozens of horses with saddles and bridles lined up along the main street of Tikitiki. He also recorded more whai and visited the Tikitiki school, which was attended by about 140 children. He described the pupils as neat, clean and alert, and enjoyed talking to them about his articles in the *School Journal*, which many of them had read.[22]

James McDonald's photographs of local people demonstrating the
stages of making a tāruke kōura, taken at Waiomatatini in 1923.

On 26 March, Buck, Andersen and McDonald travelled north to Te Araroa, where they stayed at the local hotel. Best, who was still ill, returned to the Bungalow, Ngata's home at Waiomatatini, where Margaret Buck nursed him. That afternoon the team recorded three karakia, including one chanted by Tūhaka Kōhere,[23] and Andersen collected more whai.

The next morning, Wī Repa welcomed them in front of the wharenui with a speech that they recorded.[24] Tūhaka Kōhere, Wharemuka Taotu, Mere Arihi Houkāmau, Ani Kane Roki, Heremia Puha and Waiheke Puha then recorded a series of classic Ngāti Porou waiata[25] that Ngata later published, with extensive explanatory notes, in *Nga Moteatea* (NM 1, 2 and 209, among others). The following day, Andersen collected a series of string figures, and McDonald took photographs of plaiting techniques and different types of netting for Te Rangihīroa.

The Bungalow at Waiomatatini, with Puputa pā on the
hill beyond, and the drawing room of the Bungalow in 1923.
Photographs by James McDonald.

That evening at Te Araroa they showed films of the Whanganui River and Gisborne expeditions that Te Rangihīroa narrated to the lively audience, while Andersen demonstrated a couple of string games and played a recording of Māori music. They were given a supper of crayfish with kārengo (a sweet-tasting seaweed) and cake. They headed back to Waiomatatini the next morning.

On Good Friday, 31 March, the team stayed quietly at the Bungalow, writing up their field notes. Best was now out of bed, but he was still very weak. The next day Te Rangihīroa, Andersen and McDonald attended a church service conducted by one of the Kōhere brothers. They climbed the hill behind the marae to look at Puputa pā, an ancient fortified site now used as a burial ground, before joining the others for dinner in the wharenui. In the afternoon they went by buggy to the mouth of the Waiapu River to film the kupenga kōkō kahawai (netting kahawai). That evening, some of the party played croquet while Andersen played Te Kani's songs on the piano and talked with a young woman about the 1919 Hui Aroha in Gisborne, which she had attended as a nursemaid for Ngata's children.[26]

The next day, 1 April, Buck, Andersen and McDonald travelled by horseback to Tūhaka Kōhere's house, where Andersen admired the garden with its citrus trees, grapevines and flowers. They stayed the night there, playing waiata on the phonograph. The next day they returned to the mouth of the Waiapu River, where McDonald filmed the casting of a kahawai net: the sea was rough, and no fish were caught. Two days later, back at Waiomatatini, Andersen and Buck helped to dig and stack kūmara in the rua kūmara (storage pits), while McDonald filmed the process. As Andersen remarked, 'Mrs Ngata is always cheery and laughing, so are her old woman friends; we younger ones began to be quiet as our backs began to protest against the unusual labour.'[27] That afternoon they recorded a whakaaraara — a chant to alert a fortified pā.[28] It must have been about this time, too, that McDonald photographed several series of images of women weaving, and the fine mats produced by the women at Waiomatatini.

The Kaua sisters, Heneriata Te Paea Collier (left) and Erana Heihi, weaving at Waiomatatini in 1923. Photograph by James McDonald.

Rua kūmara storage pit, photographed by James McDonald on the East Coast in 1923.

In the evening, a party from Te Araroa arrived at Porourangi wharenui to farewell the expedition team. When Buck and Andersen joined them, Andersen spoke jovially in English, ending his speech with a Danish song, which Te Rangihīroa interpreted as Andersen expressing his ardent desire to settle down with one of the local widows. As Andersen wrote in his journal, 'They enjoy fun, and I enjoy seeing them enjoy it.' The night was clear and starry, and wrapped up in rugs and leaning on pillows, they listened to the speeches, which went on until after midnight. When they returned to the wharenui in the morning, the Te Araroa people had already left, so Andersen went up the hill and wrote a song of farewell, which he decided he would sing on his last night at Waiomatatini.[29] Andersen had taken a fancy to a fifteen-year-old local girl, Meretuhi (Mary) Maxwell, who acted as their buggy driver; and over the days that followed he often went to see her.

On 4 April, Paratene Ngata, Apirana's father, recorded a pao for the team.[30] Te Rangihīroa was still determined to catch some kōkopu, and the next day he, Andersen, McDonald and Paratene Ngata, built a stone fish weir in a channel of the Waiapu River. Early the following morning when Te Rangihīroa went to check, he found just a single upokororo or grayling (*Prototroctes oxyrhynchus*) in the net, a very rare native fish that had not been seen in the Waiapu for at least a decade. The following day, three more upokororo were found in the fish trap.

Still eager to catch kōkopu, on 7 April, Te Rangihīroa worked with Andersen and McDonald to build another fish trap in the river using stones, mānuka stakes and brushwood. Ngata returned from Rotorua, and when they played him the songs that they had recorded at Te Araroa on the phonograph, they found that Ngata knew all but one of them. Early the next morning when Te Rangihīroa and Andersen visited the fish trap, they were astonished to find twenty-six upokororo in the trap; they left them there so that McDonald could photograph their haul after breakfast.[31]

Over the days that followed, Te Rangihīroa studied local fishing methods and Best talked with various elders, recording snippets about customary practices in his notebook; Andersen recorded a series of string games; and on 9 April McDonald photographed an elder, Iehu Nukunuku, playing a kōauau—or, more precisely, a 10 inch (25 centimetre) length of gas pipe with three holes bored at the lower end— while Andersen recorded the music on a wax cylinder.[32] McDonald also shot film and photographs of Te Rangihīroa and Ngata as they worked on a tukutuku panel to decorate the walls of a meeting house, and of Ngata working in the sheepyards on the family farm. In the evenings they played croquet, listened to Te Kani playing the piano, or went visiting local families with Ngata.

On 10 April, when the old man Riwai Te Miringa o Rangi finished his crayfish trap, Wī Repa teased him by pointing out an error in its manufacture and saying that his own people made much better tāruke kōura. This provoked Riwai to retort that at least

the machine and its pictures would transport him overseas. When the filming was finished, the elder stood and sang a song over his trap.[33] The next day, Ngata performed the famous East Coast haka 'Rūaumoko', delivering a speech in which he addressed future generations, saying, 'People of Ngāti Porou, this is my message to you: these songs are left for you to remember in the times to come,' and ending with a haka.[34]

On 12 April, as the expedition members were about to leave Waiomatatini, Ngata presented Andersen with a korowai; and he no doubt gave similarly important gifts to other members of the expedition.[35]

The network of relations that shaped the fourth and final Dominion Museum Ethnological Expedition reflected an intricately woven fabric of whakapapa links between Ngata and many tangata whenua, as well as his close friendship ('tō hoa aroha') with Te Rangihīroa. There were also long-standing relations of camaraderie among the expedition team members: Elsdon Best, the most senior and a renowned expert in Māori lore, but increasingly frail; Te Rangihīroa, convivial, amusing, and a dedicated student of Māori material culture; Andersen, enthusiastic and knowledgeable about string games and music, although he could speak no Māori; and McDonald, the good-humoured photographer and filmmaker.

During this fourth and last expedition, these relations were both reinforced and tested. Best was ill much of the time, and less active than he had been on previous expeditions. Te Rangihīroa was in good humour (although his wife was also unwell), delivering amusing speeches and engaging in repartee and jokes with local people. Andersen provoked laughter with his string games and songs, and some mockery for his ardent pursuit of Meretuhi (Mary) Maxwell. McDonald went up to his boots in the Waiapu River, capturing photographs and films as needed.

Local people went out of their way to help them. They saw their participation in the films and photographs as another gift, not to the team but to future generations—and so it proved.

Te Rangihīroa photographed by James McDonald setting
a hīnaki in a channel on the Waiapu River in 1923.

Iehu Nukunuku recording a gas-pipe kōauau for Te Rangihīroa
at Waiomatatini in 1923. Photograph by James McDonald.

Iehu Nukunuku playing for a group of boys at
Waiomatatini in 1923. Photograph by James McDonald.

Apirana Ngata (left) and Te Rangihīroa, weaving
a tukutuku panel together at Waiomatatini in 1923.
Photograph by James McDonald.

'THE EYE OF THE FILM'

The Tairāwhiti Film and Photographs
of 1923 through a Ngāti Porou Lens

NATALIE ROBERTSON

Te Aira (left) and Tareti, photographed by James McDonald
at Waiomatatini in 1923, holding pākōkō, a wooden clapper type
of karetao (jumping jacks or marionettes) used by women
to sort out disputes.

At home in Aotearoa, I greet the images of my ancestors verbally and speak to them as they come forth on the screen. For I know that while they have passed on, the images still live and are very much alive to me.

MERATA MITA, 'The Preserved Image Speaks Out'[1]

Standing on a sideboard in the Radio Ngāti Porou director's office in Ruatōrea (Ruatoria)[2] is a small framed black-and-white photograph of six Māori fishermen, taken during the Fourth Dominion Museum Expedition in 1923.[3] When I look at this photograph, I see the descendants of Māui, standing on the coastline he raised out of the sea. The six fishermen stand looking directly at the camera, their backs to the rocky seashore, each holding either a kupenga kōkō kehe (scoop net) or a mānuka pole. According to Ngāti Porou historian, Dr Monty Soutar, the kehe fishing pools are located at Mataahu, between Whareponga and Akuaku on the eastern seaboard of Te Ika a Māui, the great fish of Māui.[4]

One of Ngāti Porou's foundational stories begins with Māui fishing up the island: it explains how we, as tāngata moana, came to be tangata whenua in Aotearoa, the people of this land. Mātauranga ā hī ika—fishing knowledge—intertwines with Ngāti Porou cosmologies, including astronomical, navigational and environmental knowledge and relationships between humans and all other living things. Our human–fish relations include ancestors who took on the attributes of whales and were capable of long-distance ocean-going travel.[5]

From left: Apirana Pipi or Urupa, Wi Maraki, Hamuera Ngārimu, Frank Sweeney, Eruera Tuari and Wi Hunia at Mataahu, Gisborne, in 1923. Photograph by James McDonald.

A 2014 video, *Hī Ika: The Ngāti Porou Fisheries Settlement*, begins with Ngāti Porou Holding Company chairman Matanuku Mahuika holding a framed photograph of three seated men with a hīnaki—a large fish trap.[6] A widely published photograph featuring Paratene Ngata, Te Rangihīroa and a third man (probably Apirana Ngata's cousin Rāpata Wahawaha Maxwell, who is a namesake to his renowned uncle), is another of a handful of the photographs taken by James McDonald during the 1923 expedition to which Ngāti Porou currently have access.

In 1923 the brutal impacts of colonisation were taking their toll on Ngāti Porou communities. Galvanised by the terrible losses of the First World War and the 1918–19 influenza pandemic, Apirana Ngata feared that ancestral systems of cultural knowledge, particularly te reo Māori, toi (creative art forms), mahinga kai (food gathering) and mahi tahi (collective work) were in danger of vanishing, and needed to be recorded. On 1 December 1918, Ngata wrote to George W Russell, Minister of Internal Affairs, urging the government to support making phonographic sound recordings and kinematographic films in Māori communities. By 1922, Ngata saw the need to bring the ethnological team to Waiapu, his home district. Although he doesn't say so, he clearly intended that while ethnology would benefit, his own people were to be the primary beneficiaries of this enterprise. However, almost a century on, much of what was recorded during the 1923 expedition is still inaccessible to their descendants.

Today, although we know their names, the identities of the Whareponga fishermen are still missing from the public record. In Te Papa's archives they are described as 'unknown'. The photographs and film recordings McDonald produced were never formally accessioned: they exist in a space between collections and archives.[7] In Te Papa's records the photograph has a registration number (MU000523/005/0288), photographer (James McDonald), year (1923), title (Kehe Fishing on Whareponga Beach), location (Whareponga), object classification (nitrate celluloid negative) and a description: 'Six unknown Maori men fishing with handnets.'

For Māori, as the late Ngāti Apa filmmaker and writer Barry Barclay has remarked, there is an upward trajectory over the decades in which images become taonga, especially for descendants, increasing in 'vigour and relevance as decades go by'.[8] Valued as taonga, these photographs take on new life when those depicted can be identified by their descendants. This is the kaupapa or purpose behind Barclay's Mana Tūturu principle of spiritual guardianship over taonga.[9] Who were the fishermen who so confidently faced the camera? Were they posing before demonstrating the use of the kōkō stick to beat the water, sending the kehe fish towards the net? What information is lost and what is transmitted in the scant text accompanying the images? Where is the story that accompanies the image?

From left: Paratene Ngata, Rāpata Maxwell and Te Rangihīroa at Waiomatatini in 1923. Photograph by James McDonald. The thumbprint on the negative has been retained as a trace of the connection to the person who handled the original negative, possibly McDonald in 1923.

The image of the six fishermen was first published in a 1926 article by Te Rangihīroa, titled 'The Maori Craft of Netting', crediting J McDonald as the photographer, with the accompanying caption, '*Kehe* fishers on Whareponga beach: in pairs—one with net, the other with *kōkō* pole.'[10] Te Rangihīroa's caption gives a sense of the practical mātauranga behind this image. It was published again in the 1929 *Dominion Museum Bulletin* 'Fishing Methods and Devices of the Maori' by Elsdon Best, this time captioned: 'Scoop-nets for taking *kehe*, East Coast District.'[11]

Best's text focuses solely on the nets as material devices: this has the effect of losing the specific location, while the men disappear as active participants. In this way, Best's intervention reinforces asymmetrical power relationships between those publishing for what he no doubt perceived as a largely Pākehā audience, and those in front of the camera—indigenous people who were sharing their knowledge for their own descendants. Through the power of language, Best effectively erases the men from the image. In 2007, the image appeared again in sepia on a postcard, advertising on the back: 'Te hokinga mai o ngā taonga whitiāhua—screenings of archival film footage of Ngāti Porou, in association with The Film Archive and The Museum of New Zealand, Te Papa Tongarewa'.[12] This time it bore the title 'Kehe fishing on Whareponga beach 1923', reconnecting the image with place.

A weaving, cord-making, netmaking, fishing people

In his 1931 paper 'The Terminology of Whakapapa' (see page 318), Ngata describes how whakapapa works. In takiaho, one method for reciting whakapapa—complex, interwoven genealogies—fishing metaphors are used to connect people along an aho—a line or weft, in weaving. The concept was developed by coastal fishing people, based on the practice of stringing fish

through their gills. In Ngata's account, takiaho emerges both as a thing—a cord for stringing fish on—and an act of tracing linkages:

> Aho, kaha. Literally a line, string or cord. In relation to a pedigree or genealogy this is a figure that would naturally occur to a weaving, cord-making, netmaking, fishing people…Takiaho is a cord on which fish and shell fish are strung, and also a line of descent.[13]

Indeed, the takiaho itself is caught in a brief film sequence shot by McDonald on the same day as the six fishermen were photographed. In this vignette, *Te rapu kehe i Whareponga: Fishing for granite trout Whareponga*, one older man demonstrates the kehe netting method, while the other follows him with a kōkō pole. The net expert strings fish from his net onto a cord—the takiaho—threaded through their gills. The fish appear to be already dead, pre-prepared props. In the next shot, the pair face the camera, each stamping one foot, pretending to haka, holding the fish on the line, laughing at the camera and each other. They, too, remain unidentified, despite being so clearly recorded on film. However, in Te Rangihīroa's 1926 text, he credits Hemi Whangapirita of Whareponga as the person who supplied much of the information on kehe fishing techniques,[14] identifying him as the agile, white-moustached man holding the scoop net for kehe, and noting the au or needle for threading fish onto the takiaho.

In addition to referring to a line, or a line of descent, aho describes radiant light; and light as a medium for an atua in divination.[15] From a Māori perspective, historic photographs and films of ancestors, created by hihi aho, or direct rays of light imprinting onto a light-sensitive medium, remain connected to their points of origin through these aho, these whakapapa light beams. The filmmaker Merata Mita, in describing the connection between the soul and the image, says that 'the camera has power of a mystical quality'; and that 'the fusion of physics and human image has put us in touch with ourselves'.[16]

Hemi Whangapirita holding a kupenga kōkō, used for kehe fishing,
at Whareponga in 1923. Photograph by James McDonald.

On 31 August 2017, at a screening of *He Pito Whakaatu i te Noho a Te Maori i Te Tairawhiti: Scenes of Maori Life from the East Coast*—the 1923 footage shot by McDonald in Tairāwhiti—at Radio Ngāti Porou on the occasion of the station's thirtieth anniversary, I saw this for myself. It wasn't the first time the film had been screened in this community: screenings at Uepōhatu marae were held on 26 June 2007, as well as at marae in Te Araroa, Tikitiki, Rangitukia, Tokomaru Bay, Tolaga Bay, Whāngārā and Gisborne during Te Hokinga Mai, when the New Zealand Film Archive Ngā Kaitiaki o Ngā Taonga Whitiāhua showed the film to descendants in various Tairāwhiti communities.

In the mid-1980s, the Film Archive had held the first ever screenings in East Coast communities, in an effort to connect people with images, and to create bilingual subtitles.[17] Ngati Porou educator Amster Reedy provided translations for the Hui Aroha and Tairāwhiti films.[18] This screening was different though: it featured a digitally remastered version from a 4.6K scan. This is markedly sharper than the previous grainy 1980s digital copy of 35 millimetre academy aspect ratio print.[19] I set up my video camera and an audio recorder in the corner of the room to document the film screening, and to record the reactions and responses of the audience who had come to experience their ancestors come alive again on screen.

I was present at the screening in 2017 to share my research on the film and photographs with the audience, supplementing the dialogue from the elders in the room. Two screenings were attended by the older generation, including Ngāti Porou leader Morehu 'Boycie' Te Maro, then in his late eighties. Many were descendants of those who went fishing at Whareponga, or who interacted with the 1923 expedition crew. The people in the film were their nannies and papas, whether they had known them personally or not. On this occasion, the film seen was not 'a view of the Māori people' in an ethnographic sense, but rather of our own ancestors. The screening prompted many comments on the various practices, infused with great warmth and humour. Stories were shared, and they were tinged with a sadness that we didn't know the names of all the people captured on film, and that the old people who saw earlier screenings were no longer with us. Bill Hughes recalled the 2007 Te Hokinga Mai event at Uepōhatu, saying 'Nanny Hawea Mackey, Nanny Peg [Ripeka Paeatehau] Heeney, Nanny Tus [Tuhimoana Floyd] would have been alive then' in recognition that even ten years earlier, the elders who could name those on screen were present.[20]

Although any institutional records that could connect the information gathered in the 1980s, and again in 2007, have not been traced, photographs of ancestors long since past, hanging on the walls of private homes or marae, are often used to remember names and connections — our own indigenous version of a community photographic archive. On occasion, wānanga, a gathering to share ancestral knowledge, might be the catalyst to reconnect names with photographs, or it may be a tribal historian. Fortunately, in this instance, Monty Soutar recorded the names of the men directly from the daughter of Hamiora Ngārimu, Ngāti Porou kuia and silver-screen film star Keita Whakato Walker, directly onto the 2007 Te Hokinga Mai postcard,[21] from left to right: Apirana Pipi or Urupa, Wi Maraki, Hamuera Ngārimu, Frank Sweeney, Eruera Tuari, and Wi Hunia.

Today, in the Ngāti Porou community radio station, mokopuna can greet their tīpuna as 'koro' or 'pāpā' when they see them. These are familiar names within this community, and several of the men were from renowned families. For example, Hamuera Ngārimu was the younger brother of Materoa Ngārimu — a highly respected and influential female tribal leader who was deeply versed in whakapapa and tribal knowledge. Hamuera's father, Tuta, was regarded as the most senior chief of Whareponga at that time, alongside his mother Mākere, a leader in her own right. They were present in 1923 to welcome the fourth expedition to Whareponga, recording waiata and chants.

In his 1923 field notebook, Te Rangihīroa notes that the chief of Te Whānau o Te Haemata exercised the mana, the authority of the fishing grounds of that district, and that the first fish was presented to Turuhira Hine i Whakina i te rangi; grandmother to Tuta Ngārimu.[22] In 'Māori Craft of Netting', Te Rangihīroa names Tuta Ngārimu as the recipient.[23] Hamuera Ngārimu was the father of Te Moananui-a-Kiwa, a member of C Company in 28th Maori Battalion who was posthumously awarded the Victoria Cross in 1943, twenty years after this photo was taken. Their hereditary āhua — likeness, features, appearance — and the names of the six men at Whareponga live on in their many descendants.

In the case of this image, the relational cords binding the ancestors to their communities have been stretched, but not broken. Spiritually the cords remain intact. Like plucking the radial strands on a spider's web, these aho quiver when we reconnect with historic ancestral images. Photographs are a medium that link us to land and people. The āhua of the photograph — te whakaāhua — also vibrates with potentiality. These photographs offer a portal into an alternate spiral time–space realm, as do other taonga that have survived from the 1923 expedition — cinematic film, wax cylinder recordings, diaries, notebooks and published materials — connecting us with ngā pūrākau ā ngā tīpuna (stories of ancestors), so that whakapapa, waiata, whakataukī, karakia and kōrero tuku iho can be retrieved, reclaimed and reactivated. These are precious taonga, each bearing the āhua a ō tīpuna, in image, text and sound.

According to Ngāti Porou tribal leader Apirana Mahuika, all taonga in museums are tapu: 'They represent Māori history, and as such have religious and spiritual associations.'[24] Like Mita, he views taonga as living: 'The proper environment accords life to these taonga. To Māori people, death is a state which allows the living to dialogue with ancestors, either directly or through taonga.'[25] In this way, photographs are a medium that can provide a direct line through to the spiritual realm.

When I look at these historic photographs, I am in their ancestral presence. Viewing the negatives at the Museum of New Zealand Te Papa Tongarewa in Wellington was deeply emotional. Silver halide crystals on the gelatin film held traces of light that had reflected off my ancestors. As I looked at the lightbox, I was in direct communication with them.

The photographs of the river, our mother, are just as important as those of people. The silver halide may hold a trace of the mauri, the spiritual life force of the Waiapu River. These photographs are mana taonga, treasures with immeasurable prestige. The activities were recorded precisely because the techniques and material culture they highlight were vital but at risk of being lost. By instigating the expeditions, Ngata placed Māori visual culture at the centre of cultural reinvigoration.

[Re]joining the parts of the fishing net

In Ngata's exploration of whakapapa (see Appendix), when discussing the meaning of tātai—ordering or arranging things—he uses an example from Hauraki that refers to fishing and the oceanic realm: 'Ka tukua te tangata ki te tatai i nga kupenga a Marutuahu 'Join the component parts of a fishing net'.'[26] Marutūahu

was a Hauraki tipuna who had five sons, and this saying refers to the joining together of their collective net. Created from harakeke and kiekie, seine nets could be huge in scale—'several thousand metres in length'.[27] The scale of the nets required many hands to connect and hold and operate them—a mahi tahi or communal effort that reaped massive catches of fish.[28] This is reiterated by the scale of the hīnaki trap, which could be up to 4.5 metres long; for instance one in the possession of Paratene Ngata, Apirana's father, in 1923.

Tātai—the project of weaving connectedness, positioning 'individuals in sets of relationships with other people and with the environment'[29]—connects past with present, people with each other through the spiral of time. As Linda Tuhiwai Smith writes:

> The story and the story teller both serve to connect the past with the future, one generation with the other, the land with the people and the people with the story. Intrinsic in story telling is a focus on dialogue and conversations amongst ourselves and Indigenous Peoples, to ourselves and for ourselves. Such approaches fit well with the oral traditions which are still a reality in day-to-day indigenous lives.[30]

The screenings of the films from the expedition continue the practice of storytelling among ourselves. Their importance is illustrated by the rapt attention that the people give to the films. As noted by Jonathan Dennis, founder and director of the Film Archive at the time the films were first taken back to their home communities in the early 1980s: 'They are the most extensive record of their kind of traditional Māori life and activities from this period.'[31]

FOLLOWING PAGE: A hīnaki purangi stretched out to its full extent on the lawn below the Bungalow at Waiomatatini in 1923. Te Rangihīroa stands to the left, while Elsdon Best (centre) records in a notebook. Photograph by James McDonald.

Hīnaki Purangi — (Jimmy Raihi.)

Net used like purangi, but nut elongated in by title with fine mesh. acted as holding net without hinaki.

Whiti. frame at mouth. Double withy-stick.
Diameters. 45" × 48".
Total length from hoof. 15'-6".

A double page from Te Rangihīroa's notebook, showing his sketch
and notes on a hīnaki purangi, drawn from information supported
by Jimmy Raihi, and measurements recorded in Elsdon Best's
handwriting, made during the fourth expedition in 1923.

Small end, consists of 32 loops round myakekau, counting single initial one.

Put on myakekau in ordinary slip loop beginning as in figure.

Instead of going back as in ordinary bag nets a tube is formed by joining each row of meshes as it is formed.

Over the space of almost a century, however, although the films have come to light, few of the other items created or collected during the Dominion Museum expeditions—photographs, journals, wax cylinder recordings and artefacts—have made their way home. Different institutional archives hold different fragments of records, mostly hidden, and difficult to access. Snippets of the mātauranga a iwi gathered during the expeditions can be found scattered in decades-old texts, but the names of the original sources are often missing. The stories of the people and places in them and the photos remain elusive—and especially the voices of the ancestors on the wax cylinders are rarely heard by their descendants.

During the sixty-three-year gap between the making of the film and its first public showing in 1986, most of the people who had participated in the Tairāwhiti expedition had died. Even Port Awanui girl Meretuhi (Mary) Maxwell, whom Andersen named in his diary as the fifteen-year-old buggy driver for the crew, had passed away in 1983.

To join different parts of this net together, I have drawn on a range of sources—tribal oral histories, Te Rangihīroa's 1923 notebooks, the expedition diary kept by Andersen and other archival material—to analyse these connections, on film, in photographs and beyond the frame, extending into the land and the river. Reflecting on the takiaho as cords of connection shifts the emphasis from the Dominion Museum, as the archive of knowledge and material culture, to Ngāti Porou. Actively reconnecting names with faces, with places and stories, reinstates the host people as ngā tangata whenua to their rightful places as knowledge keepers. Doing so brings forward Māori narratives and rectifies their absence and erasure from the public record. It was the Māori subjects in the film who enabled McDonald to record scenes of their everyday lives. They were involved in the process of producing a lasting cultural legacy for descendants. This was explicitly intended by Ngata and other Ngāti Porou leaders, as will be seen shortly.

Much remains unknown or unrecorded about the contexts in which the films were made and the relationships beyond the frame. Fortunately, the storehouse of photographs and film from the 1923 expedition have recently been restored to a form where they can be more readily accessed. The digital remastering technologies of today provide far crisper images than those screened in the 1980s or even in 2007. This advance in technological accessibility converges with an insoluble downswing: there is no one alive today who remembers the fourth expedition, and only a few elders whose grandparents may have participated in the associated events. This work is time-critical. With a gap of almost one hundred years, memories stretch to connect unnamed faces of tīpuna ancestors who participated in the 1923 filming and photographs.

Drawing on local knowledge, I have explored the filming of two quintessential Ngāti Porou tikanga during the fourth expedition: fishing for kahawai; and the building of a stone fish trap in the Waiapu River, during which a number of the then-rare native fish species upokororo were entrapped—the last recorded catch of this fish in Aotearoa.

In investigating the first tikanga—fishing for kahawai—I used the concept of takiaho to draw out whakapapa and whanaungatanga between the key participants: farmer and community leader Panikena Kaa, Apirana's father Paratene Ngata, the filmmaker James McDonald, the instigator Apirana Ngata, at whose home the team stayed, and his lifelong friend (hoa aroha), the doctor, soldier and anthropologist, Te Rangihīroa.

I explored the second tikanga—building a pā tauremu (stone fish weir)—by analysing the events surrounding the historic catch of the upokororo fish through the lens of a maramataka (Māori lunar calendar). I consider this work vitally important—identifying locations and connecting people with times and places. As Hawaiian scholar Katrina-Ann Oliveira puts it: 'Places, like people, have genealogies.'[32]

I am familiar with the physical environment where the fishing activities took place, although radical environmental changes have occurred over the past 100 years. I have walked the riverbed, explored the beach and river mouth, bathed in the river and photographed these places, many times over many years. This tacit bodily knowledge of the environment is woven into the fabric of my research.

Holes in the net

Before looking at these filmed vignettes, it is important to discuss the minimisation at best, and erasure at worst, of the Māori scholars Ngata and Te Rangihīroa from the scholarly and public record of these expeditions, creating a gap — a hole in the net. Although these accounts accurately attribute the films to James McDonald, this privileging of the photographer is at variance with the Mana Tūturu principle of spiritual guardianship by descendants. Although McDonald made these extraordinary taonga, he did so at Ngata's initiative, and with the active involvement of people in their tribal contexts. Certainly, for the Tairāwhiti expedition, it was Te Rangihīroa who largely instigated the netting and fishing activities, as he was actively engaged in understanding how nets were made and used. McDonald focused on the 'photo business' of recording, while Andersen collected information on whai. Best, when he wasn't ill, gathered terminologies, histories and other information.

Since the film screenings of the 1980s, there has been a perception that these expeditions were led by Best, with Ngata and Te Rangihīroa as supporting actors in a Pākehā-led venture. This has often shaped views of the expedition archive.[33] Te Rangihīroa is largely absent from the scholarly record, in part because he was not yet a museum professional, unlike McDonald, Best and Andersen, and partly because he had independently arranged to join them in Tairāwhiti.[34] This may be partly due to Te Rangihīroa's own published account, which states:

Owing to the kindness of the Hon. A.T. Ngata, M.P., a party from the Dominion Museum, consisting of Messrs Elsdon Best, J. McDonald and J.C. Andersen, made an ethnological expedition to the district in 1923. I had the good fortune to be in the district at the time and to be able to assist the expedition in compiling these notes.[35]

At the time of the fourth Tairāwhiti expedition, there was an outbreak of typhoid and influenza in the district,[36] and Te Rangihīroa carried out inoculations and attended some patients during his visit to Tairāwhiti. The ethnographic study of material culture had become his passion, however, and his appearances in the film, his field notebooks and the accounts by others show that he played a pivotal role in the 1923 expedition. It has been claimed that while Ngata and Te Rangihīroa lent mana as authority and prestige to this exercise, the Pākehā present (Elsdon Best, Andersen and McDonald) exerted more control over the filmmaking.[37] But evidence shows that although McDonald was behind the camera, during his visit to Tairāwhiti he was principally directed by Ngāti Porou leaders including Apirana Ngata and his father Paratene, and by Te Rangihīroa.

On the face of it, the films and photographs belong to the genre of 'salvage and recovery' (of the 'old-time Maori', 'last of their kind', 'before they die out'). Although Ngata used the language of loss in writing to government officials to pull on funding purse strings, he and Te Rangihīroa held the view that documentation and recording could revitalise Māori arts and culture. Casting these films as totally Pākehā-led does Māori leadership and iwi participation a disservice, minimising Māori agency and rendering iwi leaders as passive. Now there is an opportunity to correct the public record and ensure that both Te Rangihīroa and Ngata, along with iwi, are accorded their rightful places in the production of these beautiful and valuable depictions of our tīpuna.

A matter of considerable importance

Silent films and still photographs are powerfully expressive subjects. I ask, what can the films and photographs tell me? Te Kawehau Hoskins and Alison Jones explain that 'Māori take for granted that the material things of the world—whether a forest, a lake, or a building—can "speak" to human beings; we are always already in relation to certain material objects.'[38] The people and places in the films and photographs speak to us across time. When I walked in the riverbed near Waiomatatini, I experienced an after-image of the film and photographs. In my mind's eye I layered expedition scenes and images over whenua and awa, aligning the hills to determine locations. To confirm these visual phantasms, I photographed sites on the riverbed. Then, using digital photographic software, I layered the historic McDonald images over the top of my images. Because the whenua and awa are already ancestral, the taonga of the film—the images carved in celluloid—becomes a 'speaking' tīpuna to me, in the same way as a carving of an ancestor. In his discussion of the Māori view of taonga, Apirana Mahuika says:

> Tribal pou or carved representatives of ancestors are likewise tapu because these figures symbolically represent ancestors who, through their whakapapa (genealogy) and by their death are very tapu. Whakapapa is tapu because of the Maori perception of creation and their theological perception of death. Namely whakapapa deals with the gods, from whom man is a descendant; whakapapa also deals with ancestors, all of whom are tapu by their association in death with those in the spiritual world. Accordingly, all taonga are tapu.[39]

By extension, the films, photographs and sound recordings, as well as the written records from the expeditions, are taonga tapu. Yet film, photography and sound technologies were not commonly held among the people, at the time. How were these received by the people and what spurred them to put on record their customary practices?

Before the 1920s and the advent of motorised road transport, the main trading gateway for the northern East Cape was Port Awanui, 6–7 kilometres south of the Waiapu river mouth. The wharenui Porourangi is located at Waiomatatini, 3.7 kilometres west of Port Awanui, where Te Wharehou, known as the Bungalow—the home of Apirana Ngata and his family—still stands. In 1922, when Ngata instigated the invitation for the ethnological expedition team to visit his home, cultural hubs like Waiomatatini in the Waiapu valley were slowly becoming depopulated. Centuries-old systems of governance, education and social, cultural and familial relationships were being turned upside down by settler colonialism, and a new order prevailed.

In 1872, Port Awanui became the first land sold out of Ngāti Porou hands to the Crown, under immense pressure from general government agent Donald McLean.[40] Under Native Land Court legislation, collectively held land was divided and households individualised. Not all tangata whenua were able to sustain a living in the communities that had been at the heart of their tribal worlds. Some coastal communities like Port Awanui were going into economic decline, and families were leaving in droves to make their lives elsewhere. This swiftly transforming environment was the setting into which the ethnological expedition brought film and still cameras, wax cylinder recording devices and notebooks, as tools to document the cultural lifeways of Ngāti Porou.

This photograph by Natalie Robertson is overlaid with a James McDonald image of Te Rangihīroa and Paratene Ngata building pā tuna with two other men on the Waiapu River in 1923.

4303

The Waiapu valley, photographed by James McDonald in 1923.

Lashing together a waka taurua

A fitting model for understanding the harnessing of two distinctive knowledge systems can be found in seine fishing canoes—waka taurua.[41] In customary fishing, waka were temporarily lashed together for the purpose of carrying large seine nets. Similarly, the Tairāwhiti expedition was a temporary vessel in which Ngāti Porou leaders joined with the expedition team to net and catch their knowledge. McDonald had been instrumental in getting government funding for the camera equipment and film, and Andersen brought with him a lightweight Edison phonograph for the wax cylinder sound recordings. Through Ngata, Ngāti Porou found in McDonald and Andersen willing collaborators, 'enthusiastic mavericks operating on the margins of government'.[42] While the expedition's waka taurua was lashed together for just three weeks, the knowledge caught in its nets is only now resurfacing.

In a show of support from a Māori filmmaker, Merata Mita wrote about McDonald's role in recording these taonga: 'By now there was an awareness by some Maori elders and scholars of the need to record and preserve, and McDonald's work was regarded as a matter of considerable importance.'[43] She adds that,

4305

4 3 0 b

'During this period, he had strong support from Te Rangihīroa (Dr Peter Buck) and Apirana Ngata, and through the patronage of these two men in particular, McDonald received the assistance of many influential Maori in the areas to which they travelled and recorded.'[44] According to Mita, the remaining record 'stands as a monument to their labour and foresight. It is among the most remarkable and rare material of its kind found anywhere in the world.'[45]

After viewing 'the McDonald films' at a screening in Hawai'i in 1989, Barry Barclay suggested that McDonald's camera was 'a bit like an outsider peering into rural life as it was then'.[46] As an indigenous filmmaker and an important critical voice in indigenous film, Barclay's viewpoint requires careful consideration. Given that the films were referred to at the time as 'the McDonald films', with little further context, his response is unsurprising. Barclay acknowledged the 'special treat it was' to see the films presented by Jonathan Dennis and Witarina Harris, an influential Ngāti Whakaue kuia who accompanied the archival screenings. As a darling of the silver screen from the silent movie era, Harris lent these occasions her considerable mana.[47] Nonetheless, the films have many hallmarks of the Western ethnographic genre of their time.

In his analysis of images of Māori in New Zealand film and television, Martin Blythe described the films as occupying 'a peculiar existence at the bicultural edge between a Pakeha-controlled technology and the Maori subjects of the film'.[48] He, too, likened the films to peering, as if through a window: 'In that sense, the films in the Eighties and beyond are a window into the past and the future, particularly for those Maori whose tipuna (ancestors) and tribal areas appear in them.'[49] Barclay has said: 'the images have great beauty; they are priceless for ethnographers and very moving for the Maori community who can feel the presence of their immediate ancestors in much the way they sense their presence in carvings in the meeting house—which to many outsiders are nothing more than sculptures'.[50]

The Tairāwhiti film is the only documentary record of life on the East Coast for the first half of the twentieth century. But who are the immediate ancestors in the film? Is the camera an outsider peering through a window into rural life? Or was it a welcomed manuhiri—a guest? Is it the contemporary commentators who are the strangers?

Waikākā beach, near the mouth of the Waiapu River and today more commonly known as Rangitukia beach, looking towards Hikurangi Maunga. Photograph by Natalie Robertson, 2020.

Hōne Ngātoto working on a tukutuku panel at Waiomatatini in 1923. Photograph by James McDonald.

From left: Eruera Moeke, Makere Rairi Ngārimu and Tuta Ngārimu, photographed by James McDonald at Whareponga in 1923.

Very little is on the public record of the people in the film and photographs, or how they came to be included, despite the apparent willingness of the people to participate. For Ngāti Porou, the tīpuna who appear in the Tairāwhiti film are influential leaders and cultural experts. For example, the only remaining Iwirākau-style carver, Hōne Ngātoto, whom Ngata had commissioned in 1908 to carve the 'Maori Room' — a study in the Bungalow[51] — demonstrates kōwhaiwhai painting in the film and McDonald photographs. Despite his reputation as a prominent tohunga whakairo, Ngātoto's name is absent from the institutional archival records.

The role of iwi manaakitanga — hospitality, generosity, sharing and care — has not yet been analysed as an affirmation of the kaupapa of the expeditions. Blythe has asked what the McDonald/Best/Andersen expeditions wanted from these films. It is equally as important, if not more so, to ask what Ngata, Te Rangihīroa and — in the case of the East Coast expedition — Ngāti Porou communities wanted from them. Regional differences and the contrasts between the 'event' films (Hui Aroha in 1919 and Rotorua in 1920) and the regional films (Tairāwhiti and Whanganui) have not been explored in sufficient depth to draw out the differences in iwi engagement. Instead, they have been, to date, treated collectively, with McDonald the filmmaker as the uniting factor in their production.

The Dominion Museum Ethnological expedition to Tairāwhiti began with a pōwhiri on the whenua of Te Aitanga a Mate at Whareponga marae on Sunday 18 March 1923. The manuhiri, Te Rangihīroa and Margaret Buck, McDonald, Andersen and Best, had travelled overland by motorcar to Waipiro on the 17 March, then onward to Whareponga along the rough rocky beach on the 18 March in a cavalcade of buggies, horses and a car. As a medical officer, Te Rangihīroa made his own way there, attending to health work in the district en route. The celestial alignments were auspicious: a new moon and a solar eclipse occurred on the day of the pōwhiri. In the Ngāti Porou maramataka, this day is known as Mutuwhenua.

Important community leaders were present, gathered together by Ngata to welcome the visitors to Whareponga. The ritual exchanges between tangata whenua and manuhiri no doubt included persuasive exhortations from Ngata to assist in sharing their knowledge, in the wake of the wartime losses and the influenza pandemic. 'Ko te kai a te rangatira, he kōrero' 'Kōrero is the food of chiefs'.[52] The generous sharing of food—and talk—is a mark of chiefly mana. Whareponga is an entry into powerful cultural narratives: there some centuries ago, the principal chief Poroumata was killed during a quarrel over fishing grounds that involved his sons. His death irrevocably shaped Ngāti Porou history.[53] One of the key pā sites, Kōkai (formerly

known as Pukenamunamu)[54] rises above the beach, where the military school Kirikiritatangi (whispering sands) was once the training ground for warriors.[55] Similarly, the group had gathered upon whenua where local knowledge around fishing tikanga abounded.

On the East Coast, the team was hosted at marae at Waiomatatini, Rangitukia and Te Araroa, as well as Whareponga, and a screening was held at the community hall in Tikitiki. Here, the role of the haukāinga (the local people) should not be underestimated, nor should the influential cultural reach of Apirana Ngata and his whānau. Ngata's wife Arihia was from Whareponga, and her family ran the local hotel. Her father, Tuta Tāmati, had been a founding member of the Polynesian Society and, along with Paratene Ngata, was one of the first honorary members of Te Aute College Students'

Association.[56] Although Tāmati had died many years earlier, it is likely that their whānau ensured that the hospitality was lavish — a point that Andersen makes in his diary.[57]

Across the district, principal whānau in Whareponga, Waiomatatini, Tikitiki, Rangitukia and Te Araroa offered manaakitanga to the expedition team.[58] Hosting Te Rangihīroa Major Peter Buck, a holder of the DSO who had been at Gallipoli, the Somme and Passchendaele, alongside the sons of local whānau, was a matter of utu (reciprocity), mana and tribal honour. The leisurely and convivial process of hui, along with the hospitality and support from Ngāti Porou leadership, suggest an alternative 'close-up' view of McDonald's camera 'peering in from the outside'. Perhaps the people in the film, photographs and sound recordings were *peering out from inside*

The Waiapu valley above Waiomatatini. The remains of the Waiapu bridge are visible in the river. Photograph by James McDonald in 1923.

their world, back at McDonald behind the camera, Andersen on his Edison phonograph, and Best with his notebook, determining how their knowledge would be recorded for their descendants.

On 19 March at Whareponga, Mākere and Tuta Ngārimu performed a taumanu: 'Aa taarai! Ka taarai tahi Tara i runga ra!' in acknowledgement of the arrival of the party of Te Rangihīroa, Te Peehi and their friends. Tuta followed with a powerful speech to the manuhiri, recorded on the wax cylinder recording: 'Ka waiho i kōnei hei taonga mā ngā uri whakatipu: We're leaving these chants as treasures for the rising generation.'[59] They had decided to share their mātauranga for the specific purpose of creating a legacy.

The means for recording their knowledge lay in accessing the technology in the hands of government institutions, in this instance the Turnbull Library and the Dominion Museum. Today, Ngāti Porou have a vision and strategy called Mana Motuhake Ngāti Porou mo ngā Uri Whakatipu (established 2012), which translates as Ngāti Porou self-determination for the future.[60]

In contributing their knowledge, I believe that the leadership of the day exercised their mana motuhake, fully aware that these recordings would travel far beyond their space and time. These images and sound recordings were their gifts, first to Ngata, then to McDonald and Andersen, who were the conduits between them and the rising generations.

Pā sites above Waiomatatini marae.
Photograph by James McDonald.

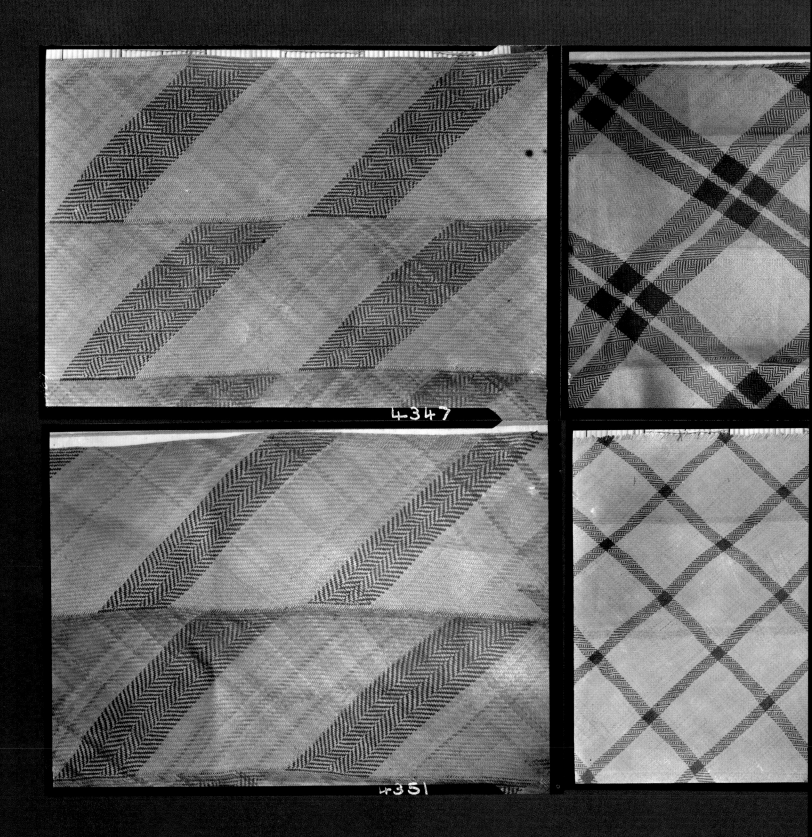

A variety of woven mats, photographed by
James McDonald at Waiomatatini in 1923.

4348

4344

4352

4354

The eye of the film

The more I explore the circumstances of the fourth expedition, the more I am struck by the powerful forces of Māori agency in the photographs and film footage. Rather than the individualistic Western model of filmmaking, where the person behind the camera can be regarded as the sole operator or auteur, this was an example of mahi tahi — collective production. I envisage the team as a prototype documentary film crew, with McDonald as cinematographer, Ngata and his father, cultural leader Paratene Ngata, as the producers, and Te Rangihīroa as director. On 18 February 1923, before the expedition, Te Rangihīroa wrote to McDonald about the still photographs he wanted:

> As regards still pictures, I think we should take a number of full and side face portraits of Maori types for the anthropological record. As regards the close up and also films to show technical detail will have ample opportunity. Also we should get some further stages of the colour designs in the floor mats.
>
> To carry on from your fire-making film, we should have the making of the fire oven, and the various stages of cooking right up to the gathering of the food into konos. We could arrange for the women to carry these with the appropriate food carrying haka up to groups of men seated in front of a good carved meeting house. I'm sure we will have plenty of material to work on.[61]

Here, Te Rangihīroa makes it plain that he is driving the filmic agenda. It is striking that he asks McDonald to photograph 'Maori types' for the physical anthropological record, and food being carried up to the marae ātea, a place usually considered tapu — although this last idea didn't come to fruition. Film scholar Angela Moewaka Barnes has noted that: 'While acknowledging the colonial interest in indigenous peoples as scientific specimens to be observed and defined, when the McDonald films are screened, they are valued as beautiful and valuable depictions of our tīpuna.'[62] Do the expedition films perpetuate a view of our ancestors as scientific specimens? Some of the portraits conform to an anthropological style. The fact that these portraits were instigated by Te Rangihīroa, however, complicates how we see his role in film direction and purpose.

Shifting across multiple positions, Te Rangihīroa appears to have directed McDonald's photography to serve his anthropological record; his engagement as a maker, and for the articles and lectures he planned in pursuit of a scholarly career. In the field, Te Rangihīroa worked closely with McDonald, making sure that he took the film sequences and photographs that he wanted to illustrate his work on netting, fishing, food preparation, cooking and portraits of individuals. On 26 March 1923, his field notebook has a list of the items 'to film' in Te Araroa:

> Torehe
> Pouraka
> Tutoko
> Matarau (Maomao)
> Matire koura

Below the list, Te Rangihīroa elaborates on particular fish and how to catch them. Later, he would use the photographs in lantern slide talks, both in Aotearoa and internationally. His 1929 field notebook records numerous lists of the photographs he took while living in Rarotonga, and travelling to Aitutaki.[63] His own photo albums reveal that Te Rangihīroa had an astute and creative eye for photographic composition. While this may not have been previously recognised as such, it was internationally groundbreaking for a Māori to be documenting Māori.

As for Ngata, he was able to attract widespread cooperation. He invited skilled and knowledgeable people to the Bungalow in Waiomatatini, and the expedition team visited other community leaders in their homes. He selected 'arts and crafts' experts for their reputations in particular practices. Ngata seems to have had little difficulty recruiting people to appear in the films and photographs, which shows the willing participation of tangata whenua in demonstrating their ancestral skills. There are numerous clues in the notebooks and diaries of the manuhiri that indicate the crucially important role that Paratene played, and the knowledge he conveyed. This documentation simply could not have been created without an invitation from Ngata, and the hospitality provided by Arihia, their daughter Te Rina, and her husband Te Kani Te Ua and other whānau.

In the years after the expedition, as recording technology advanced, Apirana Ngata developed a deepening interest in recording the practices of the people. In 1931 Ngata arranged for Materoa Reedy to travel to Wellington with a group of people to record mōteatea. In the 1940s he recorded commentaries on 1930s recordings by the Hiruharama School Choir.[64] Between the oriori 'Po! Po!' and 'Takiri Takiri Takiri', Ngata remarks: 'one looks forward to the day when recordings of these compositions rendered by experts may be made available, not only for the purposes of the scientists and the ethnologists, but for the rising generation of the young Maoris of New Zealand'.[65] Indeed, his sons William Tuakanakore Ngata and Hēnare Ngata later took up the work of recording waiata and mōteatea.

In 1928, after watching the American filmmaker Alexander Markey at work, Ngata wrote to Te Rangihīroa about the art of filmmaking:

Tai [Taipōrutu Mitchell], [Harold] Carr, Tiweka [Anaru] and [Augustus] Hamilton were there with me & we were much interested in the technique of making pictures. We decided that we could rig up a better show, where the depicting of old Maori life as far as it can be reconstructed today can be carried out in greater detail. I have recommended the Eth. Board to take up this line next summer. We have 4 good artists in NZ but no expert producer. Tai reckons I can take this part, but one must learn to look at settings with the eye of the film. Worth doing, though.[66]

Kūmara inside an oven band at Waiomatatini, 1923.
Photograph by James McDonald.

Indicating his willingness to become a producer and to learn to look with 'the eye of the film' Ngata was no doubt building on his experience of working with McDonald. Blythe puts the expedition films in a timeline: 'Significantly, until Television New Zealand's *Tangata Whenua* series in 1974, these were the only films ever produced under the auspices of the New Zealand Government in which the filmmakers themselves appear, and perhaps that only goes to suggest that these were the last films on Maori themes for some fifty years in which there was substantial Maori input.'[67] This offers a new starting point for narratives about the emergence of indigenous engagement in documentary filmmaking and photography in Aotearoa.

While the expedition films are not 'fourth cinema' — totally indigenous-led — a fuller picture of iwi-led instigation and involvement offers an opportunity to view them in a new light. As Barclay remarks, 'The quality of a hui is determined by the quality of the voice that is calling the hui ... making a film amongst your own people is like calling a hui. It takes guts to stand up and say "this matter is important and I want you to participate".'[68] For Ngata, this *was* a matter of importance. He called the hui; he called the participants. The people came because of the quality of his voice.

Barclay understood these dynamics: he had directed the 1974 Pacific Films landmark six-part documentary series 'Tangata Whenua' that Blythe cites. This series was filmed with a primarily Pākehā crew and historian Michael King as presenter. In the final episode, King interviewed Ngāti Porou leader Ngoi Pēwhairangi on important yet delicate matters of tapu. He said: 'Ngoi knew exactly what she was doing ... we were not taking pictures that morning, we were being given them.'[69]

In 1986, Barclay also directed *Ngati*, the first feature film with a Māori director. This was shot in Tairāwhiti, the homeland of Ngāti Porou writer Tama Poata. Ngoi's daughter Connie Pēwhairangi acted in the film. The lead actor, Wī Kuki Kaa — a grandson of Panikena Kaa, who features in the 1923 film — was 48 at the time of filming, a few years younger than his grandfather when he demonstrated kahawai fishing at Waiapu. This is another item on the takiaho, to hold up and examine: 'See? Here is our own Ngāti Porou film history whakapapa.'

The *Ngati* film crew were welcomed on to Iritekura marae at Waipiro, one bay along from Whareponga, where the 1923 crew had been welcomed six decades earlier. Wi Kuki Kaa must have been aware of his grandfather's role in the expedition film from family stories, the credit given to Panikena in Te Rangihīroa's 1926 publication, and the re-emergence of the 1923 films in the early 1980s, a story he may have shared with the *Ngati* crew. Barclay and Kaa may be seen as an echo of the affiliation between Te Rangihīroa and Panikena Kaa in the 1923 Tairāwhiti film.

I refer to the expedition films and photographs by their regional names, Hui Aroha, Whanganui, Rotorua Hui and Tairāwhiti, rather than giving James McDonald sole authorship. In light of new scholarship on the films, I propose that the institutions caring for these taonga should reconsider their naming processes. I do not think this detracts from McDonald's cinematographic abilities nor his instrumental role in envisioning the expeditions. Rather, it shifts the emphasis to the communities who hosted the team and shaped their work; in the case of Tairāwhiti, to Ngata and Ngāti Porou.

Hāpai: The significance of whakapapa and whanaungatanga

Through family, community and social networks, Ngata and Te Rangihīroa laid the groundwork for the Dominion Museum team and their filmmaking and photography. At the time, although colonial ruptures tore the social fabric of Ngāti Porou, systems of whakapapa as the dominant way of understanding connections did not diminish. Associations between local Māori and Pākehā colonial settlers, along with friendships with people of other tribes forged through education, war and trade, remained powerful instruments in a changing world. As Apirana Mahuika wrote: 'Like in all other iwi, the significance of whakapapa as a determinant of all mana in Ngati Porou cannot be discounted or overlooked ... [Whakapapa] survived post-European contact and continue[s] in existence today.'[70]

This was despite profound transformations in life in the region, and across the country. During the last two decades of the nineteenth century on the East Coast and elsewhere, Māori systems of justice, trade and education were being usurped by Pākehā systems. For many young Māori, growing up at a time when the Māori population was declining and Māori as a people were dismissed as a dying race, the opportunity to be educated with the tools of the Pākehā was sometimes perceived as a way of escaping a downward spiral. In the process, alternative networks were founded.

Many Māori were already involved in the Anglican Church, which had had a strong presence on the East Coast since 1834. Pivotal to these new networks were the friendships forged at Te Aute College, where bonds were established beyond the tribal context of hapū, iwi or whare wānanga. In this way, the concept of whanaungatanga 'family-making' expanded beyond hapū- and iwi-centred contexts into Pākehā systems of education, church and, later, the army. This was to have profound ramifications for Māori life in the twentieth century.

Early in the twentieth century, young men such as Apirana Ngata, Rēweti Kōhere and his brother Poihipi, Tūtere Wī Repa and Timutimu Tawhai from the East Coast, along with Māui Pōmare, Te Rangihīroa and Edward Pōhau Ellison from Te Wai Pounamu to the south and Frederick Bennett from Te Arawa, were returning from their studies to their home communities; or, as part of the Te Aute College Old Boys' Association, were earnestly railing against some Māori cultural practices, including lengthy tangihanga, customary Māori marriage systems, and a reliance on what they saw as bogus Māori spiritual and medicinal advisors — what Ngata described in a 1907 parliamentary speech as 'bastard tohungaism'.[71] Instead, they were preaching abstinence, sexual morality, health, and land reform[72] — which became intertwined with moral reform.[73] Out of this context, the Young Maori Party (YMP) was born. Fighting fire with fire, the evangelical zeal of the group aimed at meeting head on the impacts of colonisation (disease, alcohol, land sales) using other colonial tools (religion, education and health reform).

At the same time, these young men wanted to preserve language, arts and poetry as cultural practices they saw as 'desirable', as outlined in their 1909 YMP Manifesto. After the flush of righteous youthfulness had passed, they became leaders in their respective fields. Ngata, Te Rangihīroa and Pōmare recognised the uniqueness of Māori culture and set about recording songs, games, arts, ancestral stories and practices. The important roles played by these

Pākehā-educated young Māori would be vastly different from earlier Māori leaders. Nonetheless, the ability to connect through ties and networks remained a crucial skill that they used to their advantage throughout their political, religious and medical careers.

Behind this, too, were the powerful networks of Te Rangihīroa and Ngata, and the friendships forged at Te Aute. In 1898, Riwai Te Hiwinui Tāwhiri, a Ngāti Porou student at Te Aute, had invited Te Rangihīroa — a rāwaho (outsider) from Ngāti Mutunga, Taranaki — to come to the East Coast after his preliminary medical exams and work at scrubcutting.[74] As guests of Anglican minister Eruera Kāwhia, they stayed at Taumata-o-Mihi marae in the Rauru meeting house. Decorated Ngāti Porou soldier Arapeta Awatere stated, 'Here, during his school days at Te Aute College, Peter Buck was initiated by tohungas into Maaori esoteric lore';[75] and Te Rangihīroa's 's biographer, JB Condliffe, suggested that Ngata instigated this visit as a way of bringing Te Rangihīroa into contact with a Ngāti Porou way of life.

On 6 April 1923, Materoa Ngārimu, the rangatira with whom Te Rangihīroa had fallen in love in his youth — now Mrs Reedy — hosted Best and Andersen at her home. Te Rangihīroa, who was accompanied by his wife Margaret, did not attend. By this time, it was his army days and close friendship with Ngata that fuelled his connections to the East Coast, rather than an old flame.

Kauwhata: Elevating ancestral practices

To take another term from Ngata's explorations of whakapapa, the Tairāwhiti films and photographs might be understood as examples of kauwhata[76] — a practice that was used in community feasting as part of the cultural practice of manaakitanga. In the film, each vignette features Ngāti Porou experts demonstrating ancestral practices, in this sense staging each sequence to display their skill. Whakapapa and whanaungatanga were essential factors in the formation of the expedition, the choice of those who appear in the images and the practices that were displayed and given prominence in the film — fishing, netting and food-gathering practices, tukutuku

FOLLOWING PAGE: The Mōkena Kōhere memorial stone at Rangitukia, 2020. Photograph by Natalie Robertson.

4205

4198

82

4199

and kōwhaiwhai, for instance. The gender restrictions of scoop-net fishing activities meant that, unlike other film sequences from the same expedition that show women participating in preparing hāngi, diving for kaimoana and working in the fields harvesting kūmara, the trip to the Waiapu river mouth features only men.

It is this sequence at Waikākā Beach near the ngutu awa (river mouth) that offers the clearest illumination of whanaungatanga and the significance of Te Rangihīroa's presence. Through these connections, the tangata whenua elevate him (rather than Best) to a place of prominence in the proceedings. Although plans to get pictures at the Waiapu river mouth are mentioned in Andersen's diary, there is only one surviving film sequence from that location. Given the recording of Te Irimana Te Kawa Tikapa chanting the Paikea karakia at Tikapa, it is possible that the team had intended to make a visit to the river mouth from the south side the previous week; that visit may have been prevented for any number of reasons, including the tides. On 30 March, Andersen notes in his diary: 'The gear was taken into Kohere's buggy, & Dr Buck, McDonald & I rode on horses. We stayed at Kohere's place for tea & for the night.'[77] The Kōhere homestead is across the road from the Rangitukia rugby grounds (now called George Nēpia Memorial Park after the famous rugby player who married Te Huinga, Hēnare Kōhere and Ngārangi Tūrei's daughter).

Today, a memorial stone for the nationally prominent nineteenth-century tribal leader Mōkena Kōhere stands on the Hahau block, next to the house that replaced the homestead Tarata, where Poihipi Kōhere, minister for St John's Parish, once lived. The original St John's Church, situated across from Hinepare marae, was built largely by Poihipi's grandfather Mōkena Kōhere.[78] From the 1850s onwards, Kōhere had ushered in a modern style of chieftainship that, according to his descendant Rarawa Kōhere, needed to 'socialise the wider aggregations of communities aimed at addressing new and emerging issues to deal with multi-faceted relationships'.[79] In Rangitukia, the meeting between the community hosts and the guests from the

ethnological expedition — with their technological tools for recording cultural practices — was an example of this.

The team had crossed the river to Rangitukia on Good Friday, after attending a church service held by Reverend Poihipi Kōhere at Waiomatatini. After dinner at the Kōhere household that night, the team relocated to Tairāwhiti wharenui at Hinepare marae. Andersen commented that at the meeting house, 'one or two long speeches having already been made, there was more speechifying'.[80] Given Hinepare's location between the Kaa and Kōhere homesteads, it is highly likely that members of both families and other community people were present to formally welcome Te Rangihīroa and the other members of the team to Rangitukia.

Te Rangihīroa had served first as a medical officer, then as second-in-command, in the Pioneer Battalion during the First World War, along with Hēnare Mōkena Kōhere and Pekama Rongoaia Kaa, who were killed on the Somme and at Ypres respectively. Since both of these men had died overseas, with no opportunity for their whānau to lament over their bodies, the Rangitukia people must have welcomed the opportunity to share their loss with Te Rangihīroa, who had been with Hēnare when he was wounded by shellfire in the trenches. Hēnare died of his wounds on 16 September 1916, aged thirty-six, leaving behind three young children. Padre Hēnare Wainohu wrote of Hēnare's death to Poihipi Kōhere on 26 October 1916:

> Before he was taken to the dressing station that night he expressed a wish to see Major Buck (Te Rangi Hiroa). To him he said, 'I ask of you that after I am gone to place my boys, all from the Ngati-Porou Tribe, under my cousin, Lieutenant Pekama Kaa.' Major Buck replied, 'Yes, I'll carry out your wish.' Then, looking up to the major and myself, he remarked, 'I have no anxiety now, for I know the boys will be in good hands, and as for myself I shall be all right.'[81]

When he heard the news, Ngata composed 'Te Ope Tuatahi', which was both a tangi and a recruitment song. It included a verse that mentioned Hēnare; and Ngata named his youngest son Hēnare Kōhere Ngata when he was born in December 1917.

PREVIOUS PAGE: James McDonald took a series of photographs in the kūmara garden at Waiomatatini in 1923. Here, men and women are lifting and sorting the kūmara. Apirana Ngata's wife, Arihia Kane Tāmati, is in the foreground of the photographs at right.

I haere ai Henare
Me to wiwi,
I patu ki te pakanga,
Ki Para-nihi ra ia.

Farewell, O Henare,
and your 'clump of rushes'
who fell while fighting
in France.

Although the decision to promote Kaa was
not Te Rangihīroa's to make, he was no doubt
influential in passing on Kōhere's wishes to his
commanding officers.

Pekama Rongoaia Kaa, who took over from
Hēnare Kōhere, was the second child of Matewa
and Panikena Kaa — one of the well-known families
of Rangitukia — and a generation younger than
Ngata, Te Rangihīroa and the Kōhere brothers.[82]
In his monograph on his great-grandfather, Panikena
Kaa, Charl Hirschfeld states that: 'Pekama's father
Panikena knew about the incident, referring to it
in a letter (dated 21 September 1917) to Sir James
Allen … in which he expresses his pride in his son
being selected by Hēnare Kōhere to take charge
of our soldiers.'[83] On 14 August 1917, Pekama, who
was badly wounded but had refused to be moved
until his men were carried to safety — was killed
by a shell.[84] He was twenty-three years old.

Kaa's brother Hēnare also served in the Battalion, but
he was at sea, en route to Europe, when Pekama fell
in battle and so did not see his brother alive again. He
survived the war and reached the rank of corporal,
and was at Rangitukia in 1923 to greet Te Rangihīroa
and the expedition team.[85]

In 1923, during the fourth expedition to Tairāwhiti,
the Kōhere and Kaa whānau had their first chance
to host Te Rangihīroa on their own marae after
the deaths of their sons. Te Rangihīroa's personal
relationships with both of these men are part of the
backdrop to the visit to Rangitukia and the overnight
stay at the Kōhere homestead. Bound together
by war, this was also a gathering of old boys from
Te Aute College, which both Kōhere brothers,
Te Rangihīroa, Ngata and Kaa had all attended.
Rēweti Kōhere and Ngata, together with Māui
Pōmare and Timutimu Tawhai, had formed the
Association for the Amelioration of the Condition
of the Maori Race in response to an influenza
outbreak on the East Coast in 1891.[86]

This gathering reunited a group of men who sought
to hold on to their cultural values, land and language
while embracing Pākehā education. The women, who
equally exercised leadership in Ngāti Porou, were also
present to host these auspicious guests. These were
educated, worldly people who were fully involved
in local and national politics, shaping the world around
them in the face of rapid change. The evening must
have been emotion-filled. As Hirschfeld notes:

> Although they probably had not met before
> this occasion Panikena is likely to have
> welcomed Buck as someone who was a part
> of the Whānau. Buck is likely to have given
> Panikena a recitation of Pekama as a man of
> ability in the field, well admired by his troops,
> brave and cool under pressure, dignified as
> an officer and a gentleman and as a natural
> leader of men.[87]

McDonald and Andersen left the marae that evening
around midnight and walked the short distance back
to the Kōhere homestead under calm, starry skies
and a moon that was almost full. Te Rangihīroa
no doubt stayed late into the night, talking with the
families of his comrades. The next day, Andersen
wrote: 'Last night Dr Buck told a few more of his
stories, but the names slip the memory, and the
names must be remembered in the stories to have
their full value.' Given that Andersen's observations
are the only written account of these events, it
is truly a loss that he was not more conversant
with Māori and the whakapapa relationships that
underpinned these exchanges.

In Te Rangihīroa's 1923 field notebook, he names
Panikena Kaa and Riwai Raroa of Rangitukia on the
page opposite his drawings and measurements of
the kahawai scoop net. Raroa's son William was
another young soldier who had died and was buried
abroad, possibly as a result of influenza. It is highly
likely that the Raroa whānau were also present at
the wharenui. It was these connections that helped
Te Rangihīroa secure the cooperation of Ngāti Porou
fishing experts in the fieldwork that led to his 1926
article 'The Maori Craft of Netting', illustrated
by McDonald's photographs and published in the
Transactions of the New Zealand Institute.[88]

4311

The Waiapu valley, showing the cluster of mountains in and
around Hikurangi Maunga, with Aorangi in front, and Wharekia,
Taitai and Whanakau mountains visible in the distance.
Photograph by James McDonald, 1923.

The 'photo business': Kahawai fishing at the mouth of the Waiapu, 1 April 1923

In *Hī Ika: The Ngāti Porou Fisheries Settlement*, the 1923 photographs helped to demonstrate the importance of ancestral fishing knowledge in a legal context. The photographs and film taken during the 1923 expedition offer vital environmental clues and information about species in the face of increasing scarcity, and in one case, extinction. The deep cultural importance of kahawai fishing to Ngāti Porou is outlined in the Ngāti Porou Treaty of Waitangi settlement documents, where particular cultural, spiritual, historical and traditional associations with identified areas are stated:

> Statement 4. The Waiapu River has been a source of sustenance for Ngāti Porou hapu, providing water, and various species of fish, including kahawai. The kahawai fishing techniques practised at the mouth of the Waiapu River are sacred activities distinct to the Waiapu.[89]

Kahawai fishing was so integral to life in Te Riu o Waiapu (the Waiapu valley) that people drew a link between certain physical characteristics of a person and the purpose they might serve in fishing. Te Rangihīroa gives an example in his 1923 diary:

> 'E rahi te mahunga o tamaiti nei
> Hei tukituki i ngā ngaru o Waikaka.'
>
> Big-headed child born
> To pierce the waves of Waikaka.[90]

At Rangitukia, Te Rangihīroa recorded this whakataukī which refers to the act of plunging headfirst through breakers into the sea when kahawai fishing. His research into the craft of netting illuminates the link between methods and the materials and techniques used. He explains how different environments within the same rohe led to the distinctive development of the scoop net—rather than the seine net, as used at Wharekahika, another Ngāti Porou settlement.[91] Today, although the materials have changed, the body of knowledge about fishing remains crucial to Ngāti Porou identity and survival, when the ocean is te kāpata kai—the food cupboard. Today, almost a century later, the body of knowledge of earlier material usage is a valuable legacy that requires more attention.

For many generations, maramataka—Māori seasonal, lunar, stellar and solar almanacs—guided all food gathering and production. Hina, the atua of the moon, weaves cycles of regularity for time and tide.[92] Offerings and karakia were made to Tangaroa, atua of the sea; and Ngāti Porou say karakia and make offerings to Pou, atua of fish, and to tuna and other denizens of both fresh and salt waters, for abundance.[93]

Kahawai and Te Ngutu Awa

In the Porourangi Maori Cultural School Rauru-Nui-a-Toi lecture series, Ngata tells the story of Tamateaupoko, a descendant of Ruawaipu, the 'ancestress of the subtribes living on the north side of the Waiapu river'.[94] As a wartime refugee in Whāngārā, Tamateaupoko felt great anxiety when her sons disappeared over the horizon on their fishing trips:

> She wept, bewailing the risks and hardships they faced to obtain food from the ocean. And she cried 'There yonder are the foods of the streams of Ruawaipu gnawing at the shore.' Her children asked what she meant and she explained, that the streams she named abounded in the kahawai fish, which at times came of themselves to this shore, literally biting at it.[95]

These accounts accord with a saying recorded by Best during the 1923 expedition: 'Ka paaha te tonga ki konei. Ka paaha te wai' 'the suddenness of flood leaving fish on banks'.[96] However, this abundance is seasonal: the autumn equinox in late March indicates the shifting seasons, and by then, the kahawai run is usually over.

For members of the expedition, the fact that the moon was almost full on 31 March—Atua or, possibly, Rākaunui, in the maramataka—held some potential for the team's plans to go to the river mouth the next morning to film the men fishing for kahawai.

> After breakfast we rode, taking the photo business in the buggy, to the mouth of Waiapu so as to see how the 14ft kahawai net is used. A big Maori got into the shallow water where the river makes over the bar, holding the mouth of the net to the sea, & going with the current in a sweep along the beach. The

Kahawai go into the river on the tide — to eat the fresh water the Maori say — & go at great speed so that sweeping the net out with the flow the fish are caught. The surf was very heavy today, & a strong wind was blowing off the land, so our man caught no fish. Once or twice the sea threw a wave up over the narrow spit where we stood, but the wash was only an inch or two deep, except one wash which went over McDonald's boot-tops.[97]

This entry, pencilled by Andersen, recounts the first film and photographic record of Ngāti Porou tribal netting for kahawai at the mouth of the Waiapu River. It appears in a compilation of filmed scenes

that became *He Pito Whakaatu i te Noho a te Maori i te Tairawhiti*,[98] and in two photographic images. Andersen does not name the 'big Maori' who assisted the Dominion Museum team members, but Te Rangihīroa identifies him as Panikena Kaa of Rangitukia in 'The Maori Craft of Netting'.[99] Kaa's identity was further confirmed by his granddaughter Keri Kaa, who assisted the Film Archive when a print of the surviving original footage was made and screened in the 1980s.

James McDonald took a series of fishing shots on the Waiapu River during the fourth expedition in 1923. Here, Panikena Kaa (left) and possibly Riwai Raroa cast their nets into the river.

The relationship between Te Rangihīroa and the Kaa family meant that Panikena Kaa was willing to demonstrate kahawai netting for them, even though the conditions were less than optimal. The Waiapu river mouth is about three or four kilometres from the Kōhere homestead by road and then along Waikākā Beach. On the way there, the team passed by Hinepare marae, where they had spent the previous evening, then Rangitukia Native School.[100] Less than a hundred metres past the school is Whataamo, where the Kaa whānau lived.

The Taiapa whānau, later famed as carvers, lived just along the river. This short stretch of the Waiapu, on both sides, produced some of the most influential people in Ngāti Porou in the nineteenth and twentieth centuries. These families, too, had sent their well-educated sons to war, and many of them never returned. For these families, losing many of the young leaders who would have inherited these ancestral tikanga may have been the motivation to record them for future generations. Loss, grief, mutual respect, reciprocity and manaakitanga were all factors in these relationships, knotting them together. Panikena Kaa braved the heavy surf to demonstrate kahawai netting techniques for Te Rangihīroa while McDonald got his feet wet, his camera recording this tikanga for posterity.

The scene is filmed from Waikākā Beach on the northern side of the Waiapu River, looking towards the sea. With no landmarks for reference, it is impossible to know precisely where the ever-changing river mouth was at the time of filming. The brief sequence therefore provides no distinct indicators about subsequent environmental changes. One of the two photographs taken of the party arriving at Waikākā Beach shows Pohautea — the sentry hill on the south side of the river mouth — stripped bare of trees.

The image includes Kaa, Te Rangihīroa, Andersen and three other people on horseback who have accompanied them to the river mouth; these were probably Riwai Raroa along with members of the Kōhere and Kaa whānau. In the other image, the camera faces the sea, documenting Te Rangihīroa balancing his exercise book on his knee as he pencils notes from Kaa, with two men looking

The expedition arrives at Waikākā Beach, on the north side of the mouth of the Waiapu River in 1923. Pohautea is the hill behind them. Photograph by James McDonald.

on, the horse-drawn buggy carrying the 'photo business' to the left of the frame. This documentary photograph is one of only a few images from the Tairāwhiti expedition that demonstrates the sharing of knowledge from a local expert with one of the team, within the frame, on location.

Recontextualising this event from a Ngāti Porou perspective, the sequence with Panikena Kaa in particular reveals how the familial and social networks of Ngata, his whānau and those of Te Rangihīroa operated to ensure the success of the expedition. The links between Kaa, Ngata and Te Rangihīroa reveal previously unexplored nuances in the non-familial relationships; these involve what appear ostensibly to be Pākehā-controlled camera technology and Māori subjects. In this sense, the takiaho analysis proposes a relational cord along which the persons concerned are traced and their connections displayed through the filmic platform—the kauwhata.

A short resurrection

> They [the preserved image] reply in many subtle and not so subtle ways; through the clothes they are wearing, the work they are doing, the ceremonies they are performing, the body language, the facial expression, and elements of their style...and in that journey, on screen, from darkness to light, another life lives, short resurrections are made.[101]

This statement by Merata Mita aptly describes the ancestral knowledge embedded in these images. Despite its brevity, the film clip featuring Panikena Kaa resurrects the āhua (the appearance) of an expert demonstrating an important cultural practice in a threshold place between the river and the ocean. The body of water is an ancestral being— Waiapu Kōkā Huhua, 'Waiapu of many mothers'— and mother of many. This alludes not only to the great number of female leaders of the area, but also to Waiapu as home to many species and beings.

Te Rangihīroa takes field notes at Waikākā Beach in 1923 while Panikena Kaa advises him, watched by young men, possibly Kaa's sons. Photograph by James McDonald.

The Waiapu river mouth film sequence is just one minute long. It is preceded by a sequence of a woman diving for kōura at Whareponga, and followed by a fishing demonstration of the stone channel and net method at Waiomatatini. After the inter-title 'Te hi kahawai i te wahapu o Waiapu Awa. Fishing for kahawai at the mouth of the Waiapu River', Kaa enters the water, single-handedly wrestling the huge net in strong winds and the tidal currents of the river mouth. As in other sequences, McDonald steadies the camera on a tripod, maintaining a static position for each shot. The wind is whipping the waves. Entering the frame from the right, Kaa moves quickly with the current, in water above his knees, holding the scoop net down in the water. When he arrives at the spot where the river meets the ocean waves, he demonstrates the action of lifting the net up out of the water and onto his back. The inter-title, which has been inserted into the film by Ngā Taonga Sound and Vision, the national film archive body that restored it, uses the term wahapū for river mouth, whereas locally it is always referred to as the ngutu awa. The changeable river mouth is a place governed by strict protocols, ngā ture o te ngutu awa.

There are many ture (rules) to be adhered to at the ngutu awa, and in earlier years, they were strictly enforced. Nunu Tangaere said, 'if you disrespected the rules, you'd see the sea change—becoming rougher. You could even get carried out to sea and nearly drown.'[102] The agency of the sea as a being that reacts to rule-breaking by becoming rougher is explained by the worldview of the Ngāti Porou Tūturu hapū—a subtribe of the lower Waiapu River. The river mouth is a dangerous place with strong tidal currents where taniwha dwell, including my own ancestor, Taho. The act of catching kahawai is not just going fishing but an activity involving restricted tapu knowledge, where any distractions can be life-threatening.

In the film clip, Kaa wears a white shirt as a gesture of modesty. If the camera had not been present, he would have been naked, as that was (and still is) the practice when kahawai fishing at Waiapu. Being naked was a pragmatic response to keeping safe when working with the nets in a river mouth with a strong current, where clothing could be weighty and restrictive. This is one aspect of the tikanga of the river.

There are two photographs surviving of Kaa with his 4.2 metre-long kahawai scoop net. One, reproduced on the previous page, was first published in Te Rangihīroa's 'The Maori Craft of Netting'[103] and identified as 'kupenga kŏkŏ kahawai'. Te Rangihīroa was at pains to differentiate this method, 'kŏkŏ'—with short vowels, which means to 'to scoop' or 'scrape up',[104] from the more common kōkō (prodding) method, which involved use of a pole and a pointed net;[105] the former method was a speciality of Rangitukia village.

The kahawai season usually runs from December to February, with the main schools of kahawai gone by mid-March. Te Rangihīroa notes the significance of kahawai to the people of the river:

> During the kahawai season, people camped on the beach, and while the men were landing the fish, the women would clean and hang them up. Two tripods of driftwood were set up to support a crossbar, on which the cleaned fish were hung up to dry—this was called the whata. Inland people would come down to the beach with carts, and drove them away laden with dried kahawai.[106]

The filming took place a month after the usual end to the season, in a strong offshore wind and heavy surf. Why was Kaa, fisherman, farmer and community leader, prepared to demonstrate on camera the art of 'kupenga kŏkŏ kahawai' at a time when the kahawai runs were over? And, knowing that he was unlikely to catch any fish, why did he choose to be filmed—contrary to the local practice of naked net handling—in his white shirt? Certainly, Kaa was an expert net handler. One of his descendants, Charl Hirschfeld, writes:

> Physically he was strong of upright gait and possessed of deep blue eyes which made him stand out in a crowd of his immediate fellow-compatriots. In the prime of his manhood he was able to swim the channel between the tip of East Cape and Whanga o Kena (East Island), a stretch of water with powerful tides and currents. He gathered kai moana in abundance for his whanau and whanaunga and was respected for his prowess at fishing.[107]

Te Rangihīroa and others setting a hīnaki pūrangi in the Waiapu River in 1923. Photographs by James McDonald.

4290 4290

Scoop-net fishing at the river mouth is an activity that is restricted to men. Knowing that he had no control over who would see the footage in the brief resurrections of its screenings, Kaa chose to wear his shirt, indicating that he had considered how to mediate the rules of the river mouth. Although this is an ethnographic film, whose makers sought to record customary tribal ways, the tikanga was performed in a present-day manner: the white shirt is a sign that Kaa refused to be filmed naked. It does not conform to the atavistic idea of the 'ethnographic present', evident in other films of the time. It is reminiscent of other more recent recordings of scoop-net fishing in the river mouth—for example, for one of the television series, 'Waka Huia' (2016), which used archival Radio Ngāti Porou footage of Waiapu river mouth resident John Manuel teaching young men—dressed in shorts and sports shirts—the ture of netting kahawai.

These film and photographic images from the 1923 expedition offer vignettes to be lifted up for closer analysis. In this context the haukāinga had extended their manaakitanga to the expedition team; they hosted them at Hinepare marae and in their homes. This enriching of connection and the respect accorded to the honoured guests is not visible in the short moments recorded in the film. Nevertheless, McDonald's flickering film fragments and still photographs, Andersen's diaries and Te Rangihīroa's notebooks reveal deeper connections with the haukāinga than are immediately apparent. As a practical method, whakapapa offers a way to make connections in the knots along the takiaho cord. Hirschfeld's account reveals the mutual trust and respect for tikanga and the role of the camera in this deeply Māori context:

> Panikena was both a Maori modernist and traditionalist, something he lived out as part of his own life. In acceding to allowing Buck and McDonald to gather information from him personally and to permit himself thereby to be photographed was an expression of living the modernist–traditionalist contradiction. On the one hand it was about a tightly guarded centuries old method and on the other hand about ethnographic and technologic media (writing and photography) presenting the verisimilitude of something intensely Maori.

Without Panikena's approval in a heartfelt way the Buck fishing expedition at the Waiapu is likely to have lacked the success that the record now generates as a historical piece of some significance.[108]

For Mita, at the conclusion of the short resurrection of connecting with an ancestor on screen comes the time of ritual acknowledgment of 'our creator and our implacable link to the earth, its creatures, the elements and the seasons, the stars and the planets and the entire universe because that is what I have been taught and that is what those images continue to teach'.[109] This film clip is one such moment.

Maramataka and upokororo

In recording the tikanga that surrounded fishing in their region, Ngāti Porou experts were informed by the maramataka, a calendrical system based on the phases of the moon and seasonal changes. Each region or even stretch of coastline might have its own calendar, adapted to the local conditions. A comment from Paratene Ngata to Te Rangihīroa about river fishing reveals that lunar phases were on the elder's mind: he took maramataka into consideration as he guided cultural activities.

The unexpected catch of the upokororo brought gravitas to the activities of the expedition and the documentary record. In the following decades, the records kept by Te Rangihīroa would become evidence of the further decline and eventual extinction of the species. Upokororo became 'the first fish species protected under the Freshwater Fisheries Regulations 1951 (reaffirmed in 1983). It remains the only fully protected freshwater fish.'[110]

Until now, however, the photographic record and film as an evidentiary document has not been examined or analysed in detail to shed light on the events, and the cultural context, of this historic moment. As a photographer, it is startling to realise that the last-ever recorded catch of a rare species might unknowingly be caught on film. This story of a now-extinct native fish, and Mātauranga maramataka ki Waiapu, the knowledge of the almanac, brings to light aspects of hitherto unseen Ngāti Porou environmental knowledge that shaped the expedition. This has implications for documentary photographers and filmmakers working in indigenous contexts.

Today, there is resurgent interest in understanding the planetary, lunar and solar effects on the environment. Tate Pēwhairangi from Tokomaru, in his Wai 272 statement, discusses the significance of environmental knowledge at length.

> Our tipuna had so much knowledge about their environment. Whether it be fishing by the signs and at certain times of year or when to plant, grow, harvest certain crops, they knew. They knew the fish were fat when the manuka was in bloom. They knew the significance of the kowhai in bloom. They used the Milky Way te Ika o Te Rangi, and the phases of the moon for fishing and planting. They were a very knowledgeable people and worked in harmony with their environment. There was a use of the karaka berry, nikau, and other natural plants by the whanau living in those areas.[111]

These daily observations have remained essential for the lifestyle of these coastal people—including predicting the weather. Ahipene Paenga spoke of how, in his father's time, 'They knew whether it was going to be a good day for fishing...My father's generation used the cloud patterns and other natural signs to determine whether it was going to be a good day. They operated under the traditional Māori knowledge and lore.'[112] Tautini (Tini) Glover, who was raised further along the coast at Ūawa, spoke of how his grandfather had taught him about the relationship between the stars and the prevailing winds: 'He taught me about the patiki (flounder) in the Milky Way. He said the direction the tail of the patiki was facing was where the wind would come from. At night he would look up at the stars and say, there will be a southwesterly tomorrow. The next day would bring a wind just as he said.'[113]

However, Tini also observed that although he had learned from his grandfather about stars and weather patterns, he lamented that there was little application for this learning in modern conditions. Te Kapunga Dewes notes in his Wai 272 statement, 'Essential to our lifestyle was knowledge of the winds. For example, when there is a southerly it may be cold, but the sea would be calm at Horoera. The knowledge of the seasonal tides, full moon, new moon were all essential to our way of life...'[114] Winds had their own names, and they influenced fishing. Best's diary holds small clues to the relationship between the seasonal

conditions and wind factors. He notes: 'Moho fish—small, always driven ashore on third day of the parera wind, being chased by Kahawai.'[115] Dewes' statement highlights the environment in which Paratene Ngata was living and why he was so attentive to the phases when he was advising the team during the expedition. He would also have accorded them the utmost manaaki, to the point of indulging them, even when environmental conditions were not perfect.

Six recorded maramataka from Tairāwhiti eastern seaboard are analysed against the fishing events of the expedition. The first of these was recorded in the *Journal of the Polynesian Society* in 1928. Published by HW Williams, it is attributed to Hone Parehuia of Ngāti Porou.[116] This is almost certainly Hoani Te Parehuia, also known as Hoani Te Kohukoko—a leading Ngāti Ira tohunga according to Apirana Ngata, who records that Te Parehuia and his brother Wi (Wiremu Parata) Tamawhaikai (also Kohukoko) were students trained by Rangiuia, the last tohunga of Te Rāwheoro, the famed whare wānanga (school of learning) at Ūawa Tolaga Bay.[117] Ngata also mentions Wi Tamawhaikai in a 1931 letter to Te Rangihīroa about his intention to publish whakapapa in a supplement to the *Journal of the Polynesian Society*.[118] Te Parehuia's maramataka has thirty days, but no names are recorded for days fifteen and sixteen.

The second maramataka, compiled by Pineamine Taiapa, was published as 'Marama Taka a Te Maori te Tau 1946, a household calendar'.[119] It is entirely in te reo: the intended audience is evident. This thirty-day almanac has twelve months on detachable pages, each with the moonrise times and corresponding phase, and an explanatory guide. The months are transliterations of English, rather than traditional Māori names, which don't have exact correspondences with the Gregorian calendar.

What is extraordinary about this maramataka is that seasonal variations are detailed on the planting and fishing guide for each month. Taiapa also lists five seasons, which is more appropriate for Aotearoa's climate. These variations become important in the retrospective analysis of the fishing scenes recorded at Waiapu. Taiapa's maramataka aligns closely with Te Parehuia's 1928 version. In fact, the two missing lines for days fifteen and sixteen from Te Parehuia's may be able to be filled in when examined against Taiapa's maramataka.

In 1960–61 Taiapa compiled a thirty-two-day calendar specifically for Te Riu o Waiapu, that was published in the *Gisborne Herald*.[120] This is one of only two thirty-two-day almanacs on record; the other is from Hauraki, also in the eastern North Island.[121] It is vital to mention that in Taiapa's version, there are three days — Tamatea-tuhaha, Maurea, Mauri — that are underlined, with a note that states that these are not constant as months vary in length. This explains the difference between the 1946 and 1960–61 versions of Taiapa's maramataka: there are variances in the monthly sequences from twenty-nine days through to thirty-two days. In the 1946 maramataka, Taiapa names the twenty-ninth day as Mauri, with '(Omutu)' in brackets, indicating that Mutuwhenua is approaching.

Adjustments for the lunar cycle length (twenty-nine and a half days), for observable moonrises according to local geography, for seasonal activities and particular local conditions all account for these differences. Annual and seasonal adjustments suggest that the maramataka was an environmentally responsive system, as Wiremu Tawhai explains in his thesis on Te Whānau ā Apanui maramataka.[122] Taiapa's illustration on the 1960 almanac includes the first quarter (Tamatea), full-moon phase (Rākaunui) and the third quarter (Tangaroa). Furthermore, in the annual circular diagram, he shows the seasonal run of fish: kahawai, kanae, pātiki, īnanga, mangō, warehou, maomao, tāmure, tarakihi, kehe, pihapiharau, moki, hāpuku and kōura, but not upokororo.[123]

The fourth maramataka, by Mone Taumaunu, published in *Te Ao Hou* in 1962, also gives thirty days in the month.[124] His almanac provides fishing and planting advice in both Māori and English. Besides Taiapa's 1946 calendar, Taumaunu's interpretation is the only other guide to applying the maramataka for Tairāwhiti.

The fifth maramataka, a handwritten personal manuscript in 1974 by Eruera Stirling of Te Whānau ā Apanui, records thirty-one days.[125] While some of the days are not in exactly the same order, Stirling's annotations echo Taumaunu's almost word for word.

In his 2012 doctoral thesis 'Te Kore', Moana Nepia analysed Wiremu Ryland's maramataka manuscript, which is incomplete because of water damage. It offers a sixth document for comparison.[126] Finally, I have relied on Wiremu Tawhai's *Living by the Moon: Te Maramataka a Te Whānau-ā-Apanui*, published in 2019, to unpack some of the deeper meanings behind the names and activities in these maramataka. I do so with the confidence that, as a neighbouring iwi, much knowledge is shared. Indeed, Tawhai's maramataka is almost identical to those recorded by Taiapa.

Which of these maramataka is closest to the one that Paratene Ngata would have followed? As one of the senior remaining tohunga in his time, Te Parehuia contributed to Ngata's knowledge; however, his version may not have applied specifically to Waiapu. It is also incomplete, with two important days missing. The full moon, like the new moon, is a time for ensuring the maramataka is recorded accurately and environmental signs are checked. It is remarkable that these are the days not accounted for in his almanac.

For these reasons, I have favoured Pine Taiapa's 1960–61 almanac, the only one that is exclusively recorded for the Waiapu, cross-referenced with his 1946 version, which is more detailed. Taiapa was local to Rangitukia, and was raised to carry cultural and environmental knowledge. Taumaunu was from further down the coast, while Stirling was from Te Whānau ā Apanui, a neighbouring tribe but with a predominantly north-facing coastline. His wife Amiria, though, was from Ngāti Porou. Ryland's maramataka was from Tokomaru Bay.[127] Following Taiapa's maramataka and correlating this with the phases of the moon in 1923, I analyse the pā tauremu Waiapu River fishing exercise instigated by Te Rangihīroa and recorded on film, according to a Waiapu perspective.[128]

Turu

On the night after the kahawai fishing, 2 April, the moon was rising to full in the early hours at 00.39am (Gisborne/Pacific timezone), a phase called Turu. It was a perigee supermoon, and appeared closer to the earth than usual. Andersen noted that it was 'clear & starry & bright with the full moon'. Tawhai calls this a time of calm and serenity, 'when the creative spirit of the people has the opportunity to manifest itself'.[129] This proved to be a productive period for McDonald: he filmed several noteworthy sequences as fine weather allowed him to take photographs of the landscape from above Puputa pā.

According to Taiapa, Rākaunui falls on 3 April and Rākaumatohi on 4 April. While the Rākau days are considered good for fishing, the days that precede and follow the full-moon phase are better used for other efforts. Andersen's diary often misses days out or records them retrospectively, making it difficult at times to work out which day he is referring to, but his observations of the weather, stars and the moon are invaluable. Between 2 and 4 April, according to Andersen, the days were hot with a strong parera (nor'wester) blowing. Activities during the next two days of the full moon included kūmara harvesting, which McDonald filmed, with Arihia Ngata cheerfully leading the group in rolling back the kūmara vines. McDonald also made still photographs of rua kūmara at Waiomatatini. As kūmara require sun-drying before storage, the conditions were right. Taiapa notes that in April (Aperira), the full moon is a time to 'Whakaemitia nga pararareka ki ro pakoro'—to gather and store potatoes.[130] On the day of the kūmara harvesting and filming Andersen notes that, aptly, it was 'almost like a harvest moon'.

In the *He Pito Whakaatu* film, the text inter-titles inserted into the film by Ngā Taonga Sound and Vision introduce the next subject. For this one, it is: 'He auroa: Te hopu ika ki te ara toka me te kupenga ki Waiomatatini. Fishing by the stone channel and net method at Waiomatatini'. In this inter-title, 'he auroa' refers to a stone channel or fish weir. Between 5 and 8 April, the last week of the expedition, a type of fish weir called a pā tauremu[131] was built in the lower reaches of the Waiapu River, across from Waiomatatini, near a ford that was not far upriver from the former Waiapu bridge. The timecode marks the minutes and seconds of the film sequence. This scene commences at 15:30 minutes with a mid-shot of two men ankle-deep in the shallow rapids of the Waiapu River. One of the men is Te Rangihīroa; the other is Rāpata Wahawaha Maxwell, Ngata's cousin and the East Cape lighthouse keeper, according to his great-grandson, Tawhiri Maxwell.[132]

The river flows from right to left of the frame, towards another channel that has a glassy appearance. In the distance, hills taper off to the right. Both men wear hats, white shirts and shorts. One wears a waistcoat while the other has a singlet over his shirt. They are bent at the waist, picking up rocks and moving them and appear to be building a low wall in the river.

The next shot is wide, from a different angle, looking along the wall of stones. In the foreground is a pair of mānuka stakes and brushwood, forming a V-shape. The two men continue to add to their stone channel. With a subtle shift in camera angle, the filmmaker includes more of the brushwood and mānuka V-shape.

The next shot, at 16:34, reveals the location more precisely as shallow rapids flowing from a tributary into the main river. Te Rangihīroa's 1923 notebook mentions how sites for the weirs known as 'pa kokopu and pa tauremu' were selected: a dry stick was thrown into the centre of the tāheke (rapids) to pick the run of current for the mouth of the pā.[133] On the other side of the main channel, the stony riverbed extends many more metres; large dead trees lie broken on the far side.

The filmmaker is now positioned right in the flow of the rapids: we can assume, from viewing the adjacent scenes, that McDonald's tripod is in the water or just out of it, on the shingle. The two men are now adding to the mānuka trap: Maxwell is using an axe to hammer in a stake then, together, they add mānuka branches horizontally between these stakes.

Takirau-maheahea

On Thursday 5 April, it was Takirau—the eighteenth night of the lunar cycle, where the waning moon is losing its brightness. For April, Taiapa states that Takirau is a time to harvest kūmara, 'Hauhaketia nga maara kumara'—an activity that commenced two days earlier. Taumaunu describes this night as 'Takirau-maheahea, kua makoha te marama he ririki te kumara, te koura, te tuna—Kumaras planted on this day are small, also crayfish and eels'.[134] April is a time of harvest, however, not of planting. Fish may be small, but found in their multitudes. As Tawhai explains, the prefix 'taki' followed by a number rau is a multiplier, stating that Takirau is 'multitudinous but miniature'.[135]

That night, Andersen wrote up some events of the previous days:

In the afternoon Dr. Buck, McDonald & Ngata's father went along up the river & built a pa kokopu to try & catch some of that fish, — though the old man [Paratene Ngata] said it was the wrong night of the moon to set the hinaki. In speaking of it afterwards the Dr. said he had often wondered how the fish kept the run of these nights, propitious and unpropitious. 'The old man tells me it is the wrong night,' said he; 'also the wrong month, — and it would be rather strange' said he in the slow manner he adopts at times, 'if it was also the wrong year' and then his infectious laugh broke.[136]

Te Rangihīroa describes this same activity in 'The Maori Craft of Netting' as 'an experiment, for ethnological purposes', and records that 'the weir described was made in the beginning of April by members of the Dominion Museum Ethnological Expedition, under the direction of Paratene Ngata'.[137] His field notebook has several mentions of upokororo that predate the period that the 'experiment' took place.[138]

In light of his remarks, it is surprising that Te Rangihīroa did not record the days of the maramataka, given his passion for fishing knowledge. His field notebooks detail a raft of information on fishing grounds, species

Hīnaki pūrangi secured to the bank of the Waiapu River by several stakes. Photograph by James McDonald.

and seasons, on the craft of netting, even chants associated with eel bobbing — but not the optimal days of the lunar month for fishing. There is a wry tone to his 'wrong moon, wrong month, wrong year' comment and his reporting to Andersen of 'bad omens'. This suggests that, while he respects 'the old man' Paratene, he doesn't fully embrace these Māori ways of knowing.

This statement hints at a schism between the old ways and the new. However, Te Rangihīroa later acknowledges the difference between the European solar calendar and the Māori lunar calendar in his publication on netting, when he states that the former was of little use as a guide as to when fish are plentiful and in good condition. The Māori calendar, on the other hand, marked appropriate seasons for salt and freshwater fishing and of other food supplies.[139] He mentions the autumnal March eel migration rains, and that the flowering of mānuka and kōwhai holds environmental meaning. In the language of his time, he then says that: 'from Nature's calendar the Neolithic fishermen received their orders as to what traps, nets or hooks to select, and what spot to seek on inland river, coastal reef, or deep-sea fishing ground'.[140]

Te Rangihīroa may well have been motivated by a 'salvage' approach to anthropology, recording cultural practices before they died out. As a doctor trained in scientific empirical methods, and as an anthropologist, he was more in the business of understanding methods, as he saw them. However, within a few years, Te Rangihīroa published the nights of the moon for Manihiki and Rakahanga (1932) and discussed the maramataka in his letters to Ngata. Andersen's account reveals underlying tensions between the tangata whenua, who were guided by close environmental observations — a science in itself — and the manuhiri, who were educated in a Western system.

Best also misses this opportunity to record from tangata whenua, although he later published a maramataka in his 1929 *Fishing Methods and Devices of the Maori*.[141] He comments that 'on the fifth night of the lunar month eels in running streams may be found in quieter pools, lying with their heads down-stream, and easily taken by torchlight' — information he 'obtained from Ngati-Porou natives, and had

proved it correct on several occasions in the Waikawa Stream' (just north of the Waiapu river mouth). Best follows this with the patronising statement that: 'Some very quaint beliefs in connection with fish are held by natives.'[142]

As Paratene noted, it was indeed the wrong moon, the wrong month and the wrong year for catching kōkopu. At 16:56 in the film sequence, a close-up of the hīnaki pūrangi (a one-piece woven fish trap that combines the leading net and trap) is shown in position between the mānuka stakes, with a stone sitting on top of the hīnaki to hold it down. In his 1926 publication, Te Rangihīroa describes this experiment in some detail. He notes that the hīnaki pūrangi was 'in the possession of Paratene Ngata, of Waiomatatini', and that this first weir netted pāpauma and one grayling, but no kōkopu.[143] The grayling is known by many names. Among Ngāti Porou it is known as the upokororo, a name that is sadly no longer known to local fishers. In 1932, almost a decade later, Hokianga Pahau offered evidence in the Maori Land Court:

> There was a deep hole at Utangawaka — below the Trading Cos Store [near Ruatōrea] — and extending to the mouth of Te Kahika [Stream]: filled with fish called upokororo & the fish used to go up the Kahika to the swamp which got the name of the spawning place of the upokororo.[144]

Upokororo is translated roughly as 'head full of brains'. In 1926, Te Rangihīroa notes:

> Beside papauma (a native kokopu), one grayling was caught. Grayling had not been caught in that part of the Waiapu River for over twenty years. As the grayling goes in shoals, it was held that others were about, and that our experimental weir, being close to one side of the stream, had caught a fish from a flank of fish feeding further out on the rapids. The new weir was immediately built to overlap the first, and take in almost all the rest of the stream.[145]

Given that Te Rangihīroa was a visitor to the area, it is likely that Paratene Ngata was the source for this authoritative statement. This is backed up in Andersen's diary: 'They went out early to examine the catch, & found in the hinaki a grayling — upokororo — which the Dr. said was worth a hundred kokopu, it was long since the old man [Paratene Ngata] had seen one — not since 1906 or 1916; not since which (I'm not sure).'[146]

It is evident that the locals were well aware that the upokororo was no longer common in their river, though it is unlikely that they were aware it was endangered in all of New Zealand's waterways. Te Rangihīroa's record shows that the appearance of the upokororo created a flurry of activity with the rapid extension of the weir. Although he had gone against Paratene's advice, Te Rangihīroa was buoyed by the opportunity to prove that the upokororo was still present in the Waiapu River.

Paratene Ngata attaching poha to hīnaki at Waiomatatini in 1923. Photograph by James McDonald. The thumbprint on the negative has been retained as a trace of the connection to the person who handled the original negative, possibly McDonald in 1923.

Oike

The next day, Friday 6 April, dawns fine — it is now Oike. Tawhai explains that Oike can be interpreted as 'the striking of one thing against another', a collision between Oike against Korekore, an immovable phase, with the moon at this time marked by an obstructive energy;[147] the only outcome possible is that 'they join, they meld together'.[148] Although their exchange is recorded in a humorous fashion, I see Paratene and Te Rangihīroa as coming from two different perspectives, but working together as they continue to build pā tauremu, inspired by the excitement of the previous day's catch. Andersen's lyrical observations that day belie the historic event that the stone fishing channel would deliver.

> This morn I was awake before sunrise, & lay watching the light at the mouth of the river. The hills, serrating down to the opening at the mouth, were sharp and blue & the stratus cloud above them pinky purple. Bright edged clouds radiating in masses upwards further round over Port Awanui; later the purple dropped to the hills leaving the clouds lighter in hue.

> When the sun began to touch the river flats I called Dr. Buck, who wanted to go down to his fish trap. I got up too, & we met Mr. Maxwell when near the river; he was coming away, having been down to the trap already. He had the catch with him, & there were 3 more upokororo, also a smelt; cockabullies; but no kokopu. There must be many grayling about however, since 3 more were caught. The Dr. will preserve them as specimens, since it is a rare fish now.

> In the afternoon went with the Dr. & McDonald along to the river to build another pa for catching kokopu, or anything else that might come along. The water was not so cold as I thought it would be, but the stones were quite as hard as I imagined. However, I built

a considerable length of breastwork whilst the Dr. drove the stakes, tied, on the Manuka &c & set the long net. The old man came with the buggy to carry the gear — moving camera etc. — the Dr. & I rode Te Kani's horses.[149]

The 'old man' Paratene had obviously decided that this particular day held sufficient promise to build another pā tauremu. In the film, at the 17:54 timecode, Te Rangihīroa is building the pā on his own, while Paratene is in the buggy overseeing the construction and the insertion of the hīnaki.

At 19:40, seven bridge pillars are just visible in the far distance. In 1918, the Waiapu bridge had been swept away in floods. A planned rebuild was never completed, prevented by rising riverbeds caused by sediment washing downstream from inland deforestation.[150] This marker in the background assists in assessing the changing environment over the past 100 years. As the banks of the river have shifted radically, the last remaining bridge pillar — the ferrocement form, itself a marker of colonial error — offers the only distinctive measure, other than distant hills, of these changes.

Since three more upokororo had now been caught, other local people begin building their own stone channels. The 4.5 metre hīnaki is placed into the pā kōkopu and left overnight.

Korekore-whiwhia

Saturday 7 April is Korekore-whiwhia — the twentieth day of Taiapa's lunar cycle, commencing the Korekore sequence, days that are not recommended for fishing or planting. Regardless of the season, Taiapa is consistent in his message: 'He po kino, he hau, a uta te moana' — this is not a good night for fishing, the wind will blow from the land. Taumaunu's fishing and planting guide agrees: 'E hara i te ra pai mo te ono kai mo te hi ika ranei', it is not a good day for fishing. Nevertheless, the team were up again with the sun and down to the river to set the nets. According to Andersen's diary on Saturday 7 April:

After breakfast we went back to the river, & the old man bringing on the heavy gear in the buggy. I had a pair of old boots this time, so that the stones would not be so hard. We built another pa, & our success we saw had induced some Maori to build a pa on the other channel, 300 yards or more above us; this did not interfere with our stream. The old people about would not believe we had caught grayling, & there was a suggestion they might be herrings, which they resemble in shape, & [?] too as we found later, but they are broader across the body. Moving pictures were taken of the haul, which had been replaced, being taken out of the big net.[151]

In the moving picture, at the 20:00 timecode, fish are pouring from the mouth of the hīnaki pūrangi into the sack. In this scene, Best assists Te Rangihīroa (cigarette in mouth), who looks up at the camera, as if to check the scene is being recorded. From 20:05, 15 seconds are recorded of the fish being pulled out of the net. At 20:12, Te Rangihīroa pulls at one of the fish to unblock the mouth of the trap, allowing the fish to fall into the waiting sack. The next twelve seconds of footage shows the catch of fish lying on the sack on the ground. A large blowfly lands and takes off again. The fish do not move. They appear to be already dead.

Here, as in many fishing stories, the numbers caught differ between Te Rangihīroa's report and Andersen's: 'There were 26 upokororo (grayling) & they were left in the Manuka so that a picture may be taken after breakfast.'[152] From the film frame, it seems likely that there were forty fish altogether, and of these, twenty-six were upokororo. Te Rangihīroa's notes refer to some species as abundant and plentiful: he observes that within Ngāti Porou, where the matarau bag net was used for blue maomao (*Scorpis aequipinnis*), a catch could be expected to be anywhere from 700 to 2000 fish; the lower number would be considered a poor catch.[153] The size of the scoop nets and the enormous hīnaki are indicators that target species were typically caught by these devices, on the right moon, in the right month or season, in their hundreds. By that measure, forty fish, twenty-six of them upokororo, was a poor catch. Either way, it was not a good day for the upokororo.

The fate of the upokororo

The loss of biodiversity and the loss of material and cultural wealth of the indigenous people are connected.[154] For the species whose habitats are threatened or destroyed, there are no other homes for them to migrate to. As Mississauga Nishnaabeg writer and artist Leanne Betasamosake Simpson points out: 'If a river is threatened, it's the end of the world for those fish.' In the Canadian context: 'Indigenous peoples have lived through environmental collapse on local and regional levels since the beginning of colonialism—the construction of the St Lawrence Seaway, the extermination of the buffalo in Cree and Blackfoot territories and the extinction of salmon in Lake Ontario—these were unnecessary and devastating.'[155]

The impacts of species extinction within a river system have ongoing effects in terms of loss of other species, and a loss of knowledge.[156] Does it matter to the upokororo or the river that evidence is scant? Perhaps not; extinct is extinct. But history has left little remaining presence to commune with or mourn over. Te Rangihīroa later writes: 'The upokororo (*prototroctes oxyrhynchus Günther*) was once very plentiful in the upper branches of the Waiapu, Awatere, Wharekahika, and other streams. The fish travels in shoals, and frequents rivers with a shingly bottom.'[157]

No doubt this information came from Paratene Ngata, as indicated in Te Rangihīroa's field notes. For example, under a list of freshwater fish, Te Rangihīroa gives two different names supplied by Paratene Ngata for upokororo, depending on size. His notebook says: '"rehe" for small, "tirango" for large'. Of them, Ngata says: 'Very fat—caught in summer when streams are low. Traced by marks on stones, from biting or feeding on weeds = tuhoekura.'[158] This fieldnote is developed in his text:

> The grayling feeds on the freshwater algae, especially the kind known as *tuhoe-kura*. These are plentiful in the later summer and autumn months, especially March and April. The fish then become very fat and are often cleaned by twisting a stick around the entrails, which are easily withdrawn by pulling through the vent (*kotore*).[159]

Best also notes that 'Tuokura — a mossy growth on stones in creeks, [was] said to be eaten by upokororo'.[160] The word tūōkura today refers to a type of stunted treefern; the term 'tuhoe-kura' does not appear to be in current use, perhaps because this algae has disappeared from local waterways, or because, as a specialist term, its Māori name is no longer used. Te Rangihīroa's description of upokororo as 'plentiful' is incongruous. He generally stays clear of discussing conservation or environmental matters, although he was well aware that the grayling was now very rare.

Robert McDowall, a renowned freshwater fish scientist, noted that the last recorded shoal of upokororo was caught in fish traps in the Waiapu River in 1923.[161] This marked the earliest date established for extinction as 1924.[162] One of only 'three species of marine fish reported as globally extinct' in 1923, the once plentiful, sea-migratory upokororo was found in rivers all over New Zealand.[163] A 2019 study by Lee and Perry of the causes of upokororo extinction points to a perfect storm between amphidromous fish dynamics and habitat degradation.[164]

Given the excitement, it becomes all the more remarkable that there are no surviving photographs of this historic catch. McDonald clearly planned on taking a picture, but there is no evidence that he did. His photographs and filming of the building of the weir indicate he was present the previous day, so we know he was there when the fish were caught. Perhaps they were taken by the women to prepare for a meal before McDonald could make his image. Andersen's diary entry demonstrates the entanglements between the purpose of the activities, the local knowledge and the ignorance that accompanies a declining species.

> We went ahead with our pa, & about an hour or more after midday had finished, enclosing the whole branch of the river, & catching 6 more grayling whilst working. Quite ready to go home, being very hungry, could not help admiring the enthusiasm of Te Rangi Hiroa, engaging on all this work, partly in pursuit of scientific knowledge, partly for fun. It was something that the expedition should prove the existence of a fish that had not been seen by the elder people for from 16–20 years, many had never seen it at all.[165]

> 'It almost seems sacrilege,' said the Dr. in the evening when we had the fish for tea, 'eating a rare fish like this; they ought all be preserved as specimens.'[166]

This fish is known for turning to jelly not long after it comes out of the water. Like the fate of the upokororo, it is most likely that the jellified nitrate negatives of this catch, if McDonald took any photographs of it, have since disappeared. The records now show that this meal was a last supper of sorts, for the upokororo. On 8 April, as the moon entered the third quarter, the nets were pulled from the river for fear of rain. This is Korekore day, a time of scarcity, and no more upokororo were caught.

When the old net lies in a heap, a new net goes fishing

The remastered film scan is a compilation of all surviving nitrate film footage recorded by James McDonald of the 1923 expedition. Only twelve seconds of film footage of the upokororo have survived. In the fish trap sequence, there is a view of fish on the ground, showing what appears to be upokororo as well as other species. The sharper resolution makes subject identification promising, so, in 2019, I sent a screenshot to Graeme Atkins, a Te Papa Atawhai Department of Conservation ranger, for verification. He forwarded it to freshwater fish scientist Dr Jane Goodman, who through this image was able to identify the upokororo.[167] As with the now-extinct upokororo, it is highly unlikely that any other image of the fish has survived the intervening century.

> Ka pū te ruha, ka hao te rangatahi.
>
> Set aside the old net, let the new net go fishing.[168]

Like a net designed to catch fish, so too a camera, or a recording machine. Te Rangihīroa and Ngata were the progressive leaders of their generation, crafting contemporary nets to capture ancient tikanga, in the hope that this might be of benefit to future generations.

One morning at Waiomatatini, the Ngāti Porou elder Iehu Nukunuku, renowned as one of the few surviving players of taonga pūoro, was watching Te Rangihīroa making a closed-loop single-strand net while sitting on the verandah at the Bungalow. The photograph at right, shows the loop of the net wrapped around his socked foot as he weaves. Collected by McDonald, a woven net from the expedition now lies in a drawer in Te Papa's collection (ME004529) — possibly this one. Having made extensive inquiries, Te Rangihīroa thought that he had exhausted all possibilities for making this kind of net. However, Nukunuku, when he observed his technique, said, 'I do it this way', and proceeded to show him a different, double-stranded method. As Te Rangihīroa commented:

Possibly if one practised in the early morning with aged musicians or craftsmen looking on, other methods or variations might be resurrected. Therefore it were better to put on record what methods we know than wait for others that we know not of.[169]

Like Te Rangihīroa, I have sat with elders, walked the river and crafted my research net. Like McDonald, I have observed, with my camera, to leave traces of knowledge for the future generations. As Ngata advised, I have used my technological tools in conjunction with the whakapapa from my ancestors as taonga tapu to create visual stories for the next generation. Finally, while I have cast my net widely, trying to locate an image of the upokororo, or to find the names of the elders in these images, it is only through publishing this text that further information may come to light. Therefore, as imperfect as this particular suite of narratives may be, I hope they invite other stories to emerge and be shared.

Hoake ki te kāinga
Ko taku ika ki a koe
Ko te ngākau ki au.

Go on to my home
My fish will be for you
And the entrails for me.[170]

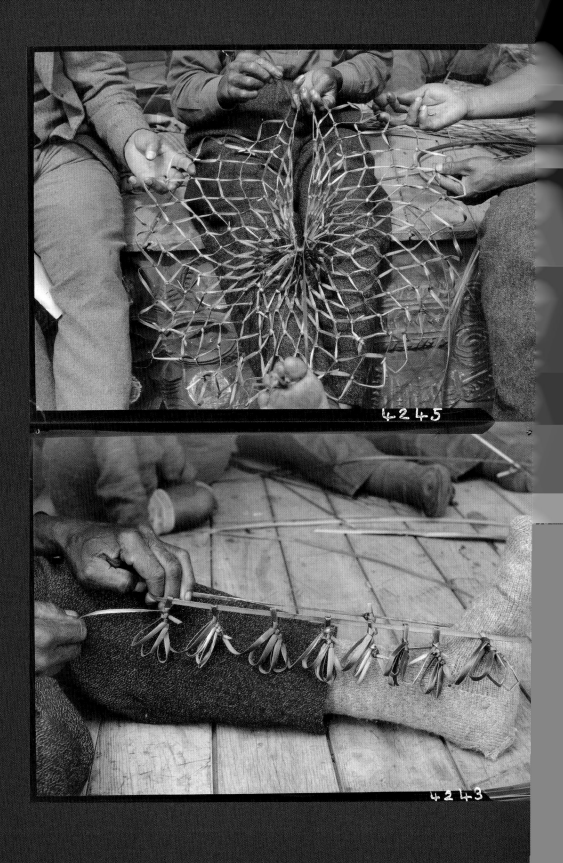

LEFT: A still from footage taken by James McDonald of the
rare, and soon to be extinct, native fish known as upokororo,
as well as mullet and other fish species, on the banks of the
Waiapu River in 1923.

Tōrehe net being woven by three people
at Waiomatatini in 1923.

Iehu Nukunuku demonstrates net weaving techni
to Te R̄angihīroa on the verandah at Waiomatati

'ALIVE WITH RHYTHMIC FORCE'

ANNE SALMOND
BILLIE LYTHBERG
CONAL McCARTHY

6

Apirana Ngata leads the haka at the Waitangi
centennial celebrations in 1940, Waitangi.

For Apirana Ngata and Te Rangihīroa, the 1923 Tairāwhiti expedition[1] was a turning point. For Te Rangihīroa, the journey led him away from Aotearoa, and towards the international discipline of anthropology. In June 1923 he delivered a lecture on 'The Old Maori: His Arts and Crafts' at the Auckland Institute, illustrated with films made by McDonald during the Whanganui and Tairāwhiti expeditions, and was 'heartily applauded at the conclusion of a most illuminating lecture'.[2] In August he applied for leave to attend the Pacific Science Congress in Melbourne and Sydney, where he presented a paper on Māori clothing, showed some of McDonald's East Coast slides, including those depicting Riwai Te Miringa o Rangi making the tāruke kōura, and gave a lecture on Māori migrations, the forerunner to his books *The Coming of the Maori* and *Vikings of the Sunrise*.

At the congress, Te Rangihīroa met leading scientists from around the Pacific Rim, and leading anthropologists, including Alfred Cort Haddon from the University of Cambridge, who he describes as 'a delightful old man, with thick white hair and dark eyebrows, a somewhat hesitating speech, a fund of humour, and a don't-give-a-damn kind of manner'. As he reported in a long letter to Ngata, Te Rangihīroa was lionised by his colleagues. He was given the honour of delivering the only public lecture during the congress at Melbourne; and when he reported to the congress on the bill that would establish the Board of Maori Ethnological Research in New Zealand, noting that 'one of the Native Races of the Pacific is assisting in carrying out one of the objects of the congress and furthermore the idea originated from within themselves', there was deafening applause. Haddon himself was so impressed that he announced that 'he regretted he wasn't a Maori'.[3]

At the Sydney congress, Te Rangihīroa met a number of Australian and American anthropologists, including Herbert Gregory from the Bishop Museum in Hawai'i, and he showed McDonald's films in the Australian Museum. He delivered another public lecture illustrated by slides from the Tairāwhiti expedition, including an image of himself and Ngata weaving a tukutuku panel, 'keeping alive the ancient arts and crafts', that was greeted with rapturous applause.

He confided in his letter to Ngata: 'On the whole, Api, I can honestly say we came out of the show more than holding our own. Whether the uneasy consciences of the Great Races are aroused or not, I cannot but say that anything to do with the Maori Race was met not only by the scientists but by the Australian public with acclamation.'[4]

A fifth Dominion Museum Ethnological Expedition to Taupō had been planned for 1924, but was postponed because of flooding. Te Rangihīroa, McDonald and Andersen all planned to go, but Best was ill, and he was intent on producing various Dominion Museum monographs.[5] That year, Te Rangihīroa's international contacts bore fruit when Gregory invited him to become an associate at the Bishop Museum and join their expedition to the Cook Islands. The ethnological expedition to Taupō had been delayed until 1926,[6] but by then Te Rangihīroa had turned his sights towards the Pacific. The following year the Bishop Museum offered him five years' fulltime research in Polynesia,[7] marking the beginning of a long and distinguished career in Pacific anthropology that included extensive fieldwork in the Cook Islands and Sāmoa, culminating in his appointment as Visiting Professor at Yale University (1932) and Director of the Bishop Museum (1936). During his long absence from New Zealand, Te Rangihīroa stayed in close touch with Ngata, often writing to him about his fieldwork and his exchanges with international anthropologists. In September 1926, for instance, he wrote to Ngata from Rarotonga:

> As you said in your last we start off with the atmosphere. The Polynesian corpuscles carry us beyond the barrier that takes a Pakeha some time to scale and the key of speech cuts out some other months. Then the plaiting technique of Wanganui, the net strokes of Waiapu etc. etc. cuts out one or two more months that Stokes will not allow for. I will be pleased to think that the Board's first venture in Polynesian research, will compare favourably with the Bishop Museum publications.[8]

In March 1927 he again confided to Ngata:

> I have worked up to the stage that I am dissatisfied with myself and want to do the best work of which I am capable. This lies in the field of anthropology. The past [studies] have gradually trained me for it. I think the time is now ripe when I should devote myself entirely to it and keep up our reputation in this branch of scientific work.

> I know I can more than hold my own with other workers in the Polynesian field... In Polynesian research, it is right and fitting that the highest branch of the Polynesian race should be in the forefront and not leave the bulk of the investigations to workers who have not got the inside angle that we have. They miss things that are significant to us.[9]

A year later, he wrote to Ngata from Hawai'i:

> I am at present representing primitive man and relying on my instincts. I listen to these other theories about myself, not that I accept them in their entirety but in order that I may look at myself as others say they look at me. I want to get their way of approach in order that I may approach myself without their assistance and without having read into me things that I don't believe I ever felt. As the Americans say, 'It's a hard line of boats.'[10]

Clearly, Te Rangihīroa found it difficult to deal with the ethnocentricism of Euro-American anthropological scholars, sharing his frustrations with Ngata, and encouraging him to share his own insights. In June 1928, Ngata responded:

> I have now to square up to your very high opinion of my capacity to write in English on the Social Organisation of the Maori. I am testing this out for my own satisfaction in a paper on 'The Application of the Genealogical Method to early New Zealand History' for the Wellington branch of the Historical Association. It is an endeavor to justify the pleas that collections of Maori whakapapa should rank with other material among the archives.

> [WHR] Rivers wrote of the Social Organisation of the Torres St. people, basing all his findings on extremely scrappy genealogical tables. If he had struck folk like the Maoris, whose education for the most part consisted of memorizing and coordinating whakapa what a noise he would of made with them in the scientific world! Rivers' estimate of the part that New Zealand should take in carrying out a full ethnographic survey of the native races under its rule should be acted up to.

War monument at Rangitukia, near the mouth of the
Waiapu River, 2020. Photograph by Natalie Robertson.

Engari kei hea he kai mahi mo tenei mo tenei maara? Ma tetahi tino tohunga rawa e whakarapopoto nga take kua kaupapa i te tini tangata kua tuhituhi nei mo taua mo te Maori me te whakaatu ki te ao i nga wahi tahapa o ena, me te waiho tahapa o ena me te waiho i nga wahi e matapouri ana.

But where is the specialist for this undertaking? It calls for an exceptional scholar to write a synopsis of the knowledge that has been written down by many people about us the Maori and it should contain a critique so that the world would know the inaccuracies, the inadequacies and doubts about some of the writings.[11]

A month later, Te Rangihīroa responded with his own reflections on metropolitan anthropology:

He [the anthropologist] is a collector with bottles ready labelled and everything must go in one or other of these bottles, the bottles that have been labelled in the university class room and not in the field that the labeller never saw.

No! Ma taua ano e wehewehe nga taonga, ma taua e whiriwhiri ki tewhea kete ki tewhea kete. Ma taua ano e raranga he kete hou mo nga taonga kaore e tika kia whaona ki nga kete tawhito. Ko wai o te Pakeha e maia ki te ki mai kia taua kei te he ta korua patu i te kai nei.

It is you and I who must separate out the items and sort them into each basket. It is you and I who must weave a new basket for the items which it would be wrong to place in the basket. Who of the Pakeha would dare to say to us, 'Your destroying of this food is wrong [i.e. you are wrong].'[12]

For Ngata, however, the journey was all about the revitalisation of te iwi Māori, and in particular, his own East Coast people. Shortly after the fourth Dominion Museum Ethnological Expedition left Waiomatatini, a long article celebrating their achievements, written by either Ngata or Wī Repa, appeared in the *Evening Post*:

Regret was expressed by nearly all the elders of the Ngatiporou people that such a visit was not made years ago, before the real men of knowledge passed away... It will be seen that the visit of this party of ethnologists to the East Coast has resulted in the recovery of much material that was on the verge of being lost. From an ethnological point of view the mission was a success. But in other directions the expedition has borne fruit. The Ngati Porou has suddenly been aroused from his indifference of many years to take an interest in his own life story as a section of mankind.[13]

From this time on, Ngata promoted ethnology, not just as a way of preserving ancestral arts — mōteatea, haka, karakia, whakairo, tukutuku, kōwhaiwhai, weaving and fishing, for instance — but as a means of inspiring pride and active engagement in Māoritanga, in being Māori. The practice and preservation of ancestral knowledge increasingly became a key element in his programme to revitalise Māori communities, ensuring that Māori people would survive and thrive *as Māori* into the future.

Over the years that followed, Ngata pursued this programme, 'kia ora ai te iwi Maori' 'to give life to the Māori people' with unflagging zeal. During the next two decades, he effectively took over the discipline of anthropology in New Zealand. In October 1923, he established the Board of Maori Ethnological Research Te Poari Whakapapa, with Te Rangihīroa as one of its members.[14] In 1924 he published a collection of ninety mōteatea; and he established the Maori Purposes Fund Board, with money from unclaimed rents from Māori land, to support Māori and Pacific ethnological research.[15] The board published many of Best's writings, for which Best was grateful although he was ambivalent about the Māori control of research funding.[16]

In 1926, inspired by Ngata, the Board of Maori Ethnological Research urged Auckland University College to include Māori as a BA subject — with no success. That same year, the Maori Arts and Crafts Act was passed, establishing the School of Maori Arts and Crafts in Rotorua and supporting the building of whare whakairo in many parts of New Zealand. In 1927 Ngata was knighted. During the following year he published the first volume of his four-volume collection *Nga Moteatea*; presented a paper, 'The Genealogical Method', to the Wellington Historical Association; and was appointed Minister of Native Affairs.[17]

While Ngata fostered ancestral arts and crafts, he was equally determined that his people should master contemporary technologies and skills — agriculture, horticulture, medicine, the law and other professions — and make a good living for themselves and their families. Over the next six years as Minister of Native Affairs, he led major initiatives in Māori education and land development, both lifelong passions, and set up scholarships and schemes in different parts of the country to foster sheep farming, cropping and dairying so that Māori could take care of their remaining lands — arousing acute jealousies and resentment in the process.[18]

In 1934 Ngata was ousted from Cabinet after an inquiry into the financial management of these schemes, although it was found that he personally had not been involved in any irregularities. When he heard about the inquiry, Te Rangihīroa was outraged, writing from Yale:

> The attack by the Audit Department and its various officials brings up to the surface a very nasty phase of Western culture. Western culture has accepted as an axiom that any member of their race or races is superior by that very fact to any member of a Native race no matter how gifted that Native may be in his own culture. By impressing this superiority complex on the races they are supposed to take care of, they have been able to govern with a minimum of grey matter.

> The Native is a fine fellow so long as he accepts an inferior position but as soon as he competes, all sorts of statements are circulated as to his inability to do without the guidance of the white man. He is constitutionally lazy, he has no business capacity, he is dishonest with money, he is shocking in his morals.

> We had it in the war when Herbert, to hide his own incapacity, told the Generals that the men were fine soldiers but he could not trust his officers. The generals believed him and the Maori Contingent or rather the subsequent Pioneer Battalion was made use of to give Pakeha officers promotion.

> So your Civil Service is angered that you have done without them in order to accomplish something. Nothing will restore them but an attack on the whole scheme to show that Maori cannot run things without Pakeha guidance and supervision. Of course they would be delighted to discredit yourself, Tai Mitchell and any of the Maori leaders. It is a purely selfish move to prevent the Maori from becoming too strong in competition.[19]

Despite the inquiry, Ngata remained a Member of Parliament until 1946, when he lost the Eastern Maori seat. For the rest of his life he dedicated himself to fostering the artistic and cultural renaissance that he and Te Rangihīroa had helped to instigate.

In 1943, Ngata wrote to Timutimu Tawhai of Te Whānau ā Apanui, who had written him a letter expressing his unease about sharing Lieutenant Ngārimu VC's whakapapa in print:

> So, my dear friend Timutimu, I put you on record in the best possible setting for the sentiments, which have been drawn from our innermost being, which some few understand and all must respect and admire.

> The time is long past, when the heirlooms and the treasures of Maori culture can be hidden in the memories of a fond few or in laboriously compiled manuscripts dedicated to descendants, who may never prize them.

> They can be forgotten, my friend, and lost. And they should not be lost. So you and I and others should have them kept, as the Pakeha keeps his records and knowledge, in print on bookshelves, that those who care may read and learn.[20]

After their long and intimate correspondence, in 1949 Ngata and Te Rangihīroa were finally reunited when Te Rangihīroa returned to New Zealand for a visit. Although Te Rangihīroa was suffering from cancer, he was as eloquent and charming as ever, and Ngata as resolute and charismatic. For these hoa aroha (loving friends), it was their last meeting. Ngata died the following year, and Te Rangihīroa died in 1951.

As for James McDonald, after returning to Wellington from Waiomatatini he set to work to assemble a collection of Māori taonga to be sent to the New Zealand Section of the 1924 Empire Exhibition in London, including artefacts purchased from Rihipeti Aperaniko of Koroniti, 'who helped us greatly in preparing articles for photography during our expedition to the Whanganui River District in 1921'.[21] In 1926 McDonald retired from the Museum, and when the Maori Arts and Crafts Act passed at the end of that year, he was appointed one of eleven members of the Board of Maori Arts, along with Ngata, Te Rangihīroa, Tai Mitchell (Ngata's Te Arawa close friend and colleague) and Archdeacon Herbert Williams, who helped to establish the Rotorua School of Maori Arts and Crafts. At this time, too, McDonald argued for the use of Māori motifs 'alive with rhythmic force', to evoke the landscape and plants of New Zealand in public buildings.

> Maori decorative designs, with their oppositions of lines and spaces, their rhythmic sequences of curve and counter-curve, of thrust and counter-thrust, are expressive of the vitality and virility of both Maori and pakeha. The forms used seem to me to be the natural incarnation of our environment. They are the essence distilled from our surroundings, and are, therefore, part and parcel of every New Zealander.
>
> From the shapes of firs and pines arose the love for certain architectural forms the Gothic architects built on their cathedrals, but from the ponga, the mamaku, the ngaio, the karaka, the pohutukawa, and other New Zealand trees arose the love for the curvilinear forms we find in the decorative art of the Maori.
>
> It is fitting that designs characteristic of our country should be wrought in the interior decoration of the portion of the Parliamentary buildings yet to be built.[22]

Passionately fond of film, McDonald bought a picture theatre in Eastbourne, Wellington, where, as his granddaughter Joyce Thorpe recalled, 'it cost sixpence to go on Saturday afternoons. All the kids went to watch silent films [with] captions.'[23] He lived for a time from this income and from the rent from several houses he and his wife May had purchased in the city; and remained active in the world of art, especially Māori carving.

In 1930, according to family accounts, McDonald became involved in Alexander Markey's infamous film *Hei Tiki*,[24] which Ngata and the Board of Maori Arts had supported, and which was largely shot around Lake Taupō.[25] When Markey fled the country with the film that had been shot and with many ancestral taonga, leaving a trail of debt behind him,[26] McDonald was one of the victims.

After losing their houses and the picture theatre, McDonald and May shifted to a bach at Tokaanu, where they could live cheaply, growing and preserving their own vegetables, and fishing from a rowboat on the lake. In 1989, their granddaughter, Joyce Thorpe, told her daughter Anne Salmond:

> …he even grew his own tobacco. There were plums, strawberries, red currants, black currants, all the vegetables you could think of. They had their preserved fruits and jams in jars. They'd get beer bottles from the pub, and take the tops off with a hot wire loop. These were covered with brown paper pasted on, and set on open shelves…An old friend came to Tokaanu to stay with them. Grandma made lovely fruit cakes, and people gave them trout. When he said to his friend that they had no money, he said, 'What do you mean? You're living like kings!'
>
> …He knew all the characters round about. It was a very happy atmosphere. He had started a carving school, because there were no carvers at Tokaanu to teach the young people…He used to visit the people at Tokaanu village. While I was there, Te Heuheu took me and Grandpa into the family mausoleum to show us the greenstone mere that would change colour when a chieftain died. Grandpa was well liked up there.

As the Māori-language newspaper *Te Waka Karaitiana* reported, 'He came to renew his acquaintanceship with the place where he, and the Hon. Te Heuheu had had fellowship in other days, in connection with the production of one of the Maori films which was produced at Tokaanu a few years back.'[27] In 1931 McDonald was invited to submit a proposal and costings for a 'model maori pa' for the New Zealand Centennial International Exhibition, producing watercolour drawings and a handwritten version of the proposal.[28]

During his time at Tokaanu, McDonald worked with Te Heuheu Tūkino V on notes on the 'Art of the Maori' (now held in the Hocken Library),[29] and helped to establish the Tuwharetoa School of Maori Arts and Crafts, an initiative parallel to the Rotorua school established under the 1926 Act.[30] Despite his lobbying efforts in Wellington, the Tūwharetoa school received no government recognition or financial support, and after McDonald died, the school came to an end.

He also worked on the refurbishment and decoration of several whare whakairo in the area, including black and white sketches in his distinctive style as medallions in the tukutuku panels in Okahukura at Otūkou pā, Lake Rotoaira;[31] and contributed to the work on Pūhaorangi at Tokaanu.[32]

When James McDonald died at Tokaanu in 1935, *Te Waka Karaitiana* printed an obituary, 'A Priest of High Crafts Passes', describing him as 'an artist of no mean Maori':

> The Maori people, their customs and equipment were the things of chief delight to this man. He was also an expert Maori carver, and no one could have detected that his carvings had not been done by a Maori. Although he was advanced in years when death overtook him, he was still learning the Maori language…He was there [in Tokaanu] painting his pictures, making his carvings, and gathering up the crumbs out of the baskets of the sacred house of Maori learning, when the call of the far distance came to him. [33]

The legacy of the expeditions

In the wake of the expeditions, in 1925 Best handed over the editorship of the *Journal of the Polynesian Society* to Johannes Andersen, a move that disturbed Ngata. He wrote to Te Rangihīroa, 'I am dishing up the whakapapa matter to put beside Nga Moteatea for the Litt D. Your comments make one hopeful of approaching the sacred tuahu [altar] of the JPS with less fear and trepidation. Under Andersen it is difficult to know how the Journal will line up.'[34]

In 1927 Andersen published his monograph on Māori string figures, although because he did not speak Māori, this did not include the chants and stories associated with the figures; and another on Māori music (1934). Ngata did not approve

of Andersen's work on mōteatea, writing to Te Rangihīroa:

> Andersen did his best work with the String Games. In regard to the songs he has a kink about bird music and a fatal facility for versification which take his mind off the reality of the Maori poetry. He has much in common with Cowan, except that Cowan is more readable. Andersen has a literary pose which offends the honest seeker after truth.[35]

In his role as Turnbull Librarian, Andersen raised funding to expand the Library's collections. His interests were eclectic, including bird song (he often whistled bird calls to his audiences, who loved it), place names, numismatics, native flora and fauna, poetry, local history and Danish literature. A popular speaker and broadcaster, Andersen was also a prolific writer on a wide range of topics. He published *Myths and Legends of the Polynesians* in 1928, following this up with *Polynesian Literature: Maori Poetry (Waiata and Tangi)* (1946) and *The Maori Tohunga and His Spirit World* (1948). Given Andersen's lack of fluency in Māori, these publications annoyed Ngata, and in 1946 Andersen was relieved of his position as editor of the *Journal of the Polynesian Society*. After a long illness, he died in Auckland in 1962.

For Elsdon Best, the Dominion Museum expeditions marked the winding down of a long and prolific career as New Zealand's foremost ethnologist. Now frail and increasingly tetchy, he did not venture out into the field again after the 1923 expedition, but remained at the Dominion Museum, where he devoted his remaining time to writing up his many monographs, based on material in his notebooks gleaned from tribal informants and often illustrated by McDonald's photographs, completing and publishing no fewer than seven books between 1924 and 1929.[36]

Many European and American anthropologists moved from the armchair to the field, but Best had done the reverse: he spent fifteen years in the Urewera, then worked for twenty years at the Dominion Museum. During his time there, Best always mixed desk-bound research with trips into tribal regions to talk to elders and observe cultural practices. The time he spent in the field far exceeded that of most of his international peers, giving him a deep understanding of Māori language and tikanga.

Best's lifelong study of Māori life impressed his international peers and many New Zealanders, winning him the Hector Medal from the New Zealand Institute and support and funding from Ngata and his allies in the Board of Maori Ethnological Research and the Polynesian Society. But by the 1920s and 1930s, younger, academically trained anthropologists such as HD Skinner and Raymond Firth were increasingly sceptical of Best's dated methods, and Māori scholars and tribal experts had a different understanding of the data he had gathered, putting it to different uses — revitalisation rather than salvage.

As Ngata wrote of the British anthropologist and collector August Pitt-Rivers' account of his trip up the Whanganui River with Best in 1924, the intentions of Pākehā ethnographers differed from Māori scholars like himself and Te Rangihīroa:

> Such a work as that of Pitt-Rivers opens up a very wide field to chaps like myself, who are perforce immersed in the problems of today and yet are desirous of touching bottom, of recovering from the phases that survive and persist today something of the polity of pre-pakeha days ...
>
> I rather think that in moments of introspection you and I, Bal [Balneavis] and many others must acknowledge that our hearts are not with this policy of imposing pakeha culture-forms on our people. Our recent activities would indicate a contrary determination to preserve the old-culture-forms as the foundations on which to reconstruct Maori life and hopes.[37]

In 1927 Ngata reported that Best's age and health meant 'active field work is not possible', adding that it was 'doubtful, also, whether he can now maintain the standard of his former studies'.[38] At the same time, some Pākehā researchers recognised that the baton was now passing to a younger generation of Māori scholars; as Andersen acknowledged, 'when the Polynesian workers themselves enter the field, as they surely will, we stammering, thumb-fingered pakeha may stand aside and rejoice in the day-dawn'.[39] Anthropologist Jeff Sissons has commented that in spite of Best's dated racial assumptions, by

the time he died in 1931, '[his] work was already taking on a new significance, informing and giving impetus to a Māori cultural renaissance'.[40] In a letter to Te Rangihīroa, announcing Best's death, Ngata gave his own, sober assessment of Best's achievements:

> While at Palmerston I received a wire from Bal that old Best had passed away. He had been ailing for some weeks — had a slight stroke also. You know all that the old chap stood for in his life — he had reached his limit some time ago. He has left a mass of material, mostly published or ready for publication, on which students can work and from which they can probably produce better results than he could have ...
>
> But his name will on the whole be associated with honest work, the laborious piecing together of legend, song and tradition by one who entered more than any other pakeha collector into the Native mind.[41]

Although Te Rangihīroa, Apirana Ngata, Elsdon Best, James McDonald and Johannes Andersen have long since died, they live on in the films and photographs made by McDonald, together with the many Māori people from the communities they visited. In the same way, the voices of those people still speak on and sing, sometimes clearly and sometimes muffled and inaudible, from the wax cylinder recordings that were collected. These traces of the relationships that shaped the expeditions still travel through space and time, spinning into the future.

This is the stuff of whakapapa; the layering of time–space coordinates that are so often reduced to 'genealogies' but are more aptly described as a 'veritable ontology'[42] — a world patterned by intricate, dynamic networks of relations among people, living and dead, and between people and other life forms. As Natalie Robertson has observed, 'in this spiral of time–space, photographs or films made in the distant past are taonga ... not dead or lifeless objects but are constantly in a process of *becoming form* as things with their own agency and interconnected relations'.[43] Nearly a century later, Riwai Te Miringa o Rangi and other ancestors 'speak' from machine-made pictures that carry something of them from place to place, from generation to generation, 'hei taonga mā ngā uri whakatipu', as a treasure for the rising generation.

Emerging from the darkness

The word 'photograph', from its Greek roots, means 'light recording'.[44] Photographic and filmic processes capture light: indeed, the light that touches the camera's subjects is the light that activates and is absorbed by volatile chemicals on the surface of negatives. Glass-plate photography, in particular, was understood by Māori to produce not merely illustrations but also manifestations of people and places. Glass-plate negatives themselves emerged from the darkness of a camera's body transformed, harnessing light to materialise presence.[45]

Thereafter, prints could be made by passing light through these negatives and onto a substrate of photographic paper or cellulose in a process of activation and transformation; and bright light allowed films to be projected—every projection a light-driven animation. The Māori descriptor for the products of the camera is whakaāhua, which conveys not only the physical outputs of photofilmic capture but also their acquisition of form in the process of transformation.[46]

From at least the late nineteenth century onwards, photographs and film images—even those produced over and over as multiples, or reproduced as poor copies—have been embraced by Māori as holding something of the mauri of their subjects. This concept of radiating energy seems especially applicable to photography and film, recording and absorbing light as it reflects off people, places and things in order to distil, be-still, or—in the case of film—animate something of their presence.

For this energy to be fully released, however, the films and photographs must be reunited with the descendants of those depicted. This can be a formidable task. In 2010, Linda Tuhiwai Smith spoke to an audience of Māori archivists and curators, describing how ancestral taonga are scattered across Aotearoa and around the globe. These taonga, she said, are 'bits and pieces all over the place'; it is vital to reconnect them to the people, 'making us whole again'.[47]

As Ngata had wished, during the Dominion Museum Ethnological Expeditions almost 200 wax cylinder recordings of waiata, karakia, whaikōrero and other oral art forms were made; and thousands of feet of nitrate film and many hundreds of photographs were taken by McDonald. Field notebooks and journals were kept and reports written by team members; and a number of artefacts were collected and taken back to the Dominion Museum. Afterwards, the surviving records were scattered across a number of different institutions and archives; some were lost, while information about particular individuals and places featured in the photographs and films is often missing or incorrect.

The photographic plates and negatives, for instance, were stored at the Dominion Museum where, over time, some of the nitrate negatives decomposed. In 1990, a curator alerted Anne Salmond and Merimeri Penfold to the damage. With funding from a University of Auckland research grant,[48] they visited the National Art Gallery and Museum Te Whare Taonga o Aotearoa—as the Dominion Museum was then called—to discuss the care of the McDonald photographic collection.[49] After receiving a warm response from Arapata Hakiwai, then curator of Māori Collections,[50] and with his strong support, funding was allocated for the restoration, copying and cataloguing of the photographs taken by McDonald.

At the Museum, photographic curators Eymard Bradley and Ross O'Rorke carried out this work over a number of years, and June Starke, a former librarian at the Alexander Turnbull Library and a volunteer at the museum, carried out extensive research into the expeditions in the Museum archives. Hakiwai urged that high-quality prints in albums should be returned to 'the people from whence they originated. The museum has been lacking in "giving back" taonga, especially historical photographs, to the areas that they were taken as it is seen as a waste of money to many people. The public relations, tribal networking and liaison must surely be in the interests of our museum to fully support this kaupapa.'[51]

Other photographs from the expeditions found their way into the Alexander Turnbull Library, no doubt through the agency of Johannes Andersen. An album of prints of the Whanganui expedition photographs, almost certainly compiled by McDonald himself, was gifted to the Turnbull Library by his daughter Marjorie McDonald.[52] The Turnbull Library also holds Best's field notebooks from the Whanganui and Tairāwhiti expeditions, and Andersen's diary also.

FOLLOWING PAGE: Six of James McDonald's negatives from the fourth expedition in 1923 laid out on a lightbox at Te Papa. Top row, from left to right: A view of the Waiapu valley; a three-quarter portrait of Paratene Ngata; the Māori room carved by Hone Ngātoto at the Bungalow, Waiomatatini, seen on page 209. Lower row: The three Waiapu Valley landscapes that appear on pages 236–37.

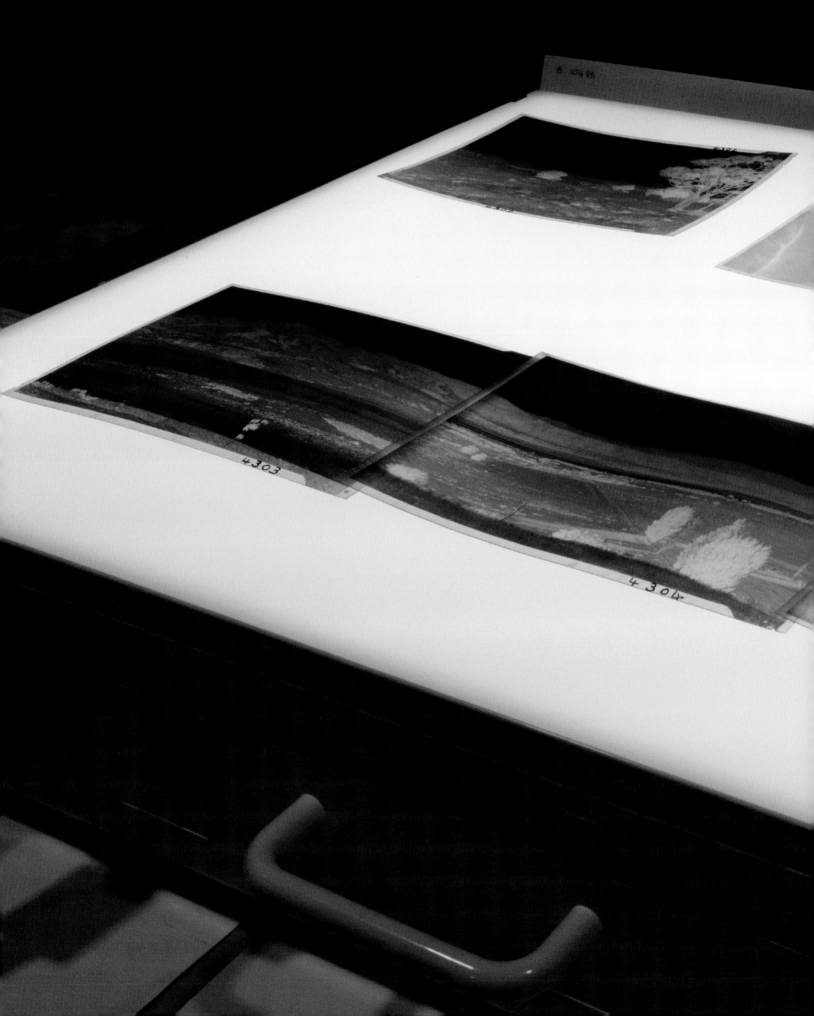

In November 1989, the National Library mounted an exhibition of McDonald's photographs, with Jo Torr as the primary researcher. Images from the expeditions, superbly printed and displayed, indicated the richness and scale of the photographic collections at the National Museum and the Alexander Turnbull Library.

As a small child during visits to Wellington, James McDonald's great-granddaughter Anne Salmond often played with a collection of his photographs, sketches, marbled notebooks and other family memorabilia, stored in cardboard boxes in her grandmother's garage. These are now held in the Salmond Family Archive. Her great-aunt Marjorie McDonald often talked to her about McDonald, and about Apirana Ngata and Te Heuheu Tūkino V, taking her to see his model pā at the Dominion Museum — experiences that first sparked her curiosity about te ao Māori.[53] For Salmond it was spine-tingling to return as an adult to visit the kaitaka worn by Paitini and given to McDonald at the Hui Aroha, and a hoeroa (long curved weapon) that McDonald had carved, now held in Otago Museum.

In 1997 when his great-great-granddaughter Amiria Salmond studied social anthropology at the University of Cambridge, she studied the family collection, along with other material, writing a research paper on the Dominion Museum expeditions that in many ways, inspired this present project.[54] Marjorie McDonald donated an extensive collection of McDonald's cartoons, sketches and manuscripts to Otago Museum in 1955 through HD Skinner, who had asked her to record memories of her father's life.[55] This collection is now held in the Hocken Library Uare Taoka o Hākena at the University of Otago.

Another major collection of photographs and other items from the Dominion Museum expeditions is held in Hawai'i at the Bishop Museum in Honolulu, where it was taken by Te Rangihīroa. The 'Buck Archive' — a vast collection of draft papers and publications, field notebooks, letters, memos, fine drawings and ephemera — includes several field notebooks from the expeditions as well as Te Rangihīroa's larger 'Technical Notebook', and Ngata's typescript, which he described as 'dishing up the whakapapa matter to put beside Nga Moteatea for the Litt D'[56] (published in the Appendix). These, like the few artefacts that can still be connected to the expeditions, are direct links with the past — thrilling to see, to hold, and to explore with gloved hands and delicate page turning.

Separate from the archives at the Bishop Museum, Te Rangihīroa's extraordinary 'Ethnographic Photo File' remains in the staff workrooms. Treated as a working tool, in a series of steel filing cabinets the file contains his working database of information on Polynesian objects and taonga, including those in museum collections as well as others encountered during fieldwork. One set of drawers holds his own research photographs, including the photographs from the Dominion Museum expeditions, along with those of fellow Bishop Museum staff members, and images clipped from other publications (a literal cut-and-paste) or received from other museums in response to requests and queries. The photographs are mounted on cards and filed according to Pacific island groups. Some objects have been taken from different angles to reveal form, carving and technique. By 1938, the collection already included 2464 photographs.[57]

Cards with Te Rangihīroa's descriptions of each object are filed in another set of drawers. These follow the same numbering system, so that a researcher can easily match the photo with the description. Often, Te Rangihīroa added his own detailed sketches of the objects and provided meticulous notes based on his observations and, less often, his particular methods of unravelling and reconstructing weaving and lashing. Here, as he promised Ngata, Te Rangihīroa was separating out ancestral objects and putting them into baskets of his own devising,[58] weaving a new (old) system of classification. The Ethnographic Photo File is a taonga in its own right, updated throughout the years and still often used. In the neighbouring storeroom, Te Rangihīroa's kahu kiwi with its fine tāniko borders and a strip of white kiwi feathers at bottom left has been preserved. It is extremely rare and precious: white kiwi are a symbol of new beginnings and renewal — a fitting adornment for Te Rangihīroa.

The new net goes fishing

In 2016, when the Te Ao Hou project began, funded by a Marsden Fund grant awarded by Te Apārangi Royal Society of New Zealand, the research team — Anne Salmond, Paul Tapsell, Conal McCarthy, Amiria Salmond, Billie Lythberg and Natalie Robertson —

walked in the footsteps of the Dominion Museum Ethnological Expedition team, seeking to reconstruct their movements. Researcher Gina Matchitt and the rest of the team worked with curators and archivists — including Athol McCredie at Te Papa; Paul Diamond at the Turnbull Library; Marie O'Connell at the Archive of Māori and Pacific Sound at the University of Auckland; Honiana Love and Lawrence Wharerau at Ngā Taonga Sound and Vision; Leah Caldeira, Karla Morgan; and Kamalu du Preez at the Bishop Museum; Dudley Meadows at Tairāwhiti Museum; Sandy Nepia at Whanganui District Library and Zandria Taare and Jessica Jacobs at the HB Williams Memorial Library in Gisborne — seeking to discover the sequence in which all of the surviving photographs from the Dominion Museum Ethnological Expeditions were made.

The team also brought together information recorded at the time in field notebooks, journals, reports and notes on the wax cylinder recordings, and where possible, collaborated with descendants to identify particular individuals and places. This enterprise is ongoing, with much work for others to do. Nevertheless, our team has brought together as much of this information as possible in this book, and on master catalogue sheets for each photograph taken during the expeditions, so that descendants can easily locate the material and use it for their own projects and purposes.

As for the wax cylinder recordings from the expeditions, they were originally stored at the Dominion Museum, where Andersen made unsuccessful attempts to transcribe them with the help of one Doreen Walsh from Auckland. The soft wax in the cylinders and the dictaphone were damaged in the process, and the documentation slips were removed from the cylinders.[59] Each time the wax cylinders were played, the quality of the recording was degraded. In 1928 Andersen arranged for the cylinders to be transferred to the Turnbull Library, but in 1956 a disastrous attempt to have six of the cylinders reproduced on modern discs by the Folklore Section in the Music Division at the US Library of Congress left all of those cylinders broken. The remaining cylinders were returned to the National Museum in 1962, and stored in the basement of Parliament Buildings.[60]

In 1958, when ethnomusicologist Mervyn McLean learned about the wax cylinders, he offered to organise the collection — a difficult task that he

discussed in detail in his catalogue, which was finally published in 1992. Some of the information on the cylinders, written in Best's Māori shorthand, was successfully deciphered by Anne Cavanaugh, secretary of the Department of Anthropology at the University of Auckland, who describes Best's shorthand system in an appendix to the catalogue.

In the 1970s, Rangi Motu, a research assistant, used dubbings of the cylinders made by the Department of Scientific and Industrial Research to prepare transcripts of the waiata, whaikōrero and other oral art forms they recorded; and these were checked by Jenifer Curnow and Merimeri Penfold. The original wax cylinders are stored at Te Papa, and digital recordings of them are in the Archive of Māori and Pacific Sound at the University of Auckland.

These remarkable taonga still hold the voices of ancestors who, 100 years ago, decided to pass on their knowledge and oral art forms to future generations. As they listen to the recordings of their forebears speaking, singing and chanting, descendants are spellbound as the hau of their ancestors, once traced in wax and now released into the airwaves, breathes in their ears. Very few have had this privilege, however. It would be marvellous if these recordings could be remastered, using contemporary technology to retrace the original cadences of song and speech, and these treasures shared with as many descendants as possible.

Films and whakapapa

Unlike the wax cylinder recordings, the artefacts and most of the photographs from the expeditions, the films shot by McDonald have been widely circulated. The screenings held at the time of the expeditions were lively affairs. As we have seen, at the 1923 Tikitiki screening of the 1921 Whanganui film, the audience called out to the people on the screen to try and influence their actions. Those who were being filmed in Tairāwhiti, such as Riwai Te Miringa o Rangi, would have known exactly what they might expect their own films to be like and how they might be received. Later that year, Te Rangihīroa's screening at Auckland Institute and his slideshow in Sydney demonstrated the mana or ancestral power of the Tairāwhiti expedition's whakaāhua, taking the light that had radiated from Riwai and his kin, land and waterways, on the first of many voyages.

After the expeditions, the films were stored at the Dominion Museum. The cellulose nitrate film base from the 1920s is highly unstable, acidic and inflammable; combustible, even in the absence of oxygen. Unless it is stored at very cold temperatures, the material decomposes, turning into a dangerous, sticky mess. For over sixty years these films were hidden away, slowly degrading. The 35mm cinematic film stored in tins would have softened and turned amber, producing toxic nitric dioxide vapours. This reaction causes the images to fade, and accelerates the deterioration. At this stage, the film literally eats away at the images.

It was not until the early 1980s that 'a jumble of fragmentary images entered the world of light',[61] when the cellulose nitrate cinematic film negatives from the Dominion Museum Ethnological Expeditions were handed over to Ngā Taonga Sound and Vision. As Ngā Taonga's preservation manager Louise McCrone remarks: 'the 1980s preservation (photochemical printing) of the film, which was completed at the Film Unit laboratory, [made] a new duplicate negative, positive and print from the original nitrate negative reels which were beginning to decompose... [T]his process introduces noise and grain into each new element.'[62]

Four historic films were compiled from surviving footage—one for each expedition—consisting of short segments centred on particular activities; each activity is introduced with an explanatory inter-title inserted by the film archive team. These extraordinary and lively silent documentary images are taonga that are deeply valued by the Māori communities in which they were made. They carry the wairua— the immaterial essence—of the people and places, customs and practices documented. Although some of this material had been shown in public, much of it had not. Since the 1980s restoration, the films have returned through multiple screenings to the communities where they were created. As Merata Mita has noted, 'material divorced from the people loses its value, the people keep it alive'.[63]

The enthusiasm and emotion with which the films and photographs were met when they were first shown almost a century ago has not abated. In 1981, when the surviving nitrate negatives of the McDonald films were found and handed over to the newly established New Zealand Film Archive, its director

Jonathan Dennis became fascinated by the decomposing fragments.[64] During the expeditions, McDonald had scratched notes onto the leader to each roll of film, with the date, location and some information about the content. This enabled the archive to piece the fragments together[65] and add subtitles that were then translated into Māori. Dennis reported in 1985 that he and eight colleagues from the archive had screened the Whanganui film for the first time, at Matahiwi marae on the Whanganui River and then at Rātana pā:

> The marae was packed, with people having come from settlements up and down the river. Some of the kuia at the showing recalled the visit of the Museum group in 1921, and identified many of those in the film. The following week the Film Archive screened the film and other rare early ones of the area, to four sell-out houses in Wanganui City.

> The McDonald Wanganui film, and other early Maori films in the New Zealand Film Archive's collection were also screened in May at the Nga Puna Waihanga (Maori Artists and Writers) hui at Ratana Pa. This special showing was attended by the Maori Queen Te Arikinui Dame Te Atairangikaahu.[66]

In September that year, the films from the Rotorua, Whanganui and the Tairāwhiti expeditions were screened at the Pacific Film Archive in California, narrated by Witarina Harris of Ngāti Whakaue.[67]

In March 1986, all four films were screened together for the first time at the Embassy Theatre in Wellington, again narrated by Witarina Harris. Dennis reported:

> Nearly 1000 people, including kaumatua representing the Whanganui, East Coast and Rotorua areas, packed the Embassy Theatre, and several hundred had to be turned away... [The films are] taonga, cultural treasures of extraordinary beauty and importance. They are unique among the films made in this country.[68]

These screenings were repeated later that year at the National Museum, and at a conservation hui in Koroniti, which Sharon Dell described in the New Zealand Film Archive newsletter:

Witarina Harris and Jonathan Harris at the opening
of *Te Maori* exhibition, Wellington, October 1986.

There is a very vocal and direct reaction to all the films on the programme. Great interest is shown in the activities and scenes depicted: the skill and panache with which cats cradle is demonstrated is commented on, the speed and technique of the weavers astounds, the making of crayfish pots and operation of eel weirs is studied intently.

The whole hall is convulsed to see children elbowed out of the way while the adults take over skipping ropes and double-dutch [skipping game], 1920s style, fills the screen. There is a contemplative silence when divinatory sticks move seemingly of their own accord. It had Elsdon Best perplexed at the time but it's not disbelief that greets the sight now. These are, however, common reactions, they mirror our own, and reflect the research value of the films as a documentary record of past activities.

Far more profound and moving is the direct communication which the films open up between the living and the dead. The children in the film are identified as the brothers and sisters of the elders amongst us. The adults are their parents, grand-parents, aunties and uncles. Most are known by name and some are greeted as though they stood before us. The effect, though tears do flow, is not maudlin. Personal characteristics are laughed at, family likenesses in the present generations are pointed out, even amongst the pigs and dogs which still wander around the village.

We all feel touched by the greatest gift our ancestors have handed down to us, their love, and their abiding presence with us. For a while the speeches provide the excuse for a song — then half the hall is up, performing song after song for us, the visitors, and for themselves, as their pride in being Ngati Pamoana manifests itself. At last the mattresses are brought out. It has been both exhilarating and draining and we have work tomorrow so we put in our earplugs and pull our sleeping bags over our heads while all around us the talk goes on and on.[69]

In early 1987 the films travelled around the world with Dennis and Harris, screening in Sydney, Melbourne, London, Paris, Münich and Berlin. In June that year, they screened at the St James Theatre in Auckland as part of a programme to welcome home to the Auckland Art Gallery the *Te Maori* exhibition that had been touring the United States and, later, New Zealand. In advance of this screening, Dennis talked with Peter Calder of the *New Zealand Herald* about how the films had been restored.

The reels of film negative, which had never been printed into a form ready for project — were a 'festering and sticky mess' when the Archive took delivery of them.

Restoration experts went to work on the film, frame by painstaking frame, repairing damage to images, splices, sprocket holes. Printers were specially adapted to accommodate the film strips which had stretched with time and the film was transferred to modern acetate safety film.

After five years of work, the film was ready for projection, and archive staff saw the results of their work — and McDonald's incomparable images — for the first time.

Dennis describes that moment as 'breathtaking, astonishing'. He speaks with breathless delight of the Maori divinatory rites — used to establish the outcome of a forthcoming battle — in which tohunga make sticks move — apparently of their own accord — along the ground.

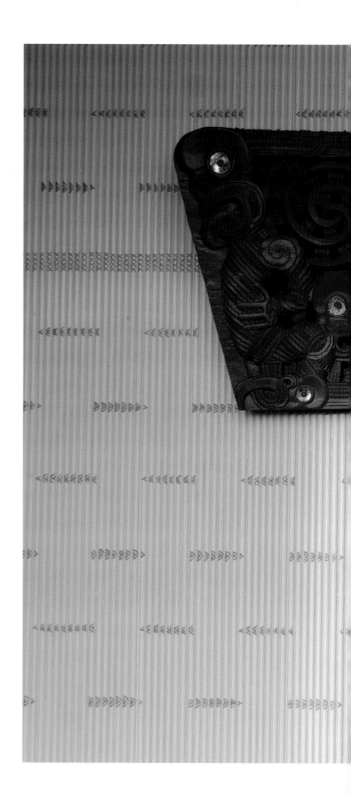

The Pororangi pare includes the three-dimensional takarangi double spirals with perforated spaces between the connecting chevron notches that create an energetic time-space vortex of continuous whakapapa.

'It was one of the greatest thrills of my life to see that the amount of time we had spent was worthwhile,' says Dennis. 'The quality of the images was beautiful, but what was even better was that the content of the films was extraordinary.'[70]

On this occasion, James McDonald's descendants—his granddaughter Joyce Thorpe, her daughter Anne Salmond and granddaughter Amiria Salmond—saw the films for the first time. The queue to get into the St James stretched along Queen Street, and as they entered the theatre, each member of the audience was handed a silver-fern leaf. In the darkened space, the silver film canisters, placed on a fine cloak, were given a pōwhiri by Ngāti Whātua, the tangata whenua. As the silent films began to play, Witarina Harris stood on the stage, narrating. People laughed, called out to people on the screen, and commented on the action. Helen Martin described the response to the screening in the *New Zealand Listener*: 'Most unexpected, at least to one who imagined that the viewing of these taonga would be a solemn affair, is the wonderfully warm, vibrant humour that flows over and out of the screen and, magically, draws you into those moments that McDonald captured so many years ago.'[71]

At the end of the screening, the films were celebrated with uproarious applause. For Joyce Thorpe and her family, it was strange to see the flickering black-and-white images on screen, knowing that the eye of their ancestor was behind the camera. He was also in the theatre, unseen but present.

Over the following years, Lawrence Wharerau, Honiana Love and other staff at Ngā Taonga Sound and Vision have screened the films at many marae and community venues, and each time they have evoked the same heartfelt reactions. According to Angela Moewaka Barnes, 'the McDonald films … are valued as beautiful and valuable depictions of our tūpuna. I attended a screening … with a predominantly Māori audience. It was a moving experience with vocal participation from the audience as tūpuna and environments were recognised.'[72]

In his 1928 paper 'The Genealogical Method', written five years after the expeditions, Ngata contrasts the immediacy of such images with the documentary records of European observers including Captain Cook and his successors. He remarks that although they 'took more or less satisfactory literary photographs of the condition of the Maori tribes as they found them in the early days', these 'do not carry conviction to those of the people they passed in review'. Here Ngata is drawing a distinction between the efficacy and potential for future impact of the 'literary' image—made with ink and paper—and the 'drawings with light' made by the camera. By 1923, Māori had long used photographs, instead of preserved heads, to illuminate whakapapa. As a complement to carvings as avatars of ancestors, hapū placed photographic portraits of their forebears at the feet of their dead, and hung the portraits in wharenui among the ancestors embodied in carved pou, poupou and tekoteko.

The ideas that Ngata was developing about whakapapa informed the Dominion Museum expeditions. Ngata regarded the recordings in film, photograph and wax cylinder as more likely to 'carry conviction' to descendants; and the expeditions he championed and the invitations he extended to McDonald with his cameras 'foresaw the genealogical value of photography to hold whakapapa and kōrero for future generations'.[73]

In his own time, Ngata also inspired a younger generation of Māori scholars. Pei Te Hurinui Jones,[74] for instance, a Tainui scholar who shared many of Ngata's interests, wrote a series of articles and books about Tainui ancestral knowledge. According to Jones, in whakairo (carving) and moko (tattoo), the takarangi (double spiral)—with its interlocking spirals linked by chevrons, each representing an ancestral pairing—echoes the chants that retrace the genealogical unfolding of the cosmos.[75] In contrast with modernity's 'arrow of time', with its unilinear, calibrated passage, in the takarangi, hau (the wind of life) surges in and out of an ancestral source, activating the everyday world and giving people direct access to their ancestors.

The vortex keeps spinning

Such ideas inspired many of Ngata's projects and in turn, his successors. As Patu Hohepa has remarked, 'Time is a moving continuum if seen through Maori language, with ego being a particle whose volition is not bound to time. Time swirls like koru patterns, three dimensional spirals.'[76] Over time, the recursive vortex keeps on spinning. In 2010–11, director Libby Hakaraia and producer Tainui Stephens co-created the television documentary *The Scotsman and the Māori*, which followed three generations of McDonald's descendants on a voyage of discovery that retraced the expeditions, visiting Pipiriki, Hiruhārama and Koroniti marae on the Whanganui River; Tokaanu, where McDonald spent his last years; and Ruatōrea, Porourangi at Waiomatatini, and Gisborne in Tairāwhiti.

In this journey, McDonald's uri (descendants—Anne Salmond, her daughter Amiria Salmond and Amiria's son Tom), with their travelling companions, came face to face with the uri of those whose āhua he had captured in still photographs and film. Led by Stephens and Hakaraia, they were welcomed on to some of the same marae where 'Mac', Ngata, Buck, Andersen and Best had stayed. In the wharenui at night, the team held 'sheetings' of films and photographs from the expeditions: a projector brought the ancestors to life on a white cotton sheet suspended from the ceiling. As always, people called out as they watched the films, naming ancestors and places and telling stories about them, giving voice to the silent films—just as the tāruke kōura maker had predicted.

Brett Graham, *Nebula 11*, 2011. Acrylic and ink on canvas, 380 × 380 mm. Private collection.

Once again, a film crew brought the latest technology into the communities: photographs of ancestors were screened from a laptop; and a portable printer was used to produce copies of the photographs for descendants as soon as they recognised their ancestors. This was yet another demonstration of the efficacy of photography in transcending space–time distance, conveying the radiating energy of mauri to new generations, whirling from te pō, the dark, invisible ancestral realm, into te ao mārama, the everyday world of light.

In addition, the efficacy of film, photographs and wax cylinders in capturing traces of mauri has been activated in evidence to the Waitangi Tribunal. In the Whanganui River claim, for instance, iwi used the Dominion Museum Expedition photographs and films to support their claims about the intimacy of their relationships with their ancestral river. When the Whanganui River Deed of Settlement was finally signed on 5 August 2014, it concluded the longest-running legal case in New Zealand history, after 148 years.

At the heart of the settlement was the legal recognition of the Whanganui River as 'its own legal entity' — a being, with its own personality and rights. The life of the river in the 1920s, and its existential entanglement with the lives of ancestors with their eel weirs and waka, were conveyed to the Tribunal in the photos and films made by the Dominion Museum Expedition team, vividly evoking the harm caused to the lives of both river and people by Crown decisions made since that time.

Some of the expeditions' film recordings have recently been digitised and enhanced by Ngā Taonga: New Zealand Archive of Film, Television and Sound, a process that has restored extraordinary details captured by the original light and sound recordings, but whose revelation was beyond the technologies then available to reproduce them in printed photographs, films and audio recordings for playback.[77] In the photographic stores at Te Papa, for example, the research team placed negatives on a lightbox and marvelled at the fine-grained information they contain, and that greatly exceeded the scope of the printing processes of their time.[78] What might be revealed if iwi descendants were to give permission for these to be printed at large scale?

Digitisation has also permitted these taonga and tīpuna to travel as digital files via electromagnetic waves. In 2017, during the filming of the documentary series 'Artefact', Anne Salmond played a digitised wax cylinder recording of Iehu Nukunuku playing a kōauau in Waiomatatini in 1923 — the first-known sound recording of a Māori musical instrument — through a mobile phone to a contemporary exponent of taonga pūoro, Horomona Horo, while Horo examined digital prints of the photographs of Nukunuku taken by McDonald made at the same time. This exchange, in turn, was recorded in sound and film, and screened on Māori Television.

In 2018 Natalie Robertson and Billie Lythberg digitised the 'Buck Archive' at the Bishop Museum, paving the way towards greater access for iwi descendants and future researchers. The lives of these illuminated records of Māori, made by Pākehā but inspired and made possible by visionary Māori leaders, are still activating networks of relations, including among the uri of those on both sides of the camera.

Ngata, Te Rangihīroa, Best and, on at least one occasion, McDonald himself were also drawn with light into the Dominion Museum Expedition photographs and films. These are part of their legacy, as not only orchestrators and facilitators but also actors and agents, along with the relations they forged. As Merimeri Penfold once chanted, 'He iwi kē, he iwi kē, titiro atu, titiro mai' — one strange people and another, looking at each other; who in the gaze of the other, see themselves, and through recognising their differences, see themselves and each other differently.

Whether present on film or as the eyes through which we see every image, as we witness the sights that McDonald, Ngata, Te Rangihīroa, Andersen and Best saw and captured, these hoa aroha cannot be disentangled from the archive, the people who hosted them, and the whakaāhua they created together for future generations:

Members of the Salmond family at Paraweka marae, Pipiriki, in 2010 during the filming of the television documentary *The Scotsman and the Māori*, made by Libby Hakaraia and Tainui Stephens. Photograph by Kerry Brown.

Hei kōnei rā koutou e te rōpu hopuhopu
o ngā takenga a te iwi Māori

Farewell until we see you again, the group
who capture the ways of the Māori people.

TE HATI PAKAROA, Whareponga, 1923[79]

E ngā iwi, hei kōrero tēnei nāku — ko ēnei
waiata waiho iho hei whakamaharatanga
ki a koutou, mō ēnei wā e haere ake nei

This is my message to you, the iwi: these songs
[and images] are left for you to remember in the
times to come

APIRANA NGATA, Waiomatatini, 1923

APPENDICES

Reconnecting Taonga
The Terminology of Whakapapa
Relationship Terms

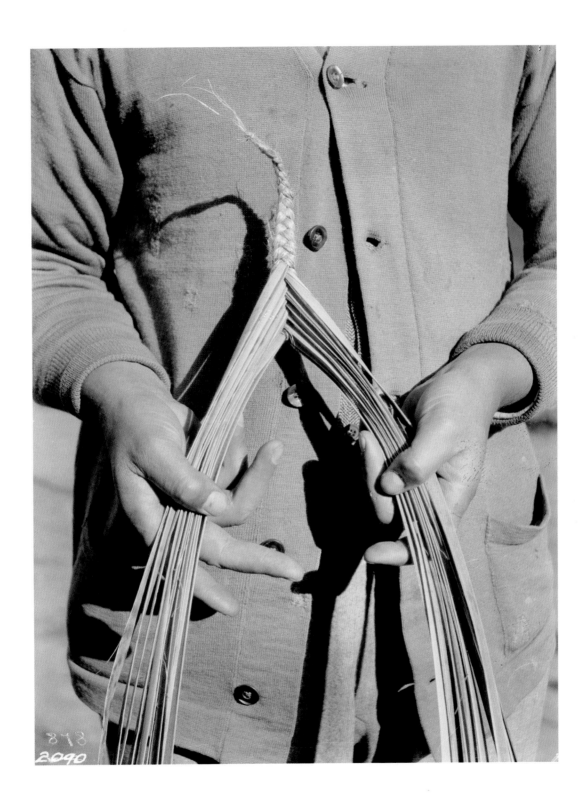

Kawe, a plaited carrier, being woven at Koroniti in 1921.
Photograph by James McDonald

RECONNECTING TAONGA

BILLIE LYTHBERG

In a plywood drawer in Te Whare Pora o Hine Te Iwaiwa (the Taonga Māori textiles store) at the Museum of New Zealand Te Papa Tongarewa sits a closed loop, single-strand net tied to an acid-free card. ME004529, the catalogue record states, is a kupenga 'net bag for koura (crayfish)' made by 'Sir Peter H. Buck' at 'Waiapu.' It is provenanced to 'J. McDonald, date collected 1921' but is almost certainly the closed-loop single strand net made by Te Rangihīroa on the verandah of the Bungalow in Waiomatatini in 1923.

The kupenga came to Te Papa in 1930 from James McDonald along with two other taonga: a kete with three handles, presented at Koroniti (ME004528) in 1920 according to the accession register, but surely this was 1921; and a hīnaki korupu trap lead (ME004527), which might one day be connected to the expeditions, though the accession register clearly distinguishes its collection date as 1930 and its locality as Tokaanu, where McDonald lived out the last of his years.

These three handwritten entries sit together, line after line, in a ledger book back of house at Te Papa. It is one of three volumes comprising the 'Museum of New Zealand Maori Collection Register': 'entries 1 to 2677'; 'entries 2678 to 5403'; and 'entries 5404 to 8187'. These replicate, update and extend the entries made in an older, single book: 'National Museum Register Ethnology.'

Reconnecting taonga at Te Papa to the Dominion Museum Expeditions involves searching the digital database made from these handwritten volumes for terms associated with the expeditions; scanning the registers for the same, as these sometimes contain information not carried across into the digital realm; and marrying accession numbers to storage shelves and drawers.

Some taonga reveal themselves quickly. The fine wooden bailer (ME003821) presented by Wirieti Nopera of Koroniti is relatively large and undeniably impressive. Its digital record describes 'A heavy tata with ornately carved anterior end, showing stylized face with pāua shell eyes. "whetu eyes". Bird/manaia like head carved on end of handle. Bailer has a hole through inside in one place.' The details are more prosaic in the National Museum Register Ethnology (NMRE), inscribed in black ink by a single hand: '1 carved baler [sic]. Koriniti. Presd. By Wirieti Nopera, of Koriniti. See Note BK. No. 2. P.179.' The handwriting is expedition member Elsdon Best's.

Its later entry in the Museum of New Zealand Maori Collection Register divides the narrative information into columns, filled in variously with entries in black ink, blue ink, and pencil. At least three hands have inscribed the information: '3821 | Carved Tata | 1 [specimen] | Koroniti [sic] | Pres: Wineti [sic] Nopera | 215" approx. See note book 2 p.179. Paua eye'. In a column headed Collector, 'Ethnol. Exped. To Wanganui?' has been scrawled in pencil.

Though it nestles on a shelf in Te Āhuru Mōwai (the Taonga Māori carving store) with other carved wooden objects, in its literary formats, the tata still keeps company with twelve other Whanganui Expedition taonga received in Koroniti, detailed in entries ME003819 to ME003830. Te Papa curator Dougal Austin directed us to the 'Blood Earth Fire' gallery to see ME003819: '1 Wooden Patu muka (made of maire-taiko) Presented by Ropata Rangitahua, of Koriniti. W.R. [Whanganui River]' according to the NMRE. The digital catalogue describes it as 'Beautifully shaped, circular cross section, indentation on bulb, flat poll. Made of Maire—taiko.' Made from a single piece of New Zealand sandalwood (*Mida salicifolia*), it is dated to the nineteenth century, and its maker is listed as 'unknown'.

Entry ME003820 is also an older taonga, made before rather than for the expeditions. Its digital record describes a toki adze blade 'Well ground, sharp, pecked butt and poll', produced between 1500 and 1820. Two old labels adhere to its surface, one overlaying the other. Though well-worn and partially concealed, the bottom label is inscribed by

Best, using the same pen, and with much the same words as its corresponding entry in the NMRE: 'Found at Koriniti. Presd. By Ropata Rangitahua', bringing a synchronous process of accessioning and labelling into sharp focus.

Of the taonga described in entries numbered ME003822–3830, only three are easily located, but each can be identified with its donor. Number ME003822, the mutu kaka named Rerehau conforms to its digital record: a bird snare of the 'Kapu type', it is 'Dark brown, plain uncarved', and, like the patu muka and toki adze, was presented by Ropata Rangitahua. However, this detail is missing from the NMRE and digital record. The mōria kākā (kiwi bone ring for the leg of a pet parrot, ME003823) named 'Ngā wai takahia', also presented by Rangitahua, is missing.

Ngā Rongo Pokiha presented the taonga described in entries ME003824–3826: two poti taro or taro baskets (ME003824 & ME003825), and a tokari (tuku taha)—a lid for a bird-storing calabash (ME003826). In a deep drawer in the Whare Pora textile stores, the poti taro labelled ME003824 has been so well stored it looks recently constructed despite being 100 years old. Its squared base softens to a circular shape at its upper extent, and eight cords, evenly spaced around the upper rim, are drawn together to affect a strong handle.

The fine weaving of Rihipeti Aperaniko, presented to the expedition in the forms of a kete kiekie (ME003827), a kete ti (ME003828), a kawe rapa carrying cord (ME003829), and makawe flax belt (ME003830), is evinced by the kete ti in the Whare Pora and elaborated in the digital catalogue: 'Made from undyed thin strips of leaf. Rather open plait, plaited keel, top & handles.'

Counterintuitively, the taonga presented at Pipiriki and Hiruhārama do not follow immediately after those presented at Koroniti in the NMRE. A series of six taonga collected elsewhere intervene before the description of ME003837 '1 Korotete basket to keep eels in. Presented by Anihana of Pipiriki'; ME003838 '1 Plaited band for pig's leg. Presented by Erueti of Pipiriki'; and ME003839 '3 calabashes in basket. Presented by Matarena [of] Hiruharama'.

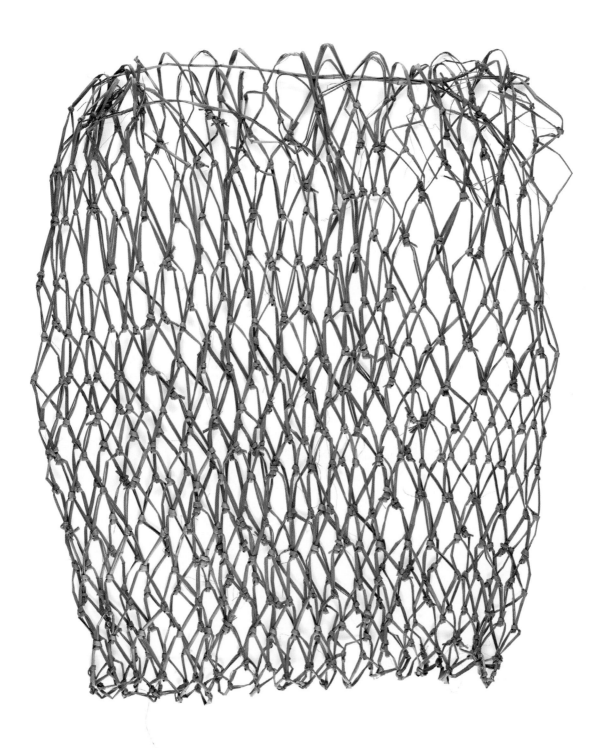

Kupenga made by Te Rangihīroa at Waiomatatini
on the Waiapu River in 1923.

Tata (bailer) collected at Koroniti,
on the Whanganui River, in 1921.

Toki (adze blade) collected at Koroniti in 1921.

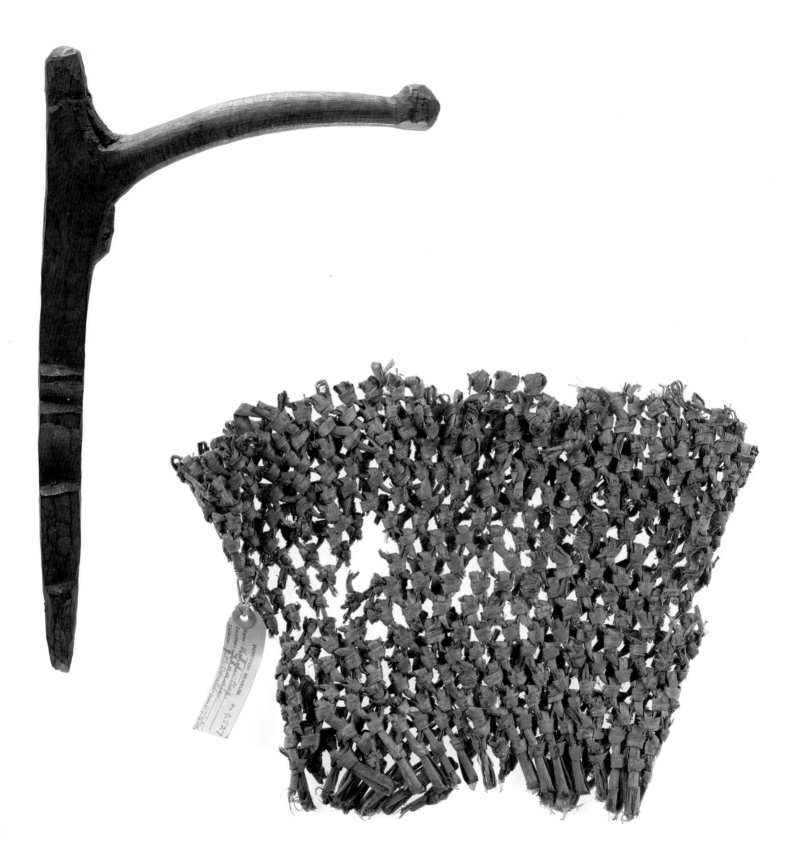

The mutu kaka (bird snare) known as 'Rerehau' collected at Koroniti in 1921.

Hīnaki (korupu trap lead), Tokaanu, 1930.

127

Date.	No.	Description of Specimen.	How acquired.	Remarks.
Jany. 28. 1921	3809	1 Korowai		
" 3 Bins.	3810	1 "		
" Bins	3811	1 " Curpn. material	Purvis Russell Collection.	
" Bins.	3812	1 Paepaeroa		
	3813	1 Korowai		
" Bins.	3814	1 Paepaeroa		
	3815	1 Carved Waka huia		
" * Cla.	3816	1 Stone adze.		
Feb. 11 "	3817	1 Paddle. Whanganui make.	Purchased £2.	
" 12 "	3818	1 Gourd. Ipu wai.	Obtd. 9 Parihaka 1880. Purchased	
March	3819	1 Wooden Patu muka (made of maire-raiko) (made of maire raiko)	Presented by Ropa... Rangitahua, of Koriniti. W. R.	
	3820	1 Stone adze. Found at Koriniti.	Presd. by Ropata Rangitahu...	
" 15 2	3821	1 Carved Baler. (Koriniti)	Presd. by Wineti Nopera, of Kori... See Note Bk. No. 2. p. 179.	
!	3822	1 Tuke (muku kaka) See Note Bk. No. 2. p. 179		c/d
"	3823	1 Maria Kaka	Pres⁴ by Ropata Rangitahua of Kori...	
"	3824	1 Poti Taro (Taro basket) See No. 2. p 189.	Presd. by Nga Rongo Pokiha of Koriniti in March 1921	
" "	3825	1 Poti Taro.	Presd. by Nga Rongo Pokiha	
" "	3826	1 Tokari (tuki tahā)	" " Te Pokiha of Koriniti	
" "	3827	1 Kete kiekie		" Rihipeti Aperaniko	
" "	3828	1 " ti (Cordyline aus.)	" of Koriniti	
/ "	3829	1 Kawe rapa		
" "	3830	1 Flax belt. (Makawe)		
April	3831	1 Stone adze	Found at Strathmore	
	3832	1 " "	14 miles from Stratford	
	3833	1 " "	...ng... up... on M... O'Callaghan's farm	

Pages 127 and 128 of the National Museum Register
Ethnology, handwritten by Elsdon Best, Museum
of New Zealand Te Papa Tongarewa.

128

Date. 1921	No.	Description of Specimen.	How acquired.	Remarks.
pril	3834	1 Stone Bowl. From Tauranga Dist.		Presd. by Colonel Ward
„ 28	3835	1 „ adze. From Richmond, Nelson.		„ „ Miss Castle
„ 30	3836	Pce. of Mata waiapu from wh. flake knives were struck.		See 2-181
„ ✓	3837	1 Korotete, basket to keep eels in. Presented by Amihama of Pipiriki		
„ ✓	3838	1 Plaited band for pig's leg.	„ „ Erueti „	
„	3839	3 Calabashes in basket.	„ „ Matarena Hirini	
Jun ✓	3840	5. Flax baskets	„ „ Te Hapai of Koriniti	roma
„ ✓	3841	1 Paddle	Presented	
	3842	1 Heitiki		
	3843	1 worked cylindrical black stone	cast also registered.	
	3844	1 „ „ pce. of bone		
	3845	1 Greenstone adze. Long & narrow		
	3846	1 „ Pekapeka. Panya		Found to be unnumbered 20-10-1921
	3847	1 „ „ „		
	3848	1 „ „		
	3849	1 „ Moria		
	3850	1 „ „		
	3851	1 „ Mako (or serpentine. ? soapstone		
	3852	1 „ „		
	3853	1 „ Kapeu. diminutive		
✓	3854	1 Tuki taha. carved.	Whanganui Dist.	c/d.
	3855	1 Stone adze 6"		
c/p *	3856	1 broken pce. of stone adze from Ship Cove. }	Presd. by Mr Drew.
	3857	1 „ „ „ „ „ „ „		
y 10/22	3858	1 Carved Pare		Lord Liverpool balm
„ ✓	3859	1 Mussel dredge		„
„ ✓	3860	1 amo. Carved post		„

Kete collected at Koroniti in 1921.

Kono (food basket) collected at Koroniti in 1921.

INTRODUCTION TO 'THE TERMINOLOGY OF WHAKAPAPA'

WAYNE NGATA

He kura ka huna
He kura ka whākina

Treasured knowledge is hidden
And then it reveals itself

Kia tīkina atu ngā kupu o te oriori a Ngāti
Kahungunu hei wāhi ake i tēnei kaupapa,

'Pinepine te kura, hau te kura,
whanake te kura i raro i Awarua.

Ko te kura nui, ko te kura roa,
ko te kura o tawhiti, nā Tūhaepō...'

Ko te kura i kōrerotia ai, e kōrerotia tonutia nei he āhuatanga whakaheke
i ngā wānanga o Hawaiki mai, ka takitakina iho ki tēnei whenua kura
e hora nei me ōna iwi. Kāti, he whenua, he whakapapa, he kōrero tonu
e whakaorioritia ana hei oranga mokopuna, hei oranga tangata. Kei konei
e āta whakaraupapahia ana e tō mātau tipuna, e Apirana, e tāea ai e tātau
te whai kia mārama ai tātau ki a tātau anō, kia mōhio ai tātau me pēhea
te whakatau, te whakarite, te whakaū i ngā tūhonohononga i waenganui
i a tātau, e tika ai tā tātau noho ki te ao. Kia whakamihia ēnei tūāhuatanga
i tukitukia e ngā momo whakawai o te ao hou i ngā tau roa, kei moa
te ngaro, me tiaki.

The relationship between Apirana Ngata and Te Rangihīroa is materialised in many things, including the letters and manuscripts they exchanged. Keith Sorrenson published 174 of their letters in *Na To Hoa Aroha, From Your Dear Friend: The Correspondence between Sir Apirana Ngata and Sir Peter Buck, 1925–50* (three volumes). Writing prepared by Ngata on the terminology associated with Māori genealogies was sent to Te Rangihīroa during their long correspondence. 'The Terminology of Whakapapa' was uncovered in the archives of the Bishop Museum and the Alexander Turnbull Library.

Ngata had proposed to write a doctoral thesis on the 'genealogical method'. In a letter dated 11 January 1931, Ngata mentions to Te Rangihīroa that he is 'dishing up the whakapapa matter along-side Nga Moteatea for the Litt. D' (*Na To Hoa Aroha*, vol. 2: 226) and cites Te Kooro Kiriahuru as his mentor. Though the thesis was never submitted, the tracts below outline an extraordinary framework for understanding how whakapapa works. Ngata explores the various material ways in which whakapapa is expressed in reo Māori 'Maori language', via meeting houses, weaving, twining and fishing techniques — whakapapa as practical ontology.

Te Kooro Kiriahuru of the Tairāwhiti was a noted genealogy expert of the late nineteenth and early twentieth centuries. He was consulted by Ngata and others in matters of genealogical knowledge and practice, and belonged to a class of tohunga who were being, and have now been, overtaken by Western models of absorbing, retaining and utilising bodies of knowledge. Te Kooro was what I would consider to be a 'tribal database and software program' of insight, wisdom and practice as it pertained to connecting the complex networks of relationships between people through and across generations, that recognised, highlighted and reinforced obligations and responsibilities of those relationships.

Modern genealogy software programs and apps continue to paint the relationship pictures we may desire, but have resulted in the loss of our ability and capacity to harness the incredible potential of our own human memory and understanding that traditional indigenous practice maintained for many generations. We are fortunate that Ngata and others were able to record experiences and learnings they gathered in the company of the likes of Te Kooro. We have much to learn if we are to gain even the smallest of insights into our own traditional ways of thinking and doing.

The manuscripts below were transcribed by Anne Salmond. The original text did not include macrons and has been left as it was written. Notes in square brackets refer to missing pages or to insertions made by Ngata in black ink or by an editor in red ink, and highlight sentences that suggest these manuscripts were written primarily for Te Rangihīroa's readership.

THE TERMINOLOGY OF WHAKAPAPA

APIRANA NGATA

[Bishop Museum MS SC Buck 6.02]

In Maori various terms are used to define a pedigree or genealogy, or the act of tracing descent or setting out genealogically the relationship of persons or groups. A people such as the Maori, which had intense pride of race and a social system based largely on the family status of its members, would be expected to evolve a rich terminology relating to the preservation and transmission of pedigrees and the processes connected therewith.

Recitation

The only process by which pedigrees were communicated and transmitted, and thus taught and preserved, was by recitation, before the art of writing was acquired from the English.

The act of recitation was described by various terms according to the figure present in the mind of the reciter. If he conceived of the line of descent as a line, cord or string along which in imagination the persons concerned in the pedigree were strung in proper sequence he would use words appropriate to the act of tracing the particular string or cord. The words he would commonly use would be 'taki' or 'hapai.' Those words would also be applicable to the idea of leading or lifting either a song or chant or story, and the reciter would become the fugleman in a massed haka or peruperu. A closely allied figure is expressed in the term 'kauwhata.' A kauwhata was a stage or frame built on which to suspend fish or bundles of food, which were tied together in such a way that the bundles straddled the cross-beams of the stage. There was a horizontal and a vertical method in the arrangement and display. It was no great step mentally to use a term which emphasised order, display and even decoration. This was the term 'tatai.'

In the term 'tahu' or 'tahuhu' (the former Eastern and the latter its equivalent among other tribes including Arawa, Tainui, Aotea and Ngapuhi) we have two conceptions, according as tahuhu is used as the first weft in the weaving of a garment, thus allied to 'taki aho' or 'hapai,' or as the ridge-pole of a house or as a stiffening rod. In the expression 'tahuhu haere' the reciter is literally tracing this first weft, picking out the eldest son of the eldest branch of a family. The second conception of a ridge-pole and of the tribe or sub-tribe or family as a house with its connected parts is the one which is more usually present in the mind of the expert genealogist.

In the word 'kauwhau' (also kauhau and kauhou) we have the basic idea of a tying together. 'Whau' and 'hou' are interchangeable as in whauwhau and houhou, and mean a tie; and 'kau' is an ancestor. It seems to be at once the oldest and the most formal expression for ancient legends and genealogies and for the act of proclaiming them.

'Whakapapa' is the term in most common use. It introduces another conception, that of placing in layers or laying upon one another. We shall develop all these terms and conceptions in detail.

(a) The line, string or cord.

Aho, kaha. Literally a line, string or cord. In relation to a pedigree or genealogy this is a figure that would naturally occur to a weaving, cord-making, net-making, fishing people. The reciter conceived a connected string on which the persons concerned in the matter of his recitation were strung along in sequence and by lifting the string displayed them prominently. The string was the aho or kaha. The act of tracing it along in memory was 'taki', and of lifting it 'hapai'.

Ex: From the song of Te Aratukutuku, who boasted of the people of Taupo: Hapainga te aho o to tupuna tama-wahine, i ariki ai ki te taniwha. E kore e tau hei whai ake mo te taki aho ariki o te wahine maru kore.

Aho is most commonly used in the expression 'aho ariki'. Takiaho is a cord on which fish or shellfish are strung, and also a line of descent.

Kaha is a rope, rauawa lashings, a line or boundary, the navel string &c., thence lineage or a line of descent, though in that connection now rarely used.

Ex: Ka hoki mai ki te whakataki i te kaha o Houmaitawhiti (T. 128)

'Taki' is to lead or bring along or to trace, and thus to recite in the days when recitation was the only method of tracing lines of descent, or history or traditions. We have it in taki tupuna, whakataki, takitaki and takiaho.

E taki ana i nga korero o mua
Ka takina te kawa.
Ka hoki mai ki te whakataki i te kaha o Houmaitawhiti, tae noa ki ana uri.
E kore e tau hei whai ake mo te takiaho ariki.
Ka takitakina te haka,
Takitakina ra, e Horo, te hu o te puoro.

'Hapai' is to raise or lift up and in the line quoted from the song of Te Aratukutuku is applied to lifting or raising the aho ariki so as to display it. It is used in the same sense as 'taki' for leading or raising the tune or tone of a song or chant.

In both taki and hapai you visualise the reciters one at each end of a line, now one now the other leading or taking the lead from the other as was the custom in the whare wananga.

'Whakaaraara' contains the same idea of lifting up or raising, and of chanting. As a noun it is a chant to keep the watch awake or give the alarm in time of war. (cf. Whakaaraara pa). As a term in relation to genealogies &c. It means to recite or explain genealogies or other formal matter. The pedigrees or legends are visualised as a matua of component parts which experts in turn will arouse.

Ex: Ara atu ano pea etahi i mahue i a au, ma tetahi atu e whakaaraara atu. He nui nga mea kei waho atu i enei katoa i whakaaraaratia atu nei e au.

(b) <u>The stage for display.</u>

'Kauwhata' is to display as on a stage or frame in tied bundles, as of fish or articles of food, the elevation giving prominence. The figure is closely allied to that denoted by taki, hapai, aho and kaha.

> Ex: E ora ana nga koromatua hai kauwhata i te riri (M. XCIX).
>   Te kauwhata o te atua. Ki te po wananga, ki te po kauwhata.

It is probably because in using these expressions, the reciter is seeking emphasis that we find them most commonly used in regard to ariki lines as in Takiaho ariki, kauwhata o te atua &c.

(c) <u>The first weft and</u>

(d) <u>The ridge-pole or stiffening rod.</u>

'Tahu or tahuhu'. Reference has been made to the double conception denoted.
We shall particularise here on the alternative figure of a ridge-pole or stiffening rod.

In the cult of genealogies, 'tahu or tahuhu' has a technical meaning. It is the act of setting out or arranging the main ancestors (connected with a common ancestor) from whom you may derive the tribe or tribes occupying a more or less extensive area. It has the idea of a horizontal arrangement with connected suspended lines that fits with both the conception of a weft and of a ridge-pole. Both weaving and house construction are so primitive that it is idle to speculate which complex derived the term from the other. The expert reciter was he who could most vividly impress on his hearers the array of related ancestors so that he might at will follow down any strand or rafter or poupou with the connected details of kaho, covering thatch or decorative tupuni. From any side or angle the suspended or propped up tahuhu challenged you to obscure it.

Te Kooro Kiriahuru, from whom I gathered enthusiasm for the cult of whakapapa, was master of the art of setting out 'tahuhu' in whakapapa. It was amazing with what ease and sureness he would after tracing out subsidiary lines in detail to the most recent date, revert to the tahuhu a little further along it to pick up connection with the next line, and so on.

In these days when recitation has given way to the written record the expert genealogist is he who can select from voluminous notes the 'tahuhu' that will most clearly display the genealogical connections of all the hapu or whanau in a territory. The Arawa canoe landed in the Bay of Plenty a crew, whose orally transmitted genealogies show them to have been of one family in the Awarua on Rangiatea from which they migrated. And so we have—

> Ko enei tangata, ko Tuamatua raua ko Uruika, ko raua te tahu nui o Te Hekengarangi,
> te tino kawai ariki, ko raua te tahu iho, tae iho ki nga uri.

On the East Coast lines you have to set out such names as Paikea, Uenuku, Ruawharo, Paoa, Whiro &c. and connect them together either under Toi or the more distant Tawhaki, Wahieroa or Rata. After some generations in New Zealand these lines converge on Porourangi, Tahu, Ruapani, Rongowhakaata and Kahungunu; you thus get the local tahuhu.

And so in naming their superior houses after main or eponymous ancestors the tribes or tribe select their immediate ancestor from the tahuhu to form in turn the subsidiary tahuhu. The internal decorations, whether carved poupou or tukutuku panels may in turn follow down from the tahuhu commemorated in the name of the house or up to the main ancestor of the tribe, or you may as in Porourangi have both systems in operation.

In tahuhu you have the same conception as in aho kaha and kauwhata of something continuous, unbroken.

(e) Orderly arrangement.

'Tatai' is to arrange or set in order, and as applied to genealogies is related to tahuhu. The idea of order or arrangement is emphasised and also of adornment. It may fit in very well as the Maori equivalent of the classical expression of adorning a tale. Hence 'tatai korero' and 'tatai tupuna' are particularly applicable to the orderly recitation of a line of ancestry or of the history of a people. Thence it was applied to the thing recited, especially the line of descent.

> Ex: Kia ata tatai i te korero, kei pokapoka, engari kia tuhono noa atu. Ka tukua te tangata ki te tatai i nga kupenga a Marutuahu (Join the component parts of a fishing net). Tatai kau ana te whetu i te rangi. Ka mutu taua tatai wahine a Tangaroa.

(f) Tying together of ancient things. [*corrected in red ink:* 'tieing']

'Kauwhau, kauhau, or kauhou' is to recite, proclaim or declare aloud legends, genealogies or traditions. I have given what I consider to be the philology of the term and its literal meaning as to the tying together of ancestors or legends.

The kau of kaumatua and of the expressions 'Na ona kau i waiho', 'he korero huna na o kau' must be one of the roots; and hou, to tie, the other. If so then the basic idea is the same as in the expressions denoting a line or string or stage or weft or ridge-pole.

> Ex: Kawhautia mai te kauwhau o te kino I pu ai te riri, i mau ai te pakanga. Whakaputa to reo ki te kauwhau riri. A raua korero e kauhau nei mo Rangi raua ko Papa. Whakaangi i runga i te kauwhau ariki.

(g) Layers.

'Whakapapa' is the term in most common use for the act of reciting a genealogy and for the genealogy itself. It introduces another conception in the reciter's mind.

Among the many meanings of the word 'whakapapa' as a verb we may select as most relevant to our subject 'to place in layers or lay upon one another'. Thus 'whakapaparanga' is a layer or series of layers, and thus a generation or generations. Whakapapa is the act of reciting in proper order these layers or generations, whether the generation is composed of one individual as in the process called taotahi or tararere or of groups related along the one plane, as brothers, sisters of cousins to the nth degree and their wives and husbands.

Whakapapa opens up the widest scope of any of the terms used for the cult of genealogies. Where taki, hapai, kauwhata, tatai or tahuhu appear limited to special lines, kauwhau and whakapapa may comprise the most extensive relationships and involve the most complicated groupings.

Kauwhau probably had a wider vogue in former days, and is still the most formal expression, but whakapapa has almost ousted all other terms in these days, where its comprehensiveness covers much shallow knowledge and laxity.

> Ex: Whakapapatia mai taua i to tipuna e korero na.
> I haere mai ia ki te whakapapa i nga kauwhau o mua.

'Whakatakoto tupuna' is an expression related to whakapapa and with the same fundamental idea of laying down according to a plan. It is rarely used.

'Whakaparu' is a term that may be associated with whakapapa if as I believe it is derived from 'paru', the thatching of bundles of raupo leaves. The association is in the idea of layering. I have not come across any example of the use of the term in regard to genealogies. Williams gives 'whakaparu wahine' as descent through the female line only.

The reciter of legends and traditions, of tribal history and genealogies thus visualises his act in turn as tracing incidents or personnel strung along strings or cords or suspended on the cross-beams of hakari stages or from the first weft of a garment or from the ridgepole of a house or from any rod used to stiffen an object, or as uncovering the layers of stored information or of thatching. In kauwhau he has the figure of ancestors tied together by blood relationship. Pervading all is the idea of order, sequence and arrangement, and in boastful mood there is a suggestion of dressing and adornment, a lifting of pedigrees from out of the ruck.

It is doubtful whether he visualised a pedigree as a tree, with its head embedded by the hairy roots in Papatuanuku and trunk and branches vainly reaching up to Rangi above. Though the word 'peka' is used for a branch of a family or tribe as in 'Patua te peka kainga, ko te peka tangata kia ora' or 'Ka whakarauoratia ko te peka tangata, ko te peka whenua ka whakamatea'. I can find no example that would support the idea of a pedigree being likened to a tree.

The fact that legends and genealogies could not be used, proclaimed or transmitted except by reciting them and that in practice this was done by groups of experts who passed the action to and fro drew into the terminology words associated with chanting and leading of tunes or chants.

Methods in recitation

(a) Taotahi or Tararere

If you pick up any family whakapapa book today, where the data was taken from the dictation of an elder towards the end of the eighth decade of last century it will reveal the following peculiarities:

1. It will give single names in each generation from the first ancestor recorded to the person then living, whose pedigree is the subject of the record.

2. If that person is also descended from a brother or sister of any ancestor after the first, the record will begin at the beginning and trace down to where the line will so descend.

3. When it happens that there is an intermarriage between ancestors in the divergent lines the reader is left to deduce the fact by noting that two ancestors traced on different pedigrees produce a child bearing the same name and having the same line descended from him.

The process of reciting genealogy in a single line of descent is called 'taotahi' and among Ngati Porou 'tararere'. It was the process favoured by the multitude, most easily cultivated and acquired. It enabled you to sort up lines with aristocratic repute and so establish bowing connection with chiefs, whom you respect—fully classed as your tuakana or tamariki or mokopuna.

The process was tedious, but for the common run of genealogist fairly safe. He traced in a direct line and did not concern himself whether a name represented a male or female, or what the intermarriages were or how many children resulted therefrom or the accepted order of their birth.

The refinements in recitation were left to the experts and among them few were able to carry in mind the ramifications of intermarriages or the orderly arrangement of families.

The process of reciting genealogy in a single line of descent is called "taotahi" and among Ngati Porou "tararere". It was the process favoured by the multitude, most easily cultivated and acquired. It enabled you to sort up lines with aristocratic repute and so establish bowing connection with chiefs, whom you respectfully classed as your tuakana or tamariki or mokopuna.

The process was tedious, but for the common run of genealogist fairly safe. He traced in a direct line and did not concern himself whether a name represented a male or female, or what the intermarriages were or how many children resulted therefrom or the accepted order of their birth.

The refinements in recitation were left to the experts and among them few were able to carry in the mind the ramifications of intermarriages or the orderly arrangement of families.

Bad arrangement or adding "tara".

(b) Whakamoe

This was the act of tracing a genealogy assigning wives to males or husbands to females. It multiplied the strain on the memory and the margin of error more than two-fold. There was the risk of juxtaposing the wrong names by quoting as that of mate a name from the next generation, above or below, or placing in the direct line of descent the name of a wife or husband. For the Maori it must be remembered was, before writing was introduced, memorising by ear and had not the further aid of memorising by sight.

Nepia Pohuhu and others of the Wairarapa Whare Wananga experts may be quoted as deferring to Te Matorohanga in the matter of reciting intermarriages. And we may quote Te Matorohanga himself:

'Kaore au e pai ki te taotahi i aku whakapapa; me ata whakamoe ano ka pai ai au.'

(c) Whakapiri

This is the act of reciting parallel lines from a common ancestor in the taotahi style for each line so as to compare their length.

In planning a marriage 'whakapiri' was used so as to keep the individuals concerned if possible on the same plane from a selected common ancestor, so that they would be tungaane and tuahine. If somebody called you by a relationship term, especially if it placed him a generation or so further than yourself from a common stock presumed to be in his mind, you would challenge him 'Kei a wai?' so as to give yourself the opportunity by 'whakapiri' of checking him.

The annotated manuscript of 'The Terminology of Whakapapa' by Apirana Ngata.

(d) Tahuhu

This is the setting forth of ~~Maui~~ [*inserted in red ink: main*] sources of the lines of descent, those sources being connected with one another. Thus in regard to the progeny of a noted ancestor, especially the eponymous ancestor of a tribe, his various wives, if more than one, would be set out in proper order either of seniority if of one family or of related families or in order of the forming of the connections if known to tradition, and the children of each marriage, and sometimes the intermarriages of these and their descendants down to points, where the genealogist may indicate the branching off of a line or lines leading to the establishment and growth of new tribes or sub-tribes.

This is the highest art and comes nearest to the modern method of constructing genealogical tables.

(e) Hikohiko

In this process the reciter deliberately skips names on the vertical line down and sometimes interpolates names on the horizontal plane—the object being not so much to trace a continuous line as to indicate the relationship of the descendant sought to be distinguished, with the outstanding ancestors of various lines of descent. This is a common feature in poetry. Rangiuia's lament is a classic instance. In poetry too there is the factor of poetic licence in the selection of names that fit in with the lilt and metre of the song as well as its theme.

(f) Ure tane and whakaparu wahine

Tracing through male or female lines. The proudest descent was reputed to be in the eldest line through males. This was rarely achieved over many generations. Descent through males only irrespective of seniority, was termed 'whakataki ure tane or ure tarewa.' It is said that the late Mahuta Tawhiao and his full brothers, as also his son Te Rata and his brothers, have their ure tarewa or ure tane in their line of descent through Pikiao, an Arawa ancestor. The converse, descent through the female line only was termed 'whakaparu wahine.' And either may be an 'ariki' line. Te Kani-a-Takirau boasted of a 'whakaparu wahine' through 'tapairu' or women of aristocratic lineage:

Ngunguruterangi
|
Hinematioro
|
Ngarangikahiwa
|
Te Kani-a-Takirau.

The tapairu were mated of course to consorts of the highest blood but not necessarily the eldest males, of the eldest branch of their respective families.

Terms defining genealogy

We have given the terms used to define the act of recitation
and the various methods used by the reciter.

Limiting the subject of recitation to cosmogonies, pedigrees or genealogies
the various terms used for these may now be given.

We have given

Aho
Takiaho
Kaha
Kauwhata
Tatai
Kauwhau (kauhau, kauhou)
Tahu or tahuhu
Whakapapa
Ure tane or ure tarewa
Whakaparu wahine

and indicated the ideas underlying them in the reciter's mind.

The list may be amplified thus:

Ara:) Common expressions with the usual meaning

Huarahi:)
    Takina mai to huarahi i a Mahaki.
    He ara tangata tonu no te kawai matua.

Kawai) The figure is that of the shoot of a creeper or gourd, spreading from

Kawei) the parent stem.

    Takinga ou kawai, kia mohiotia ai ou tipuna.

Kaweka: Is allied to kawai, but suggests idling, rambling and digressing, therefore an
indirect line of descent.

    No te wa tauware, a stray shoot.

Hikahika matua: This is an unusual expression, and according
to Williams| is a direct line of descent.

Terms for generation

We have given one—'whakapaparanga', a term derived from whakapapa meaning a layer and
thus in relation to genealogies a generation.

Other terms are—

Ahunga: From 'ahu' to foster, fashion:
    Ata whaia ki tenei ahunga tangata.
    Ko taua kuia no te ahunga i a kuoro.

Reanga: from 'rea' to spring up, grow or multiply.

Whakatipuranga or whakatupuranga—from whakatupu, to cause to grow &c.
    Ko tenei korero mo te whakatupuranga o nga tupuna o te tangata Maori.

Terms for groups of descendants

These may be classified into (a) General terms for descendants
(b) Terms for tribal or sub-tribal groups.

(a) Descendants are termed in a general way as uri, momo, aitanga, mokopuna, pori, whanau [inserted in black ink, in Ngata's hand: 'and iwi may be added']. An archaic form is ati, preserved for the most part in tribal appellations and words like mataati, and there are terms such as hoko, pu, waka, ngare, ure which fall properly into the next class. The word 'whare' should perhaps be included in this class though its use in relation to descendants appears to be limited to the expression 'whare ngaro', a line or family which has become extinct.

(b) Tribal appellations are an example of how archaic forms may linger on in names (whether of places, persons or objects). The archaic 'ati' figures prominently as in Ati-Rua, Ati-Toa from Ngati-Rua, Ngati-Toa and is the usual form in Te Ati-awa. Nga-ati and Nga-ai are contracted to Ngati and Ngai to which the final element of some ancestral patronymic is added. Sometimes however this element is a word used to commemorate some incident viz: Ngati-Kumara, Ngati-Horomoana &c. The difference in use between 'ngai' and 'ngati' appears to be one of euphony. The form 'Ngai' is more frequent on the East Coast, whose dialect is prone to abbreviate or drop consonants. Thus Ngai-Tai at Torere is the name of the same tribe as the Ngati-Tai of the Western Hauraki Gulf.

The Arawa and Tainui folk pay more punctilious attention to syllables containing consonants ahau–au, tonu–tou, mata-whaorua–matahourua &c.

As tribal prefixes aitanga- (itanga), whanau, te ngare o, te ure o are in common use. It is remarked that these relate to the act of begetting and thus to those begotten. Ati in mataati, ati-a-toa, ika-i-te-ati relates to the young, the first procured or produced, the first fish, the young men in their first fight. Its use from time immemorial with tribal names suggests an original relationship with the act of procreation, unmistakeably preserved in the form Nga-ai &c.

Te Ngare o- is a Tuwharetoa, probably a Tainui form, as Te Ure o- is distinctively Arawa. The other forms are universal but more common on the East Coast.

Te Whanau-a-Apanui
Te Whanau-a-Te Ehutu
Te Whanau-a-Maru
Te Whanau-a-Kaiaio
Te Whanau-a-Pararaki
Te Whanau-a-Tuwhakiriora
Te Whanau-a-Ruataupare
Te Whanau-a-Karuai
Te Whanau-a-Rakaihoea
Te Whanau-a-Tapuhi
Te Whanau-a-Hinetapora
Te Aitanga-a-Mate
Te Whanau-a-Rakairoa
Te Whanau-a-Te Haemata
Te Whanau-a-Iritekura
Te Aitanga-a-Hauiti
Te Aitanga-a-Mahaki
Ngai-Tai
Ngai-Tamanuhiri
Ngai-te-Rangi
Ngai-Tane.

The Ngati form is not frequent. We have Ngati-Porou, Ngati-Puai, Ngati-Horowai (these two from drowning incidents as recently happened with the Whanau-a-Apanui of Maraenui who became Ngati-Horomoana), Ngati-Rangi, Ngati-Hau, Ngati-Konohi, Ngati-Rakaipaka, Ngati-Kahungunu. It may be observed however that Aitanga and Whanau were applied formerly to subsections of a main tribe, whether this had been named or not and gradually developed into groups worthy to be deemed tribes.

The use of 'waka' and waka names for tribes should, I think, be regarded as a recent development. Our people had the Horouta canoe but never used that name as a territorial designation until the establishment of Maori Councils. Now it is not uncommon to hear some of the communities within the territory speak of themselves as Horouta—a use that may develop into the practice which has allowed Te Arawa to displace Ngaoho.

Lastly we have the word 'hoko' associated with 'ati' in the tribal names—Te hoko Ati-Rua, te hoko Ati-Puhi &c. This Hoko is connected with hoko the prefix used with the numerals 1 to 9 to signify 20 times the subjoined numeral, and there is a multitude. Hoko Ati— is then the multitude of the Members of such and such a tribe.

I have a note of 'pu' meaning a tribe. This is the 'pu' of apu—a heap or collection, not the pu meaning origin, source.

(to be continued).

Kinship terms

The Maori kinship terms express both intimate or direct kinship, as true father or mother, or brother and sister, child and grandchild and collateral or indirect relationship. But it must not therefore be assumed that they did not in fact distinguish between near and distant kin. The vocabulary contains terms that separate the latter in definite fashion.

Relatives

The general term for relatives are 'huanga' and 'whanaunga', the latter prevailing among the East Coast tribes, where huanga is practically unheard of in the colloquial. A rare term is 'pakanga'. All terms denote blood relationship, descent from a common ancestor.

This common descent is called 'puninga tahi', and relatives will claim, 'he puninga tahi matou' (we come of a common ancestor).

Near relatives are called 'tautau huanga' the figure represented is that of a string or cluster of objects. 'Pakanga kiritahi' is also used to describe near relatives, probably closer in through blood than the former term. Distant relatives are called 'epeepe', literally small objects that are attached or cling to a main object, such as a rock. The distant relatives have parted so long or so far from the common stock that they have come cold or 'mataotao', they 'awhi' or merely embrace those who have remained close to the common ancestor.

The terms however do not convey distinctions as between lineal and collateral descendants.

Lineal and collateral descent

The student must take care in seeking terms which may mark such a distinction to recognise that there may be a difference in conception between the Maori genealogist and the European sociologist, and that the former in defining relationships has a mental picture embracing on one canvas a much more extensive group than the latter. One stratifies mentally successive horizontal groups from a common stock and sees them lie equal distances from the common 'pu', or 'take' and therefore in the same relationship to one another along the common plane. His terminology thus tends to embrace all on that plane in relation to the common ancestor and to one another. The European sociologist on the other hand prefers what may be called the vertical view, and having selected a line, which for his argument he calls direct, distributes appropriate terms for the relationship of the individuals down that line. There are his terms to define kinship in the direct line, that is linear descent. Those terms are used exclusively to define kinship in the direct line. As soon as you step to one side or the other of the direct line of descent the oblique relationships are described by other terms. Once a line is selected and called direct all others become indirect in relation to it, and all kinship of persons on those lines are deemed to be collateral in relation to persons on the selected direct line. His inherent individualism and his system of inheritance and succession to property engender not only preciseness in the terminology of kin but exclusiveness and rapid lopping off of receding relatives.

The Maori genealogist visualises vertical, horizontal, and oblique relationships as radiating from a common ancestor or a group of common ancestors. Perhaps it could be truer to picture his standing at a focus and defining the connection of all those round him whether above or below directly on either side of him or radiating to or from him as on a chart. Literally he is called upon to deal with a circle of relatives, all of whom appear intimate not only on his mental chart but in the everyday life of the area they inhabit. His traditional communal system, his system of inheritance, tracing on both the maternal and paternal side if both are connected with the ancestral stock whence rights and privileges or property is derived, the tendency of his race to embrace rather than exclude those related by blood conspire to make his terminology classificatory and apparently indiscriminating. It is not that he is not aware of the distinction between intimate and distant relationships, or that there is a basis of promiscuity which is best glossed over with terms of propriety. The Maori genealogist must in the nature of the case be precise and accurate. His social system demands that he should be polite and hospitable and the precise knowledge each family has of its detailed relationships is not sought to be overridden in any way by describing their connection with others outside themselves by the same terms they apply inter se. No one is deceived and the expert is the last person to attempt to deceive by the use of terms which translated into another tongue appear to exclude whole groups of individuals.

Here is a catechism. A father (Anglice) says to his son 'Karangatia atu to papa ki te kai.' The boy may ask 'A wai?' and he might be told 'A mea—hei tungaane hoki ki to koka.' The child may by questioning learn that it is some cousin of his mother that is meant, but not a real brother. He will get at the relationship to himself of many relatives by this process, whereby he first eliminates all not in the direct line, tino or tuturu, possibly also those who are not first or second cousins and so forth. He will still be interested in many more removed than the case of the European boy whose family circle is severely circumscribed by the social or economic system.

As the Maori lad grows up he perfects his education in the loose terminology used round him. He finds any amount of mentors to swell the data he must carry through life.

If then the Maori terms for lineal and collateral descendants confuse the European investigator they provide no pitfalls for those who grow up in it and whose education in the relationship of actual individuals to himself appear to be the care of all interested in him. It is our common experience in visiting the settlements to be confronted every hour and at every turn with short courses on relationships even from those who delight to rank you on the plane of their grandparents.

Maori kinship terms may therefore be said not to emphasise distinction between lineal and collateral descendants. But the distinction is there nevertheless and the terminology suggests its presence. Terms denoting relations which in the English relationship terminology are collateral kui may be given as follows:-

Keke. In a different line: from 'ke' different. So matua keke: uncle or aunt, matua meaning someone on the plane of a parent, male or female; tamaiti keke, nephew or niece.

There are no examples of the use of the terms for more distant relatives, such as cousins of the parents or children. Papa keke: Male relation in the same generation as father and mother.

Iramutu: Nephew or niece. The word tamaiti would embrace these, but if the precise relationship is to be emphasised the word is used.

Turanga whanau: Describes the relationship of cousins. It is used to limit the terms 'tuakana', 'taina', 'tungaane', 'tuahine' so as to remove all doubt whether these are intended to convey actual relationship through actual parents, direct kinship or something more distant.

Terms denoting lineal descent

At this point it should be stated that the Maori terms which correspond to the English terms comprise relations excluded by the latter. Translation would merely confuse. Yet a statement in English must use terms that appear to correspond, and require explanation to show where they pass beyond the accepted meaning of the English terms.

We must for the occasion defer consideration of terms denoting relationship by marriage or adoption for these will only add to the confusion.

It is necessary to remember that we must tabulate our terminology for an individual on the direct line from a common ancestor and to define his relationship (1) to those in the direct line to or from himself and (2) to those who are in a different line from that ancestor, and (3) of any of those persons to himself.

The English terms are—

> Grandparents; Grand-father, grandmother
>
> Parents; father, mother
>
> Children; son, daughter
>
> Grandchildren; grandson, grand-daughter.

The individual whose relatives we are seeking to define by appropriate terms, let us say, the son on the English table.

The corresponding Maori terms may be considered in detail.

(a) <u>Grand-parents.</u>

The common term is 'tupuna,' tipuna among the East Coast tribes. (Our people experience difficulty with 'tupu', 'tupua', 'tupuna', 'tumu', 'tumuaki', where the u in tu is short. This is one of the dialectal distinctions. I explain it in the chracteristics of the two main divisions of the North Island. That which we may roughly describe as Taihauauru (including the Arawa people) were more formal and deliberate in their language, especially the ceremonial or marae language. This is evidenced in the emphasis and value given to each syllable in a word. It was necessary even to interpolate a syllable like 'nge' to make the mouthful. The Tairawhiti man was not so careful; his was a 'reo mama', and he had a partiality for 'au' instead of 'ahau', 'tou' for 'tonu', and for the tripping 'ti' instead of 'tu'.)

Whereas the English term is restricted to the actual grand-father and grand-mother the Maori term is applied to their brothers or sisters or cousins to the 'nth degree or to any person in the same generation as either of them or in any earlier generation and related to them from a common ancestor. Tupuna is in fact the equivalent of the English 'ancestor', including a grand-parent. [*Manuscript ends here*]

RELATIONSHIP TERMS

APIRANA NGATA

[ATL Ms Ngata papers (also Micro Ms 232, folder 3/7).]

1. Denoting lineal descent

(a) <u>Grandparent or ancestor</u>

Tupuna is the common term and form except among East Coast tribes where it is 'tipuna'. (Our people experience difficulty with 'tupu', 'tupua', 'tumu', 'tumuaki', where the u in tu is short. This is one of the dialectical distinctions. I explain it in the characteristics of the two main divisions of the North Island. That which we may roughly describe as Taihauauru (including the Arawa people) were more formal and deliberate in their language, especially the ceremonial or marae language. This is evidenced in the emphasis and value given to every syllable like 'nge' to make up the mouthful. The Tairawhiti man was not so careful; his was a 'reo mama', and he had a partiality for 'au' instead of 'ahau,' 'tou' for 'tonu', and for the tripping 'ti' instead of 'tu'.)

Terms less commonly or rarely used beyond certain districts are:

> Koroua: Arawa. This is also 'Karaua', an old man
> Poua
> Taua
>
> [Note. It is suggested that the roots 'tua' and 'ua' relate to the same thing—
> the back or backbone. Compare 'Papatuanuku' or Papa-tua-nuku.

In this connection one might mention 'katua'—full-grown, the adult of animals. With some tribes (I specify my own) it means the parent, more usually the mother. Also 'matua'. In 'whakamatua' there is the idea of support or stiffening or mainstay. Matua and taua are connected in the military vocabulary and generally denote the main body of a war party. Our people would then in their lines of descent use primarily those words that stand for the 'backbone', and no doubt is left that the relationship terms denoting lineal descent were first applied to direct descent and later extended for the reasons you mention in your letter to collaterals, eventually embracing tribal connections no matter how remote. [*This sentence suggests that Apirana wrote this manuscript for Te Rangihīroa, rather than as a doctoral thesis per se.*]

The Arawa use of 'koroua' is significant, as that tribe attaches the utmost importance to the 'ure tane'—the unbroken descent in the male line. The male ancestor would be uppermost in the mind of an Arawa genealogist whether on the marae or in the recitation of poetry. By the way the Tainui songs use the term freely.

'Kuia' is the sex equivalent of koroua, and is so used in poetry. But sometimes is used for 'mother' especially when the woman is of advanced years. It is probably that it meant originally an 'aged woman' and came to be applied to a mother of advanced age.

(b) <u>Parent.</u>

The general term covering both sexes may be said to be 'matua', especially in the plural, 'mātua'. I suspect though that originally 'matua' was restricted in its application to the male parent, the father, and more often designates that today. With our people the male includes the female—the latter is an afterthought. Witness our table customs, the disinclination of the female to take her meal with the males—particularly the adult males of the family or at the same time. 'Matua' and 'whaea' are contrasted among the Tainui and other folk, as unconsciously as we should contrast 'papa' and 'koka' on the East Coast or 'papa' and 'kui' among Ngati Kahungunu.

'Papa' is perhaps a more intimate term than 'matua'. A mother would use it in conversation with her child. On the other hand the use in later days by children of 'Papa' or 'E Papa' introduces the greater intimacy of the Anglicised Maori child. Williams says that the Arawa 'papara' is used only of the <u>true</u> father. That may be so, but I suspect that an Arawa gave that limitation, as I have heard Arawas speak loosely of 'papara' in the sense that 'papa' embraces collateral, or in the [sentence ends here]

Equivalents for 'papa' are:—

Koroua: Arawa, Tuwharetoa, Tainui. Among Ngapuhi means the collateral papa.

Kohake: Waikato. In Moteatea (Grey) 31 is the expression, 'Kihai whakarangona te riri a te kohake'. Ko is the root in 'koeke', 'kotiro', 'koiwha', &c. and heke is apparently the same as in 'pahake' or Whanganui or Aotea peoples.

Matua: as above

Papara: as above

Whaea: As mother has a wider vogue that any other synonymous term—practically unknown on the East Coast until the early Maori catechists introduced it from the North, the Bible then broadcasting it with unfamiliar Ngapuhi terms.

In 'whaereere' however the root 'whae' was familiarly known to East Coast folk—where 'whaereere' is the most common term for 'mother or child-bearing "wife"' or the mother of one's children—an intimate term complimentary to the factor of child-bearing.

Whaene: A euphonious variant in vogue chiefly among you Aotea folk.
[*This again points to Te Rangihīroa as the recipient.*]

The glottal closure must have induced termination by a consonant
on which emphasis could be laid as against the open and inconclusive 'a'.

Hakui: The general N' Kahungunu term for mother apart from its broad
application as an elderly or old woman.

Kui: In the N' Kahungunu district this is strictly applied only to a woman
who is a mother. Apparently an abbreviation of 'hakui.'

Kuia: More often heard in the Arawa district in the same sense as 'kui' or 'hakui'.

(Ku: would appear to be a root form. You have it in 'kuao.' Probably originated in the crooning of a child. With us 'E ku' is a term of endearment used by a mother to a loved baby and appears to reciprocated by the child. 'Kumama' is to desire or long for, used only of an invalid's fancy for certain foods.)

Karawa: Strictly 'dam' of animals, but sometimes used as 'mother' among
a section of N' Kahungunu (Rakaipaka-Rongomaiwahine).

Koka: Is distinctively Ngati Porou and probably extended to Gisborne and the Whanau-a-Apanui in the same sense as 'whaea'.

Kokara: Williams says 'Mother or true mother only'; Whaea is used more loosely. See my remarks on 'papara.' I have heard it only among Arawa.

Tia: A most unusual term, its use as mother or parent probably developed from 'tia' the navel or abdomen.

Tiaka: Derived from 'tia' and like 'karawa' is strictly the dam of animals as opposed to 'kuao' the young of animals, but often loosely applied as 'mother' of human beings.

Ukaipo: Is poetical for 'mother.' Occurs frequently in East Coast songs — Williams quotes a Tologa Bay song 'E hika, e ia, hoki mai ra ki au, ki te ukaipo o Tamakuhukuhu.'

In these intimate terms for the true mother or father two angles may be discerned:-

i.   That of the child towards the parent emphasized in the case of the female parent by endearing terms such as 'ukaipo', 'hakui', 'whaea', 'koka'.

ii. That of the third party commenting on the relationship 'kohake', 'tiaka', 'karawa', 'katua'. Neither parent nor child would use these.

(c) <u>Children.</u>

We should first deal with the terms denoting relationship towards the parents and not the relationship among children. The term of widest application is 'tamaiti' (Pl. tamariki).

For the male child or son we may accept 'tama'. But (collaterals apart) it is not distinctive. It raises in the mind of the hearer the question that possibly the eldest child is meant. So that 'tama' while defining relationship to the parents and the sex suggests also seniority among male children. And 'tama' in the 'whakatauki' may merely mean a 'child' as in the example quoted by Williams 'Kua whanau tama a Rangi' or in the better example, the Whanau-a-Apanui pepeha concerning Apanui-mutu, 'Kua whanau tama a Rongomaihuatahi, he tane', 'Rongomaihuatahi has borne a child, a son'.

'Tamahine' for daughter is less liable to confusion than 'tama.' It does mean generally a daughter but in the proper context suggests the eldest daughter. In the plural there is no such liability to confusion.

By the way in your amended 'Pakeha Pedigree' you make one mistake, viz:-

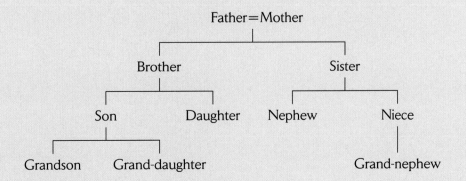

You have extended a generation too many. In tracing down the direct line of descent you must keep to the terms appropriate to the 'tahuhu' or 'aho', and use those which describe the relationship up or down and not as between individuals on the same plane. It is difficult to set it out in a table in such a way as to make the relationship terms completely relative. You can start out to describe the relationship between one generation and that which succeeds it and also the relationship of individuals on the same plane inter se. You would confuse parentage and childhood, with marital relationship or sex distinctions among children. You have only to add terms denoting order of birth (irrespective of sex) or seniority among children of either sex and you are in the soup.

Acknowledgements

The Bishop Museum and the Alexander Turnbull Library gave permission for these manuscripts to be transcribed and published.

References

Sorrenson, Maurice Peter Keith, ed. 1988, *Na To Hoa Aroha: From Your Dear Friend. The Correspondence between Sir Apirana Ngata and Sir Peter Buck 1925–1950*, vol. 1, 1925–29; vol. 2, 1930–32; vol. 3, 1932–1950. Auckland: Auckland University Press, Maori Purposes Fund Board.

'The Terminology of Whakapapa', MS SC Buck 6.02. Bishop Museum, Honolulu.

'The Terminology of Whakapapa' (continued), ATL Ms, Ngata papers, Micro Ms 232, folder 3/7. Originals in the possession of Dr Herewini Ngata, filmed at the Alexander Turnbull Library Wellington 1979.

'Relationship Terms', Ms Ngata papers (also Micro Ms 232, folder 3/7), Alexander Turnbull Library, Wellington.

NOTES

Abbreviations

DNZB Dictionary of New Zealand Biography
JPS Journal of the Polynesian Society
NMRE National Museum Register Ethnology
NZPD New Zealand Parliamentary Debates
TPNZI Transactions and Proceedings of the New Zealand Institute
AJHR Appendix to the Journals of the House of Representatives

Hei Wāhi Ake / Mihi

1   Eric Ramsden discussed with Te Ranghīroa about how his name should be written. He writes: 'I have reverted to the earlier spelling of his name, Te Rangihiroa, though on his published work he used the variant Te Rangi Hiroa. To me he admitted more than once that the form puzzled him. In his own whakapapa, written early in life, the name occurs more than once, and it was always Te Rangihiroa.' Ramsden, *A Memoir: Te Rangihiroa*, 1954, p. 6.

2   Wiremu Kaa and Te Ohorere Kaa (eds), *Apirana T Ngata*, 1996, p. 40.

Introduction

1   Tuta Ngārimu, quoted in McLean and Curnow (eds), *Catalogue of Museum of New Zealand Cylinder Recordings of Traditional Maori Songs, 1919–c.1935*, p. 143.

2   Herbert Williams, *A Dictionary of the Maori Language Edited under the auspices of the Polynesian Society and based upon the dictionaries of W. Williams and W. L. Williams*, Marcus F Marks, Government Printer, 1917. This classic dictionary of Māori was originally produced by William and his son William Leonard Williams, members of the Church Missionary Society.

3   Geoffrey Rice, *That Terrible Time*, 2020, p. 8.

4   'The 1918 Influenza Epidemic', New Zealand History online, www.nzhistory.govt.nz.

5   Rice estimates the relative death rate for Māori throughout the epidemic as seven times higher than that for Europeans: Rice, *That Terrible Time*, p. 12.

6   For a detailed account of McDonald's career as government kinematographist, see Pugsley, Christopher, *The Camera in the Crowd: Filming New Zealand in Peace and War, 1895–1920*, 2017, pp. 90–115.

7   N de B Hornibrook, 'James Allan Thomson', *DNZB*, Te Ara—the Encyclopedia of New Zealand, www.teara.govt.nz.

8   Thomson to Minister of Internal Affairs 13 February 1919, MU1/018/00011 11 3/17, Te Papa Archives Wellington.

9   Elsdon Best list, attached to Director to Ngata 17 February 1919, MU1/018/00011 11 3/17, Te Papa Archives Wellington.

10   Director to Ngata 17 February 1919, MU1/018/00011 11 3/17, Te Papa Archives Wellington.

11   Ranginui Walker, 'Hēnare Te Raumoa Huatahi Balneavis', *DNZB*, Te Ara—the Encyclopedia of New Zealand, first published 1998, www.teara.govt.nz.

12   Ibid.

13   Natalie Robertson, 'Activating Mana Rangatiratanga through Kōrero', in C Braddock (ed.), *Animism in Art and Performance*, Palgrave Macmillan, 2017.

14   See Appendix: Apirana Ngata, 'The Terminology of Whakapapa', c.1930.

15   Ibid.

16   Ibid.

17   Ibid.

18   Quoted in GV Butterworth, 'The Politics of Adaptation: The Career of Sir Apirana Ngata, 1874–1928', MA dissertation, History Department, Victoria University of Wellington, 1969, p. 37.

19   Walker, *He Tipua*, 2001, pp. 44, 47.

20   Steven Oliver, 'Rāpata Wahawaha', *DNZB*, Te Ara—the Encyclopedia of New Zealand, www.teara.govt.nz. Porter, 'History of the Early Days of Poverty Bay', 1923. Wahawaha was named Rāpata after Rāpata Whakapuhia of Tūranganui, who took him as a war captive after a battle at Tuatini pā, Tokomaru, in 1828, and took him to Gisborne. He later changed his name to Rōpata, because he preferred Donald McLean's Scottish pronunciation of his name, and it was a less vivid reminder of his time as a war captive. Wahawaha's full Māori name was Rangi Wahawaha Aruhe ki Te Puia ki Te Reinga a Tamateahiwera mā te Poaka. Te Reinga a Tamateahiwera, who was also known as Ngārangikakautu, was a tuakana to Rāpata (Wayne Ngata, pers. comm. 2021).

21   For an in-depth account of these alliances and struggles, see Soutar 2000, and Walker 2001, pp. 36–53.

22   Alan Ward, 'Donald McLean', *DNZB*, Te Ara—the Encyclopedia of New Zealand, www.teara.govt.nz. McLean made much of an affinity between Scots and Māori, a link that James Cowan also drew: 'Many a year ago colonists from the Scottish Highlands were interested to find a remarkably close resemblance beween the Gael and Maori in some of the everyday customs and in tribal beliefs and concepts … It was men like Sir Donald McLean who were the readiest to understand something of the Maori mind and to perceive the motives and the processes of reasoning which prompted actions that to most pakeha people were at first inexplicable … The average Maori of that day, had he been transported suddenly to a glen in Appin or an isle in the Hebrides, would have been able to adjust himself quickly to the tribal and village life.' Cowan in 'Cowan and Pomare', 1930, pp. 59–60.

23   Ibid., pp. 46–47. For a detailed, incisive account of the fighting between the Hauhau and Queenite factions of Ngāti Porou at this time, see Soutar 2000, pp. 248–97.

24   Walker 2001, pp. 48–49. It is likely that Rāpata's hostility towards Rongowhakaata was inspired by his period as a war captive in Tūranganui (Gisborne) after the battle of Tuatini: see Soutar, 2000, pp. 82–88.

25   Ibid., p. 48.

26   Monty Soutar, pers. comm. 2021. Katerina's sister Hera Enoka (Sarah Knox) was Monty's great-grandmother.

27   Walker 2001, pp. 50–51.

28   Hone Te Ihi was the great-grandfather of Wayne Ngata.

29   See Paratene Ngata, 1950, p. 281; and Wayne Ngata, pers. comm. 2021.

30   See Soutar 2000 for a detailed account of the distinctive origins and influence of Ngāti Porou Christianity; and Kaa 2020.

31   See Paratene's account of these events in P Ngata 1950, pp. 280–82.

32   Walker 2001, pp. 54–56.

33   Natalie Robertson, pers. comm. 2020. Co-author Natalie Robertson's great-grandmother Mabel Boyd attended the same school. Mabel's younger brothers also attended Te Aute College at the same time as Te Rangihīroa ('In 1896, fifteen-year-old Ernest Boyd was enrolled at Te Aute College, Hawke's Bay. He was joined a year later by his twin brother Arthur. Alan joined his brother at the beginning of 1898 and the three boys remained at Te Aute College until the end of 1898.' *Ancestry and Anecdotes.* Compiled by Stephanie and Ivan Hughes. June 1999.)

34   AT Ngata, 1924, History of the Waiomatatini School, in *History of the East Coast Native Schools,* ATL, PAM 1924/4460.

35   Johannes Andersen notebook, 31 March 1923.

36   Walker 2001, pp. 63–65.

37   As Rēweti Kōhere, who followed Ngata to Te Aute, recalled, Thornton was greatly admired by his students: 'I have been told again and again that there has never been a generation of Te Aute boys like the Thornton generation. John Thornton was a remarkable man in many ways. Mr. Thornton could never stand lounging about or putting one's hands in one's pockets. When he sent a boy to fetch something, the boy had to either run or step it out, but could not drag his feet. I often heard him ask a boy after the class had shown him its work, "Rangi, why must you always be the last." Constantly, in season and out of season, he watched the boys with a fatherly care and took every opportunity to teach and guide them to useful and good lives. The boys revered Mr. Thornton and among themselves always referred to him as 'Jack,' as though he were one of them. In private company Mr. Thornton was jovial and entertaining and boys felt perfectly at home with him'. (Kōhere, *The Story of a Maori Chief,* 1949, p. 75).

38   A saying from earlier times of epidemic and warfare, e.g. in *Te Karere o Poneke,* 10 February 1858, 1/17, p. 2.

39   Walker 2001, p. 65.

40   Ibid., p. 70.

41   Carey 2014.

42   Published in *Souvenir of the Ngarimu Victoria Cross investiture meeting and reception to His Excellency the Governor-General Sir Cyril Navall, G.C.B., O.M., G.C.M.G., C.B.E., A.M., Whakarua Park, Ruatoria, East Coast, 6 October, 1943,* pp. 34–38. Eruera Stirling vividly remembered Apirana performing this poem in later days.

43   Ngata 1893, p. 6.

44   Walker 2001, pp. 66.

45   W and O Kaa 1996, p. 16–18.

46   Alan Ward, 'Wiremu Pere', *DNZB,* Te Ara—the Encyclopedia of New Zealand, www.teara.govt.nz.

47   Walker 2001, pp. 71–73. In 1906 Ngata reiterated this concern, writing in *Te Pipiwharauroa,* vol. 97, pp. 3–5 that 'it was a grave misfortune for the land not to have trees … even five acres out of every hundred as reserves would be sufficient'; see Walker 2001, pp. 113–14.

48   Condliffe, JB, *Te Rangi Hiroa, The Life of Sir Peter Buck,* Whitcomb & Tombs, Christchurch, 1971, pp. 49–51

49   Sorrenson, 'Peter Henry Buck', *DNZB,* Te Ara—the Encyclopedia of New Zealand, www.teara.govt.nz. See also Condliffe 1971.

50   Condliffe 1971, p. 57.

51   Ibid., p. 30.

52   For a historical account of Te Aute, see Graham, *Whakatangata Kia Kaha,* 2009, pp. 20–60.

53   Condliffe 1971, p. 67.

54   Walker 2001, p. 75.

55   Reports and Addresses, First Conference, TACSA, pp. 7–20.

56   Quoted in Condliffe 1971, pp. 40–45; Walker 2001, p. 82.

57   Ibid., p. 83; although as Monty Soutar has pointed out, in censuses, those who were less than half Māori were counted as Europeans (Soutar 2019, p. 24).

58   Eruera Kāwhia Stirling, author Anne Salmond's mentor and teacher, who attended Te Aute and became a follower of Apirana Ngata, was named after this elder. Taumata-o-Mihi was the home of Eruera Stirling's future wife, Amiria O'Hara.

59   Ngata and Buck, ed. Sorrenson, *Na To Hoa Aroha,* vol. 1, 1986, p. 15.

60   Condliffe 1971, p. 29.

61   Ibid., p. 76.

62   Ibid., p. 77.

63   Walker 2001, p. 96; Condliffe 1971, pp. 120–21.

64   Walker 2001, pp. 83–99.

65   Ibid., p. 110.

66   Quoted in ibid., p. 111.

67   Soutar 2019, pp. 19–20.

68   Jonathan Dennis, 'James Ingram McDonald', *DNZB,* Te Ara—the Encyclopedia of New Zealand, www.teara.govt.nz.

69   *Bruce Herald,* 4 November 1868, p. 4.

70   Many thanks to Atholl Anderson for his summary of the Māori history of Lovells Flat until the 1860s (Anderson, pers. comm. 2020)

71   *Otago Daily Times,* 17 March 1928, p. 12.

72   DS Thomson, 1963. The MacMhuirich Bardic Family. *Transactions of the Gaelic Society of Inverness* 43, pp. 276–304; JWM Bannerman 1977, Edinburgh.

73   Martin McGregor 2018. The genealogical histories of Gaelic Scotland. In Adam Fox and Daniel Woolf (eds) *The Spoken Word: Oral Culture in Britain 1500–1850,* Manchester: Manchester University Press, pp. 236–289.

74   James Cowan in *New Zealand Railways Magazine,* 1 July 1935, p. 51; Box 21 F.I, DM 2/7/56, Te Papa Archives Wellington.

75   James and May might have met through her brother, the architect John Henry Brabin, who gave lessons in draughts-manship and technical drawing.

76   TE Donne, c. 1904, ATL MSX 2394, Notebook, which records that James McDonald lived at 23 Austin Street, Wellington, and was paid 275 pounds, 25 pounds less than his friend and senior James Cowan.

77   'TE Donne', New Zealand History online, www.nzhistory.govt.nz.

78   David Colquhoun, 'James Cowan', *DNZB,* Te Ara—the Encyclopedia of New Zealand, www.teara.govt.nz.

79   'Tangiwai' [James Cowan], 'Pictures of New Zealand Life', *New Zealand Railways Magazine,* 1 July 1935, p. 5.

80   *New Zealand Times,* 27 January 1906.

81   Cowan 1910, p. 107. Or, as Bernie Kernot wrote in Thomson 1998, p. 62: 'As a composition the figures represent no particular personages, nor do they represent an event either historical or mythological. They are simply a romanticised image of noble savages whose age is passing. While the old warrior looks backwards into the past, the young family appear to be facing the future, but the air of melancholy that pervades the group suggests there is no future for Maori except as a decorative embellishment of life in the colony.'

82   Neich 2001, pp. 61, 147, 155–56, 215–17.

83   TE Donne, The New Zealand Government Department of Tourist and Health Resorts, *TO* 1, 1908/495, Archives New Zealand.

84   Dominion Museum records, Letter from WJ Phillips to HD Skinner, 16 September 1955.

85   See JA Thomson, 'Special Reports: Some Principles of Museum Administration Affecting the Future Development of the Dominion Museum'. In *AJHR,* 1915, Government Printer, Wellington, pp. 9–19.

86   Elsdon Craig, *Man of the Mist: A Biography of Elsdon Best,* 1964, p. 19.

87   Ibid., p. 23.

88   Ibid., p. 24.

89   Sorrenson 1992; Rivers 1926.

90   Holman, *Best of Both Worlds,* 2010, p. 81.

91   Craig 1964, p. 50.

92   See Holman 2010 for a detailed account of the relationship with Tūtakangahau in particular.

93   Craig 1964, p. 85; Anne Cavanagh, in McLean and Curnow 1992, pp. 255–57.

94   Holman 2010, p. 216.

95   Ibid., p. 174.

96   Ibid., pp. 202–03.

97 Best, *Tuhoe,* fn 351—although as we have seen, Paitini was still alive when he and Best met again in Rotorua at the 1920 welcome to the Prince of Wales.

98 Holman 2010, pp. 220–21. See also 'E. Best 1913', MU152/012/0058, Te Papa Archives Wellington.

99 JCA to Ngata 23 September 1908; Auckland Institute and Museum Library; Andersen papers Vol. 4.

100 WJ Phillips / HD Skinner on McDonald in 16 September 1955; Skinner–Phillips 22 September 1955; Phillips–Skinner 26 September 1955 (National Museum Archives, Box labelled 'Unfiled correspondence—Phillips').

101 Johannes C Andersen, *Place Names of Banks Peninsula*, 1916–27, ATL MS Papers 0148-035

102 See for instance Thomson's first report as Director of the Dominion Museum in 1915, 'It is desirable … that phonograph records of Maori music and the rhythm of old Maori songs should be secured'

103 JA Thomson, Director: Memorandum for the Hon. The Minister of Internal Affairs, 13 February 1919, MU1/018/00011, 11/3/17, Te Papa Archives Wellington.

104 RK Dell, 'Augustus Hamilton', *DNZB*, Te Ara—the Encyclopaedia of New Zealand, www.teara.govt.nz.

105 On the extensive Māori participation in the exhibition see McCarthy 2009, pp. 119–42.

106 Kernot in Thomson (ed.) 1998, pp. 61–78. For contemporary Māori reports of the International Exhibition see *Te Pipiwharauroa* 1906 nos 104, 105.

107 Cowan, 'Official Record of the New Zealand International Exhibition of Arts and Industries', Wellington, 1910, p. 335.

108 James McDonald was author Anne Salmond's great-grandfather, and co-author Amiria Salmond's great-great-grandfather.

109 Diamond 2007, Makereti 1986.

110 Neich 2001, pp. 195–96.

111 Alan Ward, 'James Carroll', *DNZB*, Te Ara—the Encyclopedia of New Zealand, www.teara.govt.nz.

112 R Hill, *State Authority, Indigenous Autonomy*, 2004, pp. 81–83.

113 Reports of the Commission on Native Lands and Native-Land Tenure, *AJHR*, 1907, G1–G1E and 1908, Gi–iii, and G1A–1T; Walker 2001, pp. 111–20; Boast 2019, pp. 1–52.

114 Alex Frame, 'Sir John William Salmond', *DNZB*, Te Ara—the Encyclopedia of New Zealand, www.teara.govt.nz; see also Frame, *Te Mura o te Ahi*, 1995. Sir John, sometimes acclaimed as 'New Zealand's most eminent jurist', won a remarkable international reputation for his books on *Jurisprudence* (1902) and *Torts* (1907). After serving as counsel for the Office of Law Drafting (1907–10) and working closely with Ngata and Carroll as draftsman for the Native Lands Act, he was appointed Solicitor-General, and served in this role for the next decade. In 1920–24 Salmond served as a Judge on the Supreme Court of New Zealand; he represented New Zealand at the 1921–22 Washington Conference on the Limitation of Armaments. Sir John is the great-great-uncle of co-author Amiria Salmond.

115 Boast 2007, pp. 831–51.

116 See Ellis 2016.

117 Māori text in W and O Kaa 1996, p. 67.

118 Te Rangi Hiroa, 'The Coming of the Maori', Cawthron Lecture Series, vol. II, no. 2, Cawthron Institute, Nelson, 1925; *Coming of the Maori,* 2nd edn, 1929.

119 See Condliffe 1971, p. 106.

120 For a detailed account of McDonald's career in this capacity, see Pugsley 2017, pp. 92–115.

121 Ibid., pp. 102–04.

122 Interview with TEY Seddon, *Evening Post*, 23 April 1955.

123 Te Rangi Hiroa, 'He Poroporoaki— A Farewell Message', *Journal of the Polynesian Society*, vol. 60, no. 1, 1951; Condliffe 1971, pp. 111–12.

124 See Gregory, Justin, '*The SaVAge K'Lub*', *Radio New Zealand*, www.rnz.co.nz, which gives a brief explanation of the original Savage Club, and its contemporary satirical counterpart in New Zealand, and Lythberg, 'KRONKling the K'lub—from 19th Century Savages to 21st Century SaVAgery', SaVAge K'lub, 2020, www.savageklub.com.

125 Condliffe 1971, pp. 117–18.

126 Ngata to Eric Ramsden, Waiomatatini, 28 March 1950, quoted in Condliffe 1971, pp. 118–19.

127 Te Rangihīroa to Eric Ramsden, 14 September 1950, quoted in ibid., p. 120.

128 Ngata, 'Draft Statement of the Aims and Objectives of the Young Maori Party (Northern Division) in amplification of clause 2 of the Constitution', 1909. Māori Purposes Fund Board Papers: Apirana Ngata miscellanous papers 1883–1909, MS Papers-0189-011B, Alexander Turnbull Library, Wellington.

129 Carroll had strongly supported the inclusion of the Māori pā at the 1906 New Zealand International Exhibition, and the 1901 Maori Antiquities Act legislation proposed by Hamilton and Percy Smith, as well as their proposal for a national Māori museum. See McCarthy 2007.

130 Hamilton's justification for a national Māori museum is illuminating:

'Having established and maintained our position by force, it would not be human nature if complete unanimity prevailed between the conquerors and the conquered. The establishment by the ruling powers of what would practically be a monument to the forefathers of the natives, and a State Storehouse for the remaining ancestral possessions of the native race would … be a desirable, a right, and a generous thing to do.

'It would show that it is not the desire of the pakeha that the Maori Race should become as extinct as the Moa, or that the pakeha rat should entirely drive out the Kiore Maori.

'It would further show that there is no desire to destroy or lose any of the ancestral glories of the long lines of Maori chiefs who built up the Maori polity during the past centuries. Those of mixed blood will feel that they have on each side cause to be proud of their descent, and that no taint of racial animosity still exists to recall the time when their forefathers met in chivalric combat …

'It would also be a Valhalla for the Maori, a place in which the memories of their great ones can be enshrined and perpetuated … The proposal so far has me, not only with the sympathy of, but marked encouragement from many leading Maoris, whose goodwill and promised co-operation augur well for the future prospects of the project.' Augustus Hamilton 1902, 'Notes for the Information of the Members of both Houses of Parliament, in the matter of the National Maori Museum proposed to be established in Wellington to carry out the provisions of the Maori Antiquities Act of 1901, and to be a permanent memorial of the past history of the Maori People.'

131 Te Rangihīroa to Ngata, 18 May 1909, MA 31/42; Royal Anthropological Institute of Great Britain, *Notes and Queries on Anthropology*, 2nd edn, 1892, www.library.si.edu.

132 See McCarthy 2016, pp. 51–67.

133 Graham Butterworth, 'Māui Wiremu Piti Naera Pōmare', *DNZB*, Te Ara—the Encyclopedia of New Zealand, www.teara.govt.nz.

134 Te Rangihīroa, 1951, He Poroporoaki— A Farewell Message, *Journal of the Polynesian Society*, quoted in Condliffe 1971, pp. 111–12.

135 Ngata and Buck, *Na To Hoa Aroha*, vol. 1, p. 21.

136 Buck, 'On the Maori Art of Weaving Cloaks, Capes and Kilts', *Dominion Museum Bulletin No. 3*, Government Printer, Wellington, 1911, pp. 69–90.

137 Ed. Sorrenson 1987. Te Rangihīroa to Ngata, Honolulu 10 February 1931, *Na To Hou Aroha*, vol. 2, pp. 114–15.

138 Ngata to Te Rangihīroa, Waiomatatini 4 January 1929, *Na To Hou Aroha*, vol. 1, pp. 165–66.

139 Te Rangihīroa to Ngata, Honolulu 5 June 1928, *Na To Hou Aroha*, vol. 1, pp. 100–01.

140 Te Rangihīroa to Ngata, Honolulu 29 June, 1930, *Na To Hou Aroha*, vol. 2, p. 36.

141 Soutar 2019, p. 16.

142 See also Soutar 2019, p. 45.

143 Te Rangihīroa quoted in Condliffe 1971, p. 125.

144 Soutar 2019, p. 57.

145 Ibid., pp. 80–81.

146 Quoted in Condliffe 1971, pp. 127–28

147 Soutar 2019, pp. 124–25.

148 Te Rangihīroa quoted in Condliffe 1971, p. 132. See also Soutar 2019, p. 134; and for an excellent account of the role of the Maori Contingent at Gallipoli, see Soutar 2019, pp. 92–165.

149 Ibid., pp. 210–11.

150 Ibid., pp. 294–95.

151 Ibid., p. 314.

152 Ibid., p. 390.

153 Ibid.

154 *Auckland Star*, 8 February 1915; Best 1915. See also annual report 1915, p. 5. Since Te Rangihīroa left with the first Maori Contingent for Egypt in February 1915, it seems unlikely that he was in New Zealand at the same time as Rivers.

155 Rivers 1926; Skinner 1922, pp. 87–88; Slobodin 1978, pp. 51–53.

156 These reports were familiar to Best and McDonald's associates before 1923. Letter from Te Rangi Hiroa (Peter Buck) to Tarawhai (Johannes Andersen), 18.2.1923, Alexander Turnbull Library, Wellington, Johannes Andersen pers. comms. MS Papers 0148-015, Alexander Turnbull Library, Wellington.

157 See McCarthy 2007. See also Tony Bennett, Rodney Harrison, Ira Jacknis, Fiona Cameron, Ben Dibley, Nelia Dias and Conal McCarthy, *Collecting, Ordering, Governing*, Duke University Press, Durham, NC, 2017, ch. 4. For a primary source, see 'Elsdon Best Dominion Museum Maori Ethnology, 'Account of Mr Best's trip to North island' MU01/17/55, 31/1/1912, Te Papa Archives Wellington.

158 'A number of old-time and rare specimens of the art of the Kai-whakairo, which were in danger of decay, were removed from their mountings, revarnished with glue and renovated. Others now having attention are being backed with molten paraffin wax before remounting. Many of the carved slabs which were found to be visited by the wood-boring beetle were subjected to prolonged soaking in a solution of lime, … carbonate and arsenic. A large wooden Cook Island vessel with a capacity of 600 gallons was used.' James McDonald's report, Dominion Museum annual report 1916.

159 For staff activities at the Domnion Museum at this time, see the annual reports, and also McCarthy 2007.

160 Dominion Museum Annual Report 1915.

161 Elsdon Best's report, Dominion Museum annual report 1916.

162 MJ Parsons, 'Jury, Hoani Te Whatahoro', *DNZB*, Te Ara—the Encyclopedia of New Zealand, www.teara.govt.nz. On Best's trip to see Te Whatahoro Jury, see 'Offer of manuscript of Maori History by Major HP Tunuiarangi—suggesting Mr Best should interview him' (1917), MU14/002/0017 13/27/48, Te Papa Archives, Wellington.

163 MU1/017/51 'DM Wellington—Māori ethnology, Elsdon Best, proposed trip to Whanganui; Memo EB to Director (JM) 17/2/16.

164 Rice describes McDonald's text 'Some considerations for future guidance' in forming a national art collection, published in Dominion Museum annual report 1915, as 'the closest description of a strategic approach' that existed during the collection's early formative phase (Rice 2010).

165 McDonald to Undersecretary, Internal Affairs, 31 December 1918.

166 For Dominion Museum files now in the Te Papa Archives which record the organisation of the expeditions, see 'Internal Affairs Wellington–Wanganui expedition, collecting ethnological data among the Maoris (photographic and phonographic), Messers McDonald, Best and Andersen', MU1/018/00011, 11/3/17; 'Maori Ethnology: Ancient Maori Chants (Wax cylinders)', MU2/058/0008 18/0/12; 'Ethnological Expedition—East Coast, 1923', MU1/018/0010, 11/3/3.

Chapter 1 — 'Kia ora te hui aroha'

1 This was the clarion call issued to Māori to support the Hui Aroha. It was published in *Te Kopara*, 12 February 1919, no. 62, p. 5. Translation by author.

2 The goal of £25,000, first set by the trustees of the fund, was realised in April 1918. *Poverty Bay Herald*, 31 March 1919, p. 8. Translation by author.

3 *Te Kopara*, no. 62, 12 February 1919, p. 5. Translation by author. The same notice with the date of the hui, 8 April 1919, along with a full list of returning members of the Maori (Pioneer) Battalion, was published in the next issue: *Te Kopara*, no. 63, 31 March 1919, pp. 10–12.

4 *Te Kopara*, no. 64, 30 April 1919, p. 7.

5 This is the closest rendering the author could make of the Māori text. Wī Repa was a Te Aute graduate, a medical doctor and a close friend of Apirana Ngata. Translation by author.

6 The hui was first announced by Lady Carroll at Te Kapu (Frasertown) during that fundraiser. It was planned for March 1919, but that date changed when it was learnt that the ship transporting the Maori Battalion would reach New Zealand in April. *Te Kopara*, no. 54, 30 April 1918, p. 10.

7 Wī Pere was a constant recruiter and stalwart supporter of Māori soldiers. In October 1914, he gave the name Te Hokowhitu a Tū to the First Maori Contingent. He died on 9 December 1915. Soutar, *Whitiki!: Maori in the First World War*, 2019, pp. 48, 50, 218.

8 According to the Reserve Bank of New Zealand inflation calculator.

9 The goal of £25,000 was realised in April 1918. *Poverty Bay Herald*, 31 March 1919, p. 8. At a meeting held at Manutuke in June 1918 the executive council of the MSF resolved that assistance from the fund should be limited to Māori soldiers of the Eastern Maori electorate, 'but that the scheme should be extended to Maori soldiers of other districts if those districts elected to join in the scheme and provide their quota to the fund'. *Gisborne Times*, 13 June 1918, p. 6.

10 *Poverty Bay Herald*, 24 January 1919, p. 5. At the Frasertown hui, Te Arawa tribes of the Rotorua district and the Mātaatua tribes of the Whakatāne, Ōpōtiki and Urewera districts, which had not officially become contributors, were asked to join the fund. In August 1918, at Rūātoki, during the unveiling of a monument to the late Tūhoe chief Nūmia Kererū, and at a subsequent meeting at Rotorua, the Bay of Plenty tribes made a handsome contribution towards the fund. That completed the organisation of the electorate for all the purposes of the fund.

11 About 9000 New Zealanders had died by the time the influenza pandemic eased in early 1919. The death rate for Māori of 2500 was eight times that for Pākehā. The pandemic had a varying impact on Māori communities. A district like Wairoa, for example—including Whakakī, Nūhaka, Māhia, Te Reinga, Waiau, Pūtere and Mōhaka—suffered 148 deaths, while the isolated community of Waikaremoana had no cases. *Te Kopara*, no. 63, 31 March 1919, p. 7; Soutar, *Whitiki!*, p. 462; *Poverty Bay Herald*, 31 March 1919, p. 8.

12 Apirana Ngata to Hon. G.W. Russell, Minister of Internal Affairs, 1 December 1918. ACIH 16068 MA51/928 26/9/23/1 'Ethnological—Phonographic records', Archives New Zealand, Wellington.

13 Lady Carroll was chair of the fund's executive committee and Apirana Ngata was a trustee, so through the two MPs the committee not only had access to intel on troop transport movements, but they also had a direct line of communication with government ministers.

14 *Poverty Bay Herald*, 24 January 1919, p. 5.

15 Soutar, *Whitiki!*, p. 18.

16 *Poverty Bay Herald*, 9 April 1919, p. 5. See Ngata's speech of thanks to the Minister of Defence.

17 Soutar, *Whitiki!*, p. 463; *New Zealand Herald*, 31 March 1919, p. 4 published the names of the men belonging to the Auckland Provincial district; *Evening Post*, 28 March 1919, p. 4. Three hundred and thirty-six members of the Battalion had died 'on active service', including of disease, in accidents and after returning to New Zealand, as had thirteen men who had transferred to other units. Another twenty-seven had died in training.

18 Soutar, *Whitiki!*, p. 474; *Te Kopara*, no. 63, 31 March 1918, p. 9. The January 1919 issue of *Te Kopara* lists the committee members who met at Omāhu on 30 September 1918: Lady Carroll (president), Hon. AT Ngata, Dr Tūtere Wī Repa, Hetekia Te Kani Pere, Pita Te Hau, Joseph Carroll, Paraire Tomoana, Mohi Te Atahikoia, Erueti Peene, Takurua Tamarau, Wiremu Pitt (secretary). *Te Kopara*, no. 61, 12 January 1918, p. 5.

19 *Poverty Bay Herald*, 1 May 1918, p. 3; 12 October 1918, p. 5; 24 January 1919, p. 5; *Auckland Star*, 30 January 1919, p. 6. More than 1800 of the 2227 Māori and Pacific Island soldiers who had left New Zealand with the Maori Contingent and its reinforcements were still overseas. Some 346 Māori and Pacific Island recruits were at Narrow Neck camp when the war ended.

20 *Auckland Star*, 5 February 1919, p. 4.

21 *Poverty Bay Herald*, 28 January 1919, p. 7; *Auckland Star*, 6 February 1919, p. 4.

22 Phil Lascelles, *Medals and Ethnicity*, research report produced for Auckland War Memorial Museum, 2015, p. 17.

23 *Auckland Star*, 2 April 1919, p. 4.

24 *Nelson Evening Mail*, 25 March 1919, p. 4.

25 *Evening Post*, 28 March 1919, p. 4; *Poverty Bay Herald*, 7 April 1919, p. 3; *Gisborne Times*, 8 April 1919, p. 5; *Te Kopara*, 31 March 1919, no. 63, pp. 10–12 listed those soldiers from the Eastern Maori District, plus Manawatū, Whanganui and Taranaki.

26 GF Dixon to Allen, 4 April 1919, AD1, Box 951, 49/70/179 pt 1, ANZ; *Gisborne Times*, 7 April 1919, p. 5.

27 *Te Kopara*, 31 March 1919, no. 63, p. 7. Translation by author.

28 *Auckland Star*, 7 April 1919, p. 5; Tawhai Tamepo Diary, 5 April 1919, Ereatara Tamepo Family Collection.

29 Carroll travelled by the *Arahura* from Gisborne on 3 April. *Poverty Bay Herald*, 4 April 1919, p. 5.

30 Tamepo Diary, 6 April 1919.

31 *Poverty Bay Herald*, 7 April 1919, p. 3.

32 *Poverty Bay Herald*, 3 April 1919, p. 5.

33 *Poverty Bay Herald*, 28 March 1919, p. 5; 3 April 1919, p. 5.

34 *Poverty Bay Herald*, 31 March 1919, p. 8; 3 April 1919, p. 5.

35 *Poverty Bay Herald*, 5 & 7 April 1919, p. 1.

36 *Poverty Bay Herald*, 31 March 1919, p. 8. www.paperspast.natlib.govt.nz.

37 Ibid., p. 8; Soutar, *Whitiki!*, pp. 31–32, www.nzhistory.govt.nz.

38 Apirana Ngata, quoted in *Poverty Bay Herald*, 31 March 1919, p. 8.

39 Ibid., *Poverty Bay Herald*, 8 April 1919, p. 5.

40 *Poverty Bay Herald*, 1 & 3 April 1919, p. 7.

41 *Poverty Bay Herald*, 31 March 1919, p. 8; 4 April 1919, p. 5.

42 *Poverty Bay Herald*, 4 April 1919, p. 5.

43 *Poverty Bay Herald*, 3 April 1919, p. 5; *Evening Post*, 2 April 1919, p. 6; *Gisborne Times*, 4 April 1919, p. 5.

44 *Gisborne Times*, 4 April 1919, p. 5.

45 *Poverty Bay Herald*, 5, 7 April 1919, pp. 1, 3.

46 *Poverty Bay Herald*, 7 April 1919, p. 6.

47 *Poverty Bay Herald*, 13 March 1919, p. 5; *Gisborne Times*, 8 April 1919, p. 5.

48 McLean and Curnow (eds), *Catalogue of Museum of New Zealand Cylinder Recordings of Traditional Maori Songs*, 1992, pp. 27–28.

49 *Poverty Bay Herald*, 13 March 1919, p. 5; *Gisborne Times*, 8 April 1919, p. 5.

50 *Gisborne Times*, 9 April 1919, p. 2.

51 Ibid., p. 2.

52 *Gisborne Times*, 9 April 1919, p. 2.

53 Ibid.; *Poverty Bay Herald*, 29 March 1919; 7 & 8 April 1919, p. 3.

54 Dominion Museum annual report 1919, H22, p. 28.

55 *Te Kopara*, 30 April 1919, no. 64, p. 7.

56 *Gisborne Times*, 7 April 1919, p. 5; *Gisborne Times*, 9 April 1919, p. 2; *Poverty Bay Herald*, 8 April 1919, p. 3.

57 *Poverty Bay Herald*, 8 April 1919, p. 3, www.paperspast.natlib.govt.nz.

58 *Gisborne Times*, 9 April 1919, p. 2; *Poverty Bay Herald*, 8 April 1919, p. 3; Te Rangi Hiroa (Peter Buck), *The Coming of the Maori*, Maori Purposes Fund Board, Wellington, 1949, p. 391.

59 *Gisborne Times*, 9 April 1919, p. 2.

60 Ibid.

61 Ibid.; *Te Kopara*, no. 54, 30 April 1918, p. 8.

62 *Poverty Bay Herald*, 9 April 1919, p. 5; *Gisborne Times*, 19 December 1918, p. 5.

63 Tape 3, Bo 1, C21. 12 /4/19 (McL 149); translation by author.

64 *Poverty Bay Herald*, 9 April 1919, p. 5.

65 Ibid.

66 *Gisborne Times*, 9 April 1919, p. 2; Soutar, *Whitiki!*, p. 385.

67 Ibid.

68 *Gisborne Times*, 9 April 1919, p. 2.

69 Ngata took a personal interest in this waiata, and conducted extensive research on it for his later publication of song poetry, *Nga Moteatea* (1928). See 'Rangiuia's Lament', Maori Purposes Fund Board MS Papers-0189 B.141, Alexander Turnbull Library, Wellington.

70 *Press*, 10 April 1919, p. 8.

71 *Poverty Bay Herald*, 8 April 1919, p. 3 & 10 April, p. 6.

72 Only a few faded frames from this film survive in Ngā Taonga Sound and Vision Archives. Pugsley, *The Camera in the Crowd*, 2017, p. 419.

73 *Gisborne Times*, 10 April 1919, p. 5.

74 Wehipeihana (ed.), *Te Aute College*, 2005, pp. 14–16; Soutar, *Whitiki!*, p. 483.

75 *Gisborne Times*, 10 April 1919, p. 5.

76 Ibid., p. 5.

77 Ibid., p. 5, www.teara.govt.nz.

78 *Poverty Bay Herald*, 10 April 1919, p. 2; *Te Kopara*, no. 57, 12 July 1918, p. 11; Soutar, *Whitiki!*, p. 48.

79 Ngata, quoted in *Poverty Bay Herald*, 10 April 1919, p. 2.

80 *Gisborne Times*, 10 April 1919, p. 5.

81 McLean and Curnow (eds), *Catalogue*, pp. 30–33.

82 Andersen, 'Maori String Games', 1921–23, p. 84.

83 For a full list of the string games recorded at the Hui Aroha, see ibid, p. 84, and comments on ibid, p. 85.

84 Andersen, '*Maori Music with its Polynesian Background*', 1934, p. 235.

85 *Poverty Bay Herald*, 10 April 1919, p. 3.

86 Elsdon Best, Dominion Museum annual report 1919 H22, p. 27.

87 Andersen, 'Maori String Games', p. 91. According to Mate Kaiwai, a daughter of Apirana Ngata, children used to play this string game at school. The basis of the game was that you used your fingers and string to follow the example of your opponent in an attempt to catch them: pers. comm., Mate Kaiwai, 17 November 1999. Quoted in Souter, 'Ngāti Porou leadership: Rāpata Wahawaha and the Politics of Conflict', PhD thesis, Massey University, 2000, p. 183, n. 63.

88 See Andersen, *Maori String Figures*, 1927, p. 43.

89 Ibid., pp. 28, 68.

90 Dominion Museum annual report 1919, H22, p. 27.

91 Angela Ballara, 'Te Ātahīkoia, Mohi', *DNZB*, Te Ara—the Encyclopedia of New Zealand, www.teara.govt.nz; Ballara and Don Hutana, 'Hūtana, Īhāia—Hutana, Ihaia', *DNZB*, Te Ara—the Encyclopedia of New Zealand, www.teara.govt.nz.

92 McLean and Curnow (eds), *Catalogue*, pp. 33–38.

93 *Te Kopara*, no. 64, 30 April 1919, p. 10; *Gisborne Times*, 12 April 1919, p. 5.

94 *Gisborne Times*, 12 & 14 April 1919, p. 5.

95 *Te Kopara*, 30 April 1919, no. 64, p. 10; *Gisborne Times*, 12 April 1919, p. 5 and 14 April 1919, p. 6.

96 *Gisborne Times*, 10 April 1919; 7 & 11 April 1919, p. 6.

97 *Poverty Bay Herald*, 11 April 1919, p. 3; Soutar, *Whitiki!*, pp. 361, 363.

98 *Gisborne Times*, 14 April 1919, p. 5.

99 *Gisborne Times*, 14 & 15 April 1919, p. 5

100 *Gisborne Times*, 14 April 1919, p. 5.

101 McLean and Curnow (eds), *Catalogue*, pp. 39–48.

102 Tape 4, Box 2, C27, 12/4/1919; Ballara, 'Te Ātahīkoia, Mohi', *DNZB*, Te Ara—the Encyclopedia of New Zealand, www.teara.govt.nz.

103 McLean and Curnow (eds), *Catalogue*, pp. 48–51.

104 *Poverty Bay Herald*, 9 April 1919, p. 2.

105 McDonald to Undersecretary, Internal Affairs, 23 April 1919, MU1/018/00011 11/3/17, Te Papa Archives Wellington.

106 McDonald to Undersecretary, Internal Affairs, 22 April 1919, MU1/018/00011 11/3/17, Te Papa Archives Wellington.

107 *Sun*, Wellington, 20 April 1920.

108 Dominion Museum annual report 1919, H22, p. 27.

109 *Te Kopara*, 30 April 1919, no. 63, pp. 9–10.

110 Ibid., p. 10.

111 Translation by author.

112 *Gisborne Times*, 29 April 1919, p. 4; *Poverty Bay Herald*, 7 July 1919, p. 7.

Chapter 2 — 'E Tama! E te Ariki! Haere Mai!'

1 'The Prince of Wales, 1920', Te Ara— the Encyclopedia of New Zealand, www.teara.govt.nz.

2 *Evening Star*, issue 17336, 26 April 1920.

3 Ibid.

4 Neich, *Carved Histories*, 2001, pp. 250–51. This move led to the passage of the Antiquities Act, aimed to protect 'nga taonga onamata', in October 1901. See also McCarthy, *Exhibiting Māori: A History of Colonial Cultures of Display*, 2007, ch. 1.

5 *New Zealand Herald*, vol. LVII, issue 17446, 16 April 1920.

6 *Taihape Daily Times*, vol. XL, issue 3450, 4 April 1920.

7 For example, *Horowhenua Chronicle*, 16 April 1920; *Waipa Post*, vol. 12, issue 926.

8 *Colonist*, vol. LXII, issue 15349, 13 April 1920.

9 *New Zealand Herald*, vol. LVII, issue 17437, 6 April 1920.

10 While Ehau's parents had been followers of Te Kooti, his wife's father had fought against Te Kooti in the Te Arawa Contingent: Manu H Pene, 'Ehau, Kepa Hāmuera Ānaha', *DNZB*, Te Ara—the Encyclopedia of New Zealand, www.teara.govt.nz.

11 *Poverty Bay Herald*, vol. XLVII, issue 15181, 1 April 1920.

12 Johannes C Andersen, 'The Prince at Rotorua', *New Zealand School Journal*, vol. 14, no. 3, p. 194; *Poverty Bay Herald*, vol. XLVII, issue 15186, 9 April 1920; *New Zealand Herald*, vol. LVII, issue 17446, 16 April 1920.

13 *Evening Post*, vol. XCIX, issue 92, 19 April 1920.

14 For example, *Observer*, vol. XL, issue 34, 24 April 1920: 'a number of soda-water machines have been purchased and installed in the Maori Camp at Rotorua. What for? Happy, happy Maori boys and girls. Big blow out?—That [lashings] of beer rolled railward to Rotorua. Special brew, and guess it's wanted. Ten thousand natives shouting themselves hoarse in the Ka Mate want a little Kia Ora.'

Observer, vol. XL, issue 32, 10 April 1920: 'It is necessary to save money because times are hard, prices high, and likely to be higher. So the Government is spending about £30,000 in collecting, feeding and housing 5,000 Maoris at Rotorua, to show H.R.H. the Prince of Wales what the Maoris do NOT do in New Zealand … The majority of these Maoris don't know the first thing about hakas and pois, and all the rest of it, but the Government is paying huge sums to keep 5,000 idle for several weeks feeding and learning the customs and dances of the ancient tribes—vanished because communism is gone and the Maori is an individual … Under these princely circumstances the Government supplies countless tons of food to further demoralise a large mob of lazy people … [etc etc].'

15 *Taihape Daily Times*, vol. XI, issue 3450, 1 April 1920.

16 *Evening Post*, vol. XCVIII, issue 109, 5 November 1919.

17 Minute by Ngata, quoted in Undersecretary, Department of Internal Affairs, JA Thomson, 23 March 1920, National Museum archives, Box labelled Miscellaneous Correspondence 1922–24, DM 15/1/16 with DM 12/1/25.

18 JA Thomson to Undersecretary, Public Works Department, 7 February 1920, Box 5 Expeditions 1916–1935, MU1/018/00011, 11/3/17, Te Papa Archives Wellington.

19 Memorandum to Dr Thomson from JM McDonald, 7 June 1920, MU1/018/00011, 11/3/17, Te Papa Archives Wellington. It was not unusual for collection items to be 'loaned' out for use at this time—for example, carved poupou were used in the decoration of the Wellington Town Hall as a 'Maori pah' for the Citizens' Ball with the Prince of Wales. Street Decoration Committee to Thomson, 5 April 1920, MU1/018/00011, 11/3/17, Te Papa Archives Wellington. The fact that some of the spears loaned out to Ngāpuhi warriors did not return may have given museum staff second thoughts about continuing with this risky practice.

20 For example, *Evening Star*, issue 17327, 15 April 1920.

21 *New Zealand Times*, vol. XLVI, issue 10564, 15 April 1920.

22 *Sun*, 20 April 1920.

23 John Hyland in SL and IC Hughes, *Port to Pastures*, 1988, p. 75.

24 Binney, *Encircled Lands*, 2009, pp. 26, 72, 81–82, 146–47, 427.

25 McLean and Curnow (eds), *Catalogue of Museum of New Zealand Cylinder Recordings of Traditional Maori Songs, 1919–c.1935*, 1992, pp. 61–73.

26 'Fine Maori Records', *Ashburton Guardian*, vol. XL, issue 9230, 1 June 1920.

27 McDonald was not the official photographer and filmmaker for this event, the government having commissioned New Zealand Picture Supplies to film the Royal Tour (*Dominion*, vol. 13, issue 179, 24 April 1920).

28 *Otago Daily Times*, issue 17917, 23 April 1920.

29 Andersen, *Maori Music with its Polynesian Background*, 1934, pp. 433–34.

30 Andersen, 'The Prince at Rotorua', p. 196.

31 *Evening Post*, vol. XCIX, issue 98, 26 April 1920.

32 Sir Arthur William de Brito Savile Foljambe Liverpool, Second Earl, was both New Zealand's last Governor and, from 1917, its first Governor-General after the country was granted Dominion status. He became Governor in 1912, and his term was extended until July 1920 so he could welcome the Prince of Wales. Sir John Rushworth Jellicoe, First Viscount, became Governor-General from September 1920.

33 *Press*, vol. LVI, issue 16813, 20 April 1920.

34 Whakahuihui Vercoe, 'Vercoe, Henry Te Reiwhati', *DNZB*, Te Ara—the Encyclopedia of New Zealand, www.teara.govt.nz.

35 *Malborough Express*, vol. LIV, issue 99, 27 April 1920; *New Zealand Herald*, vol. LVII, issue 17456, 28 April 1920.

36 Letter from Prince of Wales to Mrs Freda Dudley Ward, MS Papers 8780-1-3, Alexander Turnbull Library, Wellington.

37 *Sun*, vol. VII, issue 1936, 29 April 1920.

38 *Press*, vol. LVI, issue 16821, 29 April 1920.

39 *Auckland Weekly News*, 6 May 1920, p. 16.

40 Ibid.

41 *Colonist*, vol. LXII, issue 15363, 29 April 1920.

42 Letter from Prince of Wales to Mrs Freda Dudley Ward, MS Papers 8780-1-3, Alexander Turnbull Library, Wellington.

43 *Otago Daily Times*, issue 17923, 30 April 1920.

44 See Neich 2001, p. 358.

45 *Te Kopara*, no. 76, 1920, pp. 3–7.

46 Andersen, 'The Prince at Rotorua', p. 196.

47 *Te Kopara*, no. 76, 30 May 1920, pp. 6–7.

48 *London Star*, 25 April 1920, quoted in *Southland Times*, issue 18861, 29 June 1920.

49 Tainui patu given to Prince of Wales, Papers relating to King's attempt to trace the patu given by Tupu Taingakawa to the Prince of Wales in 1920, apparently without Tainui approval. MS Papers-8970-221, Alexander Turnbull Library, Wellington.

50 *Otago Daily Times*, issue 17917, 23 April 1920.

51 *Otago Daily Times*, issue 17923, 30 April 1920.

52 Letter from Prince of Wales to Mrs Freda Dudley Ward, MS Papers 8780-1-3, Alexander Turnbull Library, Wellington.

53 *Waiapu Church Gazette*, vol. XVII, 11, 2 May 1927.

54 McLean and Curnow (eds), *Catalogue*, pp. 73–77.

55　*Waiapu Church Gazette*, vol. XVII, 11, 2 May 1927.

56　Dominion Museum annual report, 23 July 1920, p. 3.

57　It's interesting to note that around 1936, when Ngata was working on the restoration of the whare whakairo at Waitara in Taranaki, he wrote an article, 'The Origin of Maori Carving', that traced close links between Ngāti Tarāwhai carving and carving on the East Coast. According to Ngata, when he posed a question to 'elders of Ngati-Tarawhai at Ohinemutu, [they] acknowledged that many generations ago there had been a kai-taonga between the Ngati-Awa of Whakatane and Ngati-Tarawhai, a pakuha, an exchange of marriage gifts, and the latter received a knowledge of the art of carving from the Ngata-Awa carvers, members of the Apanui (Hurinui Apanui's forebears) family who lived at Wairaka pa, below Toi-kai-rakau's pa at Whakatane'. This article also noted close links between the Ngāti Awa school of carving with the East Coast (especially Hīngāngāroa's Te Rāwheoro whare wānanga at Ūawa) and Gisborne styles (AT Ngata, 'The Origin of Maori Carving', in *Te Ao Hou*, no. 22, 1958, pp. 30–37 and in no. 23, 1959, pp. 30–34).

58　Dominion Museum annual report, H22, 23 July 1920, p. 5; *Te Toa Takitini*, no. 15, October 1922, pp. 7–8.

59　Johannes C Andersen, 'Fish-gorges or shellfish extractors or spillikins?' *Journal of the Polynesian Society*, vol. 36, no. 143, 1927, pp. 287–89.

60　Paula Savage, 'Mair, Gilbert', *DNZB*, Te Ara—the Encyclopedia of New Zealand, www.teara.govt.nz.

61　JCA Gilbert Mair, 31 January 1923, NLR Box 5214, folder 181 Mah-Marks.

62　Memorandum from J McDonald to Director, 7 June 1920, MU1/018/00011, 11/3/17, Te Papa Archives Wellington.

63　See J Hislop, Undersecretary Internal Affairs to HRH Balneavis Secretary of Maori Board Figure Ethnological Research, 10 March 1927, 'Director: Loan of spears to Rotorua for Maori Displays', MU1/017/0065, 11/1/19, Te Papa Archives Wellington.

64　*Evening Post*, vol. C, issue 18, 21 July 1920. See also Minutes of meeting of 20 July 1920, WTu, qMS 1918–24, Wellington Philosophical Society, Historical Section, Minute Book.

65　Andersen 1920–1921, pp. 149–50; *Maori String Figures*, 1927, pp. 30–31.

66　Dominion Museum annual report, H22, 23 July 1920.

67　Dominion Museum files and photographs suggest that Tene Waitere worked on the carvings for the International Exhibition well in advance of its opening, liaising closely with Augustus Hamilton.

68　Roger Neich, 'Waitere, Tene', *DNZB*, Te Ara—the Encyclopedia of New Zealand, www.teara.govt.nz.

69　Dean Sully (ed.), *Decolonizing Conservation: Caring for Maori Meeting Houses Outside New Zealand*, Left Coast Press, Walnut Creek, CA, 2007.

70　Michael Upchurch, 'Hinemihi o Te Ao Tawhito: How a Maori meeting house in England cultivated relationships and understanding', *Museum Worlds*, no. 8, 2020, pp. 188–203.

Chapter 3 — 'Tōia Mai! Te Taonga!'

1　Diana Beaglehole, 'Hatrick, Alexander', *DNZB*, Te Ara—the Encyclopedia of New Zealand, www.teara.govt.nz.

2　Marjorie McDonald, Letter to HD Skinner, 1955, Salmond family papers.

3　Elsdon Best, Dominion Museum annual report, 20 April 1916, p. 2; Dominion Museum annual report, 19 August 1918, pp. 3–4. See also 'Collection of historical matter—Mr Elsdon Best's visit to Wanganui River' (1916), MU14/002/0001, 13/27/23, Te Papa Archives Wellington.

4　Department of Internal Affairs to…, 18 February 1921, MU1/018/00011, 11/3/17, Te Papa Archives Wellington.

5　J McDonald to J Hislop, 1 March 1921, MU1/018/00011, 11/3/17, Te Papa Archives Wellington.

6　Hatrick had a fleet of paddle steamers on the Whanganui River; see Beaglehole, 'Hatrick, Alexander', *DNZB*, Te Ara—the Encyclopedia of New Zealand, www.teara.govt.nz.

7　TW Downes, Pipiriki to Elsdon Best, 6 March 1921, MU1/018/00011, 11/3/17, Te Papa Archives Wellington.

8　James McDonald to Undersecretary Internal Affairs, 10 March 1921; Memo from Internal Affairs to Acting-Director, 14 March 1921, MU1/018/00011, 11/3/17, Te Papa Archives Wellington.

9　Koroniti, a transliteration of Corinth, is the past tense of the name that was used after missionary Richard Taylor renamed Otukopiri in the 1840s. Today the name Koriniti, present tense, is used.

10　Johannes Andersen, in *Lyttelton Times*, 20 May 1922, WTu MS Papers 148, Folder 136B, Alexander Turnbull Library, Wellington.

11　Ibid.

12　Ibid.

13　Ibid.

14　Ibid.

15　Andersen, *Maori String Figures*, 1927, p. 136.

16　Steven Oliver, 'Taumatamahoe Block Report (Wai 903 A42)', Waitangi Tribunal, 2003, p. 31.

17　McLean and Orbell, *Traditional Songs of the Maori*, 1992, p. 88, Whanganui cylinder 8, notes. For the killing of Völkner, see 'Carl Völkner' New Zealand History, online, www.nzhistory.govt.nz.

18　McLean and Orbell, *Traditional Songs of the Maori*, p. 89, Whanganui cylinder 8, notes.

19　McLean and Orbell, *Traditional Songs of the Maori*, pp. 83–88.

20　Andersen in *Lyttelton Times* 20 May 1922, WTu MS Papers 148, Folder 136B, Alexander Turnbull Library, Wellington.

21　Rihipeti and her husband, Maihi Ngarau Aperaniko, had five children, including Tita Pitaera. www.myheritage.com.

22　McLean and Orbell, *Traditional Songs of the Maori*, pp. 87–88, 92, Whanganui cylinders 7, 8.

23　Ibid., p. 87, Whanganui cylinder 7.

24　National Museum Register Ethnology, March 1921, 3827, 3828, 3829 and 3830.

25　Johannes Andersen, in *Lyttleton Times*, 20 May 1922, WTu MS Papers 148, Folder 136B, Alexander Turnbull Library, Wellington.

26　Te Rangi Hiroa, 'Maori Plaited Basketry and Plaitwork I and II, 1923, 1924.

27　McDonald to Dr Thomson, Dominion Museum, 29 April 1921, DM 6_1/1.

28　Johannes Andersen, 'Songs and Folklore: a Reminiscence of the Wanganui River', *Evening Post*, 21 December 1926

29　Best notebook, ATL MS-0195, p. 15; NMRE: '3824 Poti Taro (Taro basket) Presd by Nga Rongo Pokiha of Koroniti in March 1921, 3825 Poti Taro Presd by Nga Rongo Pokiha; 3826 Tokari (tuku taha) Presd by Te Pokiha of Koroniti'.

30　Best notebook, p. 2: 'Wooden patu muku presented by Rangitahua of Koroniti. Made of maire'; p. 6, 'Whanganui use at least some wooden beaters patu muka. Tuhoe never do'; p. 7, NMRE '3822 tuke (mutu kaka) See Best notebook No. 2, p. 179, NMRE: 3823 moria kaka, Pres by Ropata Rangitahua of Koroniti.' The mōria kākā is missing from the Museum collection. See also Best, *Forest Lore of the Maori*, 1977, p. 213: 'These *mutu* were sometimes given special names, such as one numbered 3822 in the Dominion Museum, the name of which is Rerehau; it was presented to the Museum by Rangitahua of Whanganui.'

31　Best notebook, pp. 12, 13.

32　Ibid., p. 4: 'Baler presented by Wirieti [sic] Nopera of Koroniti carved by his father Nopera. Dr. Thomson to thank him. Tahuhuroa was name of canoe it was carved for.' NMRE '3821 Carved Baler (Koroniti) Presd by Wirieti [sic] Nopera, of Koroniti (See Best Notebook No 2: 179)'.

33　Best notebook, p. 19.

34　For photographs and letters of thanks sent to Whanganui people after the expedition, see Letters J McDonald to J Hislop, 31 March and 17 May 1921, MU1/018/00011, 11/3/17, Te Papa Archives Wellington.

35　Best, *The Operiki Pa, Koroniti, Whanganui River*, 1922.

36　Best notebook, p. 15.

37　Best gave his name as Apirana; his descendants knew him as Aperahama Tukairangi.

38　This probably refers to Best notebook, p. 3: 'Raihe = fence of upright stakes; Pakonokono = of horizontal rails touching'.

39   Andersen does not name Te Rangihīroa in his account of the visit to Koroniti written for the *Lyttelton Times*, but describes him as a 'half-caste friend, a noted man both among Maori and European'.

40   Andersen in *Lyttelton Times*, 20 May 1922, WTu MS Papers 148, Folder 136B, Alexander Turnbull Library, Wellington.

41   McDonald to Dr Thomson, Koroniti, Wanganui River, 29 March 1921, DM 6_1/1.

42   Treasury invoice for 21 March to 18 April, Ethnographic Expedition Wanganui.

43   Ibid.

44   J Hislop to J McDonald, Dominion Museum Party Koroniti, 4 April 1921.

45   Treasury invoice, payment to Messrs A Hatrick & Co Ltd, Wanganui.

46   McDonald to Thomson, Hiruharama, Wanganui River, Dr. Thomson file DM 6_1/1.

47   Ibid.

48   Best field notebook, Wanganui and East Coast Expeditions 1921–23, Alexander Turnbull Library, pp. 21–23.

49   MA_B.000165, Lamprey Weir on the Whanganui River.

50   MA_B.000153, Making Hinaki Nets; MA_B.000808, Building a Lamprey Weir.

51   Best notebook, pp. 23–28.

52   Best notebook, p. 26.

53   McDonald to Thomson, Hiruharama, Wanganui River, Dr. Thomson file DM 6_1/1.

54   McLean and Curnow, *Catalogue of Museum of New Zealand Cylinder Recordings*, 1992, pp. 113, 119.

55   Ibid., pp. 105, 109.

56   Ibid., p. 102.

57   Ibid., p. 120.

58   Best notebook, p. 28.

59   McLean and Curnow, *Catalogue*, pp. 118–19. This karakia was later published in 1935 in *Journal of the Polynesian Society*, vol. 44, pp. 42–43.

60   Best notebook, p. 28.

61   Ibid., p. 29.

62   McDonald to Thomson, DM 6/1/1, 5 May 1921.

63   Dominion Museum Annual Report 1921.

64   NMRE, p. 128, '3839, 3 calabashes in basket Presented by Matarena, Hiruharama'.

65   McLean and Curnow, *Catalogue*, pp. 124–25.

66   Ibid., p. 127.

67   McDonald to Thomson, DM 5/5/21.

68   Ibid.

69   McDonald to Thomson, DM 6/1/1, 29 April 1921.

70   McDonald to Thomson, DM 6/1/1, 5 May 1921; NMRE, p. 128, '3837, 1 Korotete or basket to keep eels in. presented by Anihana of Pipiriki; s3838, 1 Plaited band for pig's leg, Presented by Erueti of Pipiriki'.

71   Andersen, in *Lyttleton Times* 20 May 1922, WTu MS Papers 148, Folder 136B, Alexander Turnbull Library, Wellington.

72   Dominion Museum annual report 1921.

73   Ngata to JC Andersen, 15 December 1921, WTu MS Papers 1187, Folder 323, Alexander Turnbull Library, Wellington.

Chapter 4 — 'Oh Machine, Speak on, Speak on'

1   Pomare, Ngata and Henare to Native Minister the Hon Sir WH Herries, 26.9.1922, MA 51, Archives New Zealand Wellington.

2   Acting Director, Memorandum for the Under-secretary Internal Affairs, 2 October 1922, 'Ethnological Expedition—East Coast, 1923', MU1/018/0010, 11/3/3, Te Papa Archives Wellington.

3   Te Rangi Hiroa to Johannes Andersen, H. 513A, 2.11.22. 'Andersen: Papers: Material relating to Ngata and Peter Buck'. MS Papers-0148-015, Alexander Turnbull Library, Wellington.

4   Te Rangi Hiroa to McDonald, 6 February 1923, Ethnological Expedition—East Coast, 1923, MU1/018/0010, 11/3/3, Te Papa Archives Wellington.

5   Ibid.

6   Acting Director, Memorandum for the Under-secretary Internal Affairs, 2 October 1922, 'Ethnological Expedition—East Coast, 1923', MU1/018/0010, 11/3/3, Te Papa Archives Wellington.

7   Acting Director, Memorandum for the Under-secretary Internal Affairs, 28 February 1923, DM 11_3/3.

8   Te Rangi Hiroa to Johannes Andersen, H. 513A, 2.11.22.

9   McLean and Curnow (eds), *Catalogue of Museum of New Zealand Cylinder Recordings of Traditional Maori Songs, 1919–c.1935*, 1992, pp. 137–40.

10   Ibid., pp. 139–41. See also 'E hika ma e! I hoki mai au i Kereruhuahua', in Ngata, *Nga Moteatea: He Maramara Rere no nga Waka Maha*, 40, pp. 134–35, which adds that Ngata 'recorded some notes dictated by Materoa Ngarimu, but these notes were not found'.

11   McLean and Curnow (eds), *Catalogue*, p. 141.

12   Ibid.

13   Ibid., pp. 140–43; translation by Rangi Motu. Note: McLean and Curnow used double vowels to indicate a long vowel sound. The editors have replaced double vowels with macrons.

14   Ibid., p. 142.

15   Name recorded in Buck to Ngata, 27 September 1923, Ngata ethnology file, Alexander Turnbull Library, Wellington.

16   Te Rangi Hiroa, 'The Maori Craft of Netting', 1926, pp. 597–646.

17   Andersen, *Maori String Figures*, 1927.

18   McLean and Curnow (eds), *Catalogue*, p. 144.

19   See Te Rangi Hiroa to James McDonald, 18 February 1923: 'Dear Mac, … I think the pictures shown at a lecture in each centre will be a good thing. The Maoris are nothing if not competitive. The sight of the arts, crafts and customs of their tribes will stimulate them to do likewise or do better if possible.' Can be found in 'Ethnological Expedition—East Coast, 1923', MU1/018/0010, 11/3/3, Te Papa Archives Wellington.

20   JC Andersen diary: Waiomatatini, Ngati Porou March–April 1923 and Tauranga December 1923, Ms-0053, Alexander Turnbull Library, Wellington, 57 pages. Transcriptions by Arawhetu Berdinner, September 2013 (pp. 1–35, with some corrections by Anne Salmond) and by Anne Salmond, April 2018 (pp. 36–57), pp. 13–14.

21   Acting Director (James McDonald) to The Undersecretary, Internal Affairs, 28 February 1923, MU1/018/0010, 11/3/3, Te Papa Archives Wellington.

22   Andersen diary 1923, p. 2.

23   McLean and Curnow (eds), *Catalogue*, pp. 144–45.

24   Ibid., p. 146.

25   Ibid., pp. 148–51.

26   Andersen diary 1923, p. 27.

27   Andersen diary 1923, p. 31.

28   McLean and Curnow (eds), *Catalogue*, p. 149.

29   Andersen diary 1923, p. 35.

30   McLean and Curnow (eds), *Catalogue*, p. 153.

31   Ibid., pp. 41–42; Andersen diary 1923, p. 18.

32   McLean and Curnow (eds), *Catalogue*, pp. 153–54; Andersen diary 1923, p. 46; Andersen, 'Maori Music with its Polynesian Background', 1933, p. 231.

33   Andersen diary 1923, pp. 10–11.

34   McLean and Curnow (eds), *Catalogue*, p. 157.

35   Andersen diary 1923, p. 26.

Chapter 5 — 'The Eye of the Film'

1   Mita, 'The Preserved Image Speaks Out', 1992, p. 73.

2   Rua a Tōrea is the ancestral name.

3   Erana Keelan Reedy is Director of Radio Ngāti Porou. The photograph was gifted to her in about 2007 by Hone Te Rito (Ngāti Porou), who worked at Ngā Taonga Sound and Vision. At that stage, the names were unknown.

4   Monty Soutar, pers. comm, June 2021.

5   See Zoe Todd, 'Refracting the State through Human-Fish Relations', in *Decolonization: Indigeneity, Education & Society: Indigenous Peoples and the Politics of Water*, vol. 7, no. 1, 2018, pp. 60–79. jps.library.utoronto.ca.

6 Te Rūnanganui o Ngāti Porou, 'Hī Ika: The Ngāti Porou Fisheries Settlement', www.ngatiporou.com.

7 The cellulose nitrate film base from that era is highly unstable, acidic and inflammable, combustible even in the absence of oxygen. Unless stored at very cold temperatures, the material decomposes, turning into a dangerous sticky mess. For over sixty years, these films were stored, slowly degrading. The 35mm cinematic film stored in tins would have softened, turned amber, producing toxic nitric dioxide vapours. This reaction fades the images and deterioration accelerates. At this stage, the film literally eats away at the images. For anyone who attempted to handle them, the chemicals pose a serious risk.

8 Barry Barclay, *Mana Tuturu: Maori Treasures and Intellectual Property Rights*, Auckland University Press, 2005, p. 102.

9 Ibid., p. 267.

10 Te Rangi Hiroa, 'The Maori Craft of Netting', *TNZI*, vol. 56, 1926, plate 106, fig. 2.

11 Best, 'Fishing Methods and Devices of the Maori', 1929.

12 The Māori name for the Film Archive, Ngā Kaitiaki o Ngā Taonga Whitiāhua, appears beneath in a minuscule 4- or 6-point font size.

13 See Appendix: Ngata, 'The Terminology of Whakapapa', p. 2.

14 Te Rangi Hiroa, 'The Maori Craft of Netting', p. 612.

15 Williams, *A Dictionary of the Maori Language*, 1957, p. 3.

16 Mita, 'The Soul and the Image', in J Dennis and J Bieringa (eds), *Film in Aotearoa New Zealand*, 1992.

17 Amiria JM Henare [Salmond] wrote that following the restoration of the expedition films in the mid-1980s, screenings were held in Gisborne, Rotorua Whanganui and on the East Coast, to which elders and descendants were invited to come and assist in providing bilingual subtitles, and to identify the people, places and activities documented in the films. In *Museums, Anthropology and Imperial Exchange*, University of Cambridge, 2008, p. 228.

18 Emma J Kelly, 'Appendix Four: Films by James McDonald of the Tangata Whenua He Pito Whakaatu a Te Maori na James McDonald 1919-1923', 2014, p. 252.

19 Louise McCrone, Preservation Manager, Ngā Taonga Sound & Vision said: 'The 1980s preservation (photochemical printing) was completed at the Film Unit laboratory, making new a duplicate negative, positive and print from the original nitrate negative reels which were beginning to decompose. In 2016, the original nitrate film fragments were scanned to 4.6k resolution on an ArriScan. From that, lower resolution files were produced for screening. The intertitles between sections were developed from original', pers. comm., email, 1 November 2016.

20 Natalie Robertson's video recording, 31 August 2017.

21 Keita Whakato Walker (née Ngārimu), also known as Kate or Kay Ngārimu, was the star of the independent 1952 film, *Broken Barrier*, directed by John O'Shea. *Te Ao Hou* stated that 'The first Māori girl to be a film star in a full-length feature film is Kay Ngarimu of Ruatoria, who is playing Rawi in the Pacific Films production Broken Barrier'. *Te Ao Hou*, July 1952, p. 37. Papers Past.

22 Te Rangi Hiroa, MS SC BUCK 7.01 (Notebook), Bishop Museum Archives, Honolulu.

23 Te Rangi Hiroa, 'The Maori Craft of Netting', p. 625.

24 Mahuika, 'Maori Culture and the New Museum', *Museum Anthropology*, vol. 15, no. 4, 1992, p. 9.

25 Ibid., p. 10.

26 See Appendix: Ngata, 'The Terminology of Whakapapa', p. 4.

27 Chris D Paulin, 'Perspectives of Māori Fishing History and Techniques: Ngā Ahua Me ngā Pūrākau me ngā Hangarau Ika o te Māori', *Tuhinga*, no. 18, 2007, p. 21. www.tepapa.govt.nz/tuhinga.

28 Ibid., p. 22.

29 Linda Tuhiwai Smith, *Decolonizing Methodologies: Research and Indigenous Peoples*, Otago University Press, 1999, p. 148.

30 Ibid., p. 145.

31 Jonathan Dennis ,'Restoring History', *Film History*, vol. 6, no. 1, Philosophy of Film History, Spring, 1994, Indiana University Press, pp. 116-27. www.jstor.org.

32 Katrina-Ann Kapā'anaokalāokeola Nākoa Oliveira, *Ancestral Places: Understanding Kanaka Geographies*, Oregon State University Press, 2014, p. 78.

33 Kelly, 'Appendix Four: Films by James McDonald of the Tangata Whenua He Pito Whakaatu a Te Maori na James McDonald 1919-1923', 2014, p. 112.

34 Blythe, in *Naming the Other*, makes no mention of him; nor do Barnes 'Ngā Kai Para i te Kahikātoa', 2011, or Barclay, 'The Held Image', 1989.

35 Te Rangi Hiroa, 'The Maori Craft of Netting', p. 598.

36 Dominion Museum annual report 1923, in the Report of the Department of Internal Affairs, p. 2.

37 Kelly, 'Appendix Four: Films by James McDonald of the Tangata Whenua He Pito Whakaatu a Te Maori na James McDonald 1919-1923', p. 60.

38 Te Kawehau Hoskins and Alison Jones, 'Non-human Others and Kaupapa Māori Reseach', in Te Kawehau Hoskins and Alison Jones (eds), *Critical Conversations in Kaupapa Māori*, Huia Publishers, Wellington, 2017, p. 49.

39 Mahuika, 'Maori Culture and the New Museum', p. 10.

40 H Hanson Turton, *Maori Deeds of Land Purchases in the North Island of New Zealand: Volume One: Awanui Block, Poverty Bay District*. www.nzetc.victoria.ac.nz. 'In the Matter of Section 6 of The Treaty of Waitangi Act, 1975 And On the Matter of Claims by H. Kaa (Wai 39), L. H. Tangaere (Wai 63), Te Rimu Trust (Wai 98), M. Reid (Wai 173), and A.T. Mahuika (Wai 272) on behalf of Te Runanga o Ngati Porou and the Ngati Porou people', Exploratory Report, 1993, p. 11.

41 Kimberley H Maxwell, Kelly Ratana, Kathryn K Davis, Caine Taiapa, Shaun Awatere, 'Navigating towards marine co-management with Indigenous communities on-board the Waka-Taurua', *Marine Policy* 111, January 2020, 10372. www.sciencedirect.com.

42 Blythe, *Naming the Other*, p. 55.

43 Mita, 'The Soul and the Image', p. 40.

44 Ibid., p. 10.

45 Ibid., p. 40.

46 Barry Barclay, *Our Own Image: A Story of a Māori Filmmaker*, University of Minnesota Press, 1990, p. 97.

47 Ibid., p. 97.

48 Blythe, *Naming the Other*, pp. 56-57.

49 Ibid., p. 57.

50 Barclay, *Our Own Image*, p. 97.

51 Ellis, 'A Whakapapa of Tradition', 2016, pp. 268-69.

52 Dewes, 'The Case for Oral Arts', 1976, p. 75.

53 Ngata, *Rauru-nui-a-Toi and Ngati Kahungunu Origins, 1944*, Lecture 3, Victoria University of Wellington. Multilith Printing, 1972, pp. 9-12.

54 Ibid., p. 6

55 Hirini George Reedy, 'Te Tohu-a-Tuu (The Sign of Tuu): A Study of the Warrior Arts of the Maori', PhD thesis, Massey University, 1996, p. 36.

56 Walker, *He Tipua*, 2001, p. 75.

57 Johannes Andersen, Personal diary of Dominion Museum ethnological expedition. MS 0053, Alexander Turnbull Library, Wellington.

58 Tuta Ngārimu, quoted in McLean and Curnow (eds), *Catalogue of Museum of New Zealand Cylinder Recordings of Traditional Maori Songs*, 1992, p. 143.

59 Ibid.

60 *Nga Kohina o Ngati Porou*, issue 43, Pepuere 2012. www.ngatiporou.com.

61 Letter from Te Rangi Hiroa to McDonald, February 1923.

62 Barnes, 'Ngā Kai Para i te Kahikātoa', p. 87.

63 MS SC BUCK 7.01 (Notebook), Bishop Museum Archives, Honolulu.

64 Ngā Taonga Sound and Vision, 'Te Puna Wai Kōrero: Sir Apirana Ngata's Recordings of 1930s', Catalogue ref. 40516, 1983. www.ngataonga.org.nz.

65 Ibid., 10:02–10:25.

66 Ngata to Buck, *Na To Hoa Aroha*, vol. 1, p. 92.

67 Blythe, *Naming the Other*, p. 56.

68 Barclay, *Our Own Image*, pp. 12–13.

69 Ibid., p. 84.

70 Mahuika, 'A Ngāti Porou Perspective', p. 147.

71 *NZPD*, 1907, p. 519; see also Walker, *He Tipua*, p. 127.

72 Paterson, 'Rēweti Kōhere's Model Village', 2007, p. 28; Walker, *He Tipua*, pp. 69–71, 126–28.

73 Walter, 'He Wahine, He Whenua i Ngaro Ai?', 2017, pp. 104–05.

74 Ernest Boyd first attended Te Aute in 1896, aged fifteen, the same year as Te Rangihīroa started. His twin Arthur Boyd joined him the following year, and Alan Boyd began in 1898. All three Boyds remained there until the end of 1899.

75 Awatere, *Awatere: A Soldier's Story*, 2003, p. 24.

76 See Appendix: Ngata, 'The Terminology of Whakapapa', p. 3.

77 Andersen diary 1923, p. 26.

78 The original St John's Church, built in the 1850s, burnt down in 1865. The church at Rangitukia at the time of the expedition was built on the same site after Mōkena Kōhere's passing.

79 Kōhere, *The Story of a Maori Chief: Mokena Kohere and His Forebears*, 1949, p. 207.

80 Andersen diary 1923, p. 27.

81 Kōhere, *The Story of a Maori Chief*, pp. 75–76.

82 Hirschfeld, 'A Brief Monograph on Pekama Rongoaia Kaa', 2017, p. 1.

83 Ibid., p. 22.

84 Chris Pugsley, in Hirschfeld, 'A Brief Monograph', p. 29.

85 Charl Hirschfeld, email to author, 12 July 2018.

86 Walker, *He Tipua*, pp. 69–70.

87 Hirschfeld, email to author, 12 July 2018.

88 Te Rangi Hiroa, 'The Maori Craft of Netting'.

89 *Ngati Porou Deed of Settlement Schedule*: Documents, '1. Statements of Association', cl. A, 4 (2010) confirms that: 'The Waiapu River has been a source of sustenance for Ngati Porou hapu, providing water, and various species of fish, including kahawai. The kahawai fishing techniques practised at the mouth of the Waiapu River are sacred activities distinct to the Waiapu': www.govt.nz.

90 Te Rangi Hiroa, 'Kahawai fishing with scoop net Waikaka beach on left of Waiapu mouth', diary, 1923.

91 Te Rangi Hiroa, 'The Maori Craft of Netting', p. 623.

92 I owe a debt to Ngahuia Murphy for this conceptual understanding of Hineteiwaiwā as a 'weaver of time': Murphy, pers. comm. on her thesis, 'Te Ahi Tawhito', 30 December 2020. 'It is accredited to the atua wahine Hinateiwaiwa who is celebrated throughout the Pacific as the personification of the moon and women's ritual arts (Varez, 2002; Yates-Smith, 1998)': Ngahuia Murphy, 'Te Ahi Tawhito, Te Ahi Tipua, Te Ahi Nā Mahuika: Re-igniting Native Women's Ceremony', PhD thesis, University of Waikato, 2019, p. 116.

93 Te Rangi Hiroa, 'The Maori Craft of Netting', p. 623.

94 Ngata, *Rauru-nui-a-Toi and Ngati Kahungunu Origins*, Lecture 6, p. 13.

95 Ibid.

96 Best notebook 1923. MS Papers 72, Alexander Turnbull Library, Wellington.

97 Andersen diary 1923, p. 28.

98 *He Pito Whakaatua i te Noho a te Maori i te Tairawhiti: Scenes of Maori Life on the East Coast*, 35mm, black and white, silent, 26 mins, Ngā Taonga Sound and Vision.

99 Te Rangi Hiroa, 'The Maori Craft of Netting', p. 620.

100 Rangitukia Native School is now called Tāpere-Nui-a-Whātonga after the whare wānanga that was once at nearby Te Kautuku.

101 Mita, 'The Preserved Image Speaks Out', p. 73.

102 'Nga Ture o Te Ngutu Awa', *Nati Link*, issue 9, December 2015, p. 33.

103 Te Rangi Hiroa, 'The Maori Craft of Netting', 1926, plate 105, fig. 1.

104 Ibid., p. 615.

105 Ibid., pp. 615, 620.

106 Ibid., p. 622.

107 Hirschfeld 2013.

108 Hirschfeld, email to author, 12 July 2018.

109 Mita, 'The Preserved Image Speaks Out', p. 73.

110 Miskelly, 'Legal Protection of New Zealand's Indigenous Aquatic Fauna', 2016.

111 Tate Pewhairangi, Statement 13, 2000, Wai 272, p. 13.

112 Ahipene Paenga, Statement 47, 2001, Wai 272, pp. 15–16.

113 Tautini Moana Glover, Statement 10, 2000, Wai 272, p. 3.

114 Te Kapunga Matemoana Dewes, Statement 66, 2000, Wai 272, p. 21.

115 Elsdon Best notebook, MS Papers 72, p. 43, Alexander Turnbull Library, Wellington.

116 HW Williams, 'The Nights of the Moon', *JPS*, vol. 37, no. 147, 1928, pp. 338–56. www.jps.auckland.ac.nz.

117 Ngata, *Rauru-nui-a-Toi and Ngati Kahungunu Origins*, Lecture 4, 1972, p. 11.

118 Ngata to Buck, 16 October 1931, in Ngata and Buck, ed. Sorrenson, *Na To Hoa Aroha*, vol. 2, p. 226.

119 Taiapa, 'Marama taka a te Maori te Tau 1946', Thomas Adams, printer, National Library of New Zealand, ref. Eph-B-MAORI-1946-01.

120 Taiapa, 'Concise Maori Almanac, 1960–61: Plant and Fish by the Phases of the Moon', *Gisborne Herald*, 1960, Auckland War Memorial Museum.

121 Roberts, Weko and Clarke, 'Maramataka: The Maori Moon Calendar', Research Report No. 283, Lincoln University, August 2006.

122 For a full discussion, see ibid.

123 Taiapa, 'Concise Maori Almanac, 1960–61'.

124 Mone Taumaunu, *Te Ao Hou*, no. 40, September 1962. teaohou.natlib.govt.nz.

125 Eruera Stirling, handwritten manuscript, 1974, Private family records, supplied by Anne Salmond, 2020.

126 Moana Nepia, 'Te Kore: Exploring the Māori Concept of Void', PhD thesis, Auckland University of Technology, Auckland, 2012, p. 61.

127 Ibid., p. 57.

128 'Moon Phase Calendar: April 1923', Astroseek. www.mooncalendar. astro-seek.com.

129 Wiremu Tāwhai, *Living by the Moon: Te Maramataka a Te Whānau-ā-Apanui*, Huia Publishers, 2013, p. 72.

130 Taiapa, 'Maramataka, Aperira 1946, 1960–61'.

131 Te Rangi Hiroa, 'The Maori Craft of Netting', p. 639.

132 Based on cross-referencing with Hughes and Hughes, *Port to Pasture: Reminiscences and Records of Port Awanui*, Timeline: 152, Gisborne, 1988 and local knowledge (particularly Tawhiri Maxwell), and deductions from Andersen's diary, this is most likely to be Robert (Rāpata Wahawaha) Maxwell. Maxwell was a cousin to Apirana Ngata through his mother Katerina Naki's sister Hera Mauraha Nekewhare. 'In the evening we had croquet before tea; & after tea I took some beads along, and succeeded in seeing Mary. It appears she had been with them at the pa kokopu, driving the buggy to take the gear, & her father was one who helped to build the pa.' Maxwell was from Waikato, based at Port Awanui, 1920–24. Jack Maxwell—son of East Cape lighthouse keeper 1920–1924—lived in the Seaview Hotel at Port Awanui. Jack (Mary Maxwell's brother, one of twelve Maxwell siblings) says his father was mad on fishing. In Hughes and Hughes, *Port to Pasture*, 1988, p. 100.

Tawhiri Maxwell, pers. comm. with author via telephone, March 2017.

133 MSC_BUCK_ Te Rangihiroa 1923, Library and Archives Bernice Pauahi Bishop Museum, Honolulu.

134 Mone Taumaunu, *Te Ao Hou*, no. 40, September 1962.

135 Tawhai, *Living by the Moon*, pp. 24–25.

136 Andersen diary 1923, p. 35.

137 Te Rangihīroa, 'The Maori Craft of Netting', p. 640.

138 MS SC BUCK 7.04 (Notebook) Maori field notes—fishing and agricultural notes, Bishop Museum Archives, Honolulu.

139 Te Rangi Hiroa, 'The Maori Craft of Netting', p. 597.

140 Ibid., p. 598.

141 Best, *Fishing Methods and Devices of the Maori*, p. 93. www.nzetc.victoria.ac.nz.

142 Ibid.

143 Pāpauma (*Cheimarrichthys fosteri*) may be placed under a general heading of 'Kokopu', according to Best, *Fishing Methods and Devices of the Maori*, p. 190. www.nzetc.victoria.ac.nz.

144 In Suzanne Doig, *The Waiapu River, Maori and The Crown*, October 2000. Wai 272, p. 8. Waiapu Minute Book 102, 2 November 1932, fol. 316. Note: Kahika (local name for mānuka). 'Evidence of fishing for upokororo in the Mata which flows into Waiapu, in Waiapu and Tolaga Bay', Native Land Court minute book 5, 28 April 1880, fols 144–45; Waiapu Native Land Court minute book 7B, 10 February 1885, fol. 59.

145 Te Rangi Hiroa, 'The Maori Craft of Netting', p. 642.

146 Andersen diary 1923, p. 36.

147 Tawhai, *Living by the Moon*, p. 26.

148 Ibid., p. 26.

149 Andersen diary 1923, pp. 40–41.

150 Hughes and Hughes, *Port to Pasture*, 1988 Timeline: 152.

151 JC Andersen, Diary: Waiomatatini, Ngati Porou March–April 1923, p. 42.

152 Ibid.

153 Te Rangi Hiroa, 'The Maori Craft of Netting', p. 633.

154 This idea is the subject of Winona LaDuke's extensive research: see LaDuke, *All Our Relations*, 1999.

155 'Dancing the World into Being: A Conversation with Idle No More's Leanne Simpson', Naomi Klein interview with writer, spoken-word artist and indigenous academic Leanne Betasamosake Simpson, posted 5 March 2013. www.yesmagazine.org.

156 Robertson, 'Upokororo: Of Vanishing Fish and Ancestral Presence in Photography and Film', *Agency and Aesthetics: A symposium on the expanded field of photography*, Auckland Art Gallery Auditorium, 1 April 2017.

157 Te Rangi Hiroa, 'The Maori Craft of Netting, p. 636.

158 Te Rangi Hiroa 1923. MS_SC_BUCK_7.01.

159 Te Rangi Hiroa, 'The Maori Craft of Netting', p. 638.

160 Best, notebook MS Papers 72 (Elsdon Best), p. 43, Alexander Turnbull Library, Wellington.

161 McDowall, *Ikawai*, 2011, pp. 245–46.

162 Lee and Perry, 'Assessing the Role of Off-take and Source-sink Dynamics', 2019, p. 1750.

163 See 'The Most Recent Extinctions', Sixth Extinction, www.petermaas.nl.

164 Lee and Perry, 'Assessing the Role'.

165 Andersen diary 1923, p. 43.

166 Ibid.

167 Graeme Atkins, pers. comm., SMS message, 31 January 2021.

168 Mead and Grove, *Ngā Pēpeha a ngā Tīpuna*, 2001, p. 181.

169 Te Rangi Hiroa, 'The Maori Craft of Netting', p. 605.

170 Ngāti Porou saying on manaakitanga and hospitality, in Te Rangi Hiroa, 'The Maori Craft of Netting, p. 620.

Chapter 6 — 'Alive with Rhythmic Force'

1 The fourth expedition was most frequently referred to as the East Coast expedition at the time.

2 *Auckland Star*, 12 June 1923. Te Rangihīroa was appointed to the Auckland Museum Council as inaugural Chair of the Anthropology and Maori Race section around this time.

3 Buck to Ngata, 27 September 1923, Ngata Ethnology File, MS Papers-6919-0208, Alexander Turnbull Library, Wellington.

4 Ibid.

5 Taupo Ethnological Expedition 1924, MU01/18/7 & 12.

6 Proposed Ethnological Expedition to Taupo 1926, Letter Peter Buck to James McDonald, 21 May 1926.

7 Condliffe, *Te Rangi Hiroa: The Life of Sir Peter Buck*, 1971, p. 151.

8 Buck to Ngata, Rarotonga, 20 September 1926, in Sorrenson (ed.), *Na To Hoa Aroha*, vol. 1, 1986, pp. 45–46.

9 Buck to Ngata, Department of Health, Auckland, 8 March 1927, ibid., p. 48.

10 Buck to Ngata, Honolulu, 21 March 1928, ibid., p. 76.

11 Ngata to Buck, Waiomatatini, 23 June 1928, ibid., pp. 102–05. Translation by Wiremu Parker (New Zealand's first Māori news broadcaster, from 1943).

12 Buck to Ngata, Honolulu, 29 July 1928, ibid., p. 122. Trans. Wiremu Parker.

13 *Evening Post*, 18 April 1923.

14 Te Rangihīroa resigned in 1926 because of his post in Hawai'i. On Ngata's 'practical anthropology', see Sorrenson, 'Polynesian Corpuscles and Pacific Anthropology', 1982, pp. 7–28.

15 Conal McCarthy and Paul Tapsell, 'Te Poari Whakapapa: Origins, Operation and Tribal Networks of the Board of Maori Ethnological Research 1923-35', *Journal of the Polynesian Society, vol.* 128, no. 1, 2019, pp. 87–106.

16 Elsdon Best, n.d., Downes MS Papers 8051, Letter from Elsdon Best, Alexander Turnbull Library, Wellington.

17 See Ngata ,'The Genealogical Method as Applied to the Early History of New Zealand', qMS-1587, Alexander Turnbull Library, Wellington.

18 Ngata, 'Maori Land Development', in *Appendices to the Journal of the House of Representatives*, Wellington, 1931, pp. i–xxiii; see also McCarthy, 'Empirical Anthropologists Advocating Cultural Adjustments: The anthropological governance of Apirana Ngata and the Native Affairs Department', 2014, pp. 280–95.

19 Peter Buck to Ngata, Yale, 10 July 1931, in Ngata and Buck, *Na To Hoa Aroha*, vol. 3, 1988, pp. 163–64.

20 AT Ngata, *The Price of Citizenship*, Wellington, Whitcombe & Tombs, 1943, p. 5.

21 See 'Rihipeti Aperaniko, Koroniti, Wanganui River. Order to make Maori work for exhibitions', MU1/005/0056, Te Papa Archives Wellington.

22 McDonald, 'Maori Decorative Art: An Interesting Departure', *Dominion*, 8 May 1926: 'Despite the fact that the Maori of olden days was confronted by many disadvantages and technical limitations, his decorative designs express in a clear and unmistakeable way the environmental forces operating upon him. The visual impressions received from nature, from tree forms, from the swinging contours of bush-clad hills and from clouds; the feelings roused by quickly-changing and every-varying climatic conditions, and the sudden rises and falls of temperature, would develop within his mytho-poetic mind a preference for certain shapes which would be agreeable to contemplation. Once found, the form or symbol would be repeated—the Maori has an inherent love for repetition—and developed into a design alive with rhythmic force.'

23 According to Thorpe, 'There were serials and "cliff-hangers", where the girl was hanging over the cliff edge, or about to be run over by a train etc. Every session they had a lucky ticket number—two or three winners won a tiny box of Roses Chocolates—five inches by three inches, with one layer of chocolates. Once my number was called up and I went up to the stage. He leaned over and said, "What's your name, little girl?" I was staying with them at Eastbourne at the time.' Joyce Thorpe, interview with Anne Salmond, 27 November 1989, Salmond Family Archive.

24 'Grandpa lost a lot of money over it. The American producer absconded with the film, and left a lot of debts. Grandpa cashed in a lot of his assets to pay the Māori actors.' Joyce Thorpe, interview with Anne Salmond, 27 November 1989.

25 Ngata to Buck, 27 March 1928: 'The Universal Films of America sent out a filming party under one Alexander Marky— a very complete & expert crowd. Marky sought us out & in an Arts Board meeting at Rotorua early in March we decided to assist, provided he attempted consciously and honestly to depict scenes from pre-pakeha days. He is doing these at Ohiwa on the old coach road by the Ohope beach. The Matatua people have gathered there. I spent a day with them and arranging the setting of some of the scenes.

    'But as Marky took these to illustrate his story—a good one—they became incidental and sketchy. Tai, Carr, Tiweka and Hamilton were there with me & we were much interested in the technique of making pictures. We decided that we could rig up a better show, where the depicting of old Maori life as far as it can be reconstructed today can be carried out in greater detail. I have recommended the Eth. Board to take up this line next summer. We have 4 good artists in NZ but no expert producer. Tai reckons I can take this part, but one must learn to look at settings with the eye of the film. Worth doing, though', in *Na To Hoa Aroha*, vol. 1, p. 92.

26 *Hei Tiki: Adventures in Maoriland*, documentary by Geoff Steven; Peter Limbrick, 'The Flotsam and Jetsam of Film History', 2007. Although, see Peter Buck to Apirana Ngata, RMS *Makura*, 11 August 1934: 'Incidentally I saw Marky in New York and he put on his film that was made at Taupo some years ago. It is not yet released and he was trying to work in some Maori as a talky addition. I rather liked the picture although the plot may not stand against ethnological criticism. It is a sympathetic portrayal with a good tone running through it and the picture parts are real good. I saw Hori Pukehika and the sight of him brought tears to me eyes. I gave Marky a hand with one or two little things', in *Na To Hoa Aroha*, vol. 3, p. 165.

27 Translated from the article in *Te Waka Karaitiana* by Rev. JG Laughton (Maori Mission) in letter to Mrs Mary McDonald, 4 May 1936, Salmond Family Archive.

28 Salmond Family Archive.

29 Hocken Library ARC 0356.

30 'The aims and objects of the Te Tuwharetoa School of Maori Arts and Crafts are as follows:

    'To organise as a producing unit the few remaining members of the tribe with experienced technique in the various Maori crafts.

    'To establish a fund to provide for buildings, equipment, and administrative purposes.

    'To give instruction in the elements of art and decoration, in the technique of carving, plaiting, and weaving, and also in the arts of drawing, painting and modelling.

    'To create within New Zealand as well as overseas a market for the products of Tuwharetoa craftsfolk.

    'To do all things that are right and proper for the development and advancement of art culture among the Maori people, and for the preservation of the ancient art from disuse and decay': 'Old-time Art: School at Tokaanu seeking assistance: Interest among Maoris', *Evening Post*, vol. CVIII, issue 18, 22 January 1932, p. 5; see also interview with McDonald.

31 Roger Neich speculates that McDonald may be responsible for figurative painted scenes in the house Okahukura at Otūkou pā, Lake Rotoaira: Neich, *Painted Histories: Early Maori Figurative Painting*, 1993, p. 258. Images of these black-and-white scenic medallions, inset in the tukutuku panels, were shown to Anne Salmond by members of the marae community, and identified as McDonald's work.

32 Letter of welcome to James McDonald Esqre, to the opening of Puahaorangi at Tokaanu on Nov. 8th 1930: 'The Komiti Marae also wish to place on record their very high esteem and appreciation for the kindly assistance and interest you have extended to them in the whole of these preparations.' Salmond Family Archive.

33 Translated in letter from Rev. JG Laughton (Maori Mission) to Mrs Mary McDonald. 4 May 1936, Salmond Family Archive.

34 Ngata to Buck, Wellington, 16 October 1931, in *Na To Hoa Aroha*, vol. 2, 1987, p. 226.

35 Ngata to Buck, Wellington, 20 September 1930, in ibid., p. 57.

36 See Jeffrey Sissons, 'Best, Elsdon', *DNZB*, Te Ara—the Encyclopedia of New Zealand, www.teara.govt.nz; McCarthy and Tapsell, 'Te Poari Whakapapa: Origins, Operation and Tribal Networks of the Board of Maori Ethnological Research 1923–35', *Journal of the Polynesian Society*, vol. 128, no. 1, 2019. pp. 87–106; Holman, *Best of Both Worlds*, 2010.

37 Ngata to Buck, Wellington, 1 August 1928, in *Na To Hoa Aroha*, vol. 1, p. 123.

38 Ngata to James Allen, November 1927, 'Maori Ethnological—Reports', MA51-3-23, Archives New Zealand Wellington.

39 Andersen, *Myths and Legends of the Polynesians*, George G Harrup, London, 1928, p. 6.

40 Sissons, 'Best, Elsdon'.

41 Ngata to Buck, *Na To Hoa Aroha*, vol. 2, p. 216.

42 Marshall Sahlins, *Islands of History*, University of Chicago Press, Chicago, 1985, p. 14; Amiria Salmond, 'Transforming Translations (Part I): The Owner of These Bones', *Hau: Journal of Ethnographic Theory*, vol. 3, no. 3, 2013, pp. 1–32.

43 N Robertson, 'Activating Photographic Mana Rangatiratanga through Kōrero', in C Braddock (ed.), *Animism in Art and Performance*, Palgrave Macmillan, 2017, p. 47.

44 From the Ancient Greek photo (φωτω-) 'to shine', and graphia (γράφω) 'recorded'. 'Photograph', the verb, as well as 'photography', are first found in a paper read before the Royal Society on 14 March 1839: Larry Schaaf, 'Sir John Herschel's 1839 Royal Society Paper on Photography', *History of Photography*, vol. 3, no. 1, 197, pp. 47–60.

45 Lythberg, 'Ka Awatea: A Journey of Life through Light', 2016, p. 35.

46 Ibid.

47 Hakiwai, 'He Mana Taonga, He Mana Tangata', 2014, p. 192.

48 University of Auckland Research Grant papers, Salmond Family Archive.

49 Anne Salmond to Curator, Photography, National Museum Wellington, 20 July 1990.

50 Arapata Hakiwai to Anne Salmond, 5 June 1991, Salmond Family Archive:

    'Kia ora Ani, He mihi nui ki a koe i runga i nga kokiritanga o te wa. He whakaaro aroha ano ki o tatou mate e hingahinga tonu mai ana i Aotearoa. No reira, e nga kuru pounamu, e nga ariki i te po Haere, haere, haere koutou ra. Ka huri te po ka tau mai te ao. Tihei mauriora! Mauriora ki te whai-ao, ki te ao marama!

    'Greetings Anne from the head of the fish. I am writing to you on behalf of the Ethnology Department and as a kai-tiaki of our taonga to say that we are behind you and supportive of what you are doing in regards to your great-grandfather James McDonald.

    'James McDonald's involvement and contribution to the colonial museum (now National Museum of New Zealand) cannot be underestimated. His dedicated work with the Maori people who employed at the colonial museum provide Aotearoa with a rich and treasured store of knowledge for the continued benefit of future generations.

    'The ethnological trips and explorations of 1919–23 which J. McDonald actively took part in would have to be one of the most historically important events/occasions this institution has ever undertaken. The photographic images and films speak of the ebb and flow of Maoridom at a crucial time in New Zealand's history.

    'People like Maui Pomare, Apirana Ngata, Elsdon Best, P. Johansen, J. Andersen and other scholars and eminent people reinforce the importance of these historic expeditions. The many publications, sound recordings, photographic images, material culture etc provide us with a storehouse of treasures and a lasting legacy for this nation …

    'No reira. A te wa ka korero ka tutaki ano taua. Hoping you are in good and healthy spirits and keenly awaiting your reply.' (Salmond Family Archive).

51 Arapata Hakiwai to Anne Salmond, n.d., Salmond Family Archive.

52 Including Hocken Library 11.819-930; 78.176-8, 81.19; 84.31; 7307; 13003-4; 16305; 20541.

53 Salmond, 'Anne Salmond', in Deborah Shepard (ed.), *Her Life's Work: Conversations with Five New Zealand Women*, 2009, pp. 139–41; Salmond, 'Anthropology, Ontology and the Maori World', in Chris Shore and Susanna Trnka (eds), *Up Close and Personal*, 2013, p. 58.

54 Amiria Salmond, 'The Politics of Ethnographic Film', 1997.

55 This correspondence is also held in the Salmond Family Archive. See in particular M McDonald to Dr Skinner, 1 October 1955, with McDonald's list of the items she donated to Otago Museum.

56 Ngata to Buck in *Na To Hoa Aroha*, vol. 2, p. 226.

57 Reported by Peter H Buck in his Report of the Director for 1938; cited in 'Guide to Ethnographic Photo File', a typewritten manuscript prepared by Catherine C Summer, 1985, now accompanying the Ethnographic Photo File in the Bishop Museum collection.

58 Buck to Ngata, Honolulu, 29 July 1928, in *Na To Hoa Aroha*, vol. 1, p. 122.

59 McLean and Curnow (eds), *Catalogue of Museum of New Zealand Cylinder Recordings of Traditional Maori Songs*, 1992, p. 14.

60 Ibid., p. 17.

61 Dennis, 'Uncovering and Releasing the Images', 1992, p. 61.

62 Pers. email comm., Louise McCrone to Natalie Robertson, 1 November 2016.

63 Mita, 'The Preserved Image Speaks Out', in National Archives of Canada, *Documents that Move and Speak: Audiovisual Archives in the New Information Age*, 1992, p. 75.

64 See Kelly, 'Appendix Four: Films by James McDonald of the Tangata Whenua He Pito Whakaatu a Te Maori na James McDonald 1919–1923, The New Zealand Film Archive catalogue with The National Museum', 2014, pp. 77–95 for an account of the restoration and screenings of the McDonald films.

65 See Jonathan Dennis: 'The negatives were in very poor condition and some had begun to decompose badly. First, the films had to be painstakingly repaired by hand, then carefully reprinted on to stable acetate film stock', in *Nga Kai-Tiaki o nga Taonga Whitiahua, New Zealand Film Archive newsletter*, no. 14, April 1986, p. 3.

66 Dennis, in *Nga Kai-Tiaki o nga Taonga Whitiahua*, no. 12, September 1985, p. 3.

67 Witarina later went to work for Ngata in Wellington. She was a founding member of Ngati Poneke Young Maori Club and the Māori Women's Welfare League. See Dennis, in *Nga Kai-Tiaki o nga Taonga Whitiahua, no. 13*, December 1985, p. 3.

68 Dennis, in *Nga Kai-Tiaki o nga Taonga Whitiahua*, no. 14, April 1986, p. 1.

69 Sharon Dell, in *Nga Kai-Tiaki o nga Taonga Whitiahua*, no. 16, February 1987, pp. 3–4. See also Angela Moewaka Barnes: 'While acknowledging the colonial interest in indigenous peoples as scientific specimens to be observed and defined, when the McDonald films are screened, they are valued as beautiful and valuable depictions of our tūpuna. I attended a screening of the McDonald films with a predominantly Māori audience. It was a moving experience with vocal participation from the audience as tūpuna and environments were recognised', Barnes, 'Ngā Kai Para i te Kahikātoa', 2011, p. 87.

70 Calder, 'Restored Images of Past', *New Zealand Herald*, Weekend Magazine, 27 June 1987.

71 Quoted in Dennis in *Nga Kai-Tiaki o nga Taonga Whitiahua*, no. 18, September 1987, p. 1.

72 Barnes, 'Ngā Kai Para i te Kahikātoa', 2011, p. 87.

73 Robertson, 'Activating Photographic Mana Rangatiratanga through Kōrero', in C Braddock (ed.), *Animism in Art and Performance*, 2017, p. 57.

74 See Bruce Biggs, 'Jones, Pei Te Hurinui', *DNZB*, Te Ara—the Encyclopedia of New Zealand, www.teara.govt.nz.

75 Pei Te Hurinui Jones, *King Potatau*, Polynesian Society (NZ), Wellington, 1959. In collaboration with Brett Graham, 2012, *Takarangi Loop*. www.vimeo.com.

76 Patu Hohepa, unpublished note, n.d.

77 The newly digitised films are always given their first public screenings at marae. In Whanganui, for example, *Scenes of Māori Life on the Whanganui River* was narrated by Lawrence Wharerau and accompanied by taonga pūoro. www.ngataonga.org.nz.

78 Robertson, 'Activating Photographic Mana Rangatiratanga through Kōrero', p. 54.

79 Trans. Rangi Motu, in McLean and Curnow (eds), *Catalogue*, 1992.

GLOSSARY

aho
a line, string or cord, commonly used for fishing line. See also: kaha. Also describes radiant light; to shine, and the medium for an atua in divination

āhua
likeness or appearance

atua
powerful ancestor or ancestral being

au
needle for threading fish onto the takiaho

awa
river

haka taparahi
haka (war dance) without weapons

hāngi
hāngī, an earth oven where food is cooked with steam and heat from heated stones

hapū
kinship group or subtribe, consisting of a number of whānau sharing descent from a common ancestor

harakeke
flax (*Phormium tenax*)

hau
breath, life force

haukāinga
local people

hihi aho
ray of light

hika ahi
producing fire from wood by friction

hīnaki
eel trap

hīnaki pūrangi
eel net

hoa aroha
close, loving or lifelong friendship

hoeroa
long, curved weapon made of whalebone

kaha
a line, rope or cord. See also: aho

kahu kiwi
kiwi feather cloak

kaimoana
seafood or shellfish

kāinga
home, dwelling or village

kaioraora
song of defiance, cursing

kaitaka
a highly prized cloak made of flax fibre with a tāniko ornamental border

karanga
ceremonial call of greeting

karengo
a sweet-tasting seaweed

kaupapa
purpose, topic, proposal or matter for discussion

kauwhata
the recitation of ancestral stories or genealogies using the mnemonic device of a kauwhata, a stage or frame on which food is tied in bunches and displayed

kawe mate
mourning ceremony at another marae subsequent to the tangihanga and burial

kehe
marblefish (*Aplodactylus arctidens*)

kō
digging stick

kōkō
to use a scoop net for fishing

kōauau
cross-blown flute, traditionally made of wood, bone or a species of kelp

kōkopu
cockabully (*Galaxias fasciatus*)

kono
food basket

kōrero tuku iho
ancestral stories

koroua
elderly man or grandfather

kotiate
short weapon of wood or bone with a notch on both edges of the flat blade

kōura
crayfish

kōwhaiwhai
painted, often symmetrical, scroll patterns, usually painted onto whare rūnanga rafters

kuia
elderly woman or grandmother

kupenga kōkō kahawai
scoop net to catch kahawai

kupenga kōkō kehe
scoop net to catch kehe

kura
knowledge or school

mahi tahi
working together, collectively

mahinga kai
place to gather food

mana
ancestral power, prestige, authority, control, influence, status, charisma

mana motuhake
self-determination

manaaki
support, hospitality, caring for

manaakitanga
the process of showing respect, hospitality, kindness and caring for others

manuhiri
guest or visitor

maramataka
Māori seasonal almanac

marae ātea
open area in front of the wharenui where formal welcomes to visitors take place and issues are debated

mātauranga
knowledge, wisdom or understanding

mātauranga ā hī ika
knowledge of fishing

mauri
life force

moemoeā matakite
prophetic dream

mōteatea
lament, ancestral chant, sung poetry

moko
tattoo

mokopuna
grandchildren or descendant

muka
prepared flax fibre

ngeri
short haka without weapons

ngutu awa
river mouth

niu
divination

oriori
genealogical, geographical chant

pā auroa
eel weir

pā harakeke
flax bush

pā kōkopu
kōkopu weir

pā tauremu
weir with two fences on either side of the
river, leading to a hīnaki pūrangi in the centre
to catch fish or eel

paepae tuatara
village latrine, a sacred place where
karakia were performed

pao
short song

pao aroha
love song

pao whaiāipō
love song

papatipu rūnanga
ancestral land council

parera
northwester

pātere
taunting song

peruperu
war dance, a leaping haka

piharau
lamprey (*Geotria australis*)

piupiu
waist-to-knees garment made of flax

poroporoaki
speech of farewell

pouhaki
flagpole

pōwhiri
ceremonial welcome

pūkana
dilating of the eyes

pūtorino
large flute, usually made of wood
and played as a flute or trumpet

raupō
bulrush (*Typha orientalis*)

rāwaho
outsider

rohe
district, region, area of land

rua kūmara
kūmara storage pits

taiaha
long wooden weapon

tāheke
river rapids

takarangi
double spiral

takiaho
cord on which fish or shellfish are
strung, also a line of descent

tangata moana
people of the Pacific

tangata whenua
indigenous people, born of the whenua

tangi
song of mourning

tangihanga
funeral, rites for the dead

tāniko
plaited border

taniwha
ancestral guardians

taonga pūoro
traditional musical instruments

taonga tapu
precious treasure

tapatapa huahua
chant

tapatapa kai
karakia for planting kai

tapatapa kūmara
karakia for planting kūmara

tāruke kōura
crayfish trap (usually wicker)

tātai
to order or arrange

tau manu
chant or incantation to entice birds

tau marae
song of welcome to marae

taumaunu
song

tauparapara
karakia, or incantation, to begin a speech

te ao mārama
the world of light

te kāpata kai
the food cupboard

te pō
the darkness

tewhatewha
hand weapon

tikanga
correct procedure, custom, practice

tikumu
mountain daisy, (*Celmisia spectabilis*
subsp. *spectabilis*)

tinatina
comic ditty

tohunga whakairo
master carver

toi
art

tuakana
elder cousin of the same gender

tukutuku
ornamental lattice-work

tūpuna
grandparent/ancestor. Tīpuna
in East Coast dialect

ture
rules

tūtū ngārahu
haka in preparation for battle

upokororo
grayling (*Prototroctes oxyrhynchus*)

uri
descendants

utu
reciprocity

utu piharau
lamprey weir

waiata aroha
love song

waiata kaioraora
cursing song

waiata poi
poi song

waiata tangi
lament

wairua
immaterial essence, spirit

waka
canoe

waka taurua
double waka

wero
traditional challenge

whai
string game

whakaaraara
watch songs

whakaaraara pā
sentry chant

whakaahua
to photograph, portray or film

whakairo
carving

whakapapa
genealogy, lineage

whakataukī
proverb or significant saying

whaikōrero
oratory, formal speech

whanaungatanga
relationship, kinship, a sense
of family connection

whare wānanga
school of learning

whare whakairo
carved meeting house

wharekai
dining hall

wharenui
meeting house

wharepuni
guesthouse

whāriki
fine mats

whenua
land

BIBLIOGRAPHY

Abbreviations

DNZB Dictionary of New Zealand Biography
JPS Journal of the Polynesian Society
NMRE National Museum Register Ethnology
NZPD New Zealand Parliamentary Debates
TPNZI Transactions and Proceedings of the New Zealand Institute
DMB Dominion Museum Bulletin

Aginsky, B and Te Rangi Hiroa (Peter H Buck), 'Interacting Forces in the Maori family', *American Anthropologist*, vol. 42, 1940, pp. 195–210.

Allen, John S, 'Te Rangi Hiroa's physical anthropology', *JPS*, vol. 103, no. 1, 1994, pp. 11–27.

Andersen, Johannes C, JC Andersen diary, Waiomatatini, Ngāti Porou March–April 1923 and Tauranga, December 1923, MS 0053, Alexander Turnbull Library, Wellington. Transcription by Arawhetu Berdinner, September 2013, pp 1–35, with some corrections by Anne Salmond; and by Anne Salmond, April 2018, pp. 36–57.

'Maori String Games', *New Zealand Journal of Science and Technology*, vol. 3, no. 2, 1921–23, pp. 81–92.

'An Introduction to Maori Music I', *TPNZI*, vol. 55, 1923, pp. 743–62.

'An Introduction to Maori Music II', *TPNZI*, vol. 56, 1924, pp. 689–700.

Memoirs of the Board of Maori Ethnological Research, vol. 2: Maori String Figures, Board of Maori Ethnological Research, Wellington, 1927.

Myths and Legends of the Polynesians, George G Harrap, London, 1928.

'Maori Music with its Polynesian Background', *JPS*, vol. 42, 1933, pp. 195–252.

Maori Music with its Polynesian Background, Thomas Avery, New Plymouth, 1934.

Auckland Star, 12 June 1923. Maori Folklore; Songs and Poetry; Customs and Fishing Methods; Phonography and Cinema Records, *Evening Post*, 18 April 1923, vol. CV, issue 92.

Awatere, Arapeta, ed. Hinemoa Ruataupare Awatere, *Awatere: A Soldier's Story*, Huia, Wellington, 2003.

Balneavis, HRH, 'Board of Maori Ethnological Research: A review', *Te Wananga*, vol. 1, no. 1, 1929, pp. 3–10.

Barclay, Barry, 'The Held Image', *Art Gallery and Museums Association of New Zealand Journal*, vol. 20, no. 1, 1989, pp. 4–9.

Our Own Image: A Story of a Maori Filmmaker, University of Minnesota Press, Minneapolis, 1990.

Mana Tuturu: Maori Treasures and Intellectual Property Rights, Auckland University Press, Auckland, 2005.

Barnes, Angela Moewaka, 'Ngā Kai Para i te Kahikātoa: Māori Filmmaking, Forging a Path', PhD thesis in Film and Media Studies, University of Auckland, 2011.

Belich, James, *Making Peoples: A History of the New Zealanders from Polynesian Settlement to the End of the 19th Century*, Penguin, Auckland, 1996.

Bell, Leonard, *Colonial Constructs: European Images of Maori 1840–1914*, Auckland University Press, Auckland, 1992.

Best, Elsdon, *Some Aspects of Maori Myth and Religion*, Dominion Museum Monograph No. 1, Dominion Museum, Wellington, Government Printer, 1922.

Spiritual and Mental Concepts of the Maori, Dominion Museum Monograph No. 2, Dominion Museum, Wellington, Government Printer, 1922.

The Astronomical Knowledge of the Maori: Genuine and Empirical, Dominion Museum Monograph No. 3, Dominion Museum, Wellington, Government Printer, 1922.

The Maori Division of Time, Dominion Museum Monograph No. 4, Dominion Museum, Wellington, Government Printer, 1922.

The Operiki Pa, Koriniti, Whanganui River, Government Printer, Wellington, 1922.

Polynesian Voyagers: The Maori as a Deep Sea Navigator, Explorer and Colonizer, Dominion Museum Monograph No. 5, Dominion Museum, Wellington, Government Printer, 1923.

The Maori As He Was, Government Printer, Wellington, 1924.

Maori Religion and Mythology: Part One, Dominion Museum Bulletin No. 10, Dominion Museum, Wellington, Government Printer, 1924.

Maori Religion and Mythology: Part Two, Dominion Museum Bulletin No. 11, Dominion Museum, Wellington, Government Printer, 1924.

The Maori: Vol. One, Harry H Tombs, for the Board of Maori Ethnological Research, Wellington, 1924.

The Maori: Vol. Two, Harry H Tombs, for the Board of Maori Ethnological Research, Wellington, 1924.

'The Maori Canoe', *DMB* No. 7, Dominion Museum, Wellington, Government Printer, 1925.

'Games and Pastimes of the Maori', *DMB* No. 8, Dominion Museum, Wellington, Government Printer, 1925.

'Maori Agriculture', *DMB* No. 9, Dominion Museum, Wellington, Government Printer, 1925.

Tuhoe: The Children of the Mist, Board of Maori Ethnological Research, New Plymouth, 1925.

'The Pa Maori', *DMB* No. 6, Dominion Museum, Wellington, Government Printer, 1927.

'Fishing Methods and Devices of the Maori', *DMB* No. 12, Dominion Museum, Wellington, WAG Skinner, Government Printer, 1929.

Forest Lore of the Maori: With Methods of Snaring, Trapping and Preserving Birds and Rats..., Government Printer, Wellington, 1977.

Binney, Judith, 'Two Maori Portraits: Adoption of the Medium', in Elizabeth Edwards (ed.), *Anthropology and Photography 1860–1920*, Yale University Press, New Haven, 1992.

Encircled Lands, Bridget Williams Books, Wellington, 2009.

Blaser, Mario, 'Ontological Conflicts and the Stories of Peoples in Spite of Europe: Toward a Conversation on Political Ontology', *Current Anthropology*, vol. 54, no. 5, 2013, pp. 547–68.

Blythe, Martin, *Naming the Other: Images of the Maori in New Zealand Film and Television*, Scarecrow Press, Metuchen, NJ and London, 1994.

Boast, RP, 'Sir John Salmond and Māori Land Tenure', *Victoria University of Wellington Law Review*, vol. 38, no. 4, 2007, pp. 831–52.

'Re-thinking individualisation: Māori land development policy and the law in the age of Ngata (1920–1940)' [online], *Canterbury Law Review*, vol. 25, 2019, pp. 1–52.

Brewis, Alexandra A and John S Allen, 'Biological Anthropological Research in the Pacific', *JPS*, vol. 103, no. 1, 1994, pp. 7–10.

Buck, Peter (Te Rangi Hiroa), 'Maori Somatology: Racial Averages I', *JPS*, vol. 31(1), 1922, pp. 37–44.

'Maori Somatology: Racial Averages II', *JPS*, vol. 31(3) 1922, pp. 145–53.

'Maori Somatology: Racial Averages III', *JPS*, vol. 31(1), 1923, pp. 159–70.

'Maori Somatology: Racial Averages IV', *JPS*, vol. 32(2), 1923, pp. 21–28.

'Review of *The Racial History of Man* by Roland B. Dixon', *JPS*, vol. 32, 1923, pp. 248–49.

Butterworth, GV, 'The Politics of Adaptation: The Career of Sir Apirana Ngata, 1874–1928', MA dissertation, History Department, Victoria University of Wellington, 1969.

Cameron, Fiona, 'From "Dead Things" to Immutable, Combinable Mobiles: HD Skinner, the Otago Museum and University and the Governance of Māori Populations', *History and Anthropology*, vol. 25, no. 2, 2014, pp. 208–26.

Cameron, Fiona and Conal McCarthy, 'Two Anthropological Assemblages: Maori "Culture Areas" and "Adaptation" in New Zealand Museums and Government Policy', *Museum and Society*, vol. 13, no. 1, 2015, pp. 88–106.

Carey, Jane, '"A Happy Blending?": Maori Networks, Anthropology and "Native" Policy in New Zealand, the Pacific and Beyond', in Jane Carey and Jane Lydon (eds), *Indigenous Networks: Mobility, Connections and Exchange*, Routledge, London, 2014, pp. 167–93.

Chapman, Robert, 'Voting in the Māori Political Sub-system 1935–1984', in E McLeay (ed.), *New Zealand Politics and Social Patterns: Selected Works*, Victoria University Press, Wellington, 1999, pp. 226–57.

Condliffe, JB, *Te Rangi Hiroa: The Life of Sir Peter Buck*, Whitcombe & Tombs, Christchurch, 1971.

Cowan, James, 'Celt and Maori', in James Cowan and Sir Maui Pomare, *The Legends of the Maori, vol. I*, Harry H Tombs, Wellington, 1930.

Craig, Elsdon, *Man of the Mist: A Biography of Elsdon Best*, AH & AW Reed, Wellington, 1964.

Cubitt, Sean, *The Practice of Light—a Genealogy of Visual Technologies from Print to Pixels*, MIT Press, Cambridge MA, 2014.

Davy, Sarah, 'Oral History as Tradition. Recording, Performance and the Dominion Museum Expeditions 1919–1923', n.d., unpublished, Salmond Family Archive.

De la Cadena, Marisol, 'Indigenous Cosmopolitics in the Andes', *Cultural Anthropology*, vol. 25, no. 2, 2010, pp. 334–70.

Dennis, Jonathan, 'Uncovering and Releasing the Images', in National Archives of Canada, *Documents that Move and Speak: Audiovisual Archives in the New Information Age/ Ces documents qui bougent et qui parlent: Les archives audiovisuelles à l'âge de l'information*, Proceedings of a symposium organised for the International Council of Archives by the National Archives of Canada, Ottawa, 30 April–3 May 1990, KJ Saur, Münich, 1992, pp. 60–65. Copy in Natalie Robertson's possession.

'Guardians of the Treasure: A moving image archive in Aotearoa (New Zealand)', *Museum International*, vol. 46, no. 4, 1994, pp. 8–10.

'Restoring History', *Film History*, vol. 6, no. 1, *Philosophy of Film History*, Spring, 1994, pp. 116–27.

Dewes, Te Kapunga, 'The Case for Oral Arts', in Michael King (ed.), *Te Ao Hurihuri: Aspects of Maoritanga*, Hicks Smith, Wellington, 1976.

Diamond, Paul, *Makereti: Taking Māori to the world*, Random House, Auckland, 2007.

Doig, Suzanne, 'The Waiapu River, Maori and The Crown', Wai 272, A6, Te Rūnanga o Ngāti Porou inquiry, October 2000, p. 8.

Education Minister, 'Native Schools [In Continuation of E.-2, 1908]', *AJHR*, 1909.

Ellis, Ngarino, 'A Whakapapa of Tradition: Iwirakau Carving, 1830–1930', PhD thesis, University of Auckland, 2012.

A Whakapapa of Tradition: 100 Years of Ngāti Porou Carving 1830–1930, Auckland University Press, Auckland, 2016.

Firth, Raymond, 'Social organization and social change', *Journal of the Royal Anthropological Institute*, vol. 84, nos 1/2, 1954, pp. 1–20.

Frame, Alex, *Salmond, Southern Jurist*, Victoria University Press, Wellington, 1995.

Gardiner, Wira, *Te Mura o te Ahi: The Story of the Maori Battalion*, Reed, Auckland, 1995.

Gentry, Kynan, *History, Heritage, and Colonialism: Historical Consciousness, Britishness, and Cultural Identity in New Zealand, 1870–1940*, Manchester University Press, Manchester, 2015.

George, Lily, 'The Interweaving of People, Time, and Place: Whakapapa as Context and Method, *Pacific Studies*, vol. 33, nos 2/3, 2010, pp. 241–58.

Gibbons, Peter, 'Going Native: A Case Study of Cultural Appropriation in a Settler Society, with Particular Reference to the Activities of Johannes Andersen in New Zealand during the First Half of the Twentieth Century', PhD thesis, History Department, University of Waikato, 1992.

Graham, James, 'Whakatangata Kia Kaha: Toitū te Whakapapa, Toitū te Tuakiri, Toitū te Mana: An Examination of the Contribution of Te Aute College to Māori Advancement', PhD thesis, Massey University, 2009.

Hakiwai, Arapata, 'He Mana Taonga, He Mana Tangata: Māori Taonga and the Politics of Māori Tribal Identity and Development', PhD thesis, Museum and Heritage Studies, Victoria University of Wellington, 2014.

Henare [Salmond], Amiria, *Museums, Anthropology and Imperial Exchange*, Cambridge University Press, Cambridge, 2005.

'Nga Rakau a te Pakeha: Reconsidering Māori Anthropology', in Jeanette Edwards, Penny Harvey and Peter Wade (eds), *Anthropology and Science: Epistemologies in Practice*, Berg, Oxford, 2007, pp. 93–113.

Hill, H, 'The Maoris To-day and Tomorrow', *TPNZI*, vol. 29, 1897, pp. 150–62; vol. 35, 1903, pp. 169–86.

Hill, Richard, *State Authority, Indigenous Autonomy: Crown–Māori Relations in New Zealand/Aotearoa 1900-1950*, Victoria University Press, Wellington, 2004.

Hirschfeld, Charl, 'Panikena Hamihona Kaa (Kaa being sometimes recorded Ka or Kā), born Brannigan Samson Carr 1872-1948', 2013, unpublished manuscript in Natalie Robertson's private collection.

'A Brief Monograph on Pekama Rongoaia Kaa', 2017, unpublished manuscript in Natalie Robertson's private collection.

Holbraad, Martin, Morten Pedersen and Eduardo Viveiros de Castro, 'The Politics of Ontology: Anthropological Positions', *Cultural Anthropology Online*, 13 January 2014.

Holman, Jeffrey Paparoa, *Best of Both Worlds: The Story of Elsdon Best and Tutakangahau*, Penguin, Auckland, 2010.

Hoskins, Te Kawehau and Alison Jones, 'Non-human Others and Kaupapa Māori Reseach', in Te Kawehau Hoskins and Alison Jones (eds), *Critical Conversations in Kaupapa Māori*, Huia Publishers, Wellington, 2017.

Hughes, SL and IC, *Port to Pasture: Reminiscences and Records of Port Awanui, East Coast, Gisborne*, 1988.

Ancestry and Anecdotes, June 1999.

Jones, Pei Te Hurinui, *King Potatau: An Account of the Life of Potatau Te Wherowhero the First Maori King*, Polynesian Society, Wellington, 1959.

Kaa, Hirini, *Te Hāhi Mihinare: the Māori Anglican Church*, Bridget William Books, Wellington, 2020.

Kaa, Wiremu and Te Ohorere Kaa (eds), *Apirana T Ngata: Āna Tuhinga i te Reo Māori*, Victoria University Press, Wellington, 1996.

Kawharu, IH, *Maori Land Tenure: Studies of a Changing Institution*, Oxford University Press, Oxford, 1977.

Keenan, Danny, *Wars Without End: The Land Wars in Nineteenth Century New Zealand*, Penguin Books, Auckland, 2009.

Keesing, Felix, *The Changing Maori*, Board of Maori Ethnological Research, Thomas Avery and Sons, New Plymouth, 1928.

Kelly, EJ, 'Appendix Four: Films by James McDonald of the Tangata Whenua He Pito Whakaatu a Te Maori na James McDonald 1919-1923, The New Zealand Film Archive catalogue with The National Museum', in EJ Kelly, 'A Critical Examination of Film Archiving and Curatorial Practices in Aotearoa New Zealand through the Life and Work of Jonathan Dennis', PhD thesis, Auckland University of Technology, Auckland, 2014.

The Adventures of Jonathan Dennis: Bicultural Film Archiving Practice in Aotearoa New Zealand, John Libbey Publishing, UK, 2015.

King, Michael, *Te Puea: A Biography*, Hodder & Stoughton, Auckland, 1977.

Kōhere, Rēweti Tuhorouta, *The Story of a Maori Chief: Mokena Kohere and His Forebears*, Reed Publishing, Wellington, 1949.

The Autobiography of a Maori, AH & AW Reed, Wellington, 1951.

LaDuke, Winona, *All Our Relations: Native Struggles for Land and Life*, South End Press, Cambridge, MA, 1999.

Lee, Finnbar and George LW Perry, 'Assessing the Role of Off-take and Source-sink Dynamics in the Extinction of the Amphidromous New Zealand Grayling (*Prototroctes oxyrhynchus*)', *Freshwater Biology*, 2019, p. 1750.

Limbrick, Peter, 'The Flotsam and Jetsam of Film History: Hei Tiki and Post-colonial Rearticulations', *Journal of Visual Culture*, no. 6, 2007, pp. 247-51.

Lythberg, Billie, 'Ka Awatea: A Journey of Life through Light', in D Skinner (ed.), *Kōrero Mai Kōrero Atu*, Auckland War Memorial Museum, Auckland, 2016, pp. 27-44.

'KRONKling the K'lub: From 19th Century Savages to 21st Century SaVAgery', 2020.

Lythberg, Billie, Carl Hogsden and Wayne Ngata, 'Relational Systems and Ancient Futures: Co-Creating a Digital Contact Network in Theory and Practice', in B Onciul, S Hawke and M Stefano (eds), *Engaging Communities (Heritage Matters series)*, Boydell and Brewer, UK, 2015.

Lythberg, Billie and Conal McCarthy (eds.), *Te Ao Hou: Whakapapa as Practical Ontology*. Special issue *JPS*, vol. 128, March 2019.

Lythberg, Billie and Conal McCarthy and Amiria Salmond, 'Introduction: Transforming Worlds: Kinship as Practical Ontology', in Conal McCarthy and Billie Lythberg (eds.) *JPS*, vol. 128, March 2019, pp. 7-18.

Mahuika, Apirana, 'Maori Culture and the New Museum', *Museum Anthropology*, vol. 15, no. 4, 1992.

'A Ngāti Porou Perspective', in M Mulholland and V Tawhai (eds), *Weeping Waters: The Treaty of Waitangi and Constitutional Change*, Huia, Wellington, 2010, pp. 145-63.

Maxwell, Kimberley H, Kelly Ratana, Kathryn K Davis, Caine Taiapa and Shaun Awatere, 'Navigating towards marine co-management with Indigenous communities on-board the Waka-Taurua', *Marine Policy*, vol. 111, 2020, 10372.

McCarthy, Conal, *Exhibiting Māori: A History of Colonial Cultures of Display*, Berg, Oxford & New York, 2007.

'"Our Works of Ancient Times": History, Colonisation and Agency at the 1906-7 New Zealand International Exhibition', *Museum History Journal*, vol. 2, no. 2, 2009, pp. 119-42.

'To Foster and Encourage the Study and Practice of Maori Arts and Crafts: Indigenous Material Culture, Colonial Culture and Museums in New Zealand', in Janice Helland, Beverly Lemire and Alena Buis (eds), *Craft & Community: The Material Culture of Place and Politics, 19th-20th Century*, Ashgate, Aldershot, 2014, pp. 59-81.

'Empirical Anthropologists Advocating Cultural Adjustments: The anthropological governance of Apirana Ngata and the Native Affairs Department', *History and Anthropology*, vol. 25, no. 2, 2014, pp. 280-95.

'Historicising the "indigenous International": Museums, anthropology, and transpacific networks', in E Dürr and P Schorch (eds), *TransPacific Americas: Encounters and Engagements between the Americas and the South Pacific*, Routledge, London & New York, 2015, pp. 3-26.

'"Two Branches of the Brown Polynesians": Ethnological Fieldwork, Colonial Governmentality and the "Dance of Agency"', in Catharine Coleborne and Katie Pickles (eds), *New Zealand's Empire*, Manchester University Press, London & New York, 2016, pp. 51-67.

McCarthy, Conal and Paul Tapsell, 'Te Poari Whakapapa: Origins, Operation and Tribal Networks of the Board of Maori Ethnological Research 1923-35', *JPS*, vol. 128, no. 1, 2019, pp. 87-106.

McDonald, James, 'The Best Equipment: Knowledge is Power', pamphlet advertising the *New Zealand Journal for Science and Technology*, by James McDonald, Acting Director of the Dominion Museum, and Acting Honorary Secretary, Board of Science and Arts, n.d.

'Maori Decorative Art: An Interesting Departure', *Dominion*, 8 May 1926 (Salmond Family Archive).

McDowall, Robert, *Ikawai: Freshwater Fishes in Maori Culture and Economy*, Canterbury University Press, Christchurch, 2011.

McLean, Mervyn and Jenifer Curnow (eds), *Catalogue of Museum of New Zealand Cylinder Recordings of Traditional Maori Songs, 1919-c.1935*, Archive of Maori and Pacific Music, Anthropology Department, University of Auckland; Foundation for Research, Science and Technology, Auckland, 1992.

McLean, Mervyn and Margaret Orbell, *Traditional Songs of the Maori*, Auckland University Press, Auckland, 1992.

Mead, Hirini Moko and Neil Grove, *Ngā Pēpeha a ngā Tīpuna: The Sayings of the Ancestors*, Victoria University Press, Wellington, 2001.

Ministry for Primary Industries, Wellington. MPI Technical Paper no: 2012/32. 2.6.5. Waiapu River Catchment Study Final Report, T Barnard, L Garrett, D Harrison, H Jones, D Moore (Scion); and M Rosser, B Page, T Porou (Applied Sociology); G Fitzgerald (GNS Science); M Bloomberg (Christchurch: University of Canterbury).

Miskelly, Colin M, 'Legal Protection of New Zealand's Indigenous Aquatic Fauna: An Historical Review', *Tuhinga*, vol. 27, 2016, Museum of New Zealand Te Papa Tongarewa, Wellington, p. 83.

Mita, Merata, 'The Preserved Image Speaks Out: Objectification and reification of living images in archiving and preservation', in National Archives of Canada, *Documents that Move and Speak: Audiovisual Archives in the New Information Age/Ces documents qui bougent et qui parlent: Les archives audiovisuelles à l'âge de l'information: Proceedings of a symposium organised for the International Council of Archives by the National Archives of Canada, Ottawa, 30 April–3 May 1990*, KJ Saur, Munich, 1992, pp. 72–76. Copy in Natalie Robertson's possession.

'The Soul and the Image', in J Dennis and J Bieringa (eds), *Film in Aotearoa New Zealand*, Victoria University of Wellington, Wellington, 1992, pp. 26–54.

Morris, Rosalind, *New Worlds from Fragments: Film, Ethnography and the Representation for Northwest Coast Cultures*, Westview Press, Boulder, Colorado, c. 1994.

'Nga Ture o Te Ngutu Awa', *Nati Link*, issue 9, December 2015, p. 33.

New Zealand Government Treaty settlement documents, Ngāti Porou Settlement, Deed of Settlement Schedule—Documents, 22 December 2010.

Neich, R, *Carved Histories: Rotorua Ngati Tarawhai Woodcarving*, Auckland University Press, Auckland, 2001.

Nepia, Moana, 'Te Kore: Exporing the Māori Concept of Void', PhD thesis, Auckland University of Technology, 2012.

New Zealand Parliamentary Debates, vol. 139, 27 June–01 August 1907.

Ngā Taonga Sound and Vision, 'Te Puna Wai Kōrero: Apirana Ngata's recordings of 1930s', Catalogue ref. 40516, 1983.

Ngata, Apirana Turupa, *The Past and Future of the Maori*, Christchurch Press, Christchurch, 1893.

'The Genealogical Method as Applied to the Early History of New Zealand', paper to be read before the Wellington Branch of the Historical Association, 1930.

'The Terminology of Whakapapa', MS SC Buck 6.02, Bernice P Bishop Museum Archives, Honolulu, 1931.

Ngata, Apirana (ed.), *Nga Moteatea: He Maramara Rere no nga Waka Maha. The Songs: Scattered Pieces from Many Canoe Areas: Part I*, Board of Maori Ethnological Research, Wellington, 1928.

Nga Moteatea: He Maramara Rere no nga Waka Maha. The Songs: Scattered Pieces from Many Canoe Areas. Part II. Board of Maori Ethnological Research, Wellington, 1929.

'Anthropology and the Government of Native Races in the Pacific', in J Allen (ed.), *New Zealand Affairs*, Institute of Pacific Relations New Zealand Branch, Christchurch, 1929, pp. 22–60.

Rauru-nui-a-Toi and Ngati Kahungunu Origins, Porourangi Maori Cultural School Lectures, vols 5–7, Department of Anthropology, Victoria University of Wellington, 1972.

Ngata, Apirana and Peter Buck, ed. MPK Sorrenson, *Na To Hoa Aroha: From Your Dear Friend: The Correspondence Between Sir Apirana Ngata and Sir Peter Buck, 1925–1950*, vols 1–4, Auckland University Press, Auckland, 1986–88.

Ngata, Paratene, 'Apirana Nohopari Turupa Ngata', *JPS*, vol. 59, no. 4, 1950, p. 281.

Ngata, Wayne, Hera Ngata-Gibson and Amiria Salmond, 'Te Ataakura: digital *taonga* and cultural innovation', *Journal of Material Culture Special Issue: Digital Subject, Cultural Objects*, Amiria Salmond and Billie Lythberg (eds), vol. 17, no. 3, 2012, pp. 229–44.

Nixon, Rob, *Slow Violence and the Environmentalism of the Poor*, Harvard University Press, Cambridge MA & London, 2011.

Oliveira, Katrina-Ann Kapā'anaokalāokeola Nākoa, *Ancestral Places: Understanding Kanaka Geographies*, Oregon State University Press, 2014, p. 78.

Paterson, Lachy, 'Rēweti Kōhere's Model Village', *New Zealand Journal of History*, vol. 41, no. 1, 2007, pp. 27–44.

Paulin, Chris D, 'Perspectives of Māori Fishing History and Techniques: Ngā Ahua me ngā Pūrākau me ngā Hangarau Ika o te Māori', *Tuhinga*, vol. 18, 2007, pp. 11–47, Te Papa Tongarewa Museum of New Zealand.

Phillipps, WJ, 'Carved Maori Houses in the Eastern Districts of the North Island', *Records of the Dominion Museum*, vol. 1, no. 2, 1944, pp. 69–119.

Pitt-Rivers, GHL, 'A Visit to a Maori Village: Being some observations on the passing of the Maori race and the decay of Maori culture', *JPS*, vol. 33, no. 129, 1924, pp. 48–65.

Porter, Lieut. Colonel, *History of the Early Days of Poverty Bay: Major Ropata Wahawaha NZC MLC: A Story of His Life and Times*, Poverty Bay Herald, Gisborne, 1923.

Pugsley, Christopher, *The Camera in the Crowd: Filming New Zealand in Peace and War, 1895–1920*, Oratia Books, Auckland, 2017.

Ramos, Alcida, 'The Politics of Perspectivism', *Annual Review of Anthropology*, vol. 41, 2012, pp. 481–94.

Ramsden, E, *Sir Apirana Ngata and Maori Culture*, AH & AW Reed, Wellington, 1948.

A Memoir: Te Rangihiroa, Whitcombe & Tombs, Wellington, 1954.

Reedy, Hirini George, 'Te Tohu-a-Tuu (The Sign of Tuu): A Study of the Warrior Arts of the Maori', PhD thesis, Massey University, 1996.

Refiti, Albert, 'A "Psychedelic Method": Spatial Exposition, Perspectivism and Bricklaying', in AC Engels-Schwarzpaul and MA Peters, *Of Other Thoughts: NonTraditional Ways to the Doctorate: A Guidebook for Candidates and Supervisors*, Sense Publication, Rotterdam/Boston/Taipei, 2013.

'How the Tā–Vā Theory of Reality Constructs a Spatial Exposition of Tongan Architecture', *Heretic Papers in Pacific Thought*, 2013, alrx01-2013.

Rice, Geoffrey, *That Terrible Time: Eyewitness Accounts of the 1918 Influenza Epidemic in New Zealand*, Hawthorne Press, Christchurch, 2020.

Rice, Rebecca, 'The State Collections of Colonial New Zealand Art: Intertwined Histories of Collecting and Display', PhD thesis in Art History, Victoria University of Wellington, 2010.

Rivers, WHR, 'The Peopling of Polynesia', in WHR Rivers, ed. G Elliot Smith, *Psychology and Ethnology*, Kegan Paul, London, 1926, pp. 238–61.

Roberts, Mere, Frank Weko and Liliana Clarke, 'Maramataka: The Maori Moon Calendar', Research Report No. 283, Matauranga Maori and Bio Protection Research Team, National Centre for Advanced Bio-Protection Technologies, Lincoln University, August 2006.

Robertson, Natalie, 'Activating Photographic Mana Rangatiratanga through Kōrero', in C Braddock (ed.), *Animism in Art and Performance*, Palgrave Macmillan, London, 2017, pp. 45–65.

'Upokororo: Of Vanishing Fish and Ancestral Presence in Photography and Film', *Agency and Aesthetics: A symposium on the expanded field of photography*, Auckland Art Gallery Auditorium, 1 April 2017.

Robertson, Natalie, '"Images Still Live and are Very Much Alive": Whakapapa and the 1923 Dominion Museum Ethnological Expedition' in Conal McCarthy and Billie Lythberg (eds.) *JPS*, vol. 128, March 2019, pp. 65–86.

Sahlins, Marshall, *Islands of History*, University of Chicago Press, Chicago, 1985.

Salmond, Amiria, 'The Politics of Ethnographic Film: The Films of James McDonald 1919–1923', unpublished MPhil research essay, University of Cambridge, 1997, Salmond Family Archive.

'Transforming Translations (Part I): The Owner of These Bones', *Hau: Journal of Ethnographic Theory*, vol. 3, no. 3, 2013, pp. 1–32.

'Transforming Translations (Part II): Addressing Ontological Alterity', *Hau: Journal of Ethnographic Theory*, vol. 4, no. 1, 2014, pp. 155–87.

Salmond, Anne and Billie Lythberg, 'Spiralling Histories: reflections on the Dominion Museum East Coast Expedition and other multi-media experiments' in Conal McCarthy and Billie Lythberg (eds.) *JPS*, vol. 128, March 2019, pp. 43–64.

Salmond, Anne, 'Te Ao Tawhito: A Semantic Approach to the Traditional Maori Cosmos', *JPS*, vol. 87, no. 1, 1978, pp. 5–28.

'The Study of Traditional Maori Society: The State of the Art', *JPS*, vol. 92, no. 3, 1983, pp. 309–32.

'Theoretical Landscapes: On Crosscultural Conceptions of Knowledge', in David Parkin (ed.), *Semantic Anthropology*, ASA Monograph Series No. 22, Academic Press, London, 1983, pp. 65–87.

'Maori Epistemologies', in *Reason and Morality*, in J Overing (ed.), ASA Monograph Series No. 24, Tavistock, London, 1985, pp. 240–63.

'Towards a Local Anthropology', *Sites*, vol. 13, 1986, pp. 39–44.

'Te Tokanga-a-Noho Meeting House', in Elizabeth Edwards (ed.), *Anthropology and Photography 1860–1920*, Yale University Press, New Haven, 1992.

'McDonald among the Maori', unpublished paper, *Colonial Baggage Symposium*, Museum of Scotland, Edinburgh, 1999, Salmond Family Archive.

'Anne Salmond', in Deborah Shepard (ed.), *Her Life's Work: Conversations with Five New Zealand Women*, Auckland University Press, Auckland, 2009, pp. 136–95.

'Anthropology, Ontology and the Maori World', in Chris Shore and Susanna Trnka (eds) *Up Close and Personal: On Peripheral Perspectives and the Production of Anthropological Knowledge, Methodology and History in Anthropology*, vol. 25, Berghan, New York, 2013, pp. 58–72.

'Tears of Rangi: People, Water and Power in New Zealand', *Hau: Journal of Ethnographic Theory*, vol. 4, no. 3, 2014, pp. 285–309.

Tears of Rangi: Experiments Across Worlds, Auckland University Press, Auckland, 2017.

'The Fountain of Fish: Ontological Collisions at Sea', in Silke Helfrich and David Bollier (eds), *Patterns of Commoning*, Off the Common Books, 2015.

Salmond, Amiria JM, 'Comparing Relations: Whakapapa and Genealogical Method' in Conal McCarthy and Billie Lythberg (eds.) *JPS*, vol. 128, March 2019, pp. 107–129.

Schaaf, Larry, 'Sir John Herschel's 1839 Royal Society Paper on Photography', *History of Photography*, vol. 3, no. 1, 1979, pp. 47–60.

Sissons, Jeffrey, *Te Waimana: The Spring of Mana. Tuhoe History and the Colonial Encounter*, University of Otago Press, Dunedin, 1991.

'The Post-assimilationist Thought of Sir Apirana Ngata: Towards a Genealogy of New Zealand Biculturalism', *New Zealand Journal of History*, vol. 34, no. 1, 2000, pp. 47–59.

'Best, Elsdon', *DNZB*, Te Ara—the Encyclopedia of New Zealand.

Skinner, HD, 'Obituary, WHR Rivers', in *JPS*, vol. 31, no. 122, 1922, pp. 87–88.

Slobodin, Richard, *WHR Rivers*, Columbia University Press, New York, 1978, pp. 51–53.

Smith, Linda Tuhiwai, *Decolonizing Methodologies: Research and Indigenous Peoples*, Otago University Press, Dunedin, 1999.

Sorrenson, MPK, 'Polynesian Corpuscles and Pacific Anthropology: The Home-made Anthropology of Sir Apirana Ngata and Sir Peter Buck', in *JPS*, vol. 91, no. 1, 1982, pp. 7–28.

Manifest Destiny: The Polynesian Society over 100 Years, Polynesian Society, Auckland, 1992.

Soutar, Monty, 'Ngāti Porou Leadership: Rāpata Wahawaha and the Politics of Conflict: "Kei te ora nei hoki tātou, me tō tātou whenua"', PhD thesis, Māori Studies, Massey University, 2000.

Nga Tama Toa: The Price of Citizenship: C Company 28 (Maori) Battalion 1939–1945, Bateman, Auckland, 2008.

Whitiki! Whiti! Whiti! E!: Māori in the First World War, Bateman, Auckland, 2019.

Stirling, Eruera, as told to Anne Salmond, *Eruera: The Teachings of a Maori Elder*, Oxford University Press, Wellington, 1980.

Sully, Dean (ed.), *Decolonizing Conservation: Caring for Maori Meeting Houses Outside New Zealand*, Left Coast Press, Walnut Creek CA, 2007.

Taiapa, Pineamine, 'Marama taka a te Maori te Tau 1946', Thomas Adams, printer, National Library of New Zealand, ref. Eph-B-MAORI-1946-01.

'Concise Maori Almanac 1960–61: Plant and Fish by the Phases of the Moon', *Gisborne Herald*, 1960.

Tāwhai, Wiremu, *Living by the Moon: Te Maramataka a Te Whānau-ā-Apanui*, Huia, Wellington, 2013.

Te Awekotuku, Ngahuia, 'Introduction', in Papakura, Makareti *The Old-time Maori*, (first published 1938), New Women's Press, Auckland, 1986.

Te Manatū Taonga | Ministry for Culture and Heritage, 28th (Māori) Battalion website, 2011.

Te Rangi Hiroa (PH Buck), 'Medicine among the Maoris in Ancient and Modern Times', unpublished MD thesis, University of Otago, School of Medicine, Dunedin, 1910.

'Maori Plaited Basketry and Plaitwork I', *TPNZI*, vol. 54, 1923, pp. 705–42.

'Maori Plaited Basketry and Plaitwork II', *TPNZI*, vol. 55, 1924, pp. 346–61.

'The Passing of the Maori', *Transactions and Proceedings of the Royal Society of New Zealand*, vol. 55, 1924, pp. 362–75.

'The Maori Craft of Netting' (read before the Auckland Institute, 25 November 1924; received by the Editor, 10 November 1924; issued separately, 6 May 1926), *TPNZI*, vol. 56, 1926, pp. 597–646.

The Coming of the Maori (Cawthron Lecture), 2nd edn, Avery, New Plymouth, 1929.

Vikings of the Sunrise, Stokes, New York, 1938.

'He Poroporoaki – A Farewell Message: Personal Reminiscences on Sir Apirana Ngata', *JPS*, vol. 60, no. 1, 1951, pp. 22–31.

'Maori Field Notes – Fishing and Agricultural Notes', field notebook, 1923. MS SC BUCK 7.01, 7.03, 7.04, Library and Archives, Bishop Museum, Honolulu.

Te Rūnanganui o Ngāti Porou, 'Hi Ika: The Ngāti Porou Fisheries Settlement'.

Thomson, John Mansfield (ed.), *Farewell Colonialism: The New Zealand International Exhibition Christchurch 1906–7*, Dunmore Press, Palmerston North, 1998.

Todd, Zoe, 'An Indigenous Feminist's Take on the Ontological Turn: "Ontology" is just another word for colonialism', blog post, 2014.

'Refracting the State through Human–Fish Relations', in *Decolonization: Indigeneity, Education & Society: Indigenous Peoples and the Politics of Water*, vol. 7, no. 1, 2018, pp. 60–79.

Turton, H Hanson, *Maori Deeds of Land Purchases in the North Island of New Zealand: Volume One: Awanui Block, Poverty Bay District*.

Viveiros de Castro, Eduardo, "AND" *Manchester Papers in Social Anthropology*, Manchester University Press, Manchester, 2003.

'The Relative Native, Hau', *Journal of Ethnographic Theory*, vol. 3, no. 3, 2013, pp. 469–502.

Cannibal Metaphysics, University of Minnesota Press, Minneapolis, 2014.

'Who's afraid of the ontological wolf? Some comments on an ongoing debate', CUSAS Annual Marilyn Strathern Lecture, 30 May 2014.

Walker, Ranginui, *He Tipua: The Life and Times of Sir Apirana Ngata*, Viking, Auckland, 2001.

Walsh, Archdeacon, 'The Passing of the Maori', *TPNZI*, vol. 40, 1908, pp. 154–75.

Walter, Inano, 'He Wahine, He Whenua i Ngaro Ai? Maori Women, Maori Marriage Customs and the Native Land Court, 1865–1909', MA thesis, University of Otago, 2017.

Wehipeihana, John (ed.), *Te Aute College: Koiri 1854–2004*, Te Aute College, Pukehou, 2005.

White, Moira, 'Dixon, Skinner and Te Rangi Hiroa', *JPS*, vol. 47, no. 3, 2012, pp. 369–87.

Wi Repa, Tūtere, 'The Young Maori Party', *Otago Witness*, 20 November 1907.

Williams, HW, 'The Nights of the Moon', *JPS*, vol. 37, no. 147, 1928.

Williams, Herbert W, *A Dictionary of the Maori Language*, Polynesian Society, Government Printer, Wellington, 1917.

Films

Te Hui Aroha ki Turanga: Gisborne Hui Aroha, 35mm, black and white, silent, 10 mins, Ngā Taonga Sound and Vision.

He Pito Whakaatu i te Hui i Rotorua: Scenes at the Rotorua Hui, 35mm, black and white, silent, 24 mins, Ngā Taonga Sound and Vision.

He Pito Whakaatu i te Noho a te Maori i te Awa o Whanganui: Scenes of Maori Life on the Whanganui River, 35mm, black and white, silent, 48 mins, Ngā Taonga Sound and Vision.

He Pito Whakaatua i te Noho a te Maori i te Tairawhiti: Scenes of Maori Life on the East Coast, 35mm, black and white, silent, 26 mins, Ngā Taonga Sound and Vision.

Artefact 2018 *Series I* (Greenstone TV and Maori TV) and 2020 *Series II* (Greenstone TV and Prime).

Hei Tiki: Adventures in Maoriland, documentary by Geoff Steven.

Ngarimu, Taina, 'Waka Huia' series, Scottie Productions, 2016.

The Scotsman and the Māori, 2011, television documentary directed by Libby Hakaraia for Māori Television.

Waka Huia, 2016, *John Manuel: Last of the old time East Coast cowboys* [26 March episode], Tina Wickliffe (dir.), Scottie Productions.

IMAGE CREDITS

ABOUT THE AUTHORS

Wayne Ngata MNZM (Ngāti Ira, Ngāti Porou, Te Aitanga a Hauiti) is a board member of the Tertiary Education Commission, and board chair of Te Taumata Aronui. He is active in the revitalisation of te reo Māori, a specialist in Māori literature, a long-time advocate for Māori art, and an active supporter of the waka hourua renaissance.

Arapata Hakiwai (Ngāti Kahungunu, Rongowhakaata, Ngāti Porou, Ngāi Tahu) is the Kaihautū | Māori Co-Leader at the Museum of New Zealand Te Papa Tongarewa and shares the strategic leadership of the National Museum with the Tumu Whakarae | Chief Executive. He has extensive knowledge, relationships and experience working with iwi and museums, including helping to restore the Ruatepupuke wharenui in the Field Museum, Chicago, undertaking a research project to identify and create an international digital database of Māori and Moriori taonga, and more recently helping to return the Motunui Pātaka panels from Geneva to Taranaki. He has long advocated for the decolonisation of museums and was the Culture Commissioner for the New Zealand National Commission for UNESCO from 2015–20.

Dame Anne Salmond ONZ DBE FRSNZ FBA is James McDonald's great-grand-daughter and a Distinguished Professor of Māori Studies and Anthropology at the University of Auckland, and a leading social scientist. She is the winner of the Rutherford Medal, New Zealand's top scientific prize, and many international fellowships and awards. She is the author of a series of prize-winning books about Māori life, European voyaging and cross-cultural encounters in the Pacific, most recently *Tears of Rangi* (Auckland University Press, 2017). In 2021 she was granted the Order of New Zealand, the country's top award.

Conal McCarthy is the director of the Museum and Heritage Studies programme at Victoria University of Wellington. He has published widely on the historical and contemporary Māori engagement with museums, including the books *Exhibiting Māori: A history of colonial cultures of display* (Routledge, 2007), *Museums and Māori: Heritage professionals, indigenous collections, current practice* (Te Papa Press, 2011) and, as co-editor, *Colonial Gothic to Maori Renaissance: Essays in Memory of Jonathan Mane-Wheoki* (Victoria University Press, 2017) and *Curatopia: Museums and the future of curating* (Manchester University Press, 2019).

Amiria Salmond is James McDonald's great-great-grand-daughter and is an independent scholar and historian, who was earlier a lecturer in social anthropology and Senior Curator at the University of Cambridge Museum of Archaeology and Anthropology. She is writing a book on the history of the island of Ulbha (Ulva) in the Scottish Hebrides, which was cleared of the great bulk of its inhabitants in the mid-nineteenth century. Her publications include *Museums, Anthropology and Imperial Exchange* (Cambridge University Press, 2005) and she co-edited *Thinking Through Things: Theorising Artefacts Ethnographically* (Routledge, 2007).

Monty Soutar ONZM (Ngāti Porou, Ngāti Awa, Ngāi Tai ki Tamaki, Ngāti Kahungunu) is an award-winning historian. He has published two major research and publication projects; *Nga Tama Toa: Price of Citizenship: C Company 28 (Maori) Battalion 1939-1945* (Bateman, 2008) and *Whiti! Whiti! Whiti! E! Māori in the First World War* (Bateman, 2019). He has also made a significant contribution as a member of the Waitangi Tribunal and in the development of the Te Tai Whakaea: Treaty Settlement Stories Project at the Ministry for Culture and Heritage. He was awarded the Creative New Zealand Michael King Writer's Fellowship in 2021.

James Schuster (Te Arawa) is a Māori Built Heritage Adviser (Traditional Arts) to Heritage New Zealand Pouhere Taonga. Born and raised in Rotorua into a family that has maintained and practised Māori arts and crafts for generations, his traditional knowledge and skills have been passed down through his family. His great-great-grandfather was Tene Waitere, the renowned Ngāti Tarawhai carver.

Billie Lythberg is a Senior Lecturer in the Faculty of Business and Economics at The University of Auckland, working at the junction of business studies, anthropology and history, with a strong focus on Aotearoa and the Pacific. She co-edited *Artefacts of Encounter: Cook's Voyages, Colonial Collecting and Museum Histories* (University of Otago Press, 2016) and *Collecting in the South Sea: the Voyage of Bruni d'Entrecasteaux 1791–1794* (Sidestone Press, 2018), and co-created the *Artefact* documentary series exploring taonga Māori in collections worldwide (Māori Television, 2018 and 2020).

John Niko Maihi MNZM (Ngati Pamoana Atihaunui a Paparangi) is the son of Aperaniko Maihi (Paeroke) and Te Kahui Gray. He actively supports his iwi and his community in his capacity as kaumātua and Pou Haahi Ringatū. A former member of the Whanganui River Māori Trust Board (1988–2017), he has held significant leadership roles in the settlement of the Whanganui River Claims. John is the current chair of Te Puna Mātauranga o Whanganui Iwi Education Authority, convenes Te Pae Matua Roopu and Te Rūnanga o te Awa Tupua o Whanganui, and kaiwhakahaere of Te Rūnanga o Tūpoho and kaumātua for the Whanganui District Health Board and the Whanganui Regional Museum. He is also the kāumatua for University College of Learning Whanganui and was made an Honorary Fellow in 2010. John is Kaumātua and Cultural Advisor to the Whanganui District Council and has taken a leadership role in the development of Te Pataka o Taiaroa since its inception. In 2011, he was made a Member of the New Zealand Order of Merit for services to Māori.

Sandra Kahu Nepia (Ngāti Pamoana — Atihaunui-a-paparangi, Ngāti Hinemihi — Tuwharetoa) is marae representative for Koriniti Marae on Te Rūnunga o Tūpoho; Board member of Ngā Tangata Tiaki o Whanganui — Advisory and Audit and Risk; Pou Herenga/Heritage and Community Services Manager at the Whanganui District Library and work in iwi developments within the Whanganui District Council; and Kaikirimana for the tohu Puna Maumahara with Te Wānanga o Raukawa.

Te Wheturere Poope Gray (Ngati Kurawhatia ki Pipiriki), also known as Bobby Gray, is the grandson of Te Wheturere Robert Gray and Ngāraiti Tuatini, and son of Te Wheturere James Gray and Janet McFall. During his working years, from 1951 to the 2000s, Te Wheturere was a primary school teacher and headmaster at primary schools around the North Island. During his years in Tokoroa, Te Wheturere was part of the founding kaimahi responsible for building Papa o te Aroha Marae, and was also a respected kaumātua there once the marae was built. Now retired, he lives at his ancestral kainga, Raetiwha Rāhui in Pipiriki, where he is a respected kaumatua of Paraweka Marae.

Te Aroha McDonnell (Ngāti Hau, Ngāti Kurawhatia, Ngāti Haua, Te Atihaunui-a-Paparangi, Ngāti Maru, Ngāti Maniapoto, Ngāti Tuwharetoa) is a representative of Ngāti Hau to Te Rūnanga o Tamaupoko and Te Rūnanga o Te Awa Tupua.

Natalie Robertson (Ngāti Porou, Clann Dhònnchaidh) is a photographic and moving image artist and Senior Lecturer at Auckland University of Technology, Tāmaki Makaurau. Much of her practice is based in Tairāwhiti, her East Coast Ngāti Porou homelands, where her focus is on her ancestral Waiapu River and the protracted catastrophic impacts of colonisation, deforestation and agriculture. She has exhibited extensively in public institutions throughout New Zealand and internationally. She photographed for the award-winning book *A Whakapapa of Tradition: One Hundred Years of Ngāti Porou Carving, 1830–1930*, written by Ngarino Ellis (Auckland University Press, 2016).

ACKNOWLEDGEMENTS

First, we'd like to thank all those people who made the 1919–1923 Dominion Museum Ethnological Expeditions possible; those before and behind the lenses of still and moving image cameras, making pictures with light and carving voices into wax cylinder recordings. Without their vision for the future, and their embracing of new technologies to carry their āhua and kōrero, lamentable gaps in archives and knowledge would be wider still.

Second, our heartfelt thanks to their descendants for permission to bring these tīpuna and images back into the light, and for further addressing archival gaps through the restoration of names and whakapapa. Some gaps remain; tīpuna and taonga yet to be identified. This book's authors hope that through its publication the names and whakapapa of 'as-yet-unidentified' people who appear in some images will be restored, and other descendants will be found.

Third, we thank Te Apārangi Royal Society of New Zealand, who funded this project's research through a Marsden grant awarded in 2016, which made it possible to work with geographically dispersed collections and colleagues to reunite these taonga with their descendants.

Fourth, we thank the editors of the *Journal of the Polynesian Society*, both now and of the past, who opened space for ideas about the background to the Dominion Museum Expeditions to be tested and published. Our Marsden team's essays about the expeditions, their people, and historical and disciplinary contexts, were published as a special issue of the *JPS* in March 2019 called *Te Ao Hou: Whakapapa as Practical Ontology*.

Fifth, we thank Te Papa Press and Area Design, without whose dedication and brilliance this book would not have assumed the shape you now hold in your hands.

Finally, but by no means least, our sincere gratitude to the managers, curators and researchers in the museums and archives with whom we worked, who accepted the challenge of opening access to fragile collections of negatives, documents and recordings. Many are now digitised so descendants can more easily access these treasures for the rising generation—hei taonga mā ngā uri whakatipu.

INDEX

First published in New Zealand in 2021
by Te Papa Press, PO Box 467, Wellington,
New Zealand

www.tepapapress.co.nz

TE PAPA® is the trademark of the Museum
of New Zealand Te Papa Tongarewa
Te Papa Press is an imprint of the Museum
of New Zealand Te Papa Tongarewa
A catalogue record is available from
the National Library of New Zealand

978-0-9951031-0-8

Te Papa photography by Maarten Holl,
Melissa Irving, Dionne Ward
Design by Area Design
Digital imaging by Jeremy Glyde
Printed by 1010 Printing Asia Ltd

Front cover: Apirana Ngata (left) and
Te Rangihiroa at Waiomatatini in 1923.
Photograph by James McDonald,
Te Papa MU000523/006/0005.

Back cover: Rihipeti Aperaniko standing
in *Te Wehi o te Rangi* at Koroniti in 1921.
Photograph by James McDonald,
Te Papa MU000523/005/0426.